"THE BREAKING WAVES DASHED HIGH."

The Pine-Tree Coast

−Illustrated−

Samuel Adams Drake

Author of "Nooks and Corners of the New England Coast"

*Now longë may'st thou saile by the Coast,
Thou gentle Master, gentle Marinere.* —Chaucer

HERITAGE BOOKS
2012

HERITAGE BOOKS
AN IMPRINT OF HERITAGE BOOKS, INC.

Books, CDs, and more—Worldwide

For our listing of thousands of titles see our website
at
www.HeritageBooks.com

A Facsimile Reprint
Published 2012 by
HERITAGE BOOKS, INC.
Publishing Division
100 Railroad Ave. #104
Westminster, Maryland 21157

Copyright © 1890 Estes & Lauriat

Originally published
Boston:
Estes & Lauriat
1891

— Publisher's Notice —
In reprints such as this, it is often not possible to remove blemishes from the original. We feel the contents of this book warrant its reissue despite these blemishes and hope you will agree and read it with pleasure.

International Standard Book Numbers
Paperbound: 978-1-55613-135-6
Clothbound: 978-0-7884-9253-2

PUBLISHERS' NOTE.

THE excellent half-tone photo-etched illustrations in this volume are from originals furnished by Mr. H. G. Peabody of Boston, Mr. Harry Brown and Messrs. Jackson and Kinney of Portland, Maine. We also take this method of acknowledging favors received from the Boston and Maine Railroad Company, tending to make the *Pine-Tree Coast* more attractive in this respect.

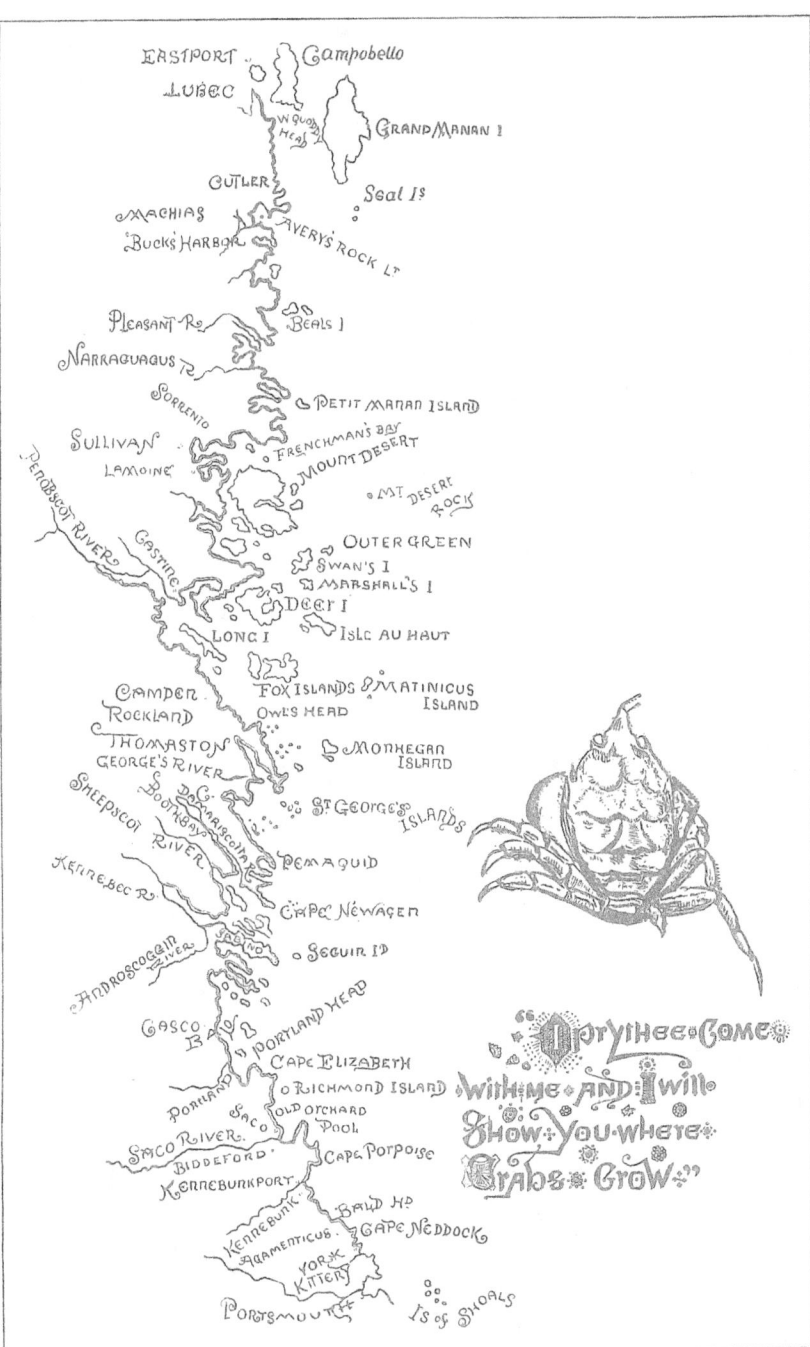

CONTENTS.

THE WEST COAST.

CHAPTER		PAGE
I.	KITTERY AND THE PISCATAQUA	17
II.	THE ISLES OF SHOALS	29
III.	A RAMBLE IN OLD YORK	44
IV.	OGUNQUIT, BALD HEAD, AND THAT SHORE	62
V.	A TURN AROUND WELLS BAY	76
VI.	AT KENNEBUNKPORT	86
VII.	THE STORY OF CAPE PORPOISE	102
VIII.	BIDDEFORD POOL	111
IX.	ON OLD ORCHARD BEACH	122
X.	FROM SCARBOROUGH TO PORTLAND HEAD	132

THE MID COAST.

XI.	A DAY IN PORTLAND	153
XII.	CASCO BAY	175
XIII.	THE GATE OF THE KENNEBEC	185
XIV.	BOOTHBAY AND ABOUT THERE	195
XV.	MONHEGAN ON THE SEA	207
XVI.	PEMAQUID THE FORTRESS	220
XVII.	THOMASTON ROUND OWL'S HEAD	236

THE EAST COAST.

XVIII.	A VOYAGE TO NORUMBEGA	253
XIX.	PENOBSCOT BAY AND ITS MOUNTAIN COASTS	259
XX.	HISTORIC CASTINE	271
XXI.	MOUNT DESERT ISLAND	289
XXII.	IN AND OUT OF BAR HARBOR	304
XXIII.	AROUND FRENCHMAN'S BAY	321
XXIV.	FROM PETIT MANAN TO MACHIAS, CUTLER, AND QUODDY HEAD	329
XXV.	EASTPORT AND QUODDY BAY	346
XXVI.	A RUN ACROSS GRAND MANAN	366

LIST OF ILLUSTRATIONS.

	PAGE
"The Breaking Waves Dashed High" Frontispiece	
Outline Map, Maine Coast.	PAGE
Head-piece	17
Old House outside Portsmouth	19
Pepperell (Portrait)	20
Fort McClary, Kittery Point	21
Wentworth Mansion, and Mouth of the Piscataqua	22
Whale's Back	23
Martello Tower, Newcastle Side	23
Whitefield at Twenty-nine (Portrait)	24
Graves of the Settlers	25
Champernowne's Grave	26
Maine Arms	28
White Island	29
Smutty-Nose Island	30
Londoner's Island	32
Sassafras	33
Appledore, from Star Island	33
Early Fishing-ship	34
Fisherman	35
Landing Fish, Olden Time	35
Drying-flake	36
Washing Fish	36
Carrying Fish	36
Dike, Star Island	37
Landing at Appledore	39
Time at a Standstill	41
Stone Church, Star Island	41
Camp-stool, or Table	43
Around Agamenticus	44
Across the Fields	45
Remarkable Bowlder	45
Ye Perfydious Spainyard	46
Old Meeting-house, York	47
Old Corner-stone	48
A Corner of Old Burying-ground	49
Ducking-stool	49
Summit of Agamenticus	50
A Lord Mayor's Procession	51

	PAGE
Canadian equipped for a March	54
Junkins' Garrison, Scotland	55
About York Harbor	56
Boon Island Light	57
Life-preserver	61
Hard Fare	62
Fronds	63
Early Morning — The Nubble, York Beach	64
Summer Night on the Coast	65
January and May	67
Union Bluff, York	67
Bald Head Cliff	69
An Aged Seamark	71
Deep-sea Codfish	73
An Original Woodcut	74
Old-time Utensils	75
Great Hill Headland, Wells Bay	76
The Settler's Chimney-corner	77
Ancient Lamp	78
The Lonely Grave	79
Spectacles	79
A Flanker	79
Leaden Casement	80
The Mail-carrier	81
Natural Fungus	82
A Summer Sunset	86
The Shipyard as it was	87
The Wreck Ashore	88
The Tristram Perkins House	89
Mitchell's Garrison	89
Congregational Meeting-house	90
The Temperance Movement	91
The Wading-place	92
Gooch's Creek	93
North Pier and Beach	93
Retired Lobsterman	94
The Old Lock	96
Old Half-moon Battery	98
Crab	99
The Bouncing Rock	100

LIST OF ILLUSTRATIONS.

	PAGE
Old Cedars, Cape Porpoise	102
Poison Ivy	103
Place of the Wreck, with Cape Porpoise Light	104
Mail-carrier (Winter)	106
War-club and Axe	107
Arrows	107
Cheese-press	107
Old Milldam, Pool Road	108
Ashore at Timber Island	111
Gate, Pool Road	112
Wood Island Light	113
Monument, Stage Island	114
Biddeford Pool	115
Weather-vane	116
Angel Gabriel	117
Road to Biddeford	118
Weather-vane	121
Dragon-fly	122
The Scavenger	123
Sand-roller	123
"Good Morning"	125
Medusæ	126
Sea-cucumber	127
Sea-urchin	128
The Contortionist	129
Spearing Flounders	130
King Philip's Wampum Belt	132
Pine-tree Device	132
Clam-digger	133
Halberd	134
Fishing-shallop, 1630	135
Ancient Flagon	136
Moccasin	137
Turnstile	137
Richmond's Island	138
Schoolhouse Porch	139
Indian Snowshoe	140
A Groat	141
Seamark	142
Portland Light	143
Gaining	144
Whitehead, Portland's Sentinel Cliff	145
The Crock	148
Block House	149
Longfellow Statue	154
Distant View of Portland	155
The Oaks	159
The One-hoss Shay	161
Public Library, Portland	162
Longfellow and his Home	163

	PAGE
Wadsworth Monument	164
Tyng Monument	164
Old Court-house, Portland	165
Views in and around Portland	167
Longfellow's Birthplace	170
Afternoon in August	173
Surf Effects, Casco Bay	177
Mrs. H. B. Stowe (Portrait)	179
The Flying Dutchman	179
Seamark	180
Half-way Rock, Casco Bay	181
Fort Popham, Kennebec River	186
Seguin Island	187
Foot-soldier of the Time	189
Indian Hunter on Snowshoes	190
Sword, Target, and Bill	191
Powder-flask of the Time	192
Getting Seaweed, Sheepscot Bay	195
The Pilot	196
A Fresh Breeze, Sheepscot Bay	197
One of the Five	198
Burnt Island, Boothbay	199
Boothbay Harbor	201
The Porgy	202
Steaming Hot	202
Seiners on the Alert	203
Cape Newagen, from Squirrel Island	204
Turnstile	205
Discovery Cross	207
Monhegan Island (Map)	208
Five Miles Away	209
A Monhegan Lad	210
Cliffs at Monhegan	214
Blue-fishing	215
Rock Inscription, Monanis	217
Old-time Fisherman	218
Pemaquid Light	220
The Oyster-shell Banks	221
Setting up a Wigwam	221
On the Damariscotta River	222
Pemaquid Point	223
A Summer Idyl	225
Arrow-heads	226
Mounting the Hill	227
Fort Frederick and Environs (Map)	228
A Snug Harbor, Pemaquid	230
The Graves	233
Tail-piece	235
Out on a Lark	236
Montpelier, General Knox's Mansion	238
Port Clyde	239

LIST OF ILLUSTRATIONS.   13

	PAGE		PAGE
General Knox's Monument	241	Schooner Head	301
Owl's Head, Penobscot Bay	243	Turtle Lake, Mount Desert	304
Matinicus Light, Penobscot Bay	247	A Bit of Bar Island	305
Tail-piece	250	Bar Harbor, from Bar Island	306
Morions, Discovery Period	253	Eagle Lake, Mount Desert	307
Dawn of Discovery	253	Tennis-player	309
Samuel Champlain (Portrait)	254	The Buckboard Wagon	310
Saint Malo	255	Cliffs, Sargent's Mountain, from Jordan's	
André Thévet (Portrait)	256	Lake	311
The Rockland Stage	259	Traveller's Room, Somesville House	314
Pumpkin Island, Penobscot Bay	261	Woods, Turtle Lake, Mount Desert	315
The Camden Mountains	263	Clock, Somesville	317
Rockport Basin, looking towards Owl's		The Ovens, Mount Desert	319
Head	264	Mount Desert, from Sullivan Harbor	321
Head of the Harbor	265	Wet	321
In Bean's Shipyards	265	A Sunny Point at Lamoine	322
Climbing the Mountain	266	Bits of Sullivan Harbor	323
Fort Knox, Bucksport	267	Petit Manan Light	325
Evening in the Harbor	269	The Wharf in December	326
Ancient Cannon (Head-piece)	271	Whistling-buoy, Schoodic Point	327
Doorway, Castine	271	A Fisherman's Cottage	329
Site of Fort Pentagoet	272	The Carrying Place	330
Harbor Shore, Castine	273	Avery's Rock, Machias Bay	331
Inscription Plate	275	Sand Cove, Petit Manan	333
Pine-tree Shilling	275	Along Shore	334
Unitarian Church, Castine	277	Old Man's Island	337
Elisha Perkins House, Castine	277	Entrance to Little River Harbor	341
The Old "Tub"	279	Where they pry up the Sun	346
Picked up at Castine	279	West Quoddy Head, Lubec	347
Main Street, Castine	280	Sir T. M. Hardy (Portrait)	352
Ferry, Bagaduce River	281	The Invader	353
Ferryman	282	High and Dry	354
Kinch's Mountain	282	Low-water Mark	355
Sir John Moore	283	Meadow Brook Cove, Campobello	356
Relic of the Occupation	284	East Quoddy Light, Campobello	357
Goose Falls, Cape Rosier	285	An Arm of Passamaquoddy Bay	359
Bass Harbor, Mount Desert Island	289	Chamcook Mountain	360
Anemone Cave, Mount Desert	290	Along the Wharves, Saint Andrews, N.B.	361
Gentleman	293	A Bit of Joe's Point, on the Saint Croix.	362
Gentlewoman, 1605	293	De Monts' Island	363
Lawyer	294	Under Joe's Point, Saint Andrews, N.B.	363
Sargent's Mountain, from the Sound	295	Boat-house and Wharf, Grand Manan	366
Bell Buoy	296	Trend of the Headlands	368
Somes' Sound	297	Cliffs and Beach, Grand Manan	369
Wharf and Sawmill, Somesville	298	Swallow-tail Point, Grand Manan	372
Rocks, Mount Desert	299	Sea-gull Cliffs, Grand Manan	375
Otter Cliff, Mount Desert	300	Southern Cross, Grand Manan	379

THE WEST COAST.

THE PINE-TREE COAST.

CHAPTER I.

KITTERY AND THE PISCATAQUA.

"Travel in the younger sort is a part of education; in the elder, a part of experience."— BACON.

I HAVE come up the coast as far as Portsmouth, that historic vestibule, so to speak, through which all travellers should pass. Upon seeing the mountains of luggage encumbering the railway station, one would be apt to fancy that all roads led to the Maine coast.

At Portsmouth, we meet the Piscataqua coming down out of the highlands. After gathering up its tributary streams in the broad basin above the city, it moves majestically on to the ocean like an army taking the field.

It is a noble river here, broad, deep, and swift, with the city skirting it on one side, and the country on the other. An ancient, thousand-legged bridge creeps across from shore to shore, carrying the railway and public road on its creaking back; also giving time for a long look down the picturesque windings of the river, as it turns now to the right, now to the left, in its progress toward the ocean. No sooner has the city receded behind us than the monster shiphouses, drooping ensigns, and tall chimneys of the Navy Yard rise above the elms that hang long mantles of brilliant green about the opposite shores, down

to the water's edge. We peer into the shady nooks beneath, where every half-hid cottage seems a veritable haven of rest. What a charming contrast there is between these graceful forms, this brilliant coloring, and inviting repose, and the hard lines, dull glare, and smothered noises of the city we have left!
While we are looking at it, the river suddenly disappears behind grassy banks of velvety green, which advance out into the stream from either shore, as if eager to touch the hem of its life-giving garment. Beyond this vanishing-point extends the low, flat line where the coast breaks off and the sea begins, though we do not yet see the ocean itself. But we know it is there. A fresh sea-breeze comes up the river to cool our impatience. It ripples across yonder grassy point like a cat's-paw on the water. Throw open the windows and let it blow in our faces! What an instant transformation that one puff from Old Ocean's vigorous lungs has effected in the countenances of all the company!

Five short minutes have sufficed to take us across the frontiers of two sovereign states, without further formality than showing our tickets to the conductor. The locomotive, encased in its harness of steel, stands impatiently puffing out a column of steam as we alight. The Pine-Tree State is under our feet.

Kittery [1] occupies the extreme southwest corner of Maine. Here begin the twenty-four hundred miles of seacoast over which we are about to travel — to travel as men did before the age of steam had struck out all the romance of it or before resigning themselves to methods of locomotion as insipid as they are wearisome and unproductive, and in which one's only purpose in life seems to be to kill time. This may be "doing" a country, but it is not seeing it.

Kittery now stretches along the Piscataqua from the great bridge to the sea. About midway of its course, the river throws off a large arm, at the east, called Spruce Creek, thus dividing Kittery Foreside from Kittery Point. When we have said that probably three-fourths of the whole area of Kittery is washed by different arms of the sea, it will be seen why the contiguous shores and highlands must make unusually fine sites for these villages, besides rendering them as accessible by water as by land. In short, whatever direction one may take he is always running up against some creek, harbor, or wandering stream to diversify the landscape or refresh the eye.

A string of islands extends close along the Kittery shore. Perhaps the most famous one of all is Badger's Island, on which in the neighborhood of a hundred and fifty vessels, large and small, have been built, first and last, including the *America*, seventy-four, which was presented to Louis XVI.

In walking from the station to the Navy Yard, about the first thing to attract particular notice will be the new library building, which Kittery owes to the generosity of the late Arabella Rice. The village really seems holding up its head the higher for it. When one looks about him at the number of wealthy people who never leave a penny out of the family, one honors all the more the memory of such a giver. This is practical benevolence indeed; this is true fame!

From books to bombs the transition is somewhat violent, I admit, but inevitable here. Only a short walk onward takes one across the bridge leading into the Navy Yard grounds.[2] Faith, the place is as peaceful as a country churchyard! Pert little sparrows were chirruping about the big guns in the artillery park, just as if they knew them to be only so much old iron encumbering the ground, or had heard the official utterance so lately given out, that this once famous dockyard was little better than a ruin. Going to ruin for want of timely attention to its needs would have more aptly expressed, perhaps, its present condition.

All the world loves a sailor. When did our own Yankee tars ever fail to uphold the honor of the dear old gridiron? Not since it first floated from the truck of yonder ship, now daubed over with unseemly ochre, and desecrated with a roof of pine boards, thus converting it into a sort of Noah's Ark, adapted

OLD HOUSE OUTSIDE PORTSMOUTH.

for the reception of some floating menagerie. In truth, one almost expects to see the sign "For Sale, or To Let" hung out over her side! Tell me, messmate, what ship is that, which Davy Crockett would have cleverly hit off as "half horse and half alligator." "That, sir," says my amiable conductor, with a shrug, "is the frigate *Constitution*."

"What, that nondescript thing,—that Old Ironsides?"

We went up over the dear old barky's side, where Hull received Dacres' sword; Bainbridge, Lambert's; and Stewart, not to be outdone, took a brace of them under his arm at once. Shade of Bellona! And must we then board this historic battle-ship through a landlubber's door, instead of by the gangway? Once more I read that inspiriting motto affixed over the cabin front, so familiar to every schoolboy in his teens, "Don't give up the ship!" then gave a glance at the rough rafters overhead, in some doubt as to where I was standing, and grew hot and cold over the crowding recollections of a glorious past, confronted by the evidences about me that they have given up the ship at last to rust and neglect.

Really the indignity of which this famous war-ship is the subject calls loudly for another stanza from the poet Holmes. She should be first stripped of all this unseemly gear, her leaks stopped, her cannons mounted, her sails bent, and then she should be anchored off the national capital, not indeed as a bulwark or defence,— since her fighting days are over,— but as a legacy from the heroic period of our history, to the flabby patriotism of these degenerate days. Then, indeed, should we once more see Old Ironsides as fancy paints her: —

> "With roomy decks, her guns of mighty strength,
> Whose low-laid mouths each mountain billow laves,
> Deep in her draught, and warlike in her length,
> She seemed a sea-wasp flying on the waves."

The road ambles pleasantly on over the hills, by the river, till it comes to Spruce Creek, which is crossed by one of those relics of barbarism, a toll-bridge. It then mounts the opposite bank to a rather spacious plot of ground, about which stand the village meeting-house, the ancient burial-ground, and one or two old-time mansions of rather better appearance than the houses we have been seeing on our way hither.

PEPPERELL.

The gambrel-roofed house at the left is best known as the Sparhawk mansion, from its having been the residence of the first, the real Sir William Pepperell's grandson, whose father was Colonel Nathaniel Sparhawk, merchant, and whose mother was the first baronet's only daughter, Elisabeth. Old Sir William had been bitterly disappointed in not being able to transmit his title and estates through direct male descent; but Andrew, his only son, died a bachelor at twenty-five, after thwarting the long-cherished plan of marrying him to Hannah Waldo, the daughter of Sir William's bosom friend and companion in arms.³ The two old friends had made the match over their wine; but Andrew played fast and loose with the lady, until forbearance ceased to be a virtue on her part, and when at last he did appear on the day fixed for the wedding, the high-spirited young lady told him she would never marry him — never. So the match was broken off then and there.

Sir William mourned his son as David mourned for Absalom, and would not be comforted. He then made his grandson, Sparhawk, his heir, on condition of Sparhawk taking the name of Pepperell, which the young man did; and the title was also confirmed to him some years after his benefactor's death, though his enjoyment of it, in the land of his birth, was short-lived, indeed, as the new baronet's loyalty to his king drove him into exile within a year after obtaining his brevet. So that he, into whose lap riches and a title had dropped without his ever stretching forth a hand, had now suddenly to pack off, leaving his all to the mercy of those who were just now his tenants, but whom the turn of events had made his masters. His fall naturally carried with it much of that traditional respect in which the family name had always been held, and when confiscation opened wide the door to greed and plunder, and all uncharitableness besides, not many cared to remember what they owed to Sir William Pepperell, Senior, the man of the people.

The house opposite to the meeting-house was built by the first Lady Pepperell, after her distinguished husband's death. She died here in 1789, after living thirty years a widow — years, some of which were passed in affluence, some embittered by seeing the vast property accumulated with so much patient industry swept away by confiscation, her daughter's husband an exile, and the family name become the synonym for Tory and renegade. Never in the history of our country has there been a more conspicuous fall from a high estate, or a more complete illustration of the vanity of riches. Not thirty years after the death of the conqueror of Louisburg, none were so poor as to do him reverence.

FORT McCLARY, KITTERY POINT.

It would seem that the doom of the Pepperells was to be transmitted to all who should inhabit that house. A blight seemed to have fallen upon it, which consumed the lives and fortunes of a family, until its evil destiny was fully accomplished. In all the world there is nothing so painful as the history of a family predestined to misfortune. Let us draw the veil of silence over it and pass on.

It is not much farther to the breezy hill-top where Fort McClary commands the river's mouth. The war left it unfinished; peace finds it neglected and dismantled. An old block house crowns the height picturesquely. The view from the ramparts is as beautiful as it is extensive. I stood there at sunset, watching the fading splendors of the day die away into the softer radiance of a glorious rising moon. Away out on the distant horizon a dusky cloud hung low over the still sea. The west wind, a herald of fine weather, had driven it off to its lair, where it sullenly crouched as if biding its time. Upon the darkening waves the great white moon was beginning to scatter her silvery scales. At the opposite shore of the harbor, Fort Constitution showed a pale light, and the island at the mouth of the river, another; and still farther out, across the struggling, sparkling, dancing moonglade, the Isles of Shoals were just visible in the gathering gloom. Suddenly a light shot out of the darkness; then it as suddenly vanished, and all seemed blacker than before. That was White Island Light going its rounds. It is no stupid fixed light, like those I saw winking and blinking at the moon's beams below me, but darts its clear ray into every nook and corner of the wilderness of waters, up and down the long reaches of

WENTWORTH MANSION AND MOUTH OF THE PISCATAQUA.

the coast, as if searching out some ship to guide or some heart to cheer. O sailor on the stormy sea, be this thy nightly hail!

> "Lead, kindly Light! amid the encircling gloom,
>   Lead thou me on;
>   The night is dark, and I am far from home;
>   Lead thou me on."

The reverse of the hill drops us gently down among the houses at Kittery Point.

Kittery Point has grown to be a place of considerable resort for people who do not demand of the landlord his list of attractions in advance, but are content to live outside the bustle of the so-called fashionable colonies, into which a continued round of gayety intrudes its unwelcome reminders of the great noisy world all too prominently.

The Point has an interesting history, much of which is associated with the fortunes of a single family, — a family of merchants, or, if you will, traders, —

" Peering in maps for ports, and piers, and roads."

WHALE'S BACK.

And this neighborhood is intimately associated with the rise of the Pepperells, as that a little way back is with what may be termed their decline and fall. The portly gambrel-roof house in which Sir William lived and died is still a prominent landmark here, even in the midst of a crowding settlement; perhaps quite as much on account of its unusual size, fine situation, and well-known history as anything else, for it is certainly plain to homeliness, though it looks good for another century. We say at once that this house was not built for show, but use. It further informs us that the builders were plain, substantial men, to whom the refinements of life were neither known nor necessary. And when the day of ease and luxury, for which they had toiled, came at last, and the old house was stuffed full, from garret to cellar, with plate, paintings, fine furniture, rare old china, old wines, and all that, Sir William certainly showed a sturdy independence in sticking to the homely mansion which held for him the tenderest associations of his whole life: we like him for this trait. It is a fact that prosperity never turned this steady head: we honor him for that.

A few steps beyond the Pepperell mansion is the Bray homestead. It looks, perhaps, just a trifle rustier and grayer than it did fifteen years ago, but is still enjoying a hale old age. It is much older than the Pepperell mansion, of which it is in some sort the progenitor; for John Bray, shipwright, gave the house-lot on which the mansion stands to William Pepperell, fisherman, when William married Margery, Bray's daughter. In course of time a second William Pepperell came upon the scene, who was destined to make some noise in the world; and who, as the thrifty son of a thrifty father, enlarged the house his sire had built, married him a wife, and jogged on comfortably with the old folks, in spite of that odious old adage which says that no roof is broad enough to cover two families at once.

MARTELLO TOWER, NEWCASTLE SIDE.

Just below the mansion, at the waterside, are the wharves where the Pepperells transacted their extensive business. The space between was formerly a fine grass-lawn. At the back of the house, in the grounds where the baronet lies buried, was the orchard, and the two or three fine elms still standing about here are the sole relics of an avenue that we are told once reached as far as the village church.

Nobody holds such a distinctive place in the community nowadays as these Pepperells did in the day of their prosperity. When anything of moment was being talked of, the question with one and all would be, What does Colonel Pepperell say? If a man had saved a few pounds against a rainy day, he begged Colonel Pepperell to take care of it for him. If he wanted to borrow, Colonel Pepperell was his banker. Indeed, all roads led to the Pepperell wharves or warehouses; for whether a man had something to sell or something to buy, he must look here alike for his market. Pepperell owned whole townships. He gave employment to half the county. All this denotes a man of large capacity, of influence; a man of substance and authority among men, — in short, a potential factor wherever he might elect to cast in the weight of his support.

WHITEFIELD AT TWENTY-NINE.

The discerning eye of William Shirley singled out this self-made man of the people to lead the undisciplined New England yeomanry against Louisburg. The world has usually argued that poor soldiers ought to have the best generals, but in this case the general was to be no better than his men. Flattered, yet perplexed by the offer, which was artfully made, Pepperell asked George Whitefield what he honestly thought about it. The great preacher advised against its acceptance, as any man in his senses was bound to do. Shirley's flattery had, however, taken effect. Pepperell's ambition was kindled; he had faith in his destiny, and his own private interests were as much at stake as any man's in the province. So he buckled on his yet undrawn sword, raised his now historic standard, opened his purse liberally, and went and took Louisburg in defiance alike of all military maxims and precedent, as of the predictions of the wiseacres of his time. Good luck and audacity fought with him, and he won. I had almost forgotten that audacity is the first of military maxims. It is quite safe to say, however, that if Pepperell had foreseen the difficulties that lay in his path, he would have thought twice before undertaking the task cut out for him.

When Sir William came home from England, with his honors thick upon him, he adopted a style of living more befitting his station. He set up a coach, had a barge manned by black oarsmen in livery, increased the number of his household servants, and kept open house for all who claimed its hospitality. It was then that he set about those schemes for beautifying his estate, of which, unfortunately, so few traces remain to-day. So much for revolutions.

Maine has thus had the honor of producing two men of very dissimilar character who received especial marks of distinction at the hands of royalty. The difference between them is that Sir William Phips bought his title with Spanish gold, while Sir William Pepperell won his in the trenches of Louisburg.

Just a word more about the expedition itself.

When the Duke of Newcastle, the incompetent minister of George II., was appealed to by Governor Shirley to defend Nova Scotia, he broke out with, "Oh! — yes — yes — to be sure — Annapolis must be defended — troops must be sent to Annapolis. Pray, where is Annapolis? — Cape Breton an island? wonderful! Show it me on the map — so it is, sure enough. (To the bearer of the dispatch), "My dear sir, you always bring us good news. I must go tell the king that Cape Breton is an island."

From the high ground about Fort McClary one gets an excellent view of Gerrish's Island, the outermost land of Kittery, and probable seat of its earliest settlement. Its situation is hardly surpassed on the whole coast of Maine. Lying, as it does, at the entrance to the Piscataqua, it looks broad off to sea, commands the whole breadth of Ipswich Bay, sees all the ships sail in and out of port, counts all the harbor lights, and hears the wash of the restless waves along its storm-dented coast. Within the river's mouth it encloses a quiet basin where many a vessel has rode out the gale that would else have sent her to the bottom. Cutts' Island, from which Gerrish's is barely divided by a strip of marsh, continues the coast as far as Brave Boat Harbor, an inlet separating Kittery from York.

GRAVES OF THE SETTLERS.

Though identified with the history of Kittery from so early a day, not many years ago these islands contained only a few scattered farmhouses to which one rough road led the way. Visitors were then few and far between. And save where a few clearings had subdued it to the farmer's hand, the greater portion still lay tossed and tumbled about, in rocky pastures, wooded fells, or low-lying fens bristling with rough thickets, quite as the first settlers found it. The best land had little value, and the worst none at all. But note the changes of time. Within a few short years the old owners have been bought off, and their humble dwellings replaced by handsome residences. The old breakneck bridge across Chauncy's Creek has given place to a modern structure, new roads have been opened, hotels built, and such general transformation effected that identification of the old sites has become difficult, to say the least. I missed those sturdy-looking, weather-beaten old farmhouses, with their mammoth chimneys and long well-sweeps. Somehow they seemed more closely knit to the nature of the place — to that blending of simplicity, wildness, and seclusion; that absence of everything which recalls the city to us, and is our ideal of a country life. Yet one can but look on at all this uprooting of old landmarks with a shrug of submission. Pray Heaven they do not uproot all the old traditions as well!

The tide is ebbing fast, uncovering the flats as it goes out. We do not find the pungent, salty exhalations it sends forth at all unpleasant, or the noonday heat, which an hour ago was stifling us, so oppressive. A light air, cool and refreshing, brings with it the fragrance it has just brushed from the sweet-scented, red-and-white clover-fields that border upon the sea.

For many, Cutts' Island holds a sentimental interest from its having been sometime the home of an English gentleman, of whom there is little else to say except that he was of gentle blood. Not far from the Thaxter residence there is a rough-walled inclosure in which many generations of the Cuttses lie buried

CHAMPERNOWNE'S GRAVE.

without stone or monument. Even the graves themselves are half hid under a covering of coarse, wiry grass and tripping vines. In one corner, beneath a heap of loose stones, like those of the wall beside it, tradition lays the bones of that Francis Champernowne[4] whose father obtained a grant of this island as far back as the year 1636. These Champernownes were of pure Norman descent, and were related by marriage to the famous Raleighs and Gilberts — bold navigators all. Sir Ferdinando Gorges, the founder of Maine, made every effort to induce men of quality to cross the sea, and realize his hopes. The sequel is well shown by this lonely grave with
"only cobblestones
To tell us where are Champernowne's poor bones."

But here we are at last at the outer shore of the island where the untamed billows come straight in from Old Ocean's heaving bosom. We could hear the noise of their fall when we were back among the woods — a confused hum like that of the wind in the tree-tops. It is our first greeting. So let us take our stand on this rock, and look about us.

Was there ever such a ragged-looking coast? Two thousand miles of rocks and sands and tumbling surf! Bays eating their way into it; rivers gnawing their way out of it; storms crushing and ice grinding it everywhere; yet showing its teeth as grimly and viciously as if all this hard pounding did but nerve it to sterner defiance, and like an untamed lion, growling the louder at every blow the ocean deals it.

It would be strange indeed to find a league of such coast without its story of shipwreck. In the equinoctial gale of March, 1876, the brig *Hattie Eaton*, bound from Cienfuegos to Boston, struck on this very island, and all on board perished except the first mate. This was the way it happened: Finding that he was driving on a lee shore, and that nothing else could save them, Captain Cook steered for what looked like a strip of smooth water among the roaring breakers. It was their last hope. On forged the unlucky brig to her doom. A monster breaker lifted her between two rocks, where she was left immovably wedged within only a few cables' lengths of the shore. The rocks held her fast, while the seas were pounding her to pieces, and flooding her deck with water. People ran up and down the shore, eager to give aid, but only to find themselves helpless witnesses of the work of destruction; for it was certain death to attempt to reach the vessel, in the teeth of such a surf as broke between ship and shore. The captain, as brave a man as ever faced death without flinching, worked his way out over the bow, to where he could make himself heard by those on shore, and stood there calmly shouting out his farewell messages to his wife and owners, until a death-dealing wave swept him away from his hold on the rigging.

Thus, one by one, the crew were torn from their places of refuge, to be dashed lifeless against the sharp rocks. It was a terrible scene for the spectators — almost too much for flesh and blood to bear. Once, and only once, by taking hold of hands, and thus forming a sort of living chain, they succeeded in getting near the brig by making a desperate rush out in the wake of a receding breaker, when the foremost man seized the mate's outstretched hand, and dragged him back to the shore more dead than alive. All the rest perished.

---

[1] There is reason to believe that the settlement, begun on the south bank of the river, quickly extended itself to the north side. Both came under the general head of the Piscataqua plantations. Kittery was the first town incorporated in Maine, 1647. It had an immense territory, including much of what is now York County. Thus Eliot and all the Berwicks formed part of original Kittery. Most of the men who were prominent in the settlement of Portsmouth also took part in settling this corner of Maine.

[2] In 1806 the government bought Fernald's Island for public purposes, and has since acquired Seavey's, the next adjoining one. Before this, several cruisers of the old navy had been built in the private yards of this river, as ship-timber and masts could be had here in greater abundance than in any other New England port. The *Kearsarge* is the most famous

war-ship this yard has so far turned out; but the want of any settled policy with regard to maintaining either this or other dockyards renders it doubtful if we shall be able to build a navy when we want it most.

[3] Andrew Pepperell died after a short illness contracted by crossing the river, late at night, after attending a gay party at Portsmouth. Within a few weeks Miss Waldo gave her hand to Crown Secretary Flucker, by whom she had a daughter, Lucy, who became Mrs. General Knox. See chapter on Thomaston.

[4] It would be more surprising to find one of these early graves marked by any stone. Champernowne is called Gorges' nephew, because his father and Sir Ferdinando married sisters. For the rest, he did little to cause his name to be remembered. He is first found at Portsmouth, where he owned property as early as 1646.

MAINE ARMS.

WHITE ISLAND.

CHAPTER II.

THE ISLES OF SHOALS.

"I marked the plunge of the muffled deep
On its sandy reaches breaking." — INGELOW.

PERHAPS no part of the Maine coast has had such distinguished and appreciative annalists as the half-dozen fragments of wave-worn rock, thrust up from the bottom of the sea at her southeast border, like the cast-off remnants of a continent. A delightful half-day might be spent simply in turning over the literature to which the Isles of Shoals have given rise. By what happy accident, we ask, are the men and women who have written about these islands both gifted and distinguished; or is there really something inspiring or out of the common in this much-talked-of little archipelago?

In his "American Note-Books" Mr. Hawthorne seems to have taken out his note-book the moment he found himself alone. For instance, he says: "It is quite impossible to give an idea of these rocky shores, — how confusedly they are bound together, lying in all directions: what solid ledges, what great fragments thrown out from the rest! Often the rocks are broken square and angular, so as to form a kind of staircase; though for the most part, such as would require a giant to stride over them. . . . But it is vain to try to express this confusion. As much as anything else, it seems as if some of the massive materials of the world remained superfluous after the Creator had finished, and were carelessly thrown down here, where the millionth part of them emerge from the sea, and in the course of thousands of years have become partially bestrewn with a little soil. . . . Pour the blue sea about these islets, and let the surf whiten and steal up from their points, and from the reefs about them (which latter whiten for an instant and then are lost in the whelming and eddying depths), the northwest wind the while raising thousands of whitecaps, and the evening sun shining solemnly over the expanse, — and it is a stern and lovely scene."

In Lowell's "Pictures from Appledore," we have the environment of the Isles set out in verse, — verse in which the rugged energy of the rhythm sends the salt spray tossing about us again with all its wildness and freedom.

SMUTTY-NOSE ISLAND.

"Away northwest is Boone Island light;
You might mistake it for a ship,
Only it stands too plumb upright,
And like the others does not slip
Behind the sea's unsteady brink.
 * * * * *
Look northward, where Duck Island lies,
And over its crown you will see arise,
Against a background of slaty skies,
 A row of pillars still and white,
 That glimmer, and then are out of sight.
 * * * * *
Look southward for White Island light;
 The lantern stands ninety feet o'er the tide.
There is first a half-mile of tumult and fight,
Of dash and roar and tumble and fright,
 And surging bewilderment wild and wide,
Where the breakers struggle left and right.
 Then a mile or more of rushing sea,
 And then the lighthouse slim and lone."

Even the gentle Mrs. Partington has a struggle between her sense of the ridiculous and her feeling for the sublime, with the one or the other alternately getting the upper hand, as she pens her parody of Byron's famous ode because she must: —

THE ISLES OF SHOALS.

> "'The Isles of Shoals! The Isles of Shoals!
> Where tuneful Celia loved and sung,
> Where the free billow ever rolls,
> Where Oscar rose and Cedric sprung;
> The summer glory gilds their shore,
> And crowns the cliffs of Appledore."

Then there is Mrs. Thaxter, who so often

> " Lit the lamps in the lighthouse tower;"

for her father, Thomas B. Laighton, who kept the light, had taught her how to tend them as well as he could himself. But the daughter saw some things that the father could not. Nature had gifted her with poetic vision. Solitude had strengthened its contemplative side. The islands were not only her home, they were her world of worlds, where every day showed something new; therefore their wild crags and hidden nooks were her books to read in. One might almost call her a child of the sea. She has, therefore, given us the best account of them, in many respects, that has yet been written. Her versified story of the "Wreck of the Pocahontas" gives one terrible passing glimpse at a scene of which landsmen know little, though most dwellers by the sea have heard with a shudder that sound they will never forget, — the minute-gun at sea!

> "When morning dawned, above the din
> Of gale and breakers boomed a gun!
> Another! We who sat within
> Answered with cries each one."

So Mrs. Thaxter's monody over the "Spaniards' Graves," on Smutty-Nose Island, is an outburst of womanly tenderness for those poor watchers who, from a foreign strand, in sunny Spain, in vain

> "Questioned the distance for the yearning sail."

And so we might go on enlarging the list of those who have enriched the islands with the best thoughts that have sprung up, like flowers among rocks, into perennial bloom. Mr. John W. Chadwick, Mr. John Scribner Jenness, and Miss Sarah O. Jewett have made valuable contributions to the literary symposium, not to speak of the letter-writers whose name is legion, and whose effusions have gone adrift on the great ocean of forgetfulness, along with the flotsam and jetsam of Time.

It is again Mrs. Partington who assists us to an apropos verse: —

> "The city and the country's muse
> — Reporter's pen and artist's brush —
> Here let their admiration loose,
> And with ecstatic raptures gush,
> While every soul-enchanted guest
> Says, 'Other isles and scenes be — blessed!'"

All this advances us at least one stage in our inquiry. Perhaps a rapid retrospect of the history of the islands will advance us another.

Although frequented from a very early day by fishing-ships, no trace of anything like permanent settlement is found here until after 1630, nor is it possible to fix with any degree of confidence a date to which such settlement should be assigned. All we know is that these islands were resorted to from year to year, long before they were thought of as a place of abode. That they were ever inhabited at all is hard to believe after seeing what nature seems to have brought forth in a fit of the ague, and cast aside with unnatural hand.

We are quite sure that De Monts and Champlain saw the islands when making their famous, but fruitless, exploration of the New England coast in 1605, because Champlain has given the bearings of islands and coast in such a way as to make that point clear; but it was reserved for Captain John Smith to formally give them a name and place in the cartography of the coast. "No lot for me," he cries out in bitterness of spirit, "but Smith's Isles, which are a many of barren rocks, the most overgrown with such shrubs and sharpe whins you can hardly passe (through) them; without either grasse or wood, but three or four short shrubby old cedars." His wail thus becomes descriptive. This was in 1614. Though Smith had thus given them his own name, that fact does

LONDONER'S ISLAND.

not seem to have deterred him from giving them a very indifferent character, as we read it, his reference to them being chiefly prompted by their importance as a landmark for the Piscataqu'

The Isles of Shoals is a later designation. Though many have given a guess at it, nobody seems to know just when it became attached to the group, or by whom it was conferred, or for what reason; though we think it might be traced to the fishing-ships, like so many other names with which our coast is sprinkled.

Yet none of these was the first who hailed Old Agamenticus. Many a swart and bearded Basque of Saint Jean de Luz, or Portingal of Lisbona, saw him shake off the morning mists long, long before. But they had merely sheered off, cursed it for barring their way to the west, and desperately bore away again for the delusive passage to Cathay. For a hundred years, at least, this virgin continent was not thought worth the spending of a few hundred pounds to explore it.

The little bark that Captain Gosnold sailed in 1602 belonged to Sir Walter Raleigh. Raleigh asserts that Gosnold and his companion, Gilbert, ran away with her. They were supposed to have gone to look for the lost Virginian colony, but made port under Cuttyhunk Island instead, built a fort there, cut cedar and sassafras wood, saw the people, and so began the history of New England. An odd beginning, it must be confessed.

This first New England cargo ever shipped to a foreign port somewhat appeased Sir Walter's wrath against his nephew, as it more than saved the charge of the voyage. In the letter from which these facts are taken, Raleigh angrily refers to his kinsman as "my Lord Cobham's man," but in a postscript he so far relents as to say "all is confiscate, but he shall have his own again."

SASSAFRAS.

A not unpleasing mystery, therefore, hangs over these islands. When it breaks away, we see a few poor fishermen's huts perched on the rugged cliffs of Appledore, to which a steep path winds up the rocks from the harbor shore. We know not whence they came or how. We may never know.

For a hundred years the islands afford few materials for history. They were first included in the charter granted to Gorges and Mason in 1622, by which the province of Maine was formally endowed with a name, if little else. Though this instrument does not mention the Shoals, it took in all islands lying within five leagues of the coast. Seven years later, in 1629, when the

APPLEDORE, FROM STAR ISLAND.

Province of New Hampshire was created for Mason's benefit, new charters carried the line, dividing the two provinces, through the middle of the Shoals, thus permanently attaching half to Maine and half to New Hampshire.

Gorges and Mason had already spent about three thousand pounds during

the period covered by these patents, in trying to establish a commercial plantation on the Piscataqua, and had failed; but their efforts brought the Shoals more and more into notice as a fishing-station, and so ships were constantly coming and going, either upon Gorges' business or their own, between the years 1623 and 1629.

The two fathers of New England colonization would not give in beaten yet. In the year 1631 they took six London merchants into partnership with themselves, procured another compact little patent, embracing both sides of the Piscataqua, as high up as Dover Point, and again set about the task of building up a great nursery for shipping and mariners. The Isles of Shoals were put into this patent as common property.

This promising association lasted, however, but two years before it was dissolved as tending more to bankrupt its promoters than meet their expectations of honor or profit.

Mason died in 1635. The indefatigable Gorges obtained, in 1639, from the king, a new charter of the Province of Maine, constituting him lord-proprietor. Once more the north half of the Shoals came under his authority. No record remains to show just at what time the islands received separate names: but Appledore,[1] Duck, Smutty-Nose, Malaga, and Cedar were those then set apart to Sir Ferdinando; Star, White, and Londoner's remaining to New Hampshire.

This anomalous, and in some respects ridiculous, partition carried jurisdiction with it, so that when it became necessary to extend municipal government to the islands, Maine's half was annexed to Kittery, and New Hampshire's to Newcastle for convenience' sake.

EARLY FISHING-SHIP.

What had long been, perhaps, only a rendezvous for occasional fishing-ships began to show its first permanent settlers at about this time; yet there is, as we have said, no definite period at which we can separate the actual from the floating population. The first occupants were guided to Appledore, no doubt, by the spring existing there at which ships had been in the habit of filling their water-casks.

It is said that these settlers had built a meeting-house before 1641, and though I do not find the statement verified by any record, it is known that the Rev. Benjamin Hull, of York, sometimes went over to preach at the islands at about this time. Rev. Richard Gibson, an Episcopal missionary, is also found preaching to the islanders, and marrying and baptizing them according to the ordinances of the Church of England, no later than the year 1642. His stay was, however, of short duration. At this time Massachusetts claimed jurisdiction over the islands.[2] In an evil hour, Gibson, who was a Gorges man, stirred up the islanders to revolt; but he had reckoned without his host here, for the news no sooner reached Boston than an officer was despatched to take Gibson into custody. His whilom followers, if he had any such, seem to have left him to shift for himself, which meant, in his case, a lodging in Boston gaol until such time as he should make a sufficiently humble apology to appease his captors, and so regain his liberty. He was then told to leave the country, and not to stand on the order of his going.

What progress the islands were making during the next few years becomes a matter of inference rather than of certainty. They were attached, in 1652, to the newly created county of Yorkshire, which comprised all the Maine settlements to which Massachusetts had extended her government. The next year we find them granted a local court for the trial of petty causes, with a constable to serve writs, keep order, and the like, but denied the town charter they asked for, as not yet being in a capacity to carry on their own affairs. Six years later they put in another petition to the same effect, and with the same result.

By 1660, however, Star, Smutty-Nose, and Appledore are supposed to have contained forty families — possibly two hundred persons. The islanders had built a church, and were maintaining a minister. They therefore now obtained the long-desired privilege, by an order of 1661, constituting them the township of Appledore.

FISHERMAN.

Anything like a coherent story of what was going on during the next quarter-century is quite out of the question. It was a rude little republic in which all codes were reduced to their simplest terms. The governing power would seem to have forgotten it, the islanders to have remembered that authority, when an exertion of it was the only way out of their disputes. There could be but one business for all afloat or ashore, — catching, curing, and housing fish gave employment to the whole population. There were no fields to till or flocks to tend. Probably most of the work of handling fish was done by women, as it is in Newfoundland to-day, and perhaps the Shoals women

LANDING FISH, OLDEN TIME.

were just as ignorant, coarse, and hard featured. If so, we need not ask what the men were like, or why a peremptory order should have banished women from the islands.

Thick fog shuts down over the islands during the decade next after their incorporation. When it lifts, we find that most of the Appledore settlers have gone over to Star. Just at what time, or for what reason, this removal took place, does not clearly appear, though we think the better landing on Star may have had something to do with it. It is usually referred to fear of the Indians; but except that Star Island is the smaller of the two, we find no capacity for defence in it not possessed by Appledore. Moreover, the Indians of Maine were never banded in hostility to the whites until Philip's War broke out in 1675, or five years after the removal came about. So the moving cause is not yet found.

DRYING-FLAKE.

The dispersion operated, however, to the prejudice of the islanders, because they were now politically divided between two colonies and two counties. Smutty-Nose and Appledore therefore prayed to be joined to the same county with Star, which, from this time forward, became the seat of government,[3] though it was not until 1715 that town privileges were newly conferred upon the settlers of Star under the name of Gosport.

As remote as these islands seem from such dangers, their inhabitants were kept in continual alarm throughout the terrible years 1676 and 1677; and though no actual assault upon them is mentioned, the traditions of Star Island affirm not only that the invading savages did land on that island, but they assert — and the hiding-place is still pointed out — that the women and children were forced to conceal themselves among the holes and caverns about the shore. Betty Moody's Hole thus has a tragic interest for visitors.

WASHING FISH.

Some time after their removal to Star, the islanders built a new meeting-house, with a bell. Their first pastor here was the Rev. Joshua Moody, of Salisbury, Massachusetts, who continued to preach the gospel, though without regular ordination over them, from about the year 1707 until 1730, when his mantle fell upon the Rev. John Tucke.

CARRYING FISH.

Here begins the first orderly account we have of the islands. A book of records was begun in 1731, in which the first entry made is a notice to the qualified voters to meet at the house of Captain Robert Downes for the purpose of extending a call to the Rev. John Tucke to be their minister. Singularly enough, we owe the first authoritative announcement that the islands were peopled at all to the Rev. Mr. Hull's missionary labors, so long before. This act of establishing a minister permanently among them probably came none too soon, and it marks a new era in the history of the Shoals. From far and near the clergy united to make the ordination an occasion of unusual solemnity, as indeed all felt it to be. Mr. Fitch, of Portsmouth, preached the sermon. Samuel Moody, of York, a man of sonorous texts, quick to grasp a forcible illustration, said in his prayer, "Good Lord, thou hast founded thy church here upon a rock: may the gates of hell never prevail against it."

Certain extracts from the records serve to show the state of education prevailing among the islanders, whose forefathers had perhaps no other books than the score and tally, — the best of them indeed being scarce able to write or spell in a legible hand.

DIKE, STAR ISLAND.

Each man agreed to give one quintal of merchantable fish toward the minister's salary. His cow was exempted, by popular vote, from the rule ordering all cows off the island, or kept from running at large, by a given date. But we do confess ourselves a bit staggered by the vote granting Mr. Tucke ground for a garden-plot. It stands recorded in "a janarel free voot past that every fall of the year when mr Run' John Tuck has his wood to carray hom evary men will not com that is abel to com shall pay forty shillings ould tenor."

That it was easier, even so long ago, to vote the minister's salary than pay it is made plain by the order directing Captain Henry Cartter and Mr. Richard Talphy "to ouer hoal the Counstabels for the money that is behind hand minstires saillary." And again when the good old man had laid down his unfruitful charge forever, a town-meeting is called to take action "concerning the Revrent John Tucke's salluary deceased."

This fine old Christian gentleman, whose pastoral charge somewhat exceeded twoscore years, seems to have held his rude parishioners within the bonds of a wholesome restraint, quite as much by the example of a pure Christian life, a patriarchal simplicity of manners, and a studied devotion to the every-day wants or interests of the humblest among them, as by his preaching. He had been long in making up his mind to accept the call to be their minister, while serving them as a missionary; but he seems at length to have felt that he could nowhere do so grateful a service to the cause of the Master as by dedicating himself to the work of weeding out the seeds of degradation and vice sowed broadcast by habitual association with pirates, smugglers, and the scum of foreign ports. While John Tucke stood at his post of duty, we hear less and less of these debasing influences. In him the islanders lost their best friend.

There is much vague allusion to the wealth and prosperity of the islands at various periods, which we find it hard to confirm; but stranger still is the assertion that "gentlemen from some of the principal towns on the seacoast sent their sons here for literary instruction," though Mr. Tucke's reputation as "an apt teacher of youth" may have brought him some few pupils from the mainland. With a single exception, the annals of the Shoals do not furnish one instance of a person of native birth who has won eminence in any direction, or who has left his impress on the time he lived in. Leaving out the ministers, the most considerable personage whom we may thus distinguish from the unknown rank and file — and small things become great in the history of these islands — is Samuel Haley, who lived, died, and is buried on Smutty-Nose, and who, while he lived, seems to have put much energetic purpose into bringing the islands up abreast of the times; for until he came to them the magical word "progress" had never been known to the island vocabulary. Samuel Haley set himself about introducing it. The harbor was notoriously unsafe, the landing scarcely practicable in rough weather. By building a mole across the ledge joining Smutty-Nose with Malaga, a small, but well-sheltered basin was enclosed, and many lives and much property eventually saved by its means. Mr. Haley also built a dock, a windmill, a brew-house, a rope-walk, a distillery, and salt works, — all objects of high utility to the islands; but the stagnation that fell upon them soon after swept away his property with the rest. Haley's old windmill was long one of the best-known sea-marks to the pilots of his day. We could almost call down the old Jewish curse upon him who removed this one picturesque feature from the bare face of the islands.

War with England, horrid war, brought with it destruction to the islanders, many of whom openly favored the royal cause; while others, from motives of self-interest, pretended to a sort of neutrality toward the belligerents. Their situation was peculiar. Either they could sell their fish, goats, and swine to the king's ships, for broad gold pieces, or they could refuse to sell and have their property taken from them by force. They could expect no help from the mainland, and they were powerless to defend themselves. Political ties had always sat lightly upon them. They had lived so long outside of all the currents of popular excitement or thought as hardly to identify themselves with what was going on in the great world about them. Like half-baked pottery,

STEAMER-LANDING AT APPLEDORE ISLAND — ISLES OF SHOALS.

they were not exactly useless vessels, nor yet quite hardened to the purposes for which they were fashioned.

But with their commerce and markets cut off the Shoals steadily declined. A great many left the islands never to return. Preaching was given up; town-meetings followed suit. A state of apathetic indolence fell upon the islanders, who appear to have forgotten the world, and whom the world seems to have forgotten, until the condition of poverty and degradation into which those who remained had lapsed became a matter of public scandal. Their reformation was then undertaken as we would now undertake missionary work.

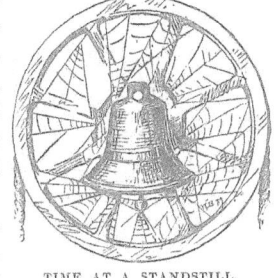

TIME AT A STANDSTILL.

A deplorable state of things revealed itself. In some drunken orgie the Shoalsmen had burned their meeting-house to the ground. Then, for want of a guiding hand, the always loosely bound society had fallen into the worst depths of immorality. Men and women were found living together, with children born to them outside of wedlock. A new generation was growing up like the weeds among their rocks, who perhaps had never heard the name of God spoken except to blaspheme with, or known any difference between one day of the week and another. Many had forgotten their own ages, for want of any record in town or church; and very few could either read or write. That such things could happen in a Christian land is indeed hard to believe; but it is all true.

The work of reform naturally began with marrying the unmarried parents, and so making their children legitimate. Preaching was resumed, and a school started. Bibles and testaments were distributed as in Congo to-day. A new church was begun, with money contributed by the coast towns, was completed in October, and dedicated in November, 1800, by the Rev. Jedediah Morse, D.D. This house was gutted by fire January 2, 1826, was rebuilt and newly dedicated in 1830, and now stands solitary and alone of all the ancient village of Gosport, a monument to this "strange, eventful history."

STONE CHURCH, STAR ISLAND.

It is strange that the Shoals should be eventually transformed into a watering-place through the agency of a self-constituted recluse — a man who had renounced all society to take up his abode on a desolate rock in the ocean. That the purpose might be still more binding, it is said he made a vow never to step foot on the mainland again. Going to live at the islands at all was indeed locking the door against the world, but going there as keeper of the lonely lighthouse was actually throwing away the key.

After some years' service as light-keeper Mr. Laighton moved over to Appledore, where he built himself a house in the shallow valley that cuts across the island from behind the cove. Appledore was then without inhabitants. This vicinity had been occupied, however, in the early history of the island, on account of its sheltered situation in winter, and for the advantage of its landing. Urged by curiosity, a few visitors dropped in. Mr. Laighton was asked to take a few summer boarders, turned the matter over in his mind, saw that it was better than leading a hermit's life, which by this time he found to have its objections, and finally acted upon the suggestion. Strange to say, the would-be hermit not only became a landlord himself, but the father of landlords as well.

Mr. Laighton also built the house near the hotel, so well known as the Thaxter cottage, in which Mr. Hawthorne tells us that he drank apple-toddy, and where so many distinguished guests have since been entertained.

Before Mr. Laighton built on Appledore the island was said to be haunted by the spectre of the ancient constable of the isles, — Phillip Babb [4] by name, — who lived, died, and was buried, tradition says, at or near the spot on which the hotel now stands. To make the story more interesting, "Old Babb" was said to have been a pirate. Some even avouched to having seen the apparition itself. Fear, therefore, kept the islanders from setting foot on Appledore after dark, till Mr. Laighton effectually laid the ghost by building over the restless constable's bones.

Meantime the enterprise shown on Appledore quickly communicated itself to poor, run-down Gosport, first by the opening of one modest public house, then of a second, and finally of a monster hotel called the Oceanic, for which an eligible site was only found by pulling down many of the fishermen's cabins then standing along the harbor front. The projectors of this scheme, of whom Mr. John R. Poor and Mr. Nathan Mathes were the head, first acquired a title to the whole island. The Oceanic was opened to the public for the season of 1873.[5] Thus, by the so-called hand of improvement, was the ancient village of Gosport swept off the face of the island to which, like some lonely sea-bird, it had clung with precarious hold for more than two hundred years. In all New England we do not recall a similiar instance of a whole village being improved out of existence. That is why we have been at some trouble to restore its history.

---

[1] First called Hog Island in an order of 1647 directing John Reynolds to remove his swine from that island.

[2] New Hampshire, 1641, had formed a political union with Massachusetts. In ten years the chiefs of this colony put forward a claim to the whole of Maine as far as Casco Bay.

[3] There was no government at all from 1679 to 1685, or next to none, as the king had dissolved the union, just referred to in Note 2, when New Hampshire entered upon a period of almost anarchy.

[4] It is a thousand pities to spoil a good ghost story ; but that affirming "Old Babb" to have been one of Kidd's men, whose shipmates murdered him that his ghost might guard

their hidden treasure, lacks, I regret to say, even that semblance of probability which is indispensable to all such tales. Phillip Babb was old enough to have been Kidd's grandfather.

[5] The rivalry thus established between Star and Appledore was not of long continuance. After suffering the loss of their fine hotel by fire, the proprietors of Star Island built another, with the same name; but this they at length sold out to the Laighton Brothers, who have thus acquired all the hotel property of the islands. These gentlemen were quietly resting in the supposed goodness of their title to Appledore, when the State of Maine publicly invited tenders for the purchase of all the islands originally belonging to her, of which Appledore was one, on the ground that they had never been granted away under province or state. In the meantime, however, actual settlers had been buying and selling their homesteads for two centuries and a half without having their titles questioned. Upon investigation Smutty-Nose was found to have been granted by Massachusetts to Mr. Samuel Haley in consideration of building a sea-wall and dock at that island. The assumed rights of Maine to the others were purchased by the Laightons, who are now sole lords of the Isles.

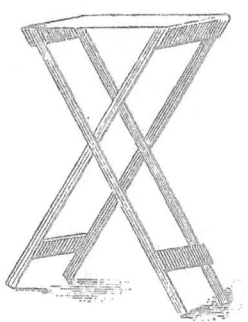

CAMP-STOOL, OR TABLE.

AROUND AGAMENTICUS.

CHAPTER III.

A RAMBLE IN OLD YORK.

"I will talk with you, walk with you." — *Merchant of Venice.*

I HAVE come back to Kittery in order to get to York Harbor.
Though, in sooth, she have a hundred harbors, Maine has not one really good one for sixty miles, as the coast runs; that is to say, from Kittery to Portland. It is true that two or three short tidal rivers afford indifferent harbors; but they are at all times difficult of access, and in bad weather are rather to be shunned than run for by strangers.

It follows that for want of commerce or ports, this part of the coast is deserted by all shipping save a few lazy coasters, which creep in and out of the cracks in the shore, but never put to sea so long as there is a cloud in the sky. In fact, your coasting captain is notoriously the most timid of mortals.

The natural features of this strip of coast are long stretches of sand between jutting promontories of granite, — at the mouths of the river marshes, in the areas of low-ground swamps, against which the sea has piled up the beaches.

As if to retrieve her mistakes here, nature has set up at one end of this coast a most commanding landmark. This is Mount Agamenticus,[1] the extreme outpost of the great White Mountains. No sailor can mistake it for any other land. It stands up solitary and alone, — a dome of green set on a low undulating base, — the natural landfall and guide to one of the best harbors in our waters, and, as we have said, the only one for many leagues up and down the coast. Agamenticus is therefore no accidental freak of nature, as it would be if placed in some dangerous or inaccessible spot.

Then again, Agamenticus River, next the sea, had been from a remote period a principal habitation of the natives, until the plague came among them and swept them away like moths before a consuming flame. There is a touch of irony in the plea put forth at this time, that God destroyed these barbarians in

ACROSS THE FIELDS.

REMARKABLE BOWLDER.

order to make room for the white people to come in and enjoy what had been merely made ready to their hands. The doctrine of the survival of the fittest is therefore neither new nor novel in our history.

I have always thought that these

considerations had much to do with Sir Ferdinando Gorges' choice of Agamenticus as the metropolis of his province.

Mount Agamenticus thus stands a perpetual monument to the barbarians over whose villages the destroying angel passed and left a desert. Not even the mandate of a prince of the blood [2] could deprive them of this distinction. In this respect they certainly have the advantage of Gorges, who has no monument either in Old or New England, except an insignificant fort in Portland Harbor. Consequences are thus not only unpitying, but sometimes grotesque.

Yet it does seem as if York, of all places, ought to commemorate the name of Gorges, that dark and scheming politician of two eventful reigns.

A strange fatality seems to have pursued the illustrious personages who took an active part in colonizing New England, while success was reserved to men of more humble origin. Sir Humphrey Gilbert perished by shipwreck; Raleigh, by the headsman; Southampton was put in the Tower; Popham died while his colony was on the sea; and Gorges lived only to see all his cherished projects crumble to dust.

A chapter might be written to be entitled "The Singularities of Sir Ferdinando Gorges, Knight." [3] He drew his descent from an old Norman family, and was the kinsman of Raleigh, whose example seems to have struck deep root in the minds of all the adventurous spirits around him. No record of his birth or education is found: no tomb is raised to his memory. The leading events in his life may be briefly summed up: A soldier with Leicester in Holland, and with Henry IV. in France; follower of Essex in power, siding with Essex in his plot against the queen, yet throwing his patron over to save himself; foremost patron of colonization; unregarded Royalist in the civil wars; man of great patience, persistency, and astuteness, coupled, we suspect, with a cold and selfish nature; in short, a man whom we can and do admire for his good qualities, but cannot bring ourselves to like in spite of his bad ones, as we do Raleigh.

Gorges had passed the greater part of his life in camps before the accession of James. That event sheathed every sword in England; for James, abandoning the warlike policy of Elizabeth, hastened to patch up a peace with "the perfidious Spaniard," in defiance of that national feeling which had become part and parcel of every Protestant Englishman's religion.

"Yᴱ PERFYDIOUS SPAINYARD."

Thus an unpopular peace, which threw out of employment all the roving and adventurous spirits who had followed the wars, — it is Gorges himself who tells us this, — was the direct cause of a revival of public interest in discovery and colonization; so that indirectly the pusillanimity of James gave rise to the settlements in Virginia and New England.

Having scanned the historic horizon beforehand, we are the better prepared to take note of the rise and fall of successive waves of emigration upon these rock-bound shores, where so many fair hopes have foundered first and last.

York is approached over a rough road skirting the coast, by a short cut across the hills from Spruce Creek, or by the branch railway from Portsmouth. It exhibits two quite distinct phases of growth, one of which is normal, and one grafted on the old root. Man, and not Providence, has thus joined them together, and with every year the fruit and foliage of the new growth is fast disguising the original flavor and character of the parent tree.

Old York, the country village, stretches itself out along the river banks, while modern York, a new plant in a strange soil, skirts the bluffs and beaches of the seashore. Old York was located with reference to the serious business of life; recent York, with regard to its idle pleasures only. Two constituents have thus come in contact, so completely antagonistic in their outward and inward aspects, that, like the ancient auguries, they can scarcely confront each other without laughing. But it is only a marriage of convenience. Perhaps the strangest thing about it all is that the transient

OLD MEETING-HOUSE.

population has come to save the permanent from the wasting process which was at work at the root of its life.

I first went to the village, and looked about me there a little. On the whole, it shows less change than one might expect. Here are the old church and cemetery, the court-house, and queer old barrack of a jail. The church has, however, made a change of front; and now stands facing on the street, instead of turning its side toward it as formerly, besides undergoing very considerable alterations both inside and out. These had hardly been completed when the church was struck by lightning,—an event which the older people were disposed to look upon as a judgment sent upon those who sacrilegiously remove the ancient landmark.

It so fell out that in turning the church around, the old corner-stone, with its date of 1747, attesting to the age of the structure, was left outside the new foundation, where it now remains, which is certainly a very curious place to find a corner-stone in.

The tall and shapely spire of this ancient house of worship is a conspicuous object for miles around.

> " ' O weathercock on the village spire,
> With your golden feathers all on fire!
> Tell me what can you see from your perch
> Above there on the tower of the church?'
>
> " 'I can see the roofs and the streets below,
> And the people moving to and fro,
> And beyond, without either roof or street,
> The great salt sea, and the fisherman's fleet.' "

What was no doubt the first house of worship in York stood at "the easterly side of the old road leading from York village to the Short Sands, a few rods from the road and near the sea." So far as I was able to ascertain, no vestige of it now remains.

OLD CORNER-STONE.

In spite of the distinction with which history invests it, there are few spots of ground in New England, I think, in which the old traditions have been suffered to die out as they have here in York. The endeavor to recover any tangible traces of the Liliputian city of Gorgeana, with its twenty-one square miles, and its twenty or thirty houses, must be equally unproductive. It is true that most of the original families have disappeared. But all that even the best informed persons can say of the past is, that if such or such a person were alive, perhaps he or she could tell you what you want to know. Why anybody should want to know about what happened before they were born is a mystery they do not attempt to fathom. They look volumes, but speak none.

The reply contains at least a suggestion. You at once go away among the gravestones. There is less change here. But there are, unfortunately, no very old stones remaining. There are, however, some long pompous inscriptions to a later generation. We are therefore driven back upon our books again.

It seems that some of the first settlers of York had come out of Bristol, in Old England, that seaport of renown, " standing commodiously for the western world." These colonists, therefore, decided to take the name of Bristol[4] for their plantation. As yet they were only transplanted Englishmen; as yet England was their native land. So it is primarily to their sentimental attachment for the place they continued to call home that we owe all those names which the late Mr. Matthew Arnold found so meaningless.

One or the other name, Agamenticus or Bristol, continued in use until superseded by that of Gorgeana,³ under the city charter of 1642.

As touching the life of the people at this early time, we have no other resource than the public records afford, and these have preserved for us only the annals of crime.

A CORNER OF OLD BURYING-GROUND.

There were no diarists like Bradford or Winthrop in this province to jot down every little passing event, every scrap of current gossip. It would be just as unfair, then, to spread out the criminal calendar and call it the history of the people of York, as to take the Newgate Calendar and declare it to be the history of the people of England. True history is not written in this way, though some writers seem to think so.

It is true that the dark side of life affords more or less insight into the beliefs and customs of the people. Thus we find that Goody Cornish, who was executed in the year 1645 at York, was the first person to suffer the death penalty in Maine, upon presumptive or circumstantial proof only. The woman had murdered her husband. What seemed to have told most strongly against her at the trial was the bleeding of the dead body whenever she came near it. Another woman was sentenced to stand in the congregation "on two several Sabbath days," wrapped in a winding-sheet, for committing adultery. Such offences as "light carriage," uncivil speeches, or profane swearing were punished by fines, imprisonment, or stripes; but there was another class of offences, such as scolding, idleness, and tale-bearing, of which the law now refuses to take cognizance, but for which those sober citizens found the ducking-stool a most efficacious remedy.

DUCKING-STOOL.

Two actions are upon record, in one of which the plaintiff prays to recover damages against a woman for saying that "she looked upon Mr. Godfrey as a dissembling man"; in the other, for calling Mrs. Godfrey in plain English a liar. Strong language to use toward the governor and his wife!

Whether the following order is still in force or not, it will tend to show

how woman was regarded in those primitive days when society was forming itself upon the old English models: "Ordered, that any woman who may abuse her husband by opprobrious language shall be put in the stocks two hours, and if incorrigible may be afterwards whipped." By these few extracts it will be seen that the so-called Blue Laws were by no means confined to the Puritan colonies, as is so generally supposed, and that the Maine colonists had a way of making laws to fit the offence as well as their neighbors.

It is a matter for regret that we should be quite in the dark as to how these people set up their primitive housekeeping, how they managed their public concerns in general, what pastimes they could safely indulge in without incurring the penalty of the law, how they divided their time between fishing and farming, what they sowed, and how their first crops turned out.

SUMMIT OF AGAMENTICUS.

Surely eye seldom dwelt on a lovelier rural landscape than the one spreading out on all sides of the village to-day. It is so different from the uncouth rocks or shaggy forests one sees everywhere about the Maine coast, as to seem even more beautiful than it is. Still, it is a lovely spot; nor can we wonder at the tenacity with which three generations held it as a forlorn hope holds out against repeated onslaughts; for this charming little valley, with its warm and sunny declivities, was certainly worth fighting for. The first comers must have thought it an earthly paradise. And the youths and maidens of that early time no doubt set the fashion for all this philandering by day and night about the beaches or cliffs, or on the placid bosom of the gently flowing river.

A LORD MAYOR'S PROCESSION, AGAMENTICUS.

A RAMBLE IN OLD YORK. 53

Alas, that we have no record of the love-making or flirtations of that most
interesting period! Nowadays it is different. In fact, our watering-places so
abound in adventures of this sort that a distinctive literature has sprung up in
consequence. Or is it a sign that the conventional round of fashionable city
life is getting somewhat stale to the literary palate?
The truth of history is often unpalatable. Supersensitive people maintain
that it should not be told at all times. But we cannot judge history as we
sometimes do people, by their concealments. What ten years of intermittent
effort had done for this plantation is easily guessed. In 1640, after obtaining
his royal charter, Sir Ferdinando sent his cousin Thomas over sea to be his
deputy on the spot. Deputy Gorges found that the settlers had stripped their
patron's mansion-house [6] of everything it contained except an old pot, a pair of
tongs, and a brace of cob-irons, which we infer were not worth the taking. On
looking about him the deputy found neither law, order, nor morality prevailing,—
a state of things not much to be wondered at when it is known that the
minister himself, George Burdett, not only set his parishioners an example of
unchaste conduct; but easily distanced them in the number and shamelessness
of his amours. One of the deputy's first acts was to ship off this gay Lothario
to England.

Though he had given the Puritan colonists some countenance, Sir Ferdinando
Gorges had no love for them, or they for him. When he died, in 1647, his
province had fallen into the hands of two factions, either of whom would
sooner have seen anarchy come than that the other should triumph. Both had
made their appeal to Massachusetts for recognition and support. The astute
Puritans, however, had no mind to pull other men's chestnuts out of the fire;
but when the monarchy fell, as it soon did, they saw their opportunity had
come for intervention of another sort, and so in 1652 Massachusetts promptly
asserted her right of domain over Gorges' whole province.

All the complicated machinery that Gorges had set up was overturned in a
moment. All the outward evidences of the lord-proprietor's chartered rights
were obliterated as quickly by forming his province into a county with the
name of Yorkshire, and by reducing his metropolis of Gorgeana to the rank of
a town, then first called York.

York is therefore the pivot upon which the history of Maine turns up to
this epoch. Gorges and his projects had now gone down the stream of time.
The epitaph to his failures is written by his own hand. It is also a confession.
"Let not therefore my evil fortunes . . . be a discouragement to any," he
sadly says, "seeing there are so many precedents of the happy success of those
who are their own masters and disposers of their own affairs."

York has also its deplorable memories. On the morning of the 5th of February,[7] 1692, the doomed village lay locked in the arms of winter. Since daybreak it had been snowing heavily, so that few of the inhabitants were yet
stirring out of doors. At this hour nothing could be heard but the muffled roar

of the sea beating against the ice-bound coast, or of the wind hurling gusts of snow against the window-panes. All else wore its usual quiet.

Suddenly a gunshot broke the stillness. At that sound the doomed village awoke. The startled settlers ran to their doors and windows. They saw themselves entrapped, surrounded. A storm of bullets drove them back. They next attempted to escape by their back doors. Death met them at the threshold. On all sides the rattle of musketry, mingled with the shrieks of the victims and yells of the assailants, drowned the voices of nature, — moaning sea and roaring storm. The village was surrounded, and retreat cut off.

CANADIAN EQUIPPED FOR A WINTER'S MARCH.

Under cover of the storm three hundred savages had crept into the village like famishing wolves upon a sheep-fold. They found no watch set or alarm given when they silently filed out of the forest into the open fields, where the peaceful homes of their victims lay in fancied security before them. The fresh snow deadened their stealthy footfall. Not even a dog barked. Not a settler dreamed that the terrible Abenakis were at his doors, until that fatal signal-gun was fired.

Then the butchery began. The savages soon burst open the doors with their axes, killing and scalping all whom they met. As fast as one house was carried, and its inmates slaughtered, the assailants first ransacked it of whatever they fancied, then ripped up and set fire to the beds, and after securing their booty, rushed off in pursuit of new victims. In a short time the village was on fire in twenty places.

At length it would seem as if the savages themselves grew weary of the slaughter, since some fourscore persons were spared the tomahawk and knife. Among these hapless captives were many aged women and little children, some of whom were set at liberty when the Indians were about to march off. Accounts differ about the number slain, Mather fixing it at fifty, others at from seventy-five to a hundred. The blow was sudden, unexpected, deadly. York became the funeral pyre of its murdered inhabitants; its flames were extinguished in the blood of the victims. No wonder Mather calls the perpetrators "bloody tygres." To call this war would be a foul libel upon the word.

Among the scattered houses, which then extended a mile and a half along the river, four or five had been expressly constructed as a defence to the rest. They were therefore called garrisons.[8] Thick walls of hewn timber made them bullet-proof, while the inmates could be doing deadly execution upon their assailants through the loopholes piercing the walls. Rude fortresses they were, yet of signal use in repelling just such attacks as the one we have now narrated.

A few resolute or desperate men succeeded in breaking through their assailants, and so gaining the shelter either of Alcock's, Harmon's, Norton's, or Preble's garrison. The enemy summoned them all to surrender, but being met with a stern defiance, they drew off without venturing to attack. Except these four every house in the village was burned to the ground.

At the time of this massacre, Shubael Dummer, the minister of York, lived down at the seaside, not far from Roaring Rock. He was shot down at his own door, in the act of mounting his horse. His wife and son were carried off

JUNKINS' GARRISON, SCOTLAND.

captives with the rest, and Mather pithily says that "one of the hell hounds" strutted about among the prisoners dressed in the clothes he had stripped from the dead body of his victim.

These Indians belonged to the missions of Father Thury at Penobscot, and Father Bigot at Kennebec, by whom the expedition had been set on foot. Before dividing their plunder, these pious savages sang the Te Deum for their victory. They also chanted matin and vesper service while on the march home, as those worthy fathers had strictly charged them not to omit the sacred offices of religion even while cutting the throats of the innocent and the helpless.

A boy four years old, called Jeremiah Moulton, who escaped the massacre, afterwards grew up to lead an avenging band against this same Kennebec tribe and mission, and exterminated both.

York Harbor may be said to have succumbed to the devastating hand of improvement. All these modern cottages in the places where the old ones had stood for so many years, reminded one of the tracts of woodland, also under my eye, where the original forest is being replaced by a second growth, yet of a different *genus*, according to the law of natural succession.

Down by the river's bank, and reached through a grassy lane that slips away from the high road almost unnoticed at your right, — a lane where daisies and buttercups peep among the grass tufts, and where larkspur, nasturtium, and sweet-peas bloom beside the houses, — there is a shady and sequestered nook. It is about the most picturesque bit of Old York I could discover remaining.

The neighborhood to which I allude might with truth be called the last stronghold of Old York. But it is evident that when the outworks have fallen the citadel cannot long hold out. Of course there is a group of old houses here, huddled together as if for mutual protection. One of them is the Barrell homestead, said to have been built by Jonathan Sayward, in 1713, who, as captain of a transport, brought home some of the spoil of Louisburg in the shape of rare old china and old brasses. The others are typical New England farmhouses, belonging to an

ABOUT YORK HARBOR.

BOON ISLAND LIGHT.

earlier period, low-walled, slant-roofed, big-chimneyed affairs, half smothered in lilacs when I saw them, half hid beneath great masses of foliage that hung about the strong-limbed elms overhead. How often I have heard just such houses ridiculed! And now they are actually building cottages to look as near like them as possible! On the other hand, the village people, taking pattern after the more modern cottages around them, are everywhere making over their old houses into new ones, so that our villages are in danger of being spoiled by the improving hand of carpenters and masons. By this means some of the oldest mansions have been so metamorphosed with paint and filigree work that their builders would never know them again. It is a curious thing, this play at cross-purposes between the old and new residents. What city people really like best about country villages is their natural charm, the fitness of things to their place and surroundings, the absence of all straining after effect. Yet it is they who have set the fashion of universal renovation.

Two superb elms stand guard between what is antique and mellowed by age, and what is new, strange, and but half naturalized. Three wharves with some dingy coal-sheds and fish-houses, three coasters with grimy hulls and half-stowed sails, announce our arrival at the harbor. It is that part of the river where a little peninsula, called Stage Neck, on which the Marshall House is situated, strikes out from the shore, thus forcing the river to make a sharp détour, and also effectually breaking off the ocean swell.

From a little circular battery, half earth, half ledge, perched at the extreme point of this neck of land, the river opens its foaming mouth, garnished with rows of jagged tusks, and exhibiting a palate of sand wide to the sea, which undulates its glossy back just outside like a monster python. Urged on by the flood tide, which sets strongly into the harbor, the long ground-swell launches billow after billow into the river's open jaws, through which they advance in successive dark ridges, to fall heavily upon the little beach, or go crashing up among the glistening rocks.

Eight or nine miles out, in plain sight, Boon Island lifts its solitary shaft aloft like an "eternal exclamation mark" to the temerity of its builders. There is no comfortable dwelling on that lonely rock, over which storms sweep unchecked. The tower is itself both house and home to the watchmen of the sea, and in great gales a prison from which there is no escape until the return of fine weather. This forlorn spot has also its forlorn story.

Long ago, the ship *Nottingham Galley*,[9] Deane master, bound from London for Boston, struck on this island on a wild December night; and as she struck, down came all her masts. In falling, the foremast lodged against the ledge, thus forming a perilous bridge over which all the ship's company crept to the inhospitable rock. During the night the ship broke up. Daylight revealed their situation to them in all its horror, though their nearness to the mainland gave hopes of a speedy rescue, the more so as they had saved next to nothing from the wreck. It will hardly be credited that they remained on this rock undiscovered from the 11th of December until the 2d of January, seeing vessels pass by them at a distance now and then, but always failing to attract the attention of those on board. During this time they built a boat out of materials saved from the wreck. That was no sooner launched than a wave thrust it back against the sharp rocks, which crushed it like an eggshell. This accident made them despair of ever quitting the island, yet their misery forced them to a second trial; for it was death to remain where they were, and no worse could befall them in any case. So they got together what few timbers remained from the wreck, made a raft of them, put two of the strongest and most resolute of the crew on board, and sent it adrift on its forlorn errand. The raft floated, or was driven, ashore, where it was found, and a search instituted for the builders. Heaven only knows what had become of its navigators. They were never more heard of again. In the meantime, however, two of the crew had died on the island, of want and exposure. Before the rest could be found and taken off they had been compelled to resort to cannibalism in order to save their own lives. And all this happened within plain sight of this spot, as I am telling you, in the year 1710.

---

[1] Mount Agamenticus is the subject of a singular Indian tradition, according to which St. Aspenquid, a prophet and saint among his people, was buried on the summit with imposing funeral rites. [Refer to John Albee's poetical rendering of the story; also to "New England Legends and Folk Lore," p. 360.]

[2] Prince Charles, afterwards Charles I., altered the name of Agamenticus to Boston.

[3] Sir Ferdinando Gorges' "Description of New England," and his "Briefe Relation" (London, 1622), put forth by the Plymouth Company, are reprinted in J. P. Baxter's "Life and Letters of Gorges" (Prince Society). Belknap's "American Biography," "Life of Captain John Mason," by John Ward Dean (Prince Society); "Vindication of the Claims of Gorges," by John A. Poor, give more or less collateral data of interest. For Gorges' share in the Essex conspiracy, consult Hume or Knight for the generally accepted view that Gorges betrayed Essex; or fuller information may be found in the biographies of Raleigh, by Edward Edwards, James A. St. John, and Edmund Gosse. Doyle's "English in America" takes the same ground.

[4] The authority for this statement is Winthrop's "Journal," II. 10; also Maverick's "Description of New England," (p. 9), in which it is said, "on the north side of this river [Agamenticus], at our great cost and charge, we [that is, Sir F. Gorges, Edward Godfrey, Alderman Hooke, of Bristol, S. Maverick, and others] settled many families, which was then called Bristol." Gorges himself asserts that Lieutenant-Colonel Walter Norton was the moving spirit in setting this plantation on foot; indeed, he refers all his own share in it to Norton's solicitation. And Gorges further says that, upon his consenting, Norton "and some of his associates hastened to take possession, . . . carrying with them their families." But Edward Godfrey declares himself "the first that ever bylt or settled" at York (Massachusetts files). His house is supposed to have been at the north side of the harbor, as the settlement began there. We cannot refer it to an earlier date than 1630.

[5] As laid out by Gorges, Gorgeana contained twenty-one square miles. He first (April, 1641) created it a borough, of which Thomas Gorges, his cousin, was named "first and next maior." This order could hardly have been put in force before it was superseded by the city charter, under which Edward Godfrey became mayor: Roger Garde, whom Winthrop calls "a

taylor," succeeding him for several terms. Gorgeana never rose above the dignity of a village, though it acquired consequence from being the residence of the deputy-governor, place of meeting for the provincial legislature and courts of justice. Rev. Benjamin Hull, who was the minister in 1643, is spoken of by Winthrop as "an excommunicated person and very contentious." The line was sharply drawn between the Royalist province and Puritan colonies when King Charles set up the royal standard, in 1642, against the Parliament. The New England Puritans believed, with much reason, that Gorges had tried to compass their ruin. The United Colonies, therefore, refused to admit Maine into their Confederacy of 1643. [Dr. Charles E. Banks is the author of a poem, entitled "Agamenticus," printed anonymously in Longfellow's "Poems of Places," and in "New England Legends."]

[6] Thomas Gorges, the first mayor, lived about half a mile above what is called Trafton's Ferry, near Gorges' Point. "The cellar of the house he dwelt in remains to this day." (Hutchson, 1–163.) Hon. David Sewall says that the salt-marshes near the head of York River brought settlers to that point "at a pretty early period." Perhaps this may account for the location of the official residence at such a distance from the harbor. (Account of York in "Massachusetts Historical Collections," 1794.)

[7] Mather gives the date of January 25, 1691. My dates are new style.

[8] Garrisons were sometimes private dwellings, and sometimes built at public charge. Hutchinson says it was thought justifiable and necessary, whatever the general rule of law might be, to erect such forts as these upon a man's own ground without special license. The two now standing in Scotland Parish are the best examples remaining of private houses adapted for defence. (McIntire's, one of those just referred to, was burned in June, 1889, after the above was written.) Alcock's was the house built by William Hooke, 1632 or 1633.

[9] Read the account of "John Deane, Master of the Nottingham," printed at Boston, 1711; also the "Watch of Boon Island," by Mrs. Thaxter, "New England Legends," p. 356. The light occupies one of the most desolate positions of any of our north-coast beacons, being six miles from the nearest land.

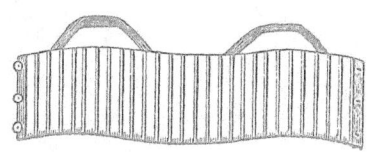

HARD FARE.

CHAPTER IV.

OGUNQUIT, BALD HEAD, AND THAT SHORE.

"What care these roarers for the name of King?" — *Tempest.*

FROM York to Ogunquit is ten miles.

One delightful May morning I swung off on foot, on the Cape Neddock road, with Ogunquit in view as my next halting-place. This excursion takes in the Long Sands, York Nubble, the Short Sands, and Bald Head Cliff, — enough, in all conscience, to be comprised in a single day's jaunt.

Spring comes slowly and reluctantly here. We sometimes wonder if it comes at all, or if it is not a fiction of the almanac makers, since it is no uncommon thing to have a killing frost in June, and there are old people who still tell of the year when there was a frost in every month.

Trees put forth their buds, and flowers come into bloom, ten days later than the same species do on the Massachusetts coast; yet the native growth is full of lusty life, and when once there comes a day or two of warm sunshine, the transformation effected by a few hours is like the work of enchantment. You believe that you can almost see the grass grow under your feet. Out come the buds and the blossoms. Up start the fronds and the flags. Only yesterday you could see the blue sky through yonder strip of naked birches. Now look! All their bare branches would seem to have caught the drops of some golden shower. To-morrow all these bright yellow beads will have burst into leaf, and the nakedness of the landscape you have looked out upon through the weary winter months have become only a grievous memory.

OGUNQUIT, BALD HEAD, AND THAT SHORE. 63

There is a fine strip of shore, rising to a bold bluff at the harbor, which stretches round the sea-front as far as Eastern Point, where the high shore breaks off abruptly and the beach begins. All along this bluff, the surface of which is roughly broken by rocky pastures, from which the first settlers turned away in disgust, a summer colony has sprung into being. There is now no land in York that is worth so much. Strange that what the builders condemned should ever have become the new foundation! It was pleasing to see that the occupants have so far very sensibly refrained from trying to convert these pastures into regular streets, lanes, and garden plots, but have left the wild growth, the sweet-scented bay and eglantine, the whortleberry and the raspberry as they found it. It is one of the choice spots of the coast, and has a charming society.

FRONDS.

York Nubble bounds the view at the left, and the Shoals at the right. A half-hour's brisk walk takes one to the beautiful gray beach known as the Long Sands.

The Long Sands join the two headlands just spoken of with a gleam of light and a frill of foam. When the tide is out, this beach is about the most popular part of all York, — its promenade, its boulevard, its recreation park. On every fine day it wears a very gay and animated appearance, each group making its dash of color on the cool gray sand, though it does seem odd to see so many people moving about without noise; for this pavement, hard and firm as it is, gives out no sound to the footfall.

We have just seen rivers running to waste; and here now is the ocean pouring its cataracts of water on the beach in pure loss, laboring to no purpose, like a giant harnessed in a treadmill.

These spacious beaches are to the rough coast-wall what cleared fields are among forests. They make spots of sunshine, tracts of alluring pleasantness, which lighten one's spirits, and lend an agreeable diversity to the scene. So we are seldom unwilling to come down off the rocks for a turn on the flat and nicely sanded floor of the beach. A very lively surf is generally running on this one, even with smooth water outside, so that there is nearly always a fine exhibition. We enjoy seeing the breakers roll in and the ships go by. We are very much delighted with the essentially panoramic effect of this noiseless flitting of sails along the sharply drawn horizon line. We seem looking on while a vast canvas is being unrolled; nor do we notice, until warned by the crash of water around us, that in our preoccupation we have nearly walked out into the surf.

At high-water mark the sea has some time thrown up a quite high and broad ridge of smoothly rounded blue and red pebbles, which makes an excellent

64   THE PINE-TREE COAST.

foundation for the road they have built upon it, above the reach of the tides. We say glibly that the sea has done this. And some one at our elbow chimes in with, "Oh, yes, of course; that is evident enough; it was the sea, to be sure." Very true; but when did it happen? Not within the memory of any living man. No one remembers the gale that heaped these millions upon millions of tons of loose stones where they have lain undisturbed for centuries. Nothing short of a tidal wave borne across the Atlantic on the back of a hurricane could have done it. When that roaring monster made his unwelcome visit here, all the low country along the coast must have been flooded with oceans of water. Only once have I met with the record of such a storm. During the great gale of August 15, 1635, the tide rose to such a height that in some places the Indians were forced to climb into trees in order to save themselves from drowning. The wind blew with such violence that there was no perceptible ebbing

EARLY MORNING — THE NUBBLE, YORK BEACH.

of the tide at all, as the raging waters were kept heaped up on the shores for so long as the gale lasted. The present century is not likely to match such a tempest as that.

Back of this sea-wall a straggling collection of small hotels and cottages, shops and pavilions stand singly and in groups as the cape is approached. Back of these extends an undrained tract of swamp steaming under the hot noonday sun.

Cape Neddock is a long tongue of land on which nothing grows but coarse, wiry grasses, — a succession of rocky knobs and deep spongy hollows, — thrust off from the main shore into the sea, which the heated rocks lap with avidity. The water lying between this cape and Eastern Point goes by the name of Long Sands Bay.

By following a cart-track for a quarter of an hour one comes to the canal, a stone's throw across, dividing the cape from the Nubble Rock. On the top of this bare crag the lighthouse-keeper's dwelling and fog-signal stand out bold

SUMMER NIGHT ON THE COAST.

and sharp against the blue sky. At the east, a clump of blanched ledges stretches off. It is an ideal sea-eyrie. The prospect comprises everything between Cape Ann and Cape Elizabeth in clear weather, and is every way admirable. Turning now toward the east, Bald Head Cliff breaks away from the shore at a few miles from us, so forming a shallow bay between.

One of the highest elevations of the cape is traversed by a stone wall which, with the battery at Stage Neck, broadly exhibits the state of our seacoast defences during the War of 1812, — no longer the last, but the worst, everything considered, which the nation has waged.

JANUARY AND MAY.

While walking about the neighborhood I met with a local proprietor, with whom I scraped an acquaintance at short notice. I began by artfully praising the locality, the air, the views, the feeling of repose. "H'm, too quiet for me. I would be willing to get out of it," he replied brusquely. Trying to fall in with his humor, I suggested that some people, certainly, would prefer less sand and more soil, less bog and more upland. "City folks like sand," he retorted. Then after a little reflection, feeling, perhaps, that he had spoken his mind too freely, he asked me to look over his place with him, — told me the age of the house, what it would cost to get lumber, who planted the willows, how hens could be raised for nothing at all, pointed out the boundaries, and mentioned the aggregate of his acres of stones and sand; all of which I listened to as a matter of course, though I thought him grown remarkably communicative all at once. When I had taken a few steps to leave him, he suddenly called out after me, "I wish some one would come along and offer me twenty thousand dollars for my place; see?" The man had taken me

UNION BLUFF, YORK.

for a land-broker or a speculator. Shade of John Law! have these people gone mad, too?

The deep nook at the head of which is the Short Sands gives one the strange idea of a large mouthful bitten out of the coast. It is by far the safest bathing beach I have ever seen, it being as flat as a floor, very broad, free from stones, well sheltered at its sides, and shelving off so gently from high-water mark that there is little danger of getting beyond one's depth. There is no undertow at all. The temperature here is something anomalous, for with the mercury registering 92° when I left Portsmouth, I found it fallen to 78° on the beach at the hour of noon.

At about a hundred paces above the present high-water mark, and stretching quite across the head of the beach, one sees a high, grassy bank on which one or two hotels are advantageously located. It is all that prevents the great tides, that always come with great storms, from forcing their way across the head of the beach, and inundating the lowlands behind it. This natural embankment has all the appearance of an artificial levee, for which, indeed, it is an excellent substitute; only, in point of fact, the winds and waves have done the work of a thousand laborers in throwing it up where we now see it, though some omniscient journalists would have us believe that its origin is a mystery. The really strange thing about it, as all must agree, is that at the cape end, where it joins the firm ground, the mound turns sharply inward, thus forming a right angle to the front, of as regular workmanship as was ever laid out by a military engineer. Indeed, if such a curiosity should be found at some inland point, it would be taken for the defensive work of a prehistoric people.

From here we betake ourselves to the humpbacked road that goes undulating off to the east. This is a part of the coast, I hasten to say, that has been long neglected, but is now beginning to find better appreciation, with improved means of access.

After going a mile or so we come to the little settlement scattered about the banks of Cape Neddock River, which is only an irregular crack in the granite wall of coast, filled by one tide and drained dry by the next, where rocks alternate with sand. The settlement, however, goes back to nearly, if not quite, as early a day as the oldest in York. During Philip's War the village here was completely destroyed, and forty persons either killed or carried into captivity.

Before the day of railroads Cape Neddock was the usual stopping-place for the mail-coach passing twice a week between Boston and Portland. Freeman's tavern had then many a notable guest under its roof. Some years ago the old tavern-stand was destroyed by fire and never rebuilt, as the railways had turned away all custom from its door, though now that travel is finding its way back into its old channels again, the ancient hostel is sadly missed.

Poor country, poor people! You think the phrase "poverty stricken" must have been invented for it. Yet there is everywhere a charming blending of sea and shore. Decrepit orchards indicate long occupation of the unfertile land; but it is also plain that one generation has merely succeeded another, as one soldier might step into the place made vacant by a fallen comrade, without growing any the better off. The granite swells lift their big backs higher in the air. Houses grow more and more unfrequent. Apparently we have reached a point where the world has come to a standstill, — where people merely plod along, and grow old.

Not above a mile from this place a remarkably bold headland lifts head and shoulders over everything around it. This is Bald Head Cliff. Upon the bleak and windy brow there is a hotel,— an object in the landscape of this coast which one is seldom, if ever, out of sight of. As it nears the cliff, the road closely hugs the shores of two romantic little coves, hollowed out of the rocks, where the waves, breaking finely at our feet, first push the loose pebbles before them up the strand, rattling loudly at being thus disturbed, then drag them clattering back again with the force of the undertow. This, then, is the natural laboratory where the process of smoothing and polishing is carried on, and those lying at our feet are the completed work. The rim of the cove where we are walking is formed of these same pebbles, the prettiest of all natural mosaics,

BALD HEAD CLIFF.

upon which the waves expend so much useless labor. Old Ocean seems in a sportive mood here, and we readily fall in with its playful mood.

Mossy ledges now thrust their bare backs above ground all about us. Everywhere the reddish-brown rocks, colored by the action of the salt air, bulge out through the thin turf piteously. In vain the grass tries to cover their nakedness. Nothing less hardy than the dwarf juniper, the whortleberry, the bayberry, or kindred shrubs, which seem to love the neighborhood of these rocks, and cling or hang about their crevices, can extract a living from the lean soil. Even these horny junipers seem to have thrown themselves flat on the ground to avoid being torn from their hold by the fierce winter gales which make everything here grow so stunted and deformed.

The iron coast now stands up stern and defiant before us, in one huge overhanging mass. We hear the *swish* and boom of water all along its base. All the near promontories sink to insignificance.

Imagine an enormous rusty-red crag lifted high up above the fume and pother going on about its feet, — a crag seamed all over its exposed face with cracks and rents, the scars of a thousand battles with storm and tempest, yet banded and knit together by great knotted veins of enduring stone in one solid mass, — against which a perpetual surf is hurling itself with the regular strokes of a trip-hammer; imagine this crag thrust out so far from the land as to expose itself to the whole fury of the Atlantic, and you may have some idea of what Bald Head Cliff is like. It is not a thing to excite admiration. Rather it amazes us by its embodiment of rugged strength, of passive against active force, as we read the history of its many conflicts on its battered front.

Feet and inches do not count here. One becomes fully absorbed in the grandeur of the combat between two such adversaries. Let us watch its progress for a few minutes. Every three or four seconds the waves launch a catapult of water full at the foot of the cliff. The shock is tremendous. A spectral column of white spray is shot high up the vertical wall, steadies itself there for an instant, bends like a reed to the wind, and then falls back into the foaming waters below with a noise like the rattle of hailstones. Then the spent wave changes from a deep black to a pale malachite-green, and is dragged back by the recoil, a broken and helpless thing.

After this onset and repulse there comes a lull, during which a hundred little cascades gush out of the old cracks and run streaming down the broken steps which the retreating wave has just left bare. You expect to see some evidence of the work the wave has just done! Summer rain trickling down the face of a statue of bronze would show just as much. Yet twice or thrice a minute, during a storm at sea, volumes of water are hurled against this cliff sufficient to sweep a village from its site without leaving a trace behind. And while you have but just thought of it, all this has been going on since the world began.

But there are all about you evidences of rack and ruin too tremendous for doubt. These tell the story of the cliff, which was so many thousand years old before it was affronted with its puerile baptismal name. It is evident that a large section of the promontory, perhaps as large as that yet remaining, has been not only demolished in course of time, but actually removed from the spot. What else can mean this smooth, sheer face, this long, level rock floor at the base, to which the south wall is joined? And where shall we look for the relics of that Cyclopean battering, the sight of which is so startling, when we are standing on the great dike, wedged into the heart of the cliff?

Taken altogether, the cliff affords most interesting ground. The dike just mentioned is perhaps the most curious thing about it, since the strata really look like regularly laid courses of stone pavement, roughly broken off at the edges, or, better still, dented by the blows of some enormous hammer. Thousands visit the place every year. You turn off the road at a deserted farmhouse, into a by-road leading to the hotel and the brow of the cliff, and on the word of an old traveller, you will find no such spacious and enrapturing sea-view for many a league up and down this storied coast.

Though it happened near fifty years ago, the wreck of the *Isidore* is one of the traditions of this locality which the visitor will often hear talked about. It was the first and last voyage of this fated ship. She had set sail from Kennebunkport on one of those deceitful November days that old sailors know and fear as weather-breeders. So it proved in this instance. A gale from the northeast struck the *Isidore* before she could get clear of the bay, forced her among the breakers, and dashed her in pieces against the rocks near Bald Head,

AN AGED SEAMARK.

without a soul on shore knowing of the tragedy or stretching forth a hand to save the crew. Most of them belonged in the river, where the ship was built. Not one was left to tell the tale. These circumstances, not to speak of a certain sorrowful ballad composed for the occasion by some local poetaster, have kept the memory of the event alive, and, indeed, to those who had friends on board the tidings of that wreck were as the tidings of a lost battle.

In the village cemetery at Kennebunkport a stone is raised to the memory of Captain Foss, the master of the *Isidore*, though his body was never found, or, for that matter, any part of the unlucky ship big enough to make a handspike of. The late Captain Kingsbury, who built the *Isidore*, told me that one day when he was walking about with Foss, under the ship's bottom, before she was launched, he said abruptly, referring to the flatness of the *Isidore's* floor, "Captain Foss, suppose you were on a lee-shore with this vessel in a gale of wind, where would you go to?"

"Where would I go?" Foss repeated after him; "why, ashore, of course."

Three miles of as picturesque country as one would wish to see, let him be ever so travelled, extend between Bald Head and the little village of Ogunquit. Monster bowlders lift their elephantine backs so often in your path, that the crooked road seems on the point of turning back, and giving up the attempt to get on in despair. There are rock studies all about that would make a rising young artist's fortune. And by the shore huge piles of desolate looking crags lean out over the sea in all manner of lawless shapes and forms, with a few sheep gravely cropping the tender shoots sprouting from the crevices, but no sound to break the stony silence, — no, not even the dull monotone of the sea.

Who would believe that such solitudes existed almost within sight and hearing of the great travelled routes?

After twisting awhile among these ledges you presently dive down into a hollow, through which a sluggish brook, skirted by scarecrow pollards, slips out under a bridge and disappears in a spongy meadow.

As Balzac says of the Burgundian peasantry, "however solitary you may think yourself, you are certain to be the focus of two eyes of a country bumpkin." An ox-cart came lumbering down the hill before me, its two clumsy beasts wagging their big heads from side to side as if keeping time to their own slow and heavy tread; while the driver, a great overgrown lout of a boy, all legs and arms, with shambling gait and stooping shoulders, whose lank hair stuck out through the cracks in his straw hat, shouted to them as if the country were made large on purpose to shout in. He checked himself long enough to stare at me, open-mouthed, then dealt his oxen a resounding thwack, hard enough to take off the skin, upon which they instantly set off down the hill at a run. In a minute or two I passed a man who was at work in his garden patch. He leaned on his hoe to watch me till I had passed the next turning of the road. At each cottage the women folk peered out through the half-drawn blinds. In this manner I entered Ogunquit, the observed of all observers.

Ogunquit is certainly the prettiest seashore village, as villages go here, between Kittery Point and Portland Head. When I had walked through it I felt the temptation to turn about and walk back again quite too strong to be resisted, even after the long tramp I had just finished. It used to be said that they built ships by the mile in Maine. Here I saw a dwelling that would justify the transfer of this bit of pleasantry to the houses. I instinctively christened it the Long House of the Ogunquits.

Perkins' Cove is one of those charming little sea-nooks deeply scooped out of the surrounding ledges. Forty fishing-boats go out from it to the adjacent fishing-grounds, and bring in cargoes worth fifteen thousand dollars every year, to be sold by pedlers through the country round. A dozen or more of these boats were drawn up on the gravel beach, where men in sea-boots and slouched hats, brown and bearded, were busy taking care of their day's catch, — some carelessly tossing the limp and slimy denizens of the sea upon the clean shingle with a pitchfork; some splitting them with sharp-pointed knives, and others standing up to their knees in the palpitating mass, as if they liked it. Two or three idlers were squatted about on their heels, watching every movement as intently as if it were an altogether novel experience; and to be frank, I soon gave myself up to the fascination which everybody has felt at seeing codfish split open, beheaded, and tossed into a basket at the rate of two or three a minute.

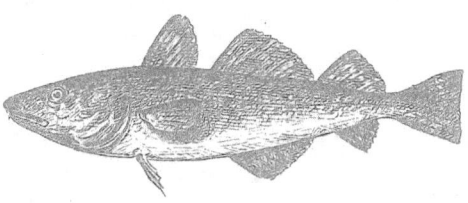

DEEP-SEA CODFISH.

One of these toilers of the sea seemed to guess my thoughts; for he drew the back of a bloody hand across his mouth, eyed me with a half-grin, spat on his whetstone, and said, as he proceeded to sharpen his knife, "Dirty work, Mister, now aint it? but it brings clean money all the same."

For a man who keeps his ears open the country store is the place of all places to get at the life of a community. The multitudinous character of a Maine storekeeper's stock in trade may be guessed from the following catalogue of items which I copied *verbatim* from a sign conspicuously displayed near a certain railway station: "Guns, Confectionery, Pressed Hay, Coffins and Caskets."

Having replaced the tavern-keeper to a certain extent, as the purveyor of local intelligence, the shopkeeper is expected to deal out the small change of local gossip to his customers; and no man could be more expert than he, not even excepting that ubiquitous person, the modern reporter, in extracting information, or embellishing it for daily consumption. It is an accomplishment for which I have the most profound admiration; for though country people in general are so inordinately inquisitive about other people's affairs, they are apt to be exceedingly close about their own.

This trait, which has made Yankee inquisitiveness proverbial, is, I take it, a relic of the inquisitorial character of the old colonial days, when every stranger was expected to give an account of himself, or be set down as a suspicious character. It was Ben Franklin who first hit upon the idea of forestalling this cross-examination in detail by calling all the bystanders about him, whenever he arrived at an inn, and addressing them as follows: "My friends, I am Ben Franklin, a printer of Philadelphia. I am travelling to collect money due for my newspaper, and believe in the Christian religion."

The guilelessness of some of these people has often reminded me of Turenne's celebrated remark about Sully, that if some one were to wring his nose, milk would flow out. A very good friend of mine once told me of a man who came into his store to buy some split peas, which he proposed to plant in order that he might raise some for family use, as he had tried and liked them. Within an hour of my arrival at Ogunquit, I myself had accosted a man whom I met in the road carrying an unusually large last year's hornets' nest in his hand. To the question of how many of the insects he supposed the hive had contained, he replied, after turning it over critically, "About three quarts."

A keen sense of the humorous, with aptness in illustration, drawn from observation in their own sphere, is another distinguishing trait. I was present at a discussion among some village philosophers, about a wedding recently solemnized in the neighborhood. The groom was described as being as poor as a church-mouse; so that the union of hearts did not promise a golden future. "Oh, never mind," said one of these graybeards; "tew pigs allers doos better'n one."

But a serpent has entered this Eden. I found that even here the farmers were selling off their land to capitalists by the hundred acres in a lump. One goodman's face expanded in a broad grin when he said that nobody wanted to buy his good land, but everybody was crazy after his poorest. They might have the "veew" and welcome, he said; he would "heave" that in. When I asked him some questions about the locality itself, he disposed of it with a monosyllable, as too trivial a thing to dwell upon, and immediately changed the subject to the price of land, showing a familiarity with the jargon of Wall Street and State Street that was quite surprising. He wanted to know how prices were going at York, and whether it was true that four acres had just been sold at Eastern Point for sixteen thousand dollars. In short, he had become a full-fledged land speculator, to whom his old occupation was already grown distasteful, and his smock frock a badge of servitude.

AN ORIGINAL WOODCUT.

But apart from the enhanced value of these shore lands, the farmers are distinctly benefited in the increased demand for farm produce of every kind, for which they now get ready cash instead of "store pay," as formerly. The storekeepers also find better profit in catering to the wants of these birds of passage, from whose plumage every one considers it a duty to pluck a feather.

The highest hill-top on which we stop to breathe, and let the cool breeze blow over us, commands a wide prospect of Wells Bay again. Change could hardly be more striking or complete, or more refreshing to the eye, for all is light and sunshine here after the darkness and gloom of those fearful crags. The coast is no longer encased in granite, but has now put on a softer and warmer raiment, as if nature herself had called a truce.

From the mouth of the Ogunquit River, — here clipped to 'Gunkit, — which falls into the sea at one end of the village, and makes its harbor, the shore sweeps grandly round till it is cut apart by the deep furrow of the Kennebunk, where the rock formation begins again.

Stretched out before us invitingly, beneath a tremulous golden mist, are the long beaches of Ogunquit and Wells, extending together for four miles, an ocean amphitheatre, with an irregular heap of dazzling sand-dunes thrown up behind them, and long levels of salt-marsh behind these again. These beaches are nearly always wrapped in a warm, luminous vapor through which the dull glitter from myriad particles of sand sends scintillations of light to a great distance. And such breakers! It is something to see, as we do here, whole troops of them advancing like prancing horsemen to the charge, three lines deep and all at once, toward the shore, up which they fling themselves in mad riot, rearing and plunging, and trampling each other down with all the action and energy of living things. But best of all is the refreshment that the sight never fails to afford us even after the most wearisome of jaunts, the coolness it brings in its train, and the sensation of real pleasure we feel at merely looking on.

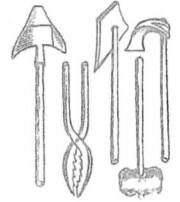
OLD-TIME UTENSILS.

Some years ago there was a sad accident at Ogunquit Beach by which four persons lost their lives while bathing. An ounce of prevention is always better than a pound of cure. Whenever there is a heavy surf running on the beach, there is always an undertow that is more or less dangerous even to good swimmers, till the sea goes down again. Want of knowledge of this fact has caused the sacrifice of many valuable lives first and last, but in the case referred to it is said that the unfortunate bathers were warned of their peril before they set out for their fatal plunge in the surf. Once within its grasp, they were quickly swept beyond the reach of assistance.

At Ogunquit Corner there is a more direct road than the one we have been travelling together, of which it behooves us to say a word, because all travellers coming from the east who may wish to ascend Agamenticus — and who does not? — need to know that this is their route. It is the old post and telegraph road to Portsmouth. At the distance of a mile from the Corner a cross-road takes one to the foot of the mountain, whence the ascent is easily made.

GREAT HILL HEADLAND, WELLS BAY.

CHAPTER V.

A TURN AROUND WELLS BAY.

"Here trembling billows marked the coast with surging foam." — BURNS.

WELLS is one of the oldest of Maine resorts, though it has been losing ground of late years to some of the later claimants for popular recognition.

But it will rise again. It must rise, because nowhere within the limits of a single township do we find so extensive an ocean frontage, with so many admirable building sites, as here in neglected Wells.

Upon leaving Ogunquit, one finds himself at the beginning of a long, sandy terrace descending by a gentle slope to the waterside, where the beach is, and the sea, and throwing wide open, as it were, throughout the six miles of curving shore that we follow without once quitting it, a large and exceedingly enjoyable prospect of the Atlantic Ocean.

At the farther end of this long plain the north shore is seen gliding out to sea again.

The three villages and two parish churches of Wells are strung out along the one street that forms part of the coast highway, making the town look much larger than it really is. Most of the houses stand at the upper side of the road, so giving to all a share in the noble ocean view; while the fields belonging to them slope away from the lower side, and when green, make as beautiful a natural esplanade as one could wish to see. The soil is, however, too sandy to be very productive, though long occupation has brought it into a condition that at first sight favors the idea of comfort and thrift to the owners. Still, there are far too many evidences of unthrift to escape notice, too few indicating improvement or confidence in the future to justify the belief that Wells is holding its own.

I had almost forgotten to mention the extensive salt-marshes, which skirt the entire shore front, and of which every farm has a portion.

These general features indicate clearly enough, perhaps, what first brought settlers to Wells. The salt-marshes offered immediate subsistence for their

THE SETTLER'S CHIMNEY-CORNER.

cattle, while such a large body of arable land, as little fertile as it looks, must have seemed an oasis to men who were accustomed to the gaunt and rocky hills of York. To these considerations should be added the valuable mill-powers furnished by several rapid streams, and the fine timber ready grown to the millwright's hand.

It is probable, therefore, that at least some of the first inhabitants found their way here from York, though it is known that the body of settlers came from Exeter, New Hampshire, with Rev. John Wheelwright,[1] who has been generally looked upon as the founder of Wells, inasmuch, also, as the first recorded grant of lands within the town's limits was made to him and his associates in 1643. Bourne[2] thinks that Edmund Littlefield,[3] who was the progenitor of all that bear his name in Wells, came here as early as 1641. He was a member of Wheelwright's church. John Gooch, from whom all of that name in Wells are descended, came from York. William Cole was another early settler. All these names are indelibly stamped upon the localities of Wells.

When we were at Old York, we felt a sincere regret at the absence of all those material evidences from which to reconstruct the life of bygone days. The historian of Wells does something to meet this want, by allowing us a peep into the privacy of the first settler's house and home. "We enter the kitchen, which is also the sitting-room and parlor. In looking around, we discover a table, a pewter pot, a hanger, a small mortar, a dripping-pan, and a skillet; no crockery, tin, or glassware; no knives, forks, or spoons; not a chair to sit on. The house contains but two more rooms, in each of which we find one bed, a blanket, and a chest. We have been through the house. And this is the house of Edmund Littlefield, the richest man in the town."

The ocean is the only thing really unchanged here. Throughout its whole extent Wells wears the unmistakable appearance of a town gone to seed; and, without irreverence, the same may be said of the family grave-yards one is constantly passing on the road.

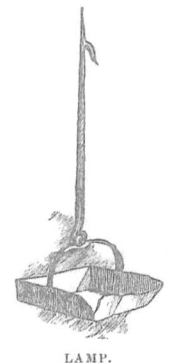
LAMP.

I think there is nothing so shocking to the feelings of most people as unconcealed insensibility to the care of the dead. I know it is apt to create an unfavorable impression of a place or a people hard to eradicate, since even barbarians manifest great veneration for the ashes of their departed ones, and try in every way to guard the place of sepulture from desecration. What, then, must be the impression caused by seeing burial lots with broken-down fences, or none at all; head-stones sticking up, here and there, out of the open commons, like unregarded stumps; or cattle trampling the graves underfoot at will? Such neglect is more than a fault: it is a crime.

Yes; the dead go quickly here. It will hardly be believed that on a public street, in a neighboring village, there is to be seen to-day a burial lot which the thrifty owner has turned into a henyard! I myself have frequently seen fowls roosting on the head-stones. There was no remonstrance that I have ever heard of. In another place, not far from the first, a citizen had pulled up all the head-stones from a lot of his, and then ploughed and planted over the graves. In this instance, some indications of disgust caused their restoration. In still another, a tomb was entered, skulls taken out, and thrown about by rude village boys in their play. And all these things are matters of common knowledge.

As we pursue our route along the highroad, two vigorous mill-streams — the Ogunquit and the Webhannet — drop down from the bluffs, cut their way through the plain to the marshes, and serpentine through these to the sea. It was on the Webhannet that Edmund Littlefield built the first saw-mill in Wells.

The high bluff above the road is the site of the mill garrison of colonial times, one of the half-dozen rallying-points for the scattered settlers, in which they were often driven to take refuge.

The street now keeps on the even tenor of its way till we come first to the cross-road leading down to Wells Beach, the houses of which we have kept in sight for the last half-hour, and next to the one peculiarly interesting spot, historically speaking, in all Wells.

THE LONELY GRAVE.

The site of the Storer garrison of the old French and Indian War period is only identified now by the angle of an old wall, solidly built of large, unhewn stones of a kind different from any found in the neighborhood, showing that they were brought here for the purpose to which they were first put. A little back from the street there is a capacious two-story farmhouse of quite attractive appearance, with a gentle slope extending down toward the river, behind it, and a gully bordered by a pine grove at its easterly side. This gully probably figured in the attack, to the disadvantage of the garrison, which stood within a gunshot of it.

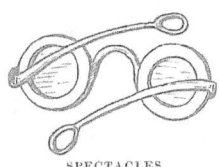

SPECTACLES.

The defence of this lonely frontier post is one of the most notable events in the annals of Indian warfare. The conditions were nowise different from those under which other garrisons had fallen, except that the man who defended this one was a soldier, every inch of him. We have all the more reason to regret the disappearance of every vestige of the ancient structure, against which the waves of fire and blood dashed themselves in vain.

It was in June, 1691, that Captain James Converse was posted in Storer's garrison with thirty-five or forty soldiers, part of whom had but just joined him, when the chief, Moxus, assaulted it at the head of two hundred warriors, expecting an easy conquest. The assault

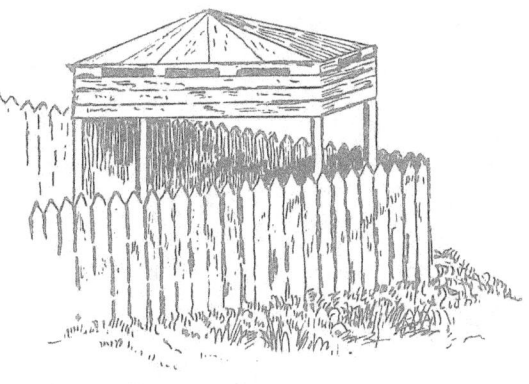

A FLANKER.

was bravely repulsed, and Moxus drew off, swearing to be revenged. When Madockawando, the Penobscot chief, heard of it, he laughed loudly. "So," said the chief, "my brother Moxus has missed it now; but next year I'll go myself and have the dog Converse out of his den."

Madockawando made good his threat in part by coming the next June, at the head of four or five hundred warriors, as he had said he would. Moxus and Egeremet were with him. The Canadian partisan Portneuf, and the Baron Saint Castin, who was by birth a gentleman, and a savage from choice, also marched with the Indians to this encounter, which one and all made no doubt of ending victoriously.

To oppose this onslaught, Converse could muster but fifteen regular soldiers of the garrison, to whom, if we should add such of the inhabitants as had sought safety in the thick walls and stout arms of their little fortress, the defenders could still count themselves but a handful. Fortunately for them, however, two sloops arrived on the 9th, with fourteen soldiers more, bringing up the garrison's complement of men to twenty-nine against an army.

It was not, however, to be a battle of numbers, but one of courage, endurance, and skill. The two sloops were anchored off in the channel, within pistol-shot of the shore, and as Converse had fully made up his mind never to yield while a man was left able to fire a shot or load a musket, the combat promised to be an obstinate one on both sides.

LEADEN CASEMENT.

The night of the 9th was an anxious one for the beleaguered garrison. As soon as it was light, contrary to their usual custom, the Indians began the fight with reckless bravado by showing themselves to the garrison in a body, also shouting out their terrible war-cries, and pouring in a harmless volley upon the besieged, as if they expected to finish the affair by a simple display of force alone. Converse's men, being well sheltered, made every shot tell, so that the savages were soon driven back to cover. They now began to see the sort of man they had to deal with. Having failed in their first attempt, they next turned their attention to the sloops, which promised them an easy prey; yet in spite of a galling fire poured in upon them at close quarters, the crews also succeeded in beating off the enemy in their turn, so that when night put an end to the fighting, our men had everywhere held their own.

The savages kept up a dropping fire throughout the night, designed to hold the besieged on the alert. In the morning they again mustered for a final and decisive assault. At a given signal they made a rush toward the garrison, yelling and firing as they came on, like fiends. Converse coolly let them come within pistol-shot. Again the loopholes were manned with stout hearts and steady hands. Only one man showed the white feather, who, when he had stammered out some words about surrendering, the captain sternly threatened with instant death if he should dare to breathe that word again.

For a time the firing was brisk. Converse's men shot from the flankers or loopholes as fast as they could take aim, the women of the garrison showing them an example of firmness by loading the muskets, and even firing them at the enemy. Again the discomfited assailants fell back out of range, presently to put in execution a second and more dangerous attempt upon the sloops. For this purpose a fire-raft was hurriedly put together, and as soon as the tide served, it was shoved off into the stream, to drift down upon the vessels. This peril, too, was providentially averted, as the wind soon drove the raft ashore, where it burned harmlessly out. With this effort the besiegers had exhausted their last resource. Many warriors had fallen in the two attacks, while the English had lost but two men in all. Converse now dared the red and white savages to another trial, but they were too thoroughly beaten to indulge even in their habitual strain of braggadocio. During the night they marched off the way they came.

Cotton Mather very neatly says of this affair, that the day was about the longest of the year, as Converse's defence was the bravest deed of the war.[4]

Bourne remarks that "it seems strange" our ancestors gave so little thought about transmitting the names of those who took part in this memorable defence to their descendants. We might add that it seems stranger still that the descendants should suffer every vestige of the brave deeds of their ancestors to pass from the sight of men.

There are one or two incidents worth relating here as going to show the sort of lives that these people led, or rather how truly it might be said of them that they carried their lives in their hands from day to day, and from hour to hour.

Ordinary travellers, for instance, had to be conducted by an armed escort from place to place, but this favor could only be granted, of course, in cases of real urgency. So did couriers who rode post-haste on public business. It was no uncommon thing for one to be found dead and scalped in the road. Regular post-routes were not established in Maine before the year 1711, letters being usually intrusted to casual travellers for conveyance. But when the routes could only be traversed

THE MAIL-CARRIER.

at the risk of life or limb, a dog was sometimes trained to the dangerous task. An authentic instance is found in which the faithful animal was shot and killed, while going his round, by some prowling savage.

So, too, occasions of rejoicing were ofttimes turned into seasons of mourning. Penhallow[5] relates an occurrence of this kind which happened at a wedding in Wells. The story runs thus: The bride's father, Captain John Wheelwright, being one of the notables of the village, his friends turned out in great numbers to witness the ceremony, and the festivities were of an exceedingly jovial character. But there were other guests not far off who had come to the wedding unbidden. After the nuptial knot had been tied, and the company was about separating to their homes, two horses were found to be missing. Some of the party went to look for the animals. They had gone but a few rods away from the house, when several gunshots were heard in quick succession. Their meaning was only too well understood. The Indians had laid a trap into which the whites had fallen. A dozen of the guests instantly mounted and rode off to the rescue, the bridegroom with the rest, since now or never was the time to show himself worthy to be the son-in-law of such a father.

NATURAL FUNGUS.

This party also fell into an ambuscade, from which the skulking savages fired as the troop passed at a gallop, killing one man outright, and unhorsing all the rest. All those who were unhurt got safely off, however, except the unlucky bridegroom, who thus suddenly found himself in the clutches of a gang of grinning savages instead of the arms of his bride. Of the first party two were shot dead on the spot, the rest taken.

The First Parish meeting-house of Wells, a conspicuous landmark of this shore, was burnt by the Indians in the year 1692, and rebuilt in 1699. George Burroughs, who was hanged at Salem for being a wizard, preached here just before that terrible madness seized upon New England which turned brother's hand against brother.

The belief in supernatural agencies was then so firmly rooted among the people, that he would have been a bold man indeed who denied their active intervention in human affairs.

There is a traditional account of Burroughs' arrest that is worthy of a place by the side of those weird legends for which the Black Forest and the Harz are famous.

According to it, the officers who were taking Burroughs to Salem conceived the idea that the devil might play them some trick if they took the road men usually travelled; so, thinking to outwit him, they started off with their prisoner to the next settlement by unfrequented paths.

They had just buried themselves in the depths of the forest, when a furious thunder-storm burst upon them. Sudden darkness spread itself in their path. The wind howled, the lightning flashed, and the thunder pealed as if the Day of Doom were indeed come. Convinced that their prisoner had really called Satan to his aid in order to compass their destruction, the terrified officers of the law now gave themselves up for lost. Presently a terrific crash, that seemed splitting earth and sky asunder, brought horses and riders to a standstill, trembling with fright. For some minutes they were blinded by the flash. Then a new terror seized them. As if fear had indeed given them wings, the horses sprang forward regardless of whip or spur. And now the terrified riders felt themselves borne along with the speed of the wind. Their steeds had yielded to the wizard's spell, and were flying through the air without a sound, as he should guide them. On they went, as if lashed by invisible hands, until with the passing away of the storm the spell was broken and a place of safety reached. It is said that the officers were so unnerved when they dismounted that the prisoner might easily have made his escape. At his trial all these circumstances were brought forward against him as so many proofs of his dealing with the Evil One.

Nothing else of interest detains us in Wells. Having come to the end of its interminable street, we pass across the boundary separating it from Kennebunk,[6] and reach the Mousam River,[7] in two lonely miles more.

If I recollect right, it was on this very road that I overheard the following colloquy between two natives, one of whom was digging in his miry field for potatoes, and the other critically looking on over the fence.

"How's 'taters?"

"'Taters?"

"Yes; how's 'taters?"

"They haint none, and them's rotten."

"Z'that so? Mine's done complete."

Potato-digger, slowly raising himself to an erect posture, "Did you perrisgreen yourn?"

"No; I jest mowed the tops off."

"Waal," resuming his digging, "when they do rot, it's the biggest ones that rots."

After turning aside to explore Hart's Beach,[8] for which Great Hill Headland is the landmark, in going two miles further we arrive at the lower village of Kennebunk, among indisputable evidence that the summer visitor has been before us. Here is still another fine beach.

There is a curious thing to be seen on what now goes by the name of Kennebunk Beach. Many rods below the present high-water mark the smooth floor is broken by what at first is taken to be, and indeed looks like, half-buried stones scattered about the polished sands. On a closer inspection these objects prove to be the stumps of large trees. A queer place this for trees to grow in, is it not, where there are ten feet of salt water at high tide? In one spot the stumps stand about in twos and threes, just as they would if a grove were cut down and the stumps left. Upon further examination it is noticed that clods of bog muck are still adhering to the roots. Some people think that the trees once grew where they now are; and if they are right, the ground must have sunk beneath them many feet, thus forming the beach about them as we see it to-day. It is more probable, I think, that in some exceptionally great flooding of the low land here, the whole grove was detached from the bog on which it stood, it being in this manner converted into an island, and then floated bodily off to its present position. Though of rare occurrence, such floating islands are not without precedent in New England.

The trite saying, that it's an ill wind blows nobody good, was never better exemplified, I am sure, than after the great gale of March 12, 1888, by which countless half-frozen fishes, of all sorts known to these waters, were tossed up on the beach, where the tide left them, to be picked up by the poor people along shore for food. These creatures had been lured back from the deep sea to their summer feeding-grounds all too soon, by a week of warm sunshine, and so had been caught by the gale in shallow waters, where the low temperature soon benumbed them, and the heavy sea threw them helpless upon the shore.

There are several old wrecks entombed among the sands of Gooch's Beach that refuse to stay buried, but rise from their graves after each great gale, as if its mad roar were a call to come forth and show its power. In a few days the sand will have covered them again, leaving no trace whatever of the skeleton in the closet.

---

[1] Rev. John Wheelwright, who was exiled from Massachusetts for preaching doctrines distasteful to the Puritan extremists; a leading actor in the religious revolt inaugurated by the famous Ann Hutchinson. Many of Wheelwright's people followed him, first to Exeter, then to Wells, though he himself afterwards went back to Massachusetts, his sentence having been revoked, and died at Salisbury in 1679, leaving descendants in Wells.

[2] Edward E. Bourne, author of a history of Wells and Kennebunk.

[3] Edmund Littlefield is said by Bourne to have built a saw-mill on the Webhannet in this year. Settlers had permission given them by Thomas Gorges, in September, 1641, to enter these lands; but it is not likely they would have wintered in Wells, though they may have picked out sites in the autumn and come back the next spring, 1642. Wells was made a town in 1653. The Ogunquit was the first boundary between York and Wells, but the line has since been moved farther west.

[4] Wells was repeatedly harried in the later wars, losing thirty-nine inhabitants at one blow in 1703; but it was never wholly deserted. The best account of the attack on Storer's garrison is found in Cotton Mather's "Decennium Luctuosum"; also in his "Magnalia."

[5] Samuel Penhallow, author of a history of the Indian Wars, 1703–10. Wheelwright's garrison, where this affair took place, was located at Gooch's Corner.

[6] Kennebunk was taken from Wells in 1820. Settlement began at the falls of the Mousam, where is located one of the handsomest villages in all Maine. Ship-building and ship-owning became its leading industry, till that business received its death-blow. Its ocean front is so cut up by marshes, creeks, streams, points, and beaches as to be almost valueless for farming purposes, though it is now being extensively availed of as a summer resort. Kennebunk is the birthplace of Hon. Hugh McCulloch, whose early home is still standing near Durell's Bridge, two miles from the sea.

[7] The Mousam, formerly Cape Porpoise River, or Meguncook, issues from ponds of that name in Shapleigh, twenty miles inland. Its water power is used by mills at Kennebunk village, but it has no harbor worthy of the name. The want of one induced, in 1793, an attempt to turn the river from its natural course into a new channel. This was finally done by damming up the stream at a point opposite the late Henry C. Hart's estate, though the hoped-for benefits were never realized, as nothing but the smallest craft can enter the Mousam. The remains of this dam and old river-bed are still to be seen. Considerable ship-

building was formerly carried on in this river, but it was soon transferred to the Kennebunk on account of the obstructions mentioned.

⁸ Hart's Beach continues the shore west of the Mousam. Mr. Charles Parsons' improvements here promise to render this locality one of the most delightful summer homes in Wells Bay. Just beyond, on the Wells side, at Lord's Beach, Mr. George C. Lord is doing for that shore what Mr. Parsons is for this. From hence to the east of the Mousam, the Kennebunk beaches overlap each other as far as the mouth of the Kennebunk River, making a scarcely broken belt of beaches for half the circumference of Wells Bay. The privateer ship *Alexander* was chased ashore at the west end of Great Hill, May, 1813, by H. M. S. *Rattler,* and made prize of.

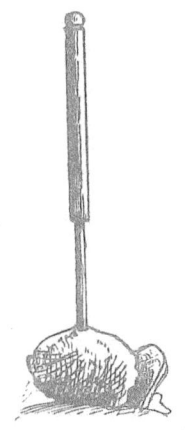

A SUMMER SUNSET.

CHAPTER VI.

AT KENNEBUNKPORT.

> "L' onda del mar divisa
> Bagna la valle e il monte
> Va passagiera in fiume
> Va prigioniera in fonte."

THE suffix "port" is of such frequent occurrence on our seaboard that the whole coast may be said to be port-holed.

Twenty-five years ago the village of Kennebunkport was comparatively unknown, or if ever known, it had been forgotten. In its general features it bears a certain family resemblance to Old York, as those who may become acquainted with both places will soon discover. York lies along the banks of a short tidal river; so does Kennebunkport. York has its old village and its new settlement; so has Kennebunkport. York, in fine, is a sort of anachronism, contemporary with George the Third and Harrison the Second; so, too, is Kennebunkport.

There has been no tantalizing steeple-chase from afar off to whet our curiosity. We have simply arrived.

Our attention is at once drawn to the amphibious character of life on the water front, by certain appearances to which we are not used at home. For instance, one sees a horse hitched at the front and a wherry at the back of the shops. It is possible then for a shopkeeper to sail up to his door, as in Venice, or go a-fishing out of his back windows, as in Holland.

When I first knew this place, both banks of the river were lined with ship-yards, that from morn till night, and from week's end to week's end, were all alive with the labor of hundreds of workmen. The moribund industry is barely kept alive in one yard now. Then, at the stroke of seven from the village belfry, the air resounded with the echoes of a thousand hammers. Now the village looks as though it had lain down and gone to sleep under its elms.

The history of one of these yards is the history of all. Within the memory of all middle-aged people ship-building was the one important industry of a hundred harbors and a hundred thousand mechanics. It was only given up when financial ruin had overtaken most of the builders, who bravely held out for the better days that never came. Beginning with the fishing-boats of a century ago, it had steadily advanced to sloops, schooners, and brigs, and from brigs to ships of the largest class afloat. It has now shrunk to its first estate,— a result involving not only the turning away of capital and the stagnation consequent upon its loss, but what is far more to be deplored, it has brought

THE SHIPYARD AS IT WAS.

about the dispersion of a distinctive body of skilled native American craftsmen, whom it would be hard to match in any branch of modern industry, or in any country. The disbanding of such a body of men can hardly be viewed in any other light than as a national misfortune.

In the days when ship-building was an American industry, as many as five first-class ships have been going up in the yards here at one and the same time. Once I counted nine vessels, large and small, on the stocks.

Then, besides the yards themselves, there were the various trades pertaining exclusively to ship-building, such as spar-making, boat-building, sail-making, rigging, pump, and block making, joining, painting, and the like. All shared the same fate, and what we now see are the fossil remains.

The records show that since the beginning of the century more than eight hundred vessels have been sent out from the shipyards of this river.[1] One finds little pleasure in retracing this chapter of history, already ancient, too often heard with incredulity or indifference, except as it serves to explain why so many signs of stagnation are visible in these seaport towns. Let the political economists tell us why prosperity goes in waves.

These decaying wharves and empty warehouses exhibit the demands of a considerable commerce. Yes; but the big seaports long ago ate up the little ones. And the railroads, by intercepting all the inland business that was once tributary to these lesser points of supply, have cut off their coasting trade; so that nature seems to have endowed them with certain franchises for progress to make void. The substance went long ago; the shadow disappeared when the

THE WRECK ASHORE.

last coasting vessel of the old fleet was sold last year. And this is the whole story in a few words.

But of all the odd changes which this state of things exhibits on the spot, perhaps the oddest is the readjustment it has called for in the seafaring population itself. To see men who have navigated big ships the world over, now turning their hands to anything they can pick up an honest living at, sets one seriously questioning whether, after all, there is such a thing as a law of natural drift, where every man finds his true level at last. Even the village gravedigger has thus been stranded by the hard logic of events.

Kennebunkport is now a well-established watering-place. Catering for the summer visitors' wants forms its unique occupation. A word or two will explain how this has been brought about.

In 1872 a few "solid men of Boston," who were looking over the coast with a view of locating a new summer resort, were attracted by the unusual advantages offered by the unoccupied shore-front here for their purpose. It was bonded or bought up, and operations begun by building a hotel, which was first

THE TRISTRAM PERKINS HOUSE.

opened to the public in the summer of 1873, under the management of that veteran landlord, Job Jenness, and by the now widely known name of the Ocean Bluff.

Before this result came about, Kennebunkport had but two geographical divisions, — Cape Porpoise, the old, original settlement, and the larger village at the river, which is its later development. The building up of the summer colony has added a third. As the history of the village goes no farther back than the middle of the last century, it lacks the interest that attaches to the older settlement at Cape Porpoise, which received its baptism in the blood of its foremost citizens. In fact, it was not until about 1740 that Paul Shackford built the first house at what is now Kennebunkport Village. The second was built by Rowlandson Bond about three years later; the third, by Gideon Walker, in 1745; and the fourth, by Eliphalet Perkins. When the road to Goff's Mill, now corresponding with Main Street, was laid out, in 1755, these were

MITCHELL'S GARRISON.

the only houses in the village, although there were several others in the neighborhood, notably that of the late Tristram Perkins, near the lock, and the one "over the river," still remaining in the Mitchell family.[2]

Let me explain that "over the river" is a term of alluring vagueness that has no reference here to the "undiscovered country" from which no traveller returns. It is more or less indefinitely applied to all the south-side region enclosed between the Wells road, the river, and the sea. It may reach as far as Bald Head Cliff and Ogunquit, or it may be limited to a circuit of the nearest beaches and the roads leading to them.

The Congregational meeting-house, which is so prominent an object when our village is approached, was not built until the year 1824. An old citizen once told me in confidence that he had helped to drink the "sperrits" that were

CONGREGATIONAL MEETING-HOUSE.

furnished when the house was raised. The times have changed since then. Old residents shake their heads mournfully and say they have nothing to live on now but these memories. In those "good old times," so feelingly referred to by the oldsters, an allowance of grog was served out every day in the shipyards, the hayfields, at a launch, at funerals, at weddings, — wherever, in short, joy was to be incited, sorrow assuaged, or labor performed. Some of the stories told about the drinking-bouts of that day would have made honest, thirsty Jack Falstaff hold his breath with admiration. But we have reformed all that.

I have already explained why the village itself has figured so little in those stirring events that belong exclusively to the older communities around it. It seems to me that I have never known one less affected by contact with the outside world.

But every medal has its reverse. I have often wondered what the gay sojourners of a summer would think if they could drop in here after Winter had laid his icy hand on the woods and streams, and some cold snap had shut up the river, or some heavy snowfall so blocked up the roads that ploughs and harrows were being used to break them out and make them passable. He would find it hard to recognize his old playground, I fear. The seashore is seldom visited then, though its moanings can be heard in the stillness of the long winter evenings,—that deep diapason which we call the rote,—or its hoarse bellowings when some gale is lashing it with destructive hand. There are pale and anxious faces by the warm firesides then, for that terrible voice of the ocean has called up memories of those who will nevermore come home from sea.

But come, let us leave these dismal fancies and betake ourselves to the promised enjoyments of the hour.

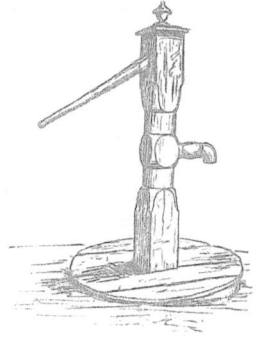

THE TEMPERANCE MOVEMENT.

Quitting the village by the road skirting the river, the shore colony is reached in going rather less than a mile. Here is also the point where the old shore road crossed this river on its winding way to the eastward.

The kernel of the settlement which has grown up on this spot was two or three fishermen's cottages, with a solitary row of balm of Gileads leaning out before them over the river's bank. Here, too, if I err not, was the dwelling-place of Trowbridge's "Old Lobsterman," whose surroundings are thus tersely depicted : —

> "A furlong or more away to the south,
> On the bar beyond the huge sea-walls
> That keep the channel and guard its mouth,
> The high, curved billow whitens and falls ;
> And the ebbing tides through the granite gate,
> On their wild errands that will not wait,
> Forever unresting, to and fro,
> Course with impetuous ebb and flow."

It is at least singular that this point should have been the site of the ancient ferry established by a colonial order of 1653, abandoned when the building of the bridges higher up suspended it as a travelled way, to be again restored as a feature of the new life of the place, which has thus shaken hands with the old across the gulf of time.

Generally speaking, when the tide was at its lowest, the river could be forded here; so that the crossing long went by the name of the Wading-Place. By and by, when the government began the granite piers[3] at the river's mouth, it became necessary to build a wharf here, in order to carry on that work with advantage, after which the locality took the name of "the government wharf." Since then it has always been found a very convenient spot for wind or tide bound vessels to tie up at. Lonely outpost, indeed, when from his wooden castle on yonder bank, only the ferryman kept solitary watch for unfrequent passengers!

There is a tradition about an adventure of Stephen Harding, who kept the ferry here long ago, that belongs to this locality.

Harding's log-house stood on the swell of ground enclosed between Gooch's

THE WADING-PLACE.

Creek and the beach and river. Tradition reports him a man of uncommon physical strength and courage,—a very giant, in fact. The Indians knew Harding well, and Harding knew them of old.

One morning, on going out of the house, he saw a band of Indians, returning doubtless from their repulse at Wells, filing across the rocks rising at the farthest end of the beach. The redskins, of course, were coming to pay him a visit.

It was now Harding's turn to be alarmed. Fortunately for him, the band was still at a distance, but there was not a moment to lose. Hurrying back to the house, Harding told his wife to take their little year-old infant, and make haste to put the creek between her and the redskins. The terrified woman snatched up the child, and ran off with it as she was told, while Harding remained behind to protect her flight, if, as he half suspected, more Indians should be lurking about there.

It turned out as he thought; for upon going into his blacksmith's shop, four Indians started up from the ground and made a rush for him. Harding now thought it time to be making his own escape. His cornfield offered the only cover at hand, so into that he plunged with rapid strides; but while running at the top of his speed, to his unspeakable dismay he suddenly came upon his wife, whom he supposed to be in safety, crouching down among the corn. The poor woman was prostrated by terror, and being no longer capable of making the least effort to save her life, had sunk down helpless within only a few rods of the house. Harding's extraordinary muscular strength was now put to the test. Taking his wife under one arm, and his babe under the other, he dashed on again for the creek, into which he plunged, getting safely over it, with his charge unharmed, too, though the savages followed him to the shore of the creek before they gave up the chase. Once across, the thick woods enabled Harding to place his wife and child in a secure hiding-place.

GOOCH'S CREEK.

All this time his favorite dog had followed close at his heels; but for fear that the animal's barking might betray them, his master was forced to kill him. All that night they lay in the woods. Late the next day, the fugitives, footsore and half-starved, reached Storer's garrison at Wells. It is probable that the Indians wished to take Harding alive, or he could hardly have escaped so easily. They showed great admiration for his prowess in this affair, often saying of him, "Much man Stephen: all same one Indian."

NORTH PIER AND BEACH.

Yonder are the piers, black and massive. Many persons who have enjoyed a quiet stroll up and down this breezy promenade, when the sea is as calm as a sleeping babe, doubtless have wondered what such thick walls of indestructible granite were intended to keep out. The river runs by quietly enough, they think. So it does. The languid sea hardly breaks outside. That is true. But then, those persons have never witnessed a storm at sea, or they would scarcely say they would give anything to see one.

Not long ago my gossip Dixey, — rest his soul! — who knew every kernel of sand on the coast, was telling me about the great gale of 1851 — the same one which swept away Minot's light ouse as if it had been a confectioner's pagoda on a show-cake, instead of a tower of iron, with iron columns deeply imbedded in solid rock. "Man!" said old Dixey to me, throwing off his habitual apathy at the bare recollection of that fearful night, "man alive! you couldn't see neither pier for three mortal hours, — yes, and more too. Breaker arter breaker

RETIRED LOBSTERMAN.

drove right over 'em, full chisel; car'd away three of them biggest granite blocks you see on the top tier, weighing seven ton apiece, and hove 'em inter the channel same's a boy would a brickbat. There they be now. Snapped copper bolts [the blocks of stone are strongly bolted together] tew inches thick, like that," the old man finished, suiting the action to the word, by breaking in two a chip he held in his hand, to show me how easily the thing was done.

For years the occurrence was talked about as one that might not happen again in a lifetime; but in the winter of 1888-89, I myself saw the seas break

AT KENNEBUNKPORT.   95

over both piers from end to end during a violent blow from the northeast, and this time a wide breach was made in the solid granite wall of the north pier, through which cataracts of water rush at every tide, thus endangering the safety of the whole structure.[4]

This river, which, when full, is charming, and when empty, only a crooked ditch, is the aquatic playground for what may be called the floating population, who find it a delightful experience

> "To let the wherry listless go,
> And wrapt in dreamy joy,
> Dip and surge idly to and fro,
> Like the red harbor buoy ;
>
> "To sit in happy indolence,
> To rest upon the oars,
> And catch the heavy earthy scents
> That blow from summer shores ;
>
> "To see the rounded sun go down,
> And with his parting fires
> Light up the windows of the town
> And burn the tapering spires."

Sometimes hemmed in between wharves, sometimes spreading out a spacious basin, the river is always running a race with itself out to sea, or back again into the land. At the village it is narrow and swift. It goes frisking along like a child, playing as it runs, making endless pirouettes in mid-stream, humming softly to itself in the gloom of yonder dripping arches, or loitering playfully awhile in some quiet reach among overhanging groves, yet ever coming back to its appointed task with renewed vigor. Let us, grown-up children as we are, imitate the river.

There is one summer visitor of by-gone days, seldom seen at the river now that it has become so populous. "Into what corner peers my halcyon's bill?" That impudent little highwayman, the king-fisher, used to make the river noisy with his loud scream of triumph as he pounced on some unlucky shiner and flew off with him to his hiding-place in the woods. He has now nearly if not quite forsaken the river. More's the pity! since he was an original denizen of the seashore, and a bird of great esteem among the ancients, who believed that if stuffed and hung up, his body would turn round with every change of the wind, and thus show from what quarter it blew.[5]

The river readily lends itself to all the caprices of the summer visitors. It is their idle voyage or race-course, their trysting-place or processional. For at the close of every season tribute is paid to the pleasures that are past, by holding a carnival of boats, which, with their illuminations, red-fire, and rockets, resemble a great fiery serpent belching forth colored flames, as it crawls slowly along the dark course of the river.

Floating up with the tide through the old lock, between banks now brightened by cultivated farms, now shadowed by thick-set woods, one comes to Durell's bridge. Nothing could be more at variance with the tragedy once enacted here than the prevailing drowsiness of a summer's day. But to my story: —

Philip Durell lived a long mile above the lock, at what is called the Landing. His isolated situation invited the attack which his absence from home made so easily successful. When he did return, at nightfall, Durell found his house plundered and desolate. He did not need to be told what the ruin about him meant, or who had been there in his absence. His wife and son, his married daughter, Mrs. Baxter, with her infant, were all gone, — all in the hands of murdering savages. The men of that day were men of action. Durell hurriedly collected his nearest neighbors, with whom he started off in pursuit.

It happened that while the Indians were ransacking Durell's house, they came across the old family Bible, which in those primitive days men believed to be the undoubted Word of God. The savages knew that this book was held in the highest veneration by the pale faces; so, in the belief that it would put them in possession of some all-powerful charm, they took it away with them. They supposed it, indeed, to be the white man's trusted oracle and guide through which he derived all his superior knowledge and power. But the march to Canada was long and the Good Book heavy, — so heavy that, notwithstanding its presumed potency, the savage who carried it threw it away at the first camping-place.

THE OLD LOCK.

Upon finding themselves closely pursued, these Indians inhumanly butchered all their prisoners except the boy, John Durell, and left them lying in their blood. John was taken to Canada, where he lived so long with his captors that he became half Indian, and wholly weaned from the habits of civilized life.

After lying buried all winter long under the snow, the stolen Bible was found by accident in the spring. I have had the pleasure of examining this historical treasure, which is looked upon with still greater veneration by its present owners on account of its history.[6] The sacred book bears indisputable evidence of the rough usage it received at that time, which was in October, 1726.

AT KENNEBUNKPORT.

Many people begin their first letter from the shore in this manner : —

"We reached the place by night
And heard the waves breaking."

It is indeed a novel experience to hear for the first time, and all night long, that measured and prolonged sound, half soothing, half threatening, come in at your open window. You may close the window and draw the curtains, but you cannot shut it out. It insensibly creeps into the consciousness like something that has power over you, and you fall asleep listening to this eternal monody of Old Ocean, with strange thoughts of what it is going to reveal to you on the morrow.

The morning shows the long coastline, lower than you had thought, sweeping grandly round from York Nubble to your feet. Twenty leagues of the Atlantic lie glistening in the sun, like a great carpet of azure silver, which is being gently shaken by unseen hands.

Charles Lamb somewhere speaks of his first view of the ocean as disappointing, because by the law of imagination "we expect to see all the sea at once, the commensurate antagonist of the land." What an idea ! That statement hardly holds water, for the reason that the imagination generally busies itself more with what we do not see than what we do. The effect of seeing nothing but water before us does, I think, produce the illusion of illimitableness. To this order of ideas the horizon line is like that separating us from futurity itself.

I have often been an interested observer of the power that the ocean exerts over different natures. Most people on getting their first glimpse of it seem to lose the power of speech, and stand as if awe-struck by the sight. Quite as often as otherwise their bewilderment finds expression in some ludicrous way, when speech does come to them. I recollect one woman who, it was evident, had never, in the whole course of her life, seen the real ocean, or possibly thought much about it, except as a place where salted fish came from. This, my countrywoman, was overheard saying, almost breathlessly, to her companion, "Mercy and truth ! I'm struck all of a heap !"

Another, who had begged her goodman honestly to tell her if this was the "truly ocean" she had heard so much about, upon receiving the assurance that there was no mistake about it, laid a trembling hand upon his arm, and with a startled look, exclaimed under her breath, "Don't it look as if it *must* run right down here and drown us all this minute !"

Yes, it is indeed the real ocean that we see stretched out there in the sun.

Blue and benignant Agamenticus is still the prominent landmark, which lends a certain grace to the outlines of the opposite coast. Farther inland the triple peaks of Bonnybeag,[7] seen above the forest, suggest both in form and color a great tidal wave advancing from the interior toward the coast, and on a clear day the White Mountains themselves, frequently white with snow in the month of May, may be seen from any elevated ground in the neighborhood.

Although there are no outlying islands in this bay, there are some very bad ledges which all gentlemen sailors will do well to steer clear of. First, and worst of all, because they lie exactly in the track of vessels bound in or out, is the clump called the Fishing Rocks, which, however, make a feature of a most charming sea-view. There used to be magnificent rock-cod and cunner fishing among these ledges, but one has need to keep a wary eye abroad there; for the breaker that rolls over them so lazily, and is so much admired from shore, would swamp a boat before one could call on St. Anthony or say Jack Robinson.

The strip of shore lying between the river and Sandy Cove forms the headland locally known as Cape Arundel, on which the summer colony has perched itself as if by instinct. Let us walk that way.

The path leads first to a dilapidated earthwork, or rather sandwork, which but for the slender beach-grass growing upon it would have been scattered to the four winds long ago. These mounds are a relic of the War of 1812.

OLD HALF-MOON BATTERY.

Knowing how averse New England was to the war, the British Cabinet determined to make her still more so by striking at her commerce and open ports. "Burn, sink, and destroy!" were the watchwords of this war. What a commentary upon our boasted civilization!

The land here is high, and the shore bold. Nothing is smoothed off. The pastures bristle with the wild native growth. Now and then some deep, broad split yawns before us, into which the sea flies foaming to our feet, or shoots up a column of spray high in the air. Here now is one to which the sonorous name of the "Devil's Cartway" has been given. And the "Devil's Armchair"[8] is its close neighbor. There's something in a name even at the shore. Only a few years ago I saw the hull of a vessel, with every stick gone out of her, wedged bolt upright in the Cartway. The next gale broke her up. Despite its name, the place proved the salvation of the crew; for if the vessel

AT KENNEBUNKPORT.

had struck half her length either to right or left, there would have been a different tale to tell.

The seashore is undoubtedly made more interesting to us all, both old and young, by the wonderful forms of animal life it exhibits, so different from anything belonging to the dry land; but only at low tide can we indulge the fancy to grope about the strange territory which the retreating waves have left bare, and the crows so regularly frequent. We have already frightened away two or three of them while picking our way out over the slippery bladder-weed, which fastens itself so strongly to every stone and every crevice, to the farthest ledges where a new growth of the edible sea-moss begins, though from its coal-black color we should never have imagined it to be the same thing we have bought of our grocer at home. Yet when exposed to sun and dew it turns first a lovely Tyrian purple, then as white as sea-foam itself. These plants give out a moist, pungent, and penetrating, though not unpleasant odor, that is new to us, — something between that arising from the steaming mould and noxious fungi of the woods and the smoke of burning brushwood in the autumn.

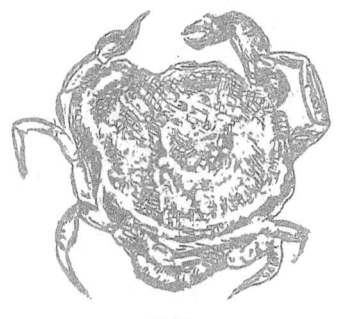

CRAB.

We are now among those secret nooks and crannies, the garden of the sea, that seem to us like the fairyland of our boyhood dreams, where little basins of liquid crystal disclose the strange forms and tints of sea-urchins and starfishes, of limpets and cockles, where the yellow, black, and purple striped cockles cling, like monster insects, to the bladder-weed, and where every step, in fact, shows us a thousand authentic tidings of invisible things, —

"Of ebb and flow and ever-during power,
And endless peace subsisting at the heart of endless agitation."

Stooping down over this shallow pool of crystal water, we espy, first of all, our own features, and next a sedentary crab who is watching us uneasily from his snug retreat under a projecting shelf of rock, all ready to make off at our slightest movement.

"Ha, ha! art thou there, truepenny?"

The coward dare not venture out of his hiding-place for fear some thief of a crow may pounce upon him, and fly away with him to her lonely haunt in yonder woods, as the great roc did with our dear old friend Sinbad, in the "Thousand and One Nights." So crabby wisely keeps close, knowing that his stout breast and back-piece, proof though they may be against beak and claws, will avail him nothing when the keen-witted crow shall have first flown up with him to a convenient height, and then let him fall headlong upon the hard rocks, crushed and bleeding, to make a meal of at her leisure.

Regaining the high ground, we next come to a colony of grisly cedars that have withstood the gales of centuries, and though still vigorous, are so shorn of all pride of leafage as to seem more like sturdy vagrants than respectable trees. Memory of man goes not back to the time when they did not stand here just as weird and fantastic-looking as they do to-day. Like very old men, they seem doomed to live on and on, in spite of themselves.

We have now gained the breezy headland overlooking Sandy Cove at the east. From this point Cape Porpoise light peeps out among the bewildering maze of broken reef and tossing foam.

In going half the length of the cove we shall come to the natural curiosity known to all the country round as the Bouncing Rock, but which a literary

THE BOUNCING ROCK.

friend, who knows how to engrave a word as well as another, has turned into Blowing Cave.

At this place the sea has undermined the softer trap-rock, which one so often sees sandwiched in between the masses of granite. Having thus bored a deep hole in the rock, the waves rush with violence into the opening, but are instantly shot out again by the compressed air, in a cloud of the finest spray, and with a hollow roar that at night sometimes startles one by its resemblance to the booming of a minute gun.

Of course the display is at its best when the sea is running high outside; for then the big waves follow each other in quick succession, while the incessant detonations of the rock, with the water-smoke constantly rising in huge, vapory puffs about it, strengthen the illusion of a fortress beleaguered by all the powers of sea and air. The best time to see the display is at half-flood or half-ebb.

[1] The class of vessels called barques was unknown to the early part of the century. They, however, took the place of the "snow," so called, which had a somewhat similar rig. At the beginning of the century ships were rarely of more than 200 tons burden. One of 300 was considered a large ship. Forty years later, ships of the largest class sometimes registered 400 tons; seldom more. But from that time to the present the increase in size and tonnage has been marked. I find that the ship *Guatimozin*, which was built here in the year 1800, is put down as of 211 tons, while the *Philena Winslow*, launched in 1876, measured 2117 tons. Since this chapter was written there has been some little revival in the prospects of shipbuilding along shore, though the demand is mostly limited to vessels suitable for the coasting trade.

[2] This "Mitchell house," which has been kept in excellent repair, was designated as a garrison, it is said. It stands between the sea-road and river, a little below the railroad crossing.

[3] The channel here was narrow, crooked, and shifting with every bad gale. Vessels coming in had to discharge part of their cargoes first; and those going out to finish their lading outside the bar, at the mouth. It was attempted to remedy these evils by constructing timber piers in 1798, the undertakers having the right to levy a small tonnage tax on vessels passing in or out. The company was finally forced to surrender its charter. The work was then assumed by the government, and the present piers were built of granite, obtained from quarries situated about two miles back from the river. The opening of these quarries led to the sudden rise and equally sudden collapse of another industry, as they were too far from tide-water to be profitable.

[4] During the great gale of November 25, 1888, a small fishing-vessel was dashed to pieces between the piers while trying to work into the river. The three men composing the crew were lucky enough to get ashore.

[5] See Shakspeare's "King Lear," Act II. Scene ii.

[6] It was printed at Cambridge, England, by the University printer, in 1638. The date is gone from the title-page, but is found at the beginning of the New Testament, where the new title-page is scrawled all over with the names of different owners.

[7] Bonnybeag is a great landmark for fishermen. The land rises all the way from the coast, making the ridge of which it forms part stand quite high, though Bonnybeag itself is only a hill when you get to it. The summit commands all the ocean between Cape Elizabeth and the Nubble. It is a shelly gneiss covered with a scrubby growth. On the summit there is a cave, called the "Devil's Den," in which five or six persons find standing-room. Bonnybeag is, I think, the Three Turks' Heads mentioned by Winthrop. Great Works River issues from Bonnybeag Pond.

[8] Two authors, Mr. J. T. Trowbridge and Professor J. B. McMaster, have chosen this locality for their summer residence.

OLD CEDARS, CAPE PORPOISE.

CHAPTER VII.

THE STORY OF CAPE PORPOISE.

"The master, the swabber, the boatswain and I,
The gunner and the mate." — *Tempest.*

YELLOW, black, and purple striped cunners swarm about these rocks. It is best to use a rod here, on account of the entangling rock-weed. For bait you have only to break off the barnacles adhering to the rocks. Large cod are often taken in the cove by simply casting the line out into deep water, without attaching a sinker. I once saw five beauties, the largest weighing seven pounds, hauled in from Bill Tynham's Rock in a few minutes. But the haddock is the best of all fish for a chowder, because its flesh is so white, firm, and flaky. And who has sung its praises like our own world-renowned Mrs. Partington?

> "Oh, chowder ! monarch of the stews —
> With onion tinctured — I am fain,
> By aid of my enraptured muse,
> To sound thy virtues in a strain ;
> The nation's glory, greatest dish
> By art conceived and born of fish ! "

Just back of the grove, under some spreading oaks, there is a pretty picnic ground to which the people of the country round have resorted, time out of mind, for their annual chowder parties. It is a custom, borrowed, no doubt, from those earlier visitors, who have left traces of their rude feasts in the shell-heaps seen all up and down the coast. In high glee, the party drive up to the spot and dismount. The men go to the rocks or fetch fire-wood. The girls go to the neighboring spring. The matrons put the kettle on. Fish are caught, water brought, and fires lighted. Meanwhile, the girls have spread a clean cloth on the thick turf. When all is ready, a fish-horn brings in all stragglers to the spot. Then, with appetites sharpened by the delicious smell of the chowder, all crowd round the steaming kettle, while the goodwife who presides over its savory contents stirs and tastes again and again with all the tantalizing deliberation of a *chef* who feels his reputation at stake. At last she gives the mixture a final stir, and, with a flourish of her ladle, pronounces it done. Then to the feast!

Daniel Webster is said to have been more vain of his skill in making a chowder than of his famous Hulseman letter. N. P. Willis, who could make a chowder as well as a verse, has left a recipe. It is a dish of which even Lucullus was ignorant.

The high ground at the head of this cove shows some old bramble-grown hollows that were once cellars, but no one now remembers either the houses or their tenants. The same thing may be seen for miles along the shore, to certify that all but the sea is barren here. There is no denying, however, that they awaken strange thoughts of those who have gone before us, and who gave up in despair all hope of extorting a livelihood from such a waste. By the same token, it calls forth a smile to see those same spots so eagerly sought after to-day. Beware the poison ivy![1] It loves these old hollows which every wholesome thing has shunned.

POISON IVY.

Before leaving the neighborhood, it will be worth our while to take a look at the rocks of the north shore, which, at low tide, spread out acres upon acres of jagged ledges, blackened as by fire, ripped up as by an earthquake, sometimes set upright in ragged rows, like grave-stones, sometimes resembling the broken tusks of some prehistoric monster that has been turned to stone, but can still bite and tear whatever the sea throws into its grinning jaws. Is it possible, we ask, that water, and water alone, has done all this? And if so, what chance would the stoutest ship that ever floated have?

It was only a year or two ago, that a north-bound schooner struck heavily on Bunkin Island reef. Look off, a short mile out, where the sea breaks so viciously at the right of yonder island! That is the very place. It was a dark winter's night, — just what the sailor most dreads, — with a cold needle-pointed drizzle freezing to everything as it fell, and the wind blowing a stiff gale from the northeast. The captain had lost his reckoning, — in fact, he was standing straight for the land without knowing it; so before any one thought of danger, the vessel was on the reef, among the roaring breakers, where no seamanship could avail. The crew gave themselves up for lost, as every monster breaker that drove in over the reef lifted the doomed vessel clear of the rocks, only to let her down again with a crash that threatened to break every timber in her stout frame. Wood and iron could not long withstand that pounding. Fearing that the masts would fall and kill them, the sailors kept below, and in terror watched for the moment when the wreck should go to pieces, and all be swallowed up in the waves. A miracle saved them. The schooner actually pounded over the reef into deeper water, where, though foundering, she still kept afloat. Once free of the rocks, she drove right on till this ragged shore again brought her up, and this time held her fast. She soon went to pieces. I saw her stem sticking up among the rocks where her perilous voyage had ended. When the tide fell, the crew got safe ashore. At four in the morning the inmates of the Cleaves cottage were aroused by a loud knocking. When the door was unbarred, there stood the shipwrecked sailors. It was the first notice the family had of the tragedy being enacted almost at their doors.

PLACE OF THE WRECK, WITH CAPE PORPOISE LIGHT.

This does not complete the catalogue of disasters; for during Thanksgiving week of the year 1886 two vessels went on the rocks of Cape Porpoise, while trying to make that harbor. One of them struck at about nine o'clock at night. It was indeed a fearful night, when all landsmen were glad to keep within doors. When day broke on the dismal scene, scarce two pieces of the wreck were left hanging together. Fortunately there was no loss of life, though the sailors only kept themselves from freezing by walking up and down the island all through the long winter night, till at daybreak the light-keeper discovered and took them off.

It is pleasant to follow the paths winding in and out among the thickset clumps of fragrant bayberry, through which the hardy raspberry and blackberry push their ripening clusters of fruit; picking a flower here or a berry there, in the long summer afternoons, and watch the reluctant twilight draw down its gray curtain over the misty sea; but pleasanter still, I think, are those clearcut days of early autumn, — days bright, and crisp, and full of invigorating tonic, — when these pastures are resplendent with the bloom of golden-rod, aster, and spiræa, and every clump shows a bewildering *mélange* of colors. Common? Ah, yes; if they were only rare, how people would go into ecstasies over them, and how highly we should prize them!

At no time is the shore visited with keener delight than in autumn. In the spring we may cull a nosegay, in summer a bouquet, but in autumn we may have flowers by the armful.

But when on some morning late in October the moist meads are sparkling with rime, it is the gentian that comes blossoming on the threshold of winter, as if to reconcile us to the change we dread so much.

> "Thou waitest late and com'st alone,
> When woods are bare, and birds are flown,
> And frosts and shortening days portend
> The aged year is near his end.
>
> "Then doth thy sweet and quiet eye
> Look through its fringes to the sky,
> Blue — blue as if that sky let fall
> A flower from its cerulean wall."

All summer we have seen the peripatetic Indian pulling up the sweet-grass with which the squaws make various small wares much in request by the summer visitors. It grows abundantly about here, and tufts of it are often seen ornamenting the best rooms of the village, in place of the traditional fly-catching asparagus branch of our grandmothers. And in many places about the roads the caraway shows first its cluster of delicate white flowers, and then its bearded seed-stalk, to remind us of the old-fashioned seed-cakes of which we were so fond.

I will simply add, in passing from a theme I love so well, that the gentian made its first appearance in this region about ten years ago. Before that time, though I had often looked for it, I had never found it. Nobody seemed to know what it was when it was found, or hold it in any esteem whatever, until the summer boarder proclaimed it the "beloved of souls that are epicures of poesy." Now its praises are on every tongue.

Cape Porpoise village is built around the shores of its harbor, which a cluster of large and small islands protects. On one of them stands the baby lighthouse of the coast.[2] This harbor — or perhaps we should say harbors, since there are two basins — is remarkable for being the only one between Portsmouth and the Saco, though the danger of attempting to run into it in bad weather needs no further illustration than is furnished by the disasters just now related.

Stage Island is naturally a place of some interest on account of its having been the home of the fishermen who first spread their flakes and built their cabins among the rocks here. The bottom being all hard sand, one may cross the harbor to the island at low tide, as the Israelites did the Red Sea. The outermost section of this island contains only a few acres. There are some old briar-choked cellars here of unknown date; also a headland commanding the north coast as far as Cape Elizabeth. Tradition says this was the burial-place of the first settlers here, but in that case the graves must have been washed into the sea long ago, for there is now no trace of them.

Obscure as its early history is, — and that should not greatly surprise us when we consider what the character of its early population was, — Cape Porpoise [3] was no less the original settlement of what is now Kennebunkport. That at the village grew up so long afterwards as to be in no way associated with the desperate struggle to hold these few acres of barren rocks against the equally determined effort to drive all the English back into the sea, whence they had come. Some of the older people remember the ruins of the ancient fort that stood on Stage Island, which, in its day, had served as a refuge from the savages, but of which not one stone now remains on another. The name Stage Island is an all-sufficient guide to the purpose for which it was first occupied. It was a good place to dry fish, and at high tide a natural fortress.

MAIL-CARRIER (WINTER).

For a long time the domestic history of this place is a blank, in consequence of the loss of its earliest records. When they do begin, the name of God is frequently found spelled with a little " g." Indeed, about all that can now be gathered of that early life comes to us in the form of remonstrance, complaint, or reproof from the governing power; so that, much to our regret, we can only infer what its primitive condition was like. All this, perhaps, sufficiently characterizes one of those isolated and primitive communities, existing almost without law, but keeping just within its limits, heeding its burdens more than its restraints, with few wants, fewer ambitions, and no education, and naturally following out the simple traditions of the fathers as their guide. Two and a half centuries have by no means eradicated all those primitive traits.

When King William's War broke out the allied tribes, whom the French supplied with guns and missionaries, rosaries and scalping-knives, marked for destruction all the coast settlements in this unlucky province, and only just failed of their purpose to extirpate them root and branch, Cape Porpoise with the rest.

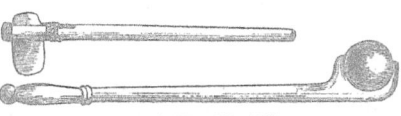

WAR-CLUB AND AXE.

Again, in 1690, the savages appeared at Cape Porpoise in force. This time they came with fleets and armies, with intent to do their work thoroughly. Those inhabitants who lived outside the defences had to fly for their lives. The rest shut themselves up in their fort on Stage Island, where, though sorely pressed, they held out until a vessel could be sent to take them off. When she sailed into the harbor, the beleaguered settlers had rammed down their last bullet and had swallowed their last mouthful. All owed their lives to the heroism of a comrade who, though wounded by a musket-ball, with Spartan bravery paddled a leaky canoe all the way to Portsmouth, and so made known their desperate situation.

ARROWS.

After this unlucky stroke the settlement remained a solitude for nearly ten years, — almost long enough for its return to a state of nature. At the end of this period some of the refugees ventured back to their broken hearthstones, but upon the renewal of hostilities, in Queen Anne's time, the place was again attacked in August, 1703, by a war-party of French and Indians, who a second time laid it waste, once more driving the settlers from their homes.

This second depopulation continued until the return of peace. In 1719 the Cape settlement was re-established with the name of Arundel, so superseding the old one given to it nearly, if not quite, a hundred years before.

Short breathing-time was allowed these impoverished people for repairing the ravages of war. Lovewell's War presently brought down upon them a new train of calamities. Anticipating that the enemy would first strike in this exposed quarter, the colonial authorities now exhorted the people to stand firm and fight it out to the last. Had it been accompanied with the means proper to its execution, the advice was excellent.

CHEESE-PRESS.

In August, 1723, the Indians again began their old work of slaughter at the Cape. When they first showed themselves, the garrisons were so weakly manned that even the women put on men's clothes and took their turns at mounting guard, in order to deceive the enemy.[4]

The story is now less picturesque, though far more grateful to narrate, than the previous chapter of strife and bloodshed. The town presently voted to build a meeting-house, but, as its historian naïvely remarks, the matter was put off until the shock of an earthquake — by much the most frightful that had happened within the memory of man — brought it up again.

OLD MILLDAM, POOL ROAD.

Then, a dispute having arisen between Cape Porpoise and Wells about their boundary, commissioners on the part of both met at the ferry-house, at the mouth of Kennebunk River, to decide the matter. Cape Porpoise laid claim to the Mousam, then called Cape Porpoise River, while Wells held out for the Kennebunk as her limit. It proved dry work, and the bottle passed freely. Finding that the Cape Porpoise men had the better case, those from Wells pushed the bottle harder. The story goes that the session being long and animated, the commissioners run up so large a score that the Cape Porpoise men were glad to yield up the territory in dispute, in consideration of the Wells men paying the scot. This amicable settlement was reached in 1660, and has never since been disturbed.

So far the history of the town has centred wholly in Cape Porpoise and its immediate vicinity; but the time came when the little hamlet at the river

THE STORY OF CAPE PORPOISE.   109

began to assume an importance at first rivalling, then overshadowing, the ancient settlement itself.

This state of things led to a protracted struggle over the question of erecting the village at the river into a new parish. The dispute waxed hotter and hotter, so warm, indeed, that one night the old meeting-house at the Cape was set on fire and burned to the ground. This summary disposition of the question led to the building of a new house in a situation equally remote from both villages; so that, as in most compromises, neither party got what it wanted, but was forced to be content with putting its opponent to as much inconvenience as itself.

The final settlement of the long-standing quarrel determined, at least, the future ascendancy of the village over the Cape.

During the Revolution a single incident signalled the existence of actual war at the Cape. The contest was near its close when one day two British cruisers made their appearance off the harbor, in which two merchant vessels were then lying at anchor. The enemy boarded and took possession of both, without meeting the least resistance. The act seems, however, to have incensed a half-witted fellow of the place, who rowed off to the vessels and boldly demanded their release. He was fired at, and badly wounded for his pains. This was the signal for an uprising. The Cape men rallied at once for an attack on the vessels. They ran first to Trott's Island, whence they crossed over to Goat Island under a heavy fire, which, however, did not stop them. Here they fell in with an armed party, who had landed to oppose them. But the blood of the Cape men was up. Stopping for neither grape nor musketry, they soon drove the invaders back to their boats, with the loss of fifteen or sixteen men killed and wounded. On the part of the Cape men, the brave Captain Burnham was killed by a ball in the chest. The enemy succeeded in getting one of their prizes out of the harbor; the other was abandoned and burnt.

The succeeding years were years of prosperity, to which the War of 1812 put a period. In 1821 the town was newly incorporated with the name of Kennebunkport. Upon referring to the causes which originally led to the change of name, we find that they no longer exist.[5] From this time forward the history of Kennebunkport is the familiar one of details belonging exclusively to its commercial or social life, and a very uneventful life it has been.

There is one thing more. By the natural expansion of a few families, whole neighborhoods often exhibit a single surname, like that of Wildes or Huff. There may be half a dozen persons of the same Christian name. The surname being dropped among themselves, it has an odd effect to hear them speaking of each other as Miss Mary Clem, Aunt Sally Josh, Aunt Hannah Eben, Aunt Sam Paulina, and so on, all being of one surname. Then the archaic words or idioms in every-day use, of vagrant or unknown origin, would set a college of comparative philology wild with delight.

[1] The leaf of the Mercury, or poison ivy, is obvate, not serrated. This plant grows among stone-walls, stone-heaps, old cellars, and the like, but is sometimes seen creeping among the grass in old burial-grounds. It has a general resemblance to the Virginia creeper, and like it turns a beautiful bright red in the autumn. Some people think that the poison is so malignant that it can be taken by merely passing the plant, if the wind blows the virus toward the passer, without either handling or touching the plant. No doubt some are more susceptible to the poison than others. There are two sorts, -- one having three, and the other five leaves, which are crinkled. A case of poisoning may be cured by applying carbolized vaseline or any simple carbolic salve.

[2] The lighthouse stands on Goat Island; it was built in 1834. The other islands are: Bunkin (most westward), Vaughan's, Green's, Folly, and Trott's.

[3] The name Cape Porpoise is referred to as early as 1624 by Levett, who speaks of it as an excellent place for fishing, though he says that "as yet no trial hath been made"; showing this Cape to have been known and named before any settlement existed on it, and disposing of the tradition that there was one prior to Levett's visit. It was included in John Stratton's grant of two thousand acres in 1631. Though incorporated in 1653, yet so late as to 1674 the settlers had neglected to lay out the town boundaries or make roads when ordered. A considerable business is done here in winter in catching lobsters for the New York market, but the laws made for the protection of this fish are but little regarded. At that season the lobster may be shipped alive in barrels.

[4] The chief Wahwa made another unsuccessful attempt at this time to surprise Harding's garrison. But in the following April three men were shot in its vicinity. The victims were buried near the clump of ledges (Butland's Rocks) lying back of the Nonantum House.

[5] Kennebunk had been the name of the Federal customs district in which Wells, Arundel, and Cape Porpoise were included, the custom-house being located at what is now Kennebunk village. Thinking themselves best entitled to it, the Arundel people also wished to take the name of Kennebunk, but being anticipated by the action of the seceders from Wells, when they were set off, and named their new town Kennebunk, Arundel still strove to retain prestige as the port of Kennebunk; hence the present name of Kennebunkport. For a fuller record the reader is referred to Bradbury's "History of Kennebunkport," which is brought down to the year 1837, or to Judge Bourne's "Wells and Kennebunk," which gives many details pertaining to the common history of these two communities.

ASHORE AT TIMBER ISLAND.

CHAPTER VIII.

BIDDEFORD POOL.

"Then a mile of warm, sea-scented beach." — BROWNING.

BEYOND Cape Porpoise we come to the bight of shallow water owning the name of Goose Rocks Bay. A cluster of isolated ledges shows above water a little way out from the land. The first comers seized upon this as the distinguishing feature, and Christopher Levett's remark about the abundance of sea-fowl he saw here probably supplies the missing link touching the name itself.

The coast, darkly bordered by a growth of low, scrubby pines, stretches on to another protruding headland at the east, from which a small island presently detaches itself. This headland is called Fortune's Rocks, and the island is Timber Island. Two small streams, Batson's River and Little River, both marshy at their mouths, where they receive the tide, fall into this bay.

At nearly every turn we take, a clump of gravestones — remorseless reminders of the road we are all travelling — starts up to confront us. This pernicious practice of burying the dead in the home lot is, I am happy to say, passing away. It still obtains, however, to some extent in the country, so making the undertaker's business much less lucrative than in the cities, where that functionary usually takes the whole estate of a deceased person; inasmuch as in the country the dead are sometimes taken to the place of interment in summer in a cart, in winter in a pung.

This allusion to graveyards naturally suggests a bit of folk-lore still current in some out-of-the-way corners. Some women lay claim — and the claim is not restricted to superannuated crones as of old — that no death can occur unless they have had "a warning," as they term it. Exactly what the nature of this warning may be, or how manifested, I have yet to learn; but I do know that full faith is accorded to those professing this gift of second sight. Among seafaring people the belief is also more or less current that a sick person will not die till the tide ebbs.

The lonely road by which one gets from Cape Porpoise to the Goose Rocks is a succession of crooks and turns among bare ledges, of winding through hill and dale, with now and then a distant glimpse of the sea opening from the brow of some windy hill, or out across the yellow marshes. The rivers have dwindled to large brooks, which come foaming down their narrow gorges with sufficient force to turn a mill-wheel. The water power and adjacent marshes show us what brought settlers here at a very early date, though what has kept them here all these years is not so clear, if one were to judge from the forlorn look of the straggling settlement we are passing through. That, however, is no affair of ours.

GATE, POOL ROAD.

At a cross-roads hamlet, where a tall guideboard "lifts its head and lies," after the manner of most country guideboards, we turn down a by-road leading to the beach, finding on our arrival there a public house, with a colony of small though neat cottages ranged along the continuous groves and hillocks. The open sea is again before us, but it is a sea without a sail, as even the fishermen avoid these shallow waters, which a moderate breeze soon tumbles about in short, choppy waves, and a gale sets in the wildest commotion. The beach itself is hard, fine-grained sand, with so gentle a slope to the water that bathing should be quite safe.

Timber Island now lies just opposite us. It was on a ledge at the easternmost point of this island that the good ship *Governor Robie*, one hundred and thirty-five days from Japan, struck one thick March morning, and was brought up "all standing," as sailors say. It had been blowing and raining all the previous day and night, — in fact, it was downright dirty weather, — but not for a moment would an old salt have condescended to call it a gale, or have clewed up anything to speak of, on account of it. When the captain turned in, he supposed the ship to be twenty miles from the nearest land! Thousands visited the scene of the disaster, some secretly hoping the vessel would go to pieces; some, like ourselves, out of curiosity to see a full-rigged ship, with everything as sound in appearance alow and aloft as when she first went to sea, standing up on the reef as straight as a monument. After many trials the vessel was pulled off, much to the disappointment of the land-sharks along shore, who look upon a wreck as their peculiar prey. A strange sort of ethics, truly! If a man should be caught in the act of robbing a wrecked railway train, he would deserve to be lynched on the spot, and public sentiment would doubtless justify the saving of time and trouble to the state. But if some unlucky ship meets a like fate, under conditions involving peril, hardship, and even life itself, the unwritten code of the shore delivers her up to be plundered by the first comers. That code needs revising.

It is only half a mile or so more to the summer colony at Fortune's Rocks, though quite two miles by the usually travelled road. Misfortune's Rocks would seem a more appropriate name, for a worse place for a ship to strike on could hardly be found in a day's journey. For this very reason, however, it is

WOOD ISLAND LIGHT.

exceedingly picturesque. If one could fancy a gigantic skeleton hand protruding above the sand and shingle, the fingers would crudely represent the knobbed ridges of hard granite that are spread apart here in the midst of a buffeting surge. Between these bare ridges the sea has scooped out ragged coves, connected them by natural causeways of loose pebbles, and in a manner walled up the marshes against its own assaults.

The outlook is now toward Biddeford Pool.[1] It should be explained that this name has attached itself to the contiguous shores as well as to the basin they enclose, so that when one asks for the Pool, the village is invariably pointed out, the dry land and not the water.

The beach lying out before us, and joining the mainland with the Pool by a narrow isthmus, has given up some of its secrets that had lain buried no one knows how long. In an autumnal gale last year this beach was deeply washed out by the floods of water poured upon it for several days together. The removal of some feet of sand, in this way, brought to light the remains of two dug-out boats such as the early settlers sometimes made use of in navigating the coast. The unlooked-for reappearance of such objects above ground, after the lapse of a century or more, perhaps, certainly awakens strange thoughts of those who have been here before us.

Crossing the clean beach in preference to the dusty road, I ascended the rocky hillock, thickly studded with cottages and boarding-houses, through which streets somehow find their way, that is at least cousin-german to the islands lying outside of it. It is a Liliputian republic, having its own church and school-house, its petty commerce and expansive sea-view. This is one of the oldest seaside resorts of Maine, as it certainly is one of the most inviting, in some respects, even if those unaccountable shiftings of population, to which the seashore forms no exception, have thrown it somewhat in the shade of late.

MONUMENT, STAGE ISLAND.

Upon gaining the high ground, a most noble and exhilarating prospect of sea and shore presents itself at one glance. Here, at our left, comes the Saco from its mountain home; right before us, Wood Island lights the entrance, and Stage Island breaks off the seas that come rolling in toward the river's mouth from the broad Atlantic. These form the anchorage known as Winter Harbor,[2] for which Wood Island's white tower[3] and Stage Island's gray beacon tell the mariner how to steer. In the distance are other islands, with the Scarborough shore lifting over them a bold promontory. Turning now to the land between, we see the whole curving expanse of Old Orchard Beach stretched out in the warm sunshine, like an odalisque of the sea, over whose slumbers those tawny headlands at right and left, these wave-washed islands, seem the grim and watchful guardians. Under fair skies the scene is like a dream of the Orient, after the grisly rocks that gird the coast with bands of iron on either side.

Upon going down to the landing-place, I found the usual clump of crazy fish-houses pervaded by the same "ancient and fish-like smell" which so violently assails one's nostrils wherever fish and men congregate in these latitudes. Swarms of flies were feeding upon the garbage thrown down upon the strand, for the tide to take or leave as it would. A dozen great hulking fellows sat around, whistling tunes, smoking pipes, whittling, or mending their lobster-traps, as if life were something to be taken easily, and work to be performed only in a sitting posture.

I went up to a man who was scrubbing the fish-scales off the inside of his wherry with the stump of an old broom, and asked him if he would set me across the gut. He barely looked up, and without pausing in his work, said he had no objection. Two birds with one stone should ever be the traveller's maxim. "Is there anything worth seeing at Wood Island?" I demanded of him. "Well," said he, glancing across the water where it rose in the offing, "there it is; see for yourself." "But," I persisted, "is there anything about it worth knowing — that is, to a stranger?" " *Yes,*' sir, ef you're a stranger, you want to keep well off to the nor'ard, so's to keep off'n the rocks." "Did anything ever happen there that you know of?" "Oh, that's what you want to know, is it?" said the fellow, straightening himself up and drawing his wet sleeve across his perspiring face. "Well, yes; Tom Cutts, of Wood Island, caught a lobster that weighed a hundred-weight."

BIDDEFORD POOL.

Here, at last, was an opening. "They tell me," said I, blandly, "that the lobster is growing scarcer and scarcer; I suppose those men," indicating them with my head, "must sometime think of Tom Cutts with regret."

"Oh, you needn't pity them," was the slow rejoinder; "small ones sells now for twice as much as big ones used to once. Them that's under lawful size, they daresn't sell, but they eat themselves. Them that has eggs, they scrape the eggs off on, and nobody knows the difference." A million young destroyed for the sake of ten cents! Here was food for thought if not for the stomach. Should we need to be further enlightened, it may be added that in one year ten million pounds of this delicious crustacean were canned in Maine alone.

"When your boat has dried off a bit, you may take me across there," I finished, astonished at this man's voluntary turning state's evidence, as it were, against his comrades. It was cleared up, however, as he was pulling me over, by his saying that he belonged to the coal schooner I saw lying out in the stream, and not to the Pool, which he seemed to owe a grudge.

The air here was tremulous with the steady roll of the surf. To an untrained ear, this sound of the sea is the sound of the sea. But to those who follow the sea, or live by its shores, the dash of the breakers against the rocks would never be mistaken for the long roll upon the beach. This noise of the rote is also an infallible sign of a change of wind or weather; for the quarter out of which it comes to your ears is that from which the wind will blow before many hours. In thick weather, pilots feel their way among the crookedest passages, safely guided only by the echo from the shores or sound of the surf. "I speak of pilots who know the wind by its scent, and the wave by its taste, and could steer to any port between Boston and Mount Desert, simply by listening to the peculiar sound of the surf on each island, beach, and line of rocks along the coast."

The Pool landing is separated from the main by a strait, not more than a cable's length in breadth, through which the tide runs as in a sluiceway into the land-locked basin called the Pool, where vessels lie snugly moored against all winds, blow high, blow low, while the outer anchorage is more or less exposed to the force of northeast gales. One easily gets the idea that the land from which the gut separates us has been joined, at some remote time, to that on the Pool village side; but while only the Power which is said to be able to remove mountains could have split the natural ridge, of which the village once apparently formed part, there is evidence everywhere to changes equally striking, and hardly less formidable, in the general structure of the coast.

On the whole, there is something singularly romantic and individual about this secluded little haven, — something that instinctively calls to mind those secret nooks of the coast of Scotland about which Scott has woven his story of the "Pirate." Then, on the one hand, there is a somewhat pleasing absence of the pretentious and exclusive side of life at the shore, and on the other, of those ingenious devices for picking the traveller's pocket, with which the so-called popular resorts so abound.

After climbing the bluff, at the farther side, I looked about me for what traces might remain of Fort Mary,[4] which defended the entrance to the river long years ago. There is really nothing to see. A sharp eye may detect here and there the fading outlines of the old work, but that is all. I found, indeed, a shallow hollow in the earth, enclosed by portions of what was evidently an angle of the embankment. In a year or two more even that will have disappeared. Vandal hands have long since carried off all that could be carried away, and time's ravages will do the rest. There was nothing in these perishing mounds to grow sentimental over; but not far from them there stands a dwelling, belonging to nearly the same period, when every man's house was so truly his castle that this one has ever since been known as the Jordan garrison.[5]

Now that we have taken a look at things as they are, give us leave, gentle reader, to roam awhile in the eventful past, for here again History beckons us to her side.

It is that sterling sailor, Champlain, who draws for us such a pretty pastoral picture of the Indian settlement as he saw it here in 1605. De Monts and he had been heartily welcomed by the simple-minded natives, who danced and sang for joy about the sands as the strange bark glided up the river to her anchorage. Champlain describes their fortress as being "a large cabin surrounded by palisades made of rather large trees, placed by the side of each other, in which they take refuge when their enemies make war upon them." Their cabins were covered with bark. The place, he says, was very pleasant, and as agreeable as any to be seen; the river alive with fish and bordered by fair meadows.

ANGEL GABRIEL.

It was a new thing to these explorers to find savages tilling the soil, and indicated a higher grade of intelligence than the Frenchmen had hitherto found among them; but to know just what the land was capable of producing was a matter of far more vital concern to the designs of De Monts. So they carefully noted what they saw growing in the Indian gardens. Maize was of course their principal crop, —

"The green-haired maize, her silken tresses laid
In soft luxuriance on her harsh brocade."

They found that the Indians' way of planting was to drop three or four kernels of corn, and as many beans, into each hill, by seeing the beans blossoming among the corn. Farmers in this part of the world follow the custom to this day, and succotash is a dish derived from the most primitive of Indian cookery. Squashes, pumpkins, and a sort of tobacco, which was probably our poke-weed, were also grown to perfection by these Indians; yet with no other tools than a clumsy wooden spade to loosen the earth, and the cast-off shell of a horseshoe crab to scrape it up with into hills. Rude husbandry this! Yet they were happy as the day is long. Civilization had not yet begun improving them out of existence.

The site of the Indian fortress is located on the gravelly ridge on the west bank, extending at the back of Mr. John Ward's house; and of the village on a neighboring piece of flat land. A spring in the neighborhood still goes by the name of the Indian Spring.

Though surprisingly few reminders of it remain, not many places surpass Biddeford in historic or romantic interest. It was here that Richard Vines,[6] that faithful follower of Sir Ferdinando Gorges, spent the memorable winter of

1616–17, in a miserable hovel, among the plague-stricken savages, in order to show Englishmen that the climate of Maine was no such terrible bugbear as Lord Popham's people had made it appear. The subsequent use of this harbor by himself and others is directly traceable, we think, to the presence of the Indians, with whom a trade in furs and goods speedily sprung up.

It is a fact that the fishery did little to develop Maine in these earlier years. Getting out lumber, masts, and shingles was about the first business to put a stamp of real progress on the country. This required the selection of sites with water powers, the erection of saw-mills, and the employment of a better sort of labor than in the fishery. To this cause the gradual rise of a new settlement at the falls, while the old remained at a standstill, must be attributed.

It is well known that a single enterprising settler and trader named William Phillips had established himself at the falls of the Saco some years before the breaking out of King Philip's War, and had built a saw and grist mill there.[7] His dwelling was built with an eye to defence; for he was in a lonely situation, and knew he could have no resource except in the thickness of his walls, should the Indians at any time declare war. His nearest neighbor, not a very desirable one at the best, lived half a mile lower down the river, on the opposite or eastern side. This was one John Bonython,[8] a man of so stubborn and intractable a spirit, so much of an Indian, in fact, that his neighbors had dubbed him the Sagamore of Saco. Bonython had a hint given him to look to himself, as the river Indians were about to fall on the settlers unawares. He took the alarm and fled to Phillips' garrison in time to see his own house in flames.

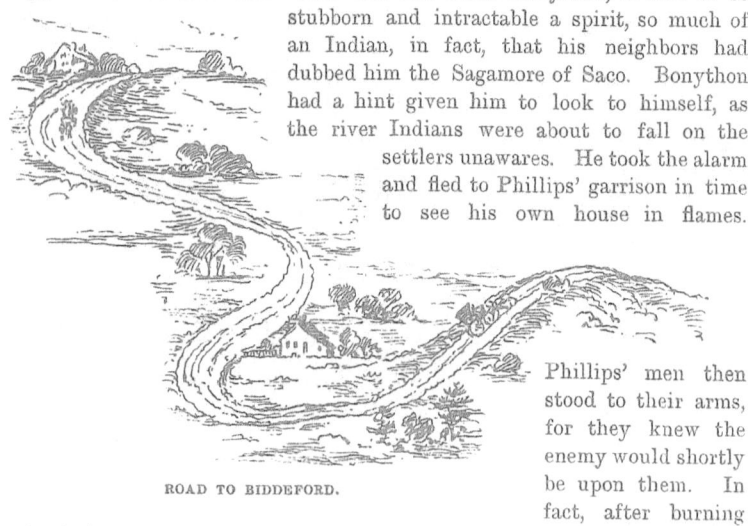

ROAD TO BIDDEFORD.

Phillips' men then stood to their arms, for they knew the enemy would shortly be upon them. In fact, after burning Bonython's house, the savages laid siege to Phillips', who, however, beat them off, with the loss of many of their warriors; though he was presently forced to abandon his post to the enemy, in spite of his gallant defence of it, because the people at the Pool were afraid to come to his assistance. Phillips' brave stand, therefore, only delayed the destruction of the weak settlement at the falls for a brief time, as the defeated savages soon came back to complete what they had left unfinished.

This is the self-same John Bonython whose portrait the poet Whittier thus draws in "Mogg Megone":—

"The hunted outlaw, Bonython!
A low, lean, swarthy man is he,
With blanket garb, and buskined knee,
And naught of English fashion on;
For he hates the race from whence he sprung,
And he couches his words in the Indian tongue."

The poet's description of the falls, as they appeared before the white men's dams and canals had shorn them of their primitive grandeur and beauty, is a much more engaging picture.

"Far down through the mist of the falling river,
Which rises up like an incense ever,
The splintered points of the crags are seen,
With water howling and vexed between,
While the scooping whirl of the pool beneath
Seems an open throat, with its granite teeth!"

On the Biddeford side the banks of the Saco are broken and hilly; on the Saco side, level and sandy. The two neighbor cities are built around the falls, six miles from the ocean, and owe their later growth to the magnificent water power, which has raised them to the rank of manufacturing centres, with the stamp of thrift and enterprise visible in their public buildings, nowhere more so than in the educational institutions.

One of the most charming episodes of a sojourn in this locality, before the steamer was withdrawn from the route, was the sail down the pleasant windings of the Saco, through the outlying islands, to the Pool. It was by far the most agreeable means of bringing the history and traditions of the Saco and its banks under one's eye, to say nothing of the gratification derived from the excursion itself. We need more such to be opened, not closed.

---

[1] Saco was the oldest, as it was the most important, settlement within the Gorges patent. The name Biddeford is from Bideford, County Devon, England, memorable as the port from which Sir Walter Raleigh despatched assistance to his unfortunate Virginia colony. Prior to 1718, both sides of the river were called Saco. The name was then changed to Biddeford. This continued till 1762, when the east side was separately incorporated by the name of Pepperellborough, in honor of Sir William Pepperell, who had once owned a large part of it. In 1805 the name of Saco was restored to this side. This confusion of names is believed to be unmatched in the annals of any municipality. Under the local designation of Winter Harbor, the Pool continued to be the chief settlement for a hundred years.

[2] The tradition is that Vines and his companions wintered at Leighton's Point, at the north side of the Pool; hence the name Winter Harbor. But no actual settlers are found here before 1630, or until Vines had received his patent. There were certainly none when Levett

arrived in 1624. It is to be regretted that the Pool should not have kept the name which served to identify it as the locality of the earliest settlement on the Saco.

[3] Wood Island, strange to say, is actually wooded. My coast pilot says you may go into Winter Harbor either from the eastward or westward of Wood Island, though the eastward passage is best, on account of some rocks, and a sand-bar lying to the west and southwest. Anchor inside of Stage Island, which makes the lee. This island, formerly known as Gibbons', has a tall stone monument. The lighthouse, built in 1808, shows a red flash. There is also a fog-bell, and on the back beach, at the Pool, a life-saving station.

[4] Fort Mary was not built till some years after Philip's War, and no doubt prevented a total desertion of the inhabitants during the next. Though nominally a fort, it served the purpose also of a trading-post, as the English supposed it would draw the tribes away from the French, while the Indians demanded the establishment of such posts. Church, who favored attacking the Indians in their own strongholds, declared the policy of supplying them with everything they wanted all wrong, and advised the abandonment of Fort Mary. In 1703 it was taken by the enemy. At that time it mounted only four cannon, and Church says was not worthy of the name of a fort. Massachusetts determined, however, to hold it; so it was strengthened and garrisoned again in 1705.

[5] Said to have been built about 1717 by Samuel Jordan, son of Dominicus, of Spurwink, who was slain by the Indians. Samuel, then a boy, was taken to Canada, learned the Indian tongue, and after his release became an object of terror to his captors, who on more than one occasion tried to take or kill him.

[6] Richard Vines has not yet found a biographer. Yet of all the minor characters of his time Vines richly deserves an enduring record. Gorges seems to have found in him the man he wanted, and Vines certainly served his patron well to the end. Vines did what Smith had, so unfortunately, been prevented from doing by his capture at sea. We do not know why Saco should have been chosen for the experiment, unless the existence of the Indian settlement there had become known through the fishing-ships. The ravages of the plague referred to may be guessed from what John Winter, of Richmond's Island, has to say about the handful remaining at Saco in 1633. Popham's failure bears so directly upon the fortunes of Saco that the student is invited to consider the sequence of events after that failure. Vines first acted as Gorges' steward or agent, until the proprietor sent his nephew, William Gorges, to establish a *de facto* government in place of the loosely jointed combination which had previously existed on the spot. This was formally done March 25, 1636, at Richard Bonython's house, which tradition locates at the east side of the river, near the lower ferry, though why the court should have been held there, instead of at the Pool, is not clear.

[7] Phillips' Garrison occupied a commanding site at what is still called the "Shipyard," though now covered with buildings, just below the bridge leading to Factory Island, and where the old Pierson house now stands, at the corner of Pierson's Lane, in Biddeford. The stone fort of later times stood on a rocky bluff, just above the bridge, in the Laconia Company's yard.

[8] Mr. Whittier himself says of " Mogg Megone," in which Bonython figures so prominently, "The poem was written in my boyish days, when I knew little of colonial history or anything else, and was included in my collected writings by my publishers against my wishes." We cannot refrain from pointing out the danger of making history serve the purpose of fiction by manipulating its facts. Probably ten young people have read "Mogg Megone" to one who has read the true story. It is needless to add that none of the events related in the poem have any historical sanction whatever, except the sacking of Norridgewock, which took place quite fifty years after Ruth Bonython is supposed to have fled there after stabbing Megone to the heart, and of which she is a frenzied witness. John, the son of Richard Bonython, one of the original patentees of Saco, was outlawed for refusing to obey a legal process, and defying the officers sent to arrest him. But for this fact he would, in all probability, have

remained unknown and unsung. Sullivan is the first to give the oft-quoted inscription on Bonython's gravestone, which still remained when Sullivan was writing his history, "at a place called Rendezvous Point."

" Here lies Bonython, Sagamore of Saco:
He lived a rogue, and died a knave, and went to Hobomoko."

There is no trace of this stone, nor have I been able to find any one who remembers it. Sullivan practised law in Biddeford, in a house now standing near the bridge, at the corner of Hill and Main streets, before he became governor of Massachusetts, and was familiar with all the traditions of the place.

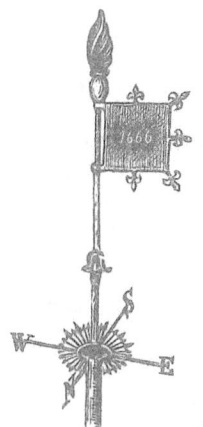

CHAPTER IX.

ON OLD ORCHARD BEACH.

"And all impatient of dry land, agree
With one consent, to rush into the sea." — COWPER.

OLD ORCHARD BEACH unites two historic settlements. This was the thoroughfare by which the old-time traveller, who had just crossed the Saco at the lower ferry, rode on to Pine Point, to be again ferried over the Dunstan to Scarborough. Certes, it was no holiday promenade when the wayfarer ran the risk of leaving his bones to moulder away among the sand-drifts we see heaped at the top of the beach! A gunshot, a puff of smoke, and it was all over with him. Yet we often read in the old chronicles of such or such a man being shot down on Saco sands, like a sandpiper nowadays, by hunters who were after human game. The prowling redskin sprang from his lair, tomahawk in hand, neatly flayed off his victim's scalp, waved it aloft with a cry of triumph, and so added one more deed of blood to the annals of the beach.

Thomas Rogers, one of the earliest settlers here, who lived near Goose Fare Brook, planted an orchard, from which the beach takes its name. The Indians burned Rogers' house to the ground soon after their repulse at Phillips' garrison; but his orchard continued for a century longer to blossom among the ruins of his homestead, — an eloquent reminder of what it cost in the old days to be a pioneer.

We turn from these records of bloodshed to something more attractive. To-day we can hardly conceive of the murderer and incendiary as plying his infernal trade in such a place; of these cool groves that whisper us on one side as the deadly ambuscade; of the sands that entice us on the other as crimsoned with the blood of unknown heroes. Yet this is no fancy picture.

One of Taine's charming bits of description fits admirably into the scene before us: "The coast stretches into the vapor its long strip of polished sand; the gilded beach undulates softly and opens its hollows to the ripples of the sea. Each ripple comes up foamy at first, then insensibly smooths itself, leaves behind it the flocks of its white fleece, and goes to sleep upon the shore it has kissed. Meanwhile another approaches, and beyond that again a new one, then a whole troop, striping the blue water with embroidery of silver. They whisper low, and you scarcely hear them under the outcry of the distant billows; nowhere is the beach so sweet, so smiling; the land softens its embrace the better to receive and caress those darling creatures, which are, as it were, the little children of the sea."

This is the picture that the summer visitor knows, all grace and feeling. There is another, known only to those who have stood here when some autumnal gale was storming along the coast as if it would crush it to atoms, when destruction rides upon the tempest, and all the world of waters seems at war with itself. Silence falls on every tongue at sight of the great ocean running riot without a guiding hand; for any disturbance in nature's orderly movements brings home to us, as nothing else can, what shadows we are and what shadows we pursue,—

THE SCAVENGER.

"and we fools of nature,
So horridly to shake our disposition
With thoughts beyond the reaches of our souls."

Scarborough and the Pool make the two horns of the crescent. On the Pool side we yet hold Wood Island so plainly that the surf is seen alternately whitening and subsiding about its seaward point. How charmingly yonder curling foam-wreath sets off the deep blue of the sea! It is like a great plain of lapis-lazuli veined with streakings of alabaster. And somehow it gives us real pleasure to see the lighthouse standing at its post out there in the offing, though the sky is without a cloud, and the sea scarcely breaks at our feet.

At the Scarborough side are other islands, on the larger of which there is a house;[1] farther off two vessels are slowly forging past each other on the same tack. One has just left port; the other is just going into it. One captain has turned his back upon his home; the other is filled with joyful anticipations; for we know his has been a long voyage by the rusty hulk, patched sails, and grimy spars alow and aloft. Still farther out, a steamer's smoke is trailing along the horizon. Our grandfathers would unhesitatingly have declared it to be a ship on fire.

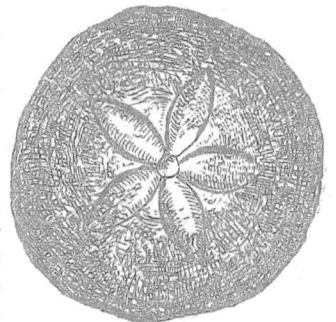

SAND-ROLLER.

Here are the sea and the dunes. A colony of hardy little pitch-pines has established itself along the head of the beach, on a ridge of firm, white sand. This is the candlewood of the early settlers, who used splints of it to light their cabins. It is the only tree that will grow here; but tough as it looks, the shock of many a storm is visible along the thinned ranks. Every tree looks as if stripped for a fight. That describes accurately a skirmish line, thrown out in front of the denser masses of forest behind it. And here before it are the charging billows. The ground beneath these pines is carpeted with fallen needles, so that one walks noiselessly about. Pale ferns vegetate in the thick shades, and at the back of the grove is a pretty pond. In truth, these seaside groves seem more like overgrown thickets than woods, so stunted are they in their growth, so roughened by exposure to the loss of the native graces of their kind. But we must not loiter here.

We have approached the group of cottages at Bay View; for be it known that Old Orchard[2] proper has thrown off its suburbs, each of which holds out its peculiar claims to public patronage. At some distance beyond us, the houses crowd thickly down upon the beach, halt there, and form a line, curving with the shore, for as far as the eye can reach. This city of the sea is Old Orchard. We try not to look that way.

The vicinity of Bay View offers much the most extensive sweep of the eye of any part of the beach, inasmuch as the Cape Elizabeth shore, with Richmond's Island lying out before it, is finely brought out from this spot. With a glass the Two Lights could probably be made out, although I could not see them with the naked eye; but by night they must shine out brilliantly. The sea-scape is certainly larger here than at any other point.

To some the beach may be always simply a playground, and nothing else, while to others it may prove a far more interesting and instructive school for the study of zoölogy than a stuffy lecture-room, presided over by a dried-up professor, with dried-up specimens. More can be learned here in a day, with an intelligent companion, than in a month with books. Every tide casts up perfect specimens; the student has only to pick them up. Finally, the man who kicks everything away from him in disgust, saying that is only a kelp-stalk, or this a dead sculpin, listens at first with incredulity, then with growing interest, and at last with actual wonder and admiration, to the story of the despised mussel-shell.

Let me strike the water with one oar, and with the other scrape the sands. Here now is something that looks so uncanny, so snake-like, as it lies stretched out at full length on the warm and glistening sands, that we almost expect to see the slimy thing start up and glide away at our approach. But no; it is only one of those despised things, — a stalk of kelp, uprooted from Neptune's garden by the last gale. But what, then, is this object to which it clings with such a death-like gripe?

This long, flexible, tubular stalk loves to attach itself to the broad back of some unsuspecting mussel, and when once its glutinous roots have taken firm hold, not even the death of one or both can dislodge it. Can it be that the instinct of the plant — if we may suppose plants possessed of such a thing; and why not? — tells it to lay hold of the first stationary object it finds anchored at the bottom, regardless of trespass or ejectment, and so secure itself against being tossed about at the sport of every wave? Does might also make right. we ask, at the bottom of the sea? At any rate, the life of the kelp is the doom of the mussel, for the strong, talon-like roots instantly clasp this fixed object as in a vise. And now comes the curious part of the story. There being no soil for this singular plant to root itself in, it adheres to the mussel's back by the power of suction, until by some chemical action the glutinous matter of the plant is so combined with the lime of the mussel-shell as to become absolutely glued to it. The mussel puts up with this forcible entry upon her premises as best she may, since her unwelcome tenant can neither be shaken off nor evicted, and she is now as fully in its power as a fawn would be in the coils of a python; but at length its growth becomes such a serious drawback to her, so to speak, that when the pangs of hunger have forced her to open her mouth, the kelp will not let her shut it again, and she soon falls a prey to the omnivorous sand-fleas or leaf-worms. So the poor mussel, like many another bearer of unsought burdens from which there is but one way of escape, finally gives up the ghost in despair.

But mark the revenge nature allows her to take of the intrusive and destroying kelp! Upon looking closely, we discover no end of tiny baby mussels cunningly hid away among the roots of the kelp, to which they have attached themselves by means of the curious fibrous ligament with which they are provided. So that the plant, which has destroyed the mother mussel, is compelled to nourish her offspring.

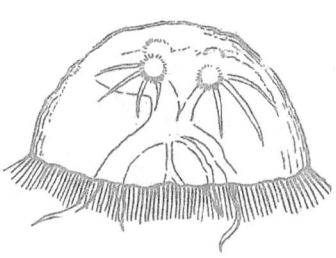

"GOOD MORNING."

Every now and then in my walk I would come across a stranded jelly-fish, or Medusa, but never before had I seen anything approaching in size these castaways of the deep sea, or at all like them in general appearance. The common Medusæ, with which our rivers and harbors are alive in summer, are seldom larger than a large saucer, and are so entirely transparent and colorless that the markings of the different organs by which this wonderful little animal lives, breathes, and has its being, may be seen through the palpitating flesh. Those I found stranded on the beach in October were of prodigious size, — as large over as my walking-stick, — all hairy round the creatures' mouths, with flesh of the color of raw beef. What more graceful objects can be imagined than the smaller Medusæ, when opening and shutting their delicately fringed bodies with a slow, wavy motion in the act of swimming? It is the very poetry of motion. These were most repulsive looking things.

Old Orchard might be called an overgrown railway station, with a Fourth of July annex. The railway ploughs a deep furrow through the mass of wooden buildings, constantly interjecting its noise, smoke, and clatter into the sentiment of the protesting sea. Nevertheless, Old Orchard is the typical watering-place for those who detest the name of solitude. An esplanade of hard, white sand, with an undulating wall of surf at the bottom, and another of warm dunes at the top, makes its front street, — a street five miles long, built, graded, swept, and kept in repair by the ocean. Cottages and hotels are ranged along the sea-front; hotels and cottages cross the dunes behind, mount the bald slopes rising at the back, and finally disappear among cool groves of pine, whose dark green instantly relieves the white glare of the sands, and the nakedness of the unshaded expanse of red roofs, peaked gables, and gaudy turrets packed in one mass underneath a broiling sun.

This assemblage of houses, accidental in everything except an eye to the main chance, has the appearance of having sprung up in a night, like a colony

MEDUSÆ.

of red, white, and orange toadstools after a summer shower. You would be willing to wager something that it was not here yesterday. Everything new, or as good as new; nothing to mellow this offensive newness or to tempt one to a second look. Shops, cafés, booths, fruit-stands, shooting-galleries, bazaars without end, crowd together in interminable rows. Every one is busily employed in catering to the wants of the army of travellers, who have come here to divert themselves, and who demand to be diverted.

You pass through a cross-fire from newsboys, hotel-porters, and bootblacks to the wooden sidewalk. A man in a soiled white apron, with sleeves rolled up, comes out of a doorway and rings a dinner-bell in your face. "Dinner, sir?" You pass on. A second brings out a gong, with which you are deafened. This performance begins again on the arrival of every train. Apparently it is always time to eat here. All at once you hear a terrible rumbling on one side of you!

ON OLD ORCHARD BEACH.

"This way, sir, to the gravity railway!" An express train thunders through the principal street, blinding you with its smoke and dust. When you open your eyes again, you see a placard before you, announcing that there is to be a political meeting at the Camp Ground. As it is near the hour, you join the crowds already streaming that way, much impressed by the variety of diversion that Old Orchard affords. On arriving at the Camp Ground, after a hot walk, you find three thousand people impatiently awaiting the arrival of the speakers. A band in uniform plays "Nearer my God to Thee." After this, one of the trustees of the Camp Ground, whose face wears a most guileless smile, mounts the rostrum, and, after clearing his throat, gently reminds the audience of the sacred character of the place by announcing that a collection will be taken up. The crowd laughs good humoredly and pays.

Having sufficiently diverted yourself, you make a bee-line for the beach again.

Here the people who live at the edge of the shore are reclining in hammocks, in various listless attitudes, reading, smoking, or looking off on the water, or at the knots of pedestrians sauntering idly about the beach, now stopping to pick up a shell, over which they hold an animated confab, or stooping curiously about some nondescript fish, on which they hold an inquest. Carriages are crossing the beach in every direction, or standing where the occupants can watch the bathers, who, if timid, are seen splashing the water about like great children, or, if bold, gambolling in the big surf-waves farther out, where their heads bob up and down like corks. Still farther out, the white gulls stoop to skim the waves with their wings, and then sail screaming off. Perhaps there will be twenty sail or more of mackerel-catchers in the offing, all headed up in the wind, with sails flapping idly in the cool breeze. A good haul to you, my mates! Here, at least, we are not bored to death. But we must on, for the day is waning.

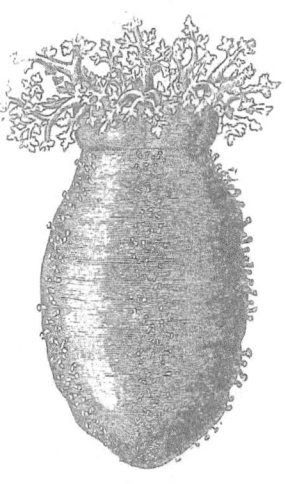

SEA-CUCUMBER.

One custom that is peculiar to Old Orchard has given rise to no end of satirical comment or downright ridicule. It is the one so long observed by the country folk, far and near, of resorting to the beach on the 26th of June in each year, in consequence of the prevailing belief that whoever, on that day, dipped in the sea would be freed from all the ills which flesh is heir to.

Formerly the anniversary was kept on St. John the Baptist's day, but by general consent it was moved forward two days. No valid objection is found to the custom of bathing even once a year, yet the question of how far it may be accepted as an evidence of lingering superstition remains unsolved to this day. It unquestionably arose in the beginning from a firm belief in the miraculous efficacy of the waters to heal the sick, make the lame walk, and the weak strong. Just how it came about is not clear. Many years ago it was reported that a cow had opened her mouth, not like Balaam's ass to reprove a prophet, but to declare the miraculous virtues of these waters. But there is no poetry about these plain country folk or their superstitions. Whenever the subject is broached, they stoutly deny any belief in the alleged healing properties of the waters; yet most of them will be found on the beach when the sacramental day comes round again. I am therefore persuaded that a strong undercurrent of credulity really exists, and that in this case actions speak louder than words. Superstition is like the undertow of the beach itself, which sometimes carries even the strongest swimmers off their feet.

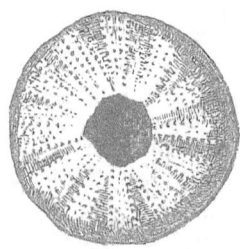

SEA-URCHIN.

The beach is the only place where one can get perfect specimens of the sort of shellfish that grow and multiply far out, where the ordinary wash of the tides does not disturb them. Here, snugly tucked away in beds of clean white sand, in quiet waters, the giant-clam, quahaug, and razor-clam [3] lead a life of undisturbed tranquillity, until some great gale turns them out of house and home.

During the winter of 1876, after a storm at sea, this beach was reported to be covered with quahaugs to the depth of a foot, and in some places two feet. I confess this sounded like exaggeration until the great gale of November 28, 1888, happened, when curiosity led me to visit the beach.

The sight that met me was supremely grand, supremely desolate, — as if in very truth the fountains of the great deep were broken up, and chaos come again. Nobody ever looked on such a spectacle without feeling awed and sobered. Everything was in the wildest commotion, — the air full of blinding spray, the sea one mass of tossing water, the clouds rolling in thick, opaque masses overhead. And at the edge of the shore the steady rush and ceaseless roar of the breakers, as they came up fifteen feet high against the beach, was echoed along the coast, was in the air, and seemed the voice of the storm crying no quarter to the groaning land. Would that I might describe those roaring monsters that shook the solid earth with the weight of their fall! Vain attempt! Three ranks deep, heaped up all the way from Ireland, they drove on up the beach, which seemed to shrink before their daring advance. Then, as they broke, they deluged the shores with rivers of foam that ran seething, bubbling, and hissing about, till the force that had launched them spent itself, and they were swept back, exhausted, into the jaws of the coming wave.

This gale will long be remembered for its disastrous effects. Hardly within the memory of man has so much sea-stuff come on shore, or have the farmers reaped such a rich harvest. All the cottages standing along the water-front showed the effects of hard usage. Bulkheads were wrecked, outhouses turned round, awnings, platforms, and walks carried away, while the wet sand lay in unsightly heaps about the house doors, some of which had been forced open by the winds and waves. All this indicated that the danger limit had been reached when the gale was at its height. The few people who remained in their houses passed a night of terror in listening to the wash of the waves beneath them, till the turning of the tide relieved their fears for the time; and for once it was Old Orchard on the sea without any straining of the situation.

At low tide the sea stood at the point ordinarily reached by the flood. High-water mark was indicated by a windrow of seaweed, mixed with broken-up woodwork, lying quite high up beyond the first line of houses. A more woebegone spectacle than this washed-out village presented would be hard to imagine, and yet it had its ludicrous side, too, in the numerous signs displayed on all sides of "Ice Cold Soda Water," "Bathing Suits to Let," and the like legends, the bare sight of which on this November day was enough to set one's teeth chattering.

Not far away, havoc of another kind had been going on unchecked. These gales are very destructive to animal life. Toward Pine Point the beach was buried to the depth of a foot or more beneath a sodden mass of water-soaked sawdust, ground-up bark, or slimy driftwood that had been lying at the bottom, no one knows how long, until this gale dislodged and cast it up. A little way off it had the appearance of a ledge of rocks. There were acres upon acres of this stuff. It was the strangest sight I ever looked upon; for mixed up with the soft and sticky mass were live lobsters, crabs, mussels, quahaugs, cockles, sea-urchins,[4] starfish, and razor-clams by the cartload. I do not exaggerate in the least in saying it — by the cartload. In fact, men were carting them off the beach, while I was recovering from my astonishment at seeing what would have fed a good-sized village going to waste, or, at best, destined to the farmers' manure-heaps. All these denizens of the deep sea had been thrown up by one tide; the next would doubtless swell the heap with fresh victims.

THE CONTORTIONIST.

Ah! if only the poor of the cities could have the benefit of such a windfall, it would be every whit as good as a miracle; but with fuel rotting upon the hills, and food rotting upon the shores, while some poor souls are freezing and some starving, nature's economy does seem now and then to need a little useful direction.

If there be a more alluring pursuit open to man's ambition than is found in poking over swaths of tangled seaweed, turning over loose stones, peering into every little puddle, or unearthing a crab just as he has comfortably scuttled himself down in the sand, it should be made known at once. What would some naturalists, who look forward to a season's dredging in the deep sea with such joyful anticipation, not have given for the privilege of carting off this palpitating rubbish? It seemed as if the dredgings of the whole Atlantic were spread out before me. I picked up two or three sea-cucumbers, torpid from cold, clammy to the touch, disgusting objects to look at when denuded of the splendid frill of tentacles, with which the head is furnished; also several hermit-crabs, all alive and kicking, — all of which now adorn my cabinet. Of a dozen persons to whom I showed the cucumber, not one knew whether it was an animal or a plant.

SPEARING FLOUNDERS.

Certainly the beach is most attractive in summer, but most imposing and instructive in winter.

Not far from the place where the shellfish came up, Little River formerly cut its way out through the beach. The railroad embankment has turned it into a new channel, thus extending the beach two miles at least, but obliterating the mark of an historic event. It was here that honest Captain Wincall, while marching to the relief of Scarborough with only eleven men, in the time of Philip's War, was set upon by more than ten times his own number of Indians. Though hard pushed, Wincall and his gallant little band kept their assailants at bay, until a chance offered itself to break through them, and gain the shelter of Foxwell's garrison at Dunstan.

The affair was, however, to have its tragic sequel; for upon hearing the firing, a party of nine men hastened from Winter Harbor to the relief of their friends. The savages laid in wait for them among the thickets, with guns cocked, and slaughtered them to a man, though not without their making a desperate fight for their lives.

This affair took place in plain sight of the garrison at Black Point, where Captain Scottow[5] was posted with some soldiers. His men begged hard to be allowed to go to the aid of the poor fellows on the beach, but Scottow turned a deaf ear to their entreaties. One of the fishermen asked him if he was not ashamed to stand still with so many armed men about him, and let those nine Winter Harbor men be murdered before their eyes. Scottow continued dumb. "Come," the speaker persisted, "put me some men into my shallop, and by the help of God, I will pull them on shore in Little River, and doubt not we shall save some of their lives." Scottow would neither stir himself nor give the order.

Hubbard adds that one of the victims of this massacre was the Thomas Rogers who lived at the other end of the beach.

At Pine Point, where the beach comes to an end, are more cottages, and the beach is again pleasantly skirted by groves. Round the point is a fishing-hamlet going back to the old, old time when Charles Pine, a noted slayer of Indians, lived here. The shell-heaps found on the south side of this point bear witness to the aboriginal feasts of long ago. But we are now within the limits of Scarborough, at the site of the old crossing-place to Black Point, — as it was first called, — now Prout's Neck.

---

[1] Stratton's Island has the house; Bluff Island adjoins it. Both belong to Scarborough. Stratton's Island is low and bare, and is so called as early as 1631, in Cammock's patent, presumably from John Stratton, an early settler. Eagle Island and Ram Island lie out opposite Bay View. Basket Island is inside of Stage.

[2] Old Orchard was taken from Saco in 1883. E. C. Staples first took in a few boarders in his farmhouse, about 1840. The beach lies at about three miles from the central part of Saco, and is a summer resort pure and simple. A branch railway connects Old Orchard proper with Ferry Beach, at the mouth of the Saco, and again by ferry with Biddeford Pool; a horse railroad with Saco, which can also be reached by the beach, there being a good road from Bay View, which cuts off the extreme corner of the shore. Old Orchard is equipped with electric lights, a fire department, an abundance of pure water, etc.

[3] John Josselyn calls the razor-clam the sheath-fish, and says it was fully as good eating as a prawn. The flesh is very plump, white, and delicate; but the fish has become too scarce to be used as food.

[4] Scientists have labelled the urchin with the extraordinary encumbrance of "strongylocentrotus," which will doubtless become very popular with the unscientific world. The animal has many other names, — as sea-chestnut, hedgehog of the sea, whore's egg, etc. It is highly esteemed as an article of food by the people living on the shores of the Mediterranean, who gather them for market by diving to the bottom for them.

[5] Joshua Scottow, merchant, of Boston; captain of the artillery company; a great proprietor at Scarborough, where Scottow's Hill is named for him. Read note 1, next chapter. He is the author of "Old Mens' Tears for their own Declensions," 1691; also, of "A Narrative of the Planting of the Massachusetts Colony." Sewall, in his diary, notices Scottow's death and funeral: "Thus the old New England men drop away."

KING PHILIP'S WAMPUM-BELT.

CHAPTER X.

FROM SCARBOROUGH TO PORTLAND HEAD.

"The ocean overpeering of his list,
Eats not the flats with more impetuous haste." — *Othello*.

PINE-TREE DEVICE.

VER marshes cleanly trenched by a network of salt-water inlets, through roads broidered with wild flowers,—where daisies blow, and the purple flower-de-luce springs up from sheaves of sword-like flag, — our way lies along the storied Scarborough shore.

The tide-water, which surges in from sea through the opening between Pine Point and the long promontory of Prout's Neck,[1] at once throws off three long, crooked arms, resembling the feelers of the octopus, that with many a snaky twist and turn reach far up through the broad levels of meadow, into the retreating land. Without doubt, these marshes first attracted settlers to the spot. They furnished an abundant crop of salt-hay, with no other labor than that of cutting, curing, and stacking it; they swarmed with the wild mallard, crane, duck, and brant, and they were bordered by clam-beds so prolific that they have never failed from that day to this, although constantly dug over for two centuries and a half. It would be quite safe to say that no spot as large as one's hand has escaped being turned up again and again.[2] And yet there is the clam-digger to-day, with his dory drawn up beside him on the flats, as busy at work as his great-great-grandfather of the same name was in his time, and just as thoughtless as he of economizing such a common thing as a clam. The marvellous fecundity of these creatures is something to which few have ever given even a passing thought. Yet they have been the source of untold wealth. Gold-fields may be worked out; clam-fields, never.

From the railroad station to Prout's Neck, which is the extreme seaward point of Scarborough, there is a straggling settlement of rather ordinary farmhouses for the whole four miles. Roads branch off at the left to the settlements on the Spurwink, or to the beaches on that side. All of these roads are good, and the drives interesting; but the way to the Neck lies over a sandy plain, offering little that calls for special mention here. Mrs. Sigourney, however, would have liked this long street for its elms and well-sweeps, if for nothing else.

This point was so early occupied that even its topographical features have a certain interest. We wish to know the whys and wherefores, as it were. There is a little cove made by a projection of this peninsula toward Pine Point. It was but an indifferent roadstead, even for the pinnaces and shallops of that day; but Winter Harbor on one side, and Richmond's Island on the other, were the real seaports of Scarborough. It was here, however, that Thomas Cammock established himself about 1636, and it was also here that the first ferry connected the long route along the seaboard.

If we shall turn our backs upon this cove, and take one of the paths leading through the wood skirting the road here, we shall presently come out at the shore of Massacre Pond, extending between us and the beach, a long, smooth sheet of water. It was here that Captain Hunnewell and eighteen more Scarborough men were slaughtered by the Indians.[3] And a little north of this pond the site of Scottow's fort is still distinguishable. Beyond this point the sand-dunes seem to have engulfed what was probably cultivated land within fifty years, as good soil is found on digging away the superincumbent sand. Prout's Neck now elevates itself to a grassy headland appropriated everywhere by summer hotels and cottages.

The Thomas Cammock who was just now referred to, who received a grant of Black Point in 1631, and is therefore considered the founder of Scarborough, is first heard of as an agent for Sir Ferdinando Gorges, at Piscataqua, in this

CLAM-DIGGER.

same year. It is not certain, however, that he took up his residence at Black Point before the year 1636. Cammock's father had made a runaway match with the Lady Frances, daughter of the Earl of Warwick, the details of which are quite romantic. A few unimportant scraps are all that have been recovered concerning Cammock himself or his stay at Black Point, probably because there is so little to be said of him.

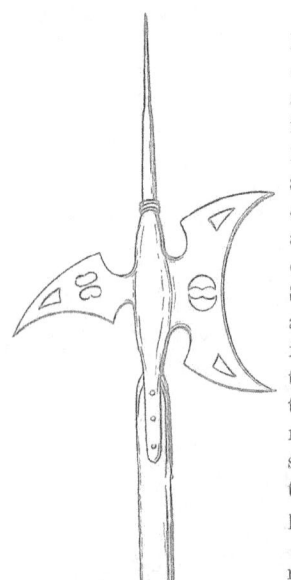

HALBERD.

But Cammock had a bachelor friend who, like himself, had been in Gorges' service, and was wholly devoted to his interest. Exact dates are unattainable, but we find Henry Josselyn, gentleman,[4] installed as a member of Cammock's household in 1638, at which time the family received a notable accession. This was no less a person than John Josselyn, brother of Henry, whose "Two Voyages" and "Rarities" are so highly prized by antiquarians. On this account the earliest annals of Scarborough are fuller and more satisfactory than are those of any other of the Maine plantations; for Josselyn was both observant and well informed, though some of his stories would do no discredit to the late Baron Munchausen himself, of famous memory. In short, we are indebted to John Josselyn for a good deal that would else have been lost to the world, and for much more that never had a place in it.

In the first place, Josselyn was a naturalist of no mean acquirements, as his "Rarities" go to prove. It is to him we owe the first discovery, or report of it, of the world-renowned sea-serpent, whose annual appearance is now looked for with such eager interest by landlords all along the New England coast. Not one of the scoffers whose incredulity is so actively aroused when the royal ophidian is mentioned has a word to say against the octopus, — of the two by much the hardest to believe in unless one has had the evidence of his own eyes. The merman is another thing — if it be proper to call it so — about which Josselyn gives us the first precise information. Then Josselyn was again the first person to describe the White Mountains by this entirely felicitous name, and he has added to the opinion that they were raised by earthquakes, his settled conviction that these awful peaks "are hollow, as may be guessed by the resounding of the rain upon the level tops." Nor do we know that this ingenious theory has ever been actually disproved. The mountains rose daily to his view, and were, he says, weather signs to people at the coast.

While searching the country round for curiosities of all sorts, John Josselyn laid his hand upon something that he had never seen before. He quickly took it off again on finding the thing was alive with hornets,[5] without adding it to his collection. Alexander or Napoleon would have done the same thing.

Longfellow has somewhere made use of the incident in the descriptive lines:—

> "I feel like Master Josselyn when he found
> The hornets' nest, and thought it some strange fruit,
> Until the seeds came out, and then he dropped it."

Josselyn also points out, what would be highly improper to-day, that a man could drink more brandy in Maine with impunity than in England. If true, this statement would go far to bear out the theory that the climate is changing. Among other "natural, physical, and chyrurgical" rarities he mentions the mineral spring at Black Point, which he says would "color a spade as if hatcht with silver."

Other glimpses Josselyn gives us of the life and manners of the people are generally in a more serious vein. At this time Scarborough consisted of about fifty dwelling houses and a magazine or storehouse. The people had "store of neat cattle and horses, 700 or 800 sheep, goats, and swine." They also had a mill to grind their corn. This is a valuable off-hand sketch of Scarborough as it existed just before the first Indian war depopulated it; for, in fact, we have none other.

FISHING-SHALLOP, 1630.

"The people," Josselyn says, "may be divided into magistrates, husbandmen or planters, and fishermen; of the magistrates some be Royalists, the rest perverse spirits; the like are the planters and fishers both; others meer fishers." There were no shopkeepers. Boston took their fish and exported it to "Lisbonne, Bilbo, Burdeaux, Marsiles, Taloon [Toulon], Rochel, Roan, etc." He goes on to explain how their trading was done: "The merchant comes in with a walking tavern, — a bark laden with the legitimate bloud of the rich grape, which they bring from Phial, Madera, etc., Brandy, Rhum and tobaco. Coming ashore, he gives them a taste or two which so charms them that they will not go to sea again till they have had their drunken frolic out." Quarrelling and fighting usually accompanied these drunken sprees.

The industrious and frugal obtained a comfortable livelihood, he says, but those "of a droanish disposition," of whom Josselyn says there were too many, grew "wretchedly poor and miserable." This does not seem so surprising when we read a little farther on that certain individuals among them "had a custom of taking tobacco, sleeping at noon, sitting long at meals; sometimes four in a day; and now and then drinking a dram of the bottle extraordinarily."

The Scarborough people were perhaps not more superstitious than their neighbors to the east or west; only Josselyn was on the spot to make a note of everything that floated in the air. He relates a fairy-tale about a certain Master Foxwell who, while lying off shore one night in his shallop, saw a weird band of men and women dancing round a blazing bonfire on the beach. They called out to him to come on shore and join their revel. True to his surname, and mistrusting that all was not as it should be, Foxwell refused to be inveigled by these dancing sirens, though he did go the next morning, finding half-burnt brands, marks of numerous footprints, and other like evidences of the midnight orgie strewed about the spot.

Among other happenings, the gentle Josselyn refers to the premature cold snap of September 15, 1664, by which the inhabitants "were shrewdly pinched"; but he himself, fortunately having "two or three bottles of excellent Passada, made a shift to bear it out." We can readily believe what he says of the wonderful number of herrings cast up at the harbor on one occasion, — so many that one "might have gone halfway the leg in them for a mile together"; but our credulity is severely tasked by his account of frogs standing a foot high, of wild turkeys weighing sixty pounds, or when he is asserting that the Indians usually delivered their speeches in regular hexameter verse. And so we reluctantly take our leave of him.

ANCIENT FLAGON.

Let us go back a little. Having sailed on a voyage to Barbadoes, Cammock left his wife and property to the care of Henry Josselyn. Cammock died while absent, and Josselyn married the widow, with whom also he took the deceased husband's whole estate. Many years of strife with his restless neighbor Cleeves on one side, and the Massachusetts authorities on the other, were followed by the appearance of a new and more formidable claimant, whose rights were to be asserted with the tomahawk and scalping-knife.

The chieftain Mogg, whose band committed most of the atrocities in this region during the continuance of Philip's War, suddenly showed himself at Black Point, at the head of a hundred warriors, in October, 1676. The inhabitants instantly fled to Josselyn's strong house for protection. Instead of burning his fingers by assaulting it, the wily Mogg demanded a parley, which was granted him; and Josselyn, who knew Mogg well, came out of the garrison to talk with him. Mogg said all the people should have leave to depart unharmed with their goods, but that he must have the place. Josselyn agreed to these terms, but on going back to the garrison he found it deserted by all except some of his own servants. No choice was therefore left him but a surrender.

The garrison was, however, reoccupied, and an effort made to maintain it. In May, 1677, Mogg again attacked it. This time the Indians met so stout a resistance that they drew off after their redoubtable leader Mogg had been made to bite the dust. Yet a more sanguinary affair took place in June, when the brave but unwary Captain Swett was led into a trap while making a scout in the neighborhood. His large force of raw soldiers and friendly Indians was speedily overpowered and cut to pieces, more than fifty being killed, including Swett himself.

During the subsequent wars, the place was twice abandoned and as often resettled. These repeated depopulations, extending over a space of thirty years, with their accompanying destruction of houses, barns, fences, — in short, every vestige of the husbandman's labor, — had so obliterated all landmarks that when new settlers came, the ancient metes and bounds were only recovered with the aid of the oldest planters. In none of the old plantations did the storm of war rage with more relentless fury or leave such utter desolation in its track. Indeed, it might be said that for forty years the history of this plantation is written in blood. What has been recounted here is meant to serve rather as a sample than stand for a history.

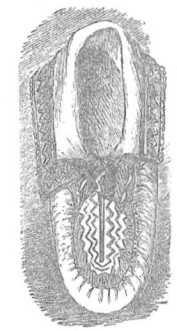

MOCCASIN.

There are two principal summer colonies at Scarborough, one of which occupies the site of the ancient settlement at Prout's Neck, the other skirting the long sand-beach to the east of it. In its physical features, the first is quite the counterpart of Biddeford Pool; the last looks out over the beach upon the broad Atlantic. At night, the Cape Elizabeth lights flash out in the east; while from the west, Wood Island now and then turns its flaming eye, red as with watching, into the darkening sea.

After visiting the points of interest in and about Scarborough, I set my face toward the Cape Elizabeth shore one sunny morning in June, with the Two Lights as my first prospective halting-place.

TURNSTILE.

May is a fickle month in Maine. The weather is apt to be damp, foggy, and overcast. Leafy June also has her vagaries, but there is now and then a day which nearly realizes that perfection which the poet Lowell claims for it.

In passing out of Scarborough by the shore road, we come directly to the brow of a moderately high hill, from which, on looking off inland, the first object we see is Mount Washington. Below us, stretched out cool and glossy among its meadows, is the Spurwink, and just beyond this stream, the long, bold promontory of Cape Elizabeth [6] forms the other side of a narrow valley, which we must first ascend in order to get to the bridge, by which it is crossed. At our right, another road descends the hillside to Higgins' beach.

Gaining the high ground on the Cape side, where there is a quaint little meeting-house, with a rather populous graveyard, we find a scattered settlement extending along the banks of the Spurwink to the sea. All this shore has been held by those owning the name of Jordan ever since the country was first settled, and through the thick and thin of old and new wars, or the thousand and one temptations to seek homes elsewhere, the Jordans have stuck to their original acres with the pertinacity of a Highland clan, and have continued to flourish

RICHMOND'S ISLAND.

until, as I was credibly informed, out of fifty or sixty scholars in the district school, there were not half a dozen of any other name.

All Cape Elizabeth is full of sudden dips, or up-starting knobs of half-bare ledges, interspersed here and there with a plantation of oaks or a forest of spruces.

From Spurwink two more miles will take us to the shore close upon Richmond's Island.[7] This island, with an outward sweep of the mainland, forms quite a deep indent, at the bottom of which there is another pretty beach, with a hotel and cottages at the back, and a gleaming line of breakers at the front. The land here slopes off finely to the water. I was quite charmed with the locality, in spite of its absurd name of Bowery Beach. We are now again upon ground having considerable historic and picturesque distinction.

Had New England definitely passed to French control, in all likelihood Richmond's Island would have retained the more poetic name of Isle of Bacchus, which Champlain first gave it, and very possibly some exiled seigneur would have been raising grapes there now, instead of the cabbages for which it is so famed. *Sic transit.* At any rate, the island has borne no inconspicuous part in the commercial annals of Maine, far back in the time when her islands were looked upon as being more available for commerce and fishery than the mainland itself.

Champlain saw some ripe grapes there, which he pronounced as fine as those of France, and he was positive that if cultivated they would produce good wine. But then Champlain had not seen France for some time. They would have proved but sour grapes, I fancy, under the present code of Maine. But a truce to these pleasantries.

We know that a certain Walter Bagnall had established himself on this island, already known as Richmond's, perhaps as early as 1628, although we do not know who he was or whence he came, nor are the fellow's antecedents of much importance. A patent for the island, with some part of the adjacent mainland, was made out to him three years later; but by this time "Great Watt," as Bagnall's contemporaries call him, was lying in the grave he had dug for himself, so to speak, by cheating and robbing the Indians, with whom he seems to have carried on a considerable trade. One night in October, 1631, a party of them passed over to the island, slew

SCHOOLHOUSE PORCH.

Bagnall and a man of his, and after plundering the trader's house, burned it to the ground, thus returning the island to its original solitude.

The next occupant was John Winter, who came out to New England as the factor of Robert Trelawney, merchant, of Plymouth, to set up a fishery at the island, patterned after that of Monhegan. Winter was on the ground in April, 1632. One of his first acts was to warn off George Cleeves[8] and Richard Tucker, who had already built on the mainland next the island, as trespassers. They left the next spring when Winter returned with men and materials for beginning active work. From this time forward, until the station was broken up by Winter's death, Richmond's Island was as well known on both sides of the Atlantic, perhaps, as Portland is to-day.

When the establishment was in its most flourishing state, Winter had about sixty men under him, for whose spiritual good Trelawney had provided, as a chaplain, one Richard Gibson, the same person who is found a little later stirring up a revolt at the Isles of Shoals. When Gibson left, the living went to the Rev. Robert Jordan,[9] who presently married Sarah Winter, through whom, at Winter's death, Jordan became possessed of the whole Trelawney property. Willis, the historian of Portland, relates that "the wife of one of Robert Jordan's descendants, needing some paper to keep her pastry from burning, took Trelawney's patent from a chest of papers, and used it for that purpose."

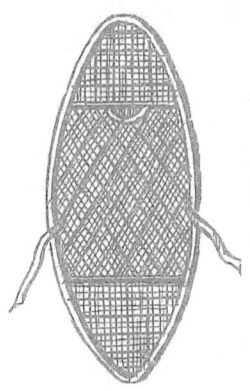

INDIAN SNOWSHOE.

Go where you will about Cape Elizabeth, you cannot help remarking the attention that is paid to the raising of cabbages; whichever way you turn you are sure to see cabbage-heads. Indeed, the cultivation of this highly nutritious vegetable is one of the earliest traditions; for I remember having read how a man's life was saved here, during the wars, by throwing himself flat on his face in his cabbage-patch. The crop of 1888 amounted to between five and six thousand tons. Just fancy it! six thousand tons of cabbage-heads raised among these rocks! One is obliged to admit that a field of the red sort looks very pretty about harvest time, — not so very unlike enormous Jacqueminot roses stuck in the ground.

It is a long mile from the point where the road turns off before you reach the Two Lights, to which we are guided by the black tips of the lanterns peering above the woods for the last half hour. These lights mark the extreme southerly limit of Casco Bay, and with Seguin at the eastern portal, they signal the entrance thirty miles out on the Atlantic. They are, in truth, the eyes of the coast, purblind by day and shining only at night, like a cat's.

It is breathing-time with the keeper; we have done our eight miles since breakfast-time, so we stretch ourselves along the soft turf for a little chat together.

FROM SCARBOROUGH TO PORTLAND HEAD.

Less than forty years ago, our lighthouse service was probably the worst among civilized nations. One man delivered all the supplies, made such repairs as he liked, and strange to say, was entrusted with about all the supervision that the whole range of coast lights received from Vermilion Bay to Quoddy Head. He had neither written nor printed instructions from anybody, nor were any provided even for the keepers, nor was there any system of instruction or examination whatever. In consequence, there was constant complaint, of the inferior quality of the oil, the polish, the frames, — everything in short, — until one day the venerable head of the lighthouse board suddenly awoke, rubbed his eyes, and fell into a paroxysm of rage on being told that the whole service was going to the devil.

Brother Jonathan, good, easy soul, submits to being victimized, until forbearance ceases to be a virtue; nor is he easily convinced of his errors, but when once fully aroused he generally sets things to rights with a steady hand. The lighthouse service is now excellent, with its duties so minutely defined that the keepers are every day expecting an order to report the number of flies that light on the tower from meridian to meridian.

A GROAT.

Fog-whistles and fog-trumpets have, as is well known, contributed greatly to the safety of coast navigation. It is not generally known, I think, that the telephone itself was originally a contrivance for sounding alarm signals, at sea or on shore, by means of certain modulated tones which could be produced by compressed air acting on the mechanism, something in the manner of the calliope, and controlled by stops on which the operator played such notes, either of simple direction or warning, as the case might require, — a musical alarm trumpet, in short.

The Two Lights of Cape Elizabeth stand up at the end of a long and narrow granite ridge raised fifty or sixty feet above the low ground around it. That gives an elevation of one hundred and fifty feet from low-water mark to the top of the lantern, or focal plane rather. They are cylindrical iron towers of exactly the same height, as bare of ornament as a bridge caisson or a Croton water-pipe. In fact, as far as looks go, they are as like as two peas in a pod. It was found necessary to place them well back from the water's edge, as the bluff on which they stand is broken off abruptly at a distance of fifty or sixty paces from the shore. They are what is called range lights, one being a first-order fixed, the other a flashing light, and very brilliant.

The outlook opened to us here, whether of sea or shore, of windy cape or tumbling surf, is uncommonly fine, if only one could get rid of the train of ideas that these roaring reefs on one hand, and the life-saving station on the other, with all its paraphernalia of life-boats and bombs, signals and beacons, so infallibly suggest. Even in the season of calm seas and serene skies these gray little cabins by the sea constantly remind us of lurking dangers, and of the heroic but ill-rewarded efforts of the men of that service to rescue their fellow-beings from a watery grave.

All about us the waters are sown with jagged reefs, and the shores closely surrounded by rugged humps of rock with narrow gullies between, into which the sea incessantly plunges in rushing coils and eddies. These dangerous rocks and reefs have an evil repute among sailors. See now how gently the sea breaks on yonder reef! The waves seem actually caressing it. Well, it was just there, on that very spot, that I once saw a ship lying a dismal wreck, with this same treacherous sea flying high over her decks.

Yonder white pillar gleaming in the east is Portland Light, three miles away; and in very clear weather Seguin can easily be made out, twenty miles away.

Lying as they do at the entrance to the most frequented harbor on the coast, the pointed reefs naturally pick up many vessels. Worst of all the shipwrecks that have happened here was that of the Allan steamship *Bohemian*, which struck on Trundy's reef and became a total loss, strewing the coast with the wreckage of ship and cargo as far as Cape Ann, where two boots came ashore each with a human foot in it.

SEAMARK.

But here is the story of a single day. September 26, 1889, ushered in a tremendous gale on the coast. It blew great guns from the northeast, and all the wide ocean for as far as eye could reach was one waste of broken water. The offing was eagerly scanned by the men of the life-patrol for any sign of a vessel in distress. At three in the afternoon, when the gale was at its height, Captain Trundy, of the life-saving station, sighted a wreck driving before it in the offing. Though there was but one chance in a hundred of a boat's living in that sea, he unhesitatingly determined to take that chance. The order was quickly given to man the life-boat. Although every man of the crew knew the desperate nature of the attempt, there was no flinching. A dozen nervous hands grasped the life-lines. Out into the surf went the buoyant life-boat, and then came the tussle at the oars to force a way out foot by foot through breakers. After getting clear of the toppling seas, which threatened to overset them, they began to thread their way through the white hedge of breakers, that only in such storms unmask the intricate network of outlying reefs and shoals. It took more than an hour to do this. Every shoal was a breaker, every breaker showed its rock of danger. Then came the long, hard pull through a tremendous sea, where a steady hand and eye at the steering oar was necessary to avoid being swamped, out to the distressed vessel. At length they came up with her, driving miserably on before the gale, a deserted wreck, rolling heavily from side to side, her mainmast broken short off, her sails and rigging dragging alongside. One moment she was wallowing deep in the trough of the sea, the next struggling up to the crest again, with the water pouring off her deluged decks in fifty streams. Finding no living thing on board, for the vessel had been left to be the sport of the gale, the life-savers abandoned the derelict to her fate, and after a stubborn fight with the curling monsters that broke all around them and repeatedly flung the boat-steerer into the bottom of the boat, steering-oar and all, they succeeded in once again running the gauntlet of the breakers to the beach.

On this same afternoon it was reported that two vessels had been sighted off the Cape, one of them bottom up. A large three-masted schooner was also made out with headgear gone, and sails split, running before the gale. Another was driven past the Lights at race-horse speed, under bare poles, into the flying scud, which swallowed her as suddenly as she had appeared. And finally two Cape fishermen, who knew every kernel of sand upon the coast, were dashed upon the rocks, escaping with their lives, but losing their boat.

The life-patrolmen's path hugs the shore. I took it from choice on account of the enticing succession of pretty coves niched in between outstretched points that I saw before me. In these coves the hardy beach-pea unfolds its white and purple blossoms within a few feet of the incessant dash of the waves. Talk about decorative art! Decorative nature has made these wan and haggard stones blossom fairly in spite of themselves. I now first remarked intruding masses of gray schist lying about among the granite.

PORTLAND LIGHT.

These look so much like huge lumps of dirty dough baked by exposure to sun and air, that one could almost fancy Holmes' giant had been flinging his pudding about again.

At Pond Cove the road again takes us up. Thence to Portland Head is but a short walk. The cliff on which the lighthouse is built is not high, but is exposed and ragged. It was certainly known by its present name as long ago as 1750, or long before the name attached to the port it defends. The lighthouse stands at the entrance to the ship channel. What we now see is the old, rough-rubble tower, topped out with brick and iron twenty feet higher. It was the first to display a light on this coast, it having been erected in the year 1790.

Ranging between east and northeast from the lighthouse are the outermost islands of Casco Bay, — the peerless bay of all the Pine-Tree Coast. Lonely Ram Island, with its tripod, is the nearest to us. At intervals the doleful ding-dong, ding-dong of a fog-bell comes to us across the water. Beyond Ram Island are the dangerous Outer Green, and Junk of Pork, — a tough morsel even for old salts. Still farther out between the capes, Half-Way Rock raises its monumental shaft of gray.

We are now entering the region of seashore cottages again, — the summer home and haunt of fashionable Portland.

Not far beyond the lighthouse we come to Cape Cottage, a favorite resort, built of dark gray stone taken from the ledges cropping out about here. John Neal, poet, journalist, lawyer, and critic, was also the author of this building. His keen appreciation for the unsurpassed beauty of the site, let us believe, was his controlling motive.

GAINING.

The Cape now begins to take on the character of a populous town. Indications of our near approach to the city meet us on every side, and admonish us, free and careless pedestrian that we are, to brush the dust from our garments, and to walk more sedately. With self-confessed reluctance, therefore, we shake off the dust of the road, and once more pass within the borders of civilization, for which we do not feel at all fitted after a week's unstinted companionship with nature. "God made the country, and man made the town."

But the sea is still there, behind us, and were we to meet the doom of Lot's wife herself, we could not help looking back.

The shore now skirts the ship channel, formed by the cluster of large and small islands that here crowd in toward the Cape, so making a family group of marked interest in a picturesque sense, of peculiar importance to the seaport they have helped to create. They are, in fact, the sea-wall of Portland and its harbor. As such they play far too important a part in maintaining the integrity of the port to be lightly passed over.

First to indentify them: The outermost one, with the large hotel crowning it, is Cushing's. That inviting-looking spot, in which so many have found an abiding charm, was the gloomy refuge of some of the survivors of the terrible massacre of 1676, when human bloodhounds were on their track. It has now no other enemy than the changeful sea. It is best known, however, to a later generation, by the superb castellated mass of crag piled on crag, set at its northern point, that from its peculiar ashen hue is known as White Head. This colossal bulwark of the isle, be it said, is without doubt the most individual ocean cliff to be met with on the coast of Maine, if not the highest; and as warden to the port over which it has watched so long, it has obtained a wide

WHITE HEAD, PORTLAND'S SENTINEL CLIFF.

celebrity, not only with those who sail the ocean, but with artists and poets, who are of all people the most susceptible to the sublime, and the quickest to show their appreciation of it. The extreme seaward projection of this cliff is so formed or broken as to present the gigantic profile of a human face to perfection. In some places the sea has hewed and hacked its way into the very bowels of the cliff, where it roars and plunges like a mad bull.

> "Beyond it the laden ships go out,
> Out in the open sea,
> To battle with danger, and storm and, doubt,
> And the ocean's treachery."

Next north is Peak's Island, which is both winter suburb and summer playground for Portland, it having a quite considerable resident population. This is where the city people run down of an afternoon, to get a mouthful of sea air and to be amused. House Island will be known by the gray walls and green ramparts of Fort Scammell. The first habitation of a white man in this region is supposed to have stood here. The north half of this island, where we see the flakes spread out, has been occupied as a fishing-station ever since Portland was a fishing-village of half a hundred houses. Great and Little Hog islands, now turned by an exacting æstheticism into Great and Little Diamond, lie next inside of Peak's, and a little to the south of it. Picturesque and useless Fort Gorges reposes on an isolated ledge. These, with Cow Island, a bare, treeless thing, complete the group of sheltering islands.

Simonton's Cove, next south of Fort Preble,[10] is the supposed scene of Major Church's fight with the Indians in 1690, if fight it can be called where one side suffers all the loss. From Church's own account of this affair, which is in his usual blustering vein, it is clear that he was not only taken by surprise, but badly beaten in the bargain.

The village existing on this side of the Cape long went by its Indian name of Purpooduck, and there were settlers living on the point where Fort Preble stands as early as the year 1658. In circumnavigating the Cape, so to speak, we have thus traversed its most ancient settlements.

At this point I was overtaken by a thunder-storm, which obliged me to take refuge under a shed, where two persons had already preceded me. The rain poured down in torrents. "Well," said one to the other, "Felt's dead; died this morning."

"I want to know if Felt's dead."

"Yes; they found him hanging to a beam in the barn; shed was piled full of wood he'd been choppin' all the week; seems as though he must have thought of something."

"Well, Felt was always forehanded, that's a fact."

¹ Black Point has been called Cammock's Neck, Prout's Neck, and Libby's Neck from successive proprietors. Prout's Neck is its present designation. The name Black Point is found in the patent of 1631. Hubbard speaks of it as if it had originated in some quarrel. It included all Scarborough until the incorporation of the township by this name in 1658, with the exception of Blue or Pine Point, opposite. The dark evergreen growth, almost universally called black growth by the first settlers, was sufficiently descriptive for fishermen and sailors. Joshua Scottow of Boston became proprietor of the Cammock patent, in 1666, by purchase of Josselyn, Cammock's heir. (Read also note 4.) The first Libby settled here.

² Scarborough clams are sent in large quantities to the Portland market to be sold fresh for family use, or salted for bait. The industry is the chief support of a large number of people; on Pine Point there is a canning factory. Besides this export demand, the clam is an important article of food to the shore people in winter. In summer they will not eat it.

³ Richard Hunnewell was a noted Indian fighter, who is said to have once beheaded an Indian with his scythe in single combat. An account of the affair in which he fell may be found in "Williamson's Maine," II. 44. The Indians next turned upon the garrison, which was only abandoned after a brave defence. It was then set on fire and burnt. Elizabeth Hammond, Hunnewell's daughter, received a grant of one hundred acres of land from Massachusetts in consideration of her father's services to the country.

⁴ Henry Josselyn, son of Sir Thomas, of Kent, Knight. A strenuous supporter of Gorges, who could not yield to the logic of events. He lost his Black Point property (see note 1) before Philip's War compelled him to abandon his residence there. Later on he is found at Pemaquid.

⁵ "The wasps breed in hives made like a great pineapple, their entrance is at the lower end; the whole hive is of an ash color, but of what matter it's made no man knows. Wax it is not, neither will it melt nor fry, but will take fire suddenly like tinder." — *New England's Rarities*.

⁶ Cape Elizabeth is mentioned by Levett in 1623, and included in the Lygonia patent of 1629–30. Robert Trelawney received a patent of it in 1631, which also included Richmond's Island. Originally, it formed part of Falmouth. It is put down on Smith's map of 1641, but assigned to a very different locality than the true one.

⁷ Richmond's Island lies half a mile off the mainland. The water between was always fordable at low tide over a strip of shingle joining it with the mainland. Under the lee of this spit was the very indifferent harbor. Government has since improved it by building a sea-wall, which gives a refuge from northeasters. Watts' Ledge lies off to the northeast of the island, and Old Anthony and the Hue and Cry rocks are bad ledges lying still farther out in this direction. The island is about three miles in circuit, is good land, and since its first settlement has nearly always been inhabited. It is now owned by R. J. Chisholm, of Portland. "The Trelawney Papers," with Mr. Baxter's memoir of George Cleeves, best elucidate the early history of this island and its surroundings. "Robert Jordan lived here some time." — HUBBARD'S *Wars*, II. 74. The island was the scene of a bloody encounter in 1676. — *Ibid.* II. 173. An earthen crock, containing money and an antique signet ring, was dug up in 1855, the incident furnishing a theme for Mr. Ilsley's historical novel. There was a wreck here, attended with loss of life, in the winter of 1886.

THE CROCK.

⁸ George Cleeves, the founder of Portland, with Tucker, first built on the mainland, next Richmond's Island, about 1630. They had cleared, planted, and enclosed within palings four feet high an acre and a quarter of ground, when driven off. The palings were to keep out wild animals. After being ousted here, they went to Casco Bay. Cleeves induced Sir Alexander Rigby to buy up the Lygonia or Plough patent, so-called, which covered forty miles square between the Kennebec and Cape Porpoise, but which had fallen into desuetude in conse-

quence of the breaking up of the company to which it was issued. Rigby made Cleeves his deputy on the spot. The Lygonia patent conferred powers of government which, of course, brought about a conflict between Cleeves and those holding under Gorges. The time of Cleeves' death is not ascertained. There is a monument to him at Portland.

⁹ Robert Jordan, the progenitor of all the Jordans in Maine, an Episcopal clergyman and Royalist, showed determined hostility to the claims of Massachusetts, on the one hand, which caused his arrest and imprisonment in 1663 ; and to those of Cleeves, on the other, though he became an assistant under the Lygonia government afterward. There is a MS. of his extant dated " From ye prison at Boston, ye 4th (7ber) 1663." Aside from personal feelings, his large property, recovered on an execution against Trelawney's heirs, was put in jeopardy when Massachusetts asserted rights to the soil and government of Maine. Jordan's house at Spurwink was burned in Philip's War, the incendiaries killing, at the same time, Ambrose Boaden, who kept the ferry there, and who lived on Scarborough side. — WILLIAMSON, I. 524.

¹⁰ Fort Preble (named for Commodore Edward Preble), with Fort Scammell (named for Colonel Alexander Scammell of the Revolutionary army), constitute with Fort Gorges, in the inner harbor, the defences of the ship channel of Portland, which the battery at Portland Head is designed to augment, and it is to be hoped render more efficient, as the heavy guns of our new cruisers now throw shot with effect nearly eight miles. The channel forts, Preble and Scammell, were built in 1807-8, and called, in derision, "embargo forts," as they were said to be designed to keep our shipping in, rather than the enemy out.

BLOCK HOUSE.

THE MID COAST.

CHAPTER XI.

A DAY IN PORTLAND.

"Often I think of the beautiful town
That is seated by the sea." — LONGFELLOW.

IF any one of the seaboard towns through which we have lately passed would require a volume to do it justice, Portland would be worth two, at least.

This is a city set on a hill. Nature has thus furnished the pedestal on which the tall steeples rise with monumental effect. As it is but four miles from the open ocean up to the wharves, one has no sooner entered the ship channel than he sees the city spires springing up in the distance.

Thrown off the southern corner of Casco Bay, the high ridge on which Portland[1] is built just escaped becoming one of that magnificent archipelago over which the city presides like a goddess of the sea, with her obsequious vassals clustered about her feet.

As we look up at it from the harbor, this long peninsula, or ridge, takes the form of a saddle, with the business portion in the seat, and the residences mostly grouped about the high bluffs rising at the opposite extremities. Wharves, warehouses, and shipping monopolize, of course, the extensive water-front; but the real heart of the city seems to beat high up on the ridge, among its steeples, while its working hands are plunged deep down into the waters of the bay. There is something about it, too, that recalls Quebec, in streets climbing up the face of steep declivities, and flights of stairs connecting what seems to us like an upper and lower town.

Of the two high bluffs just mentioned, Munjoy Hill, at the right, exhibits a wooden signal tower, reminiscent of the big ships that once sailed to every port and clime, while Bramhall's, at the left, is fringed about with a grove of evergreens, reminiscent of the vanished forest.

The greatest seaport in the world could not have a more splendid or more imposing approach. And the history of this quarter of New England could hardly be written, that did not make large mention of that steeple-crowned ridge.

But let us take a look at the city itself, as it appears in its every-day working dress. One sees at a glance that nature has more than done her part toward raising Portland to the front rank of maritime ports. We expect to read the story of two hundred and fifty years on the fronts of the buildings, the faces of the people we meet, or if not there, perhaps on the tablets in the ancient cemeteries.

Portland is certainly the prettiest little city out of doors. Every man, woman, and child has an inalienable freehold in pure air, generous sunshine, and the most exquisite of sea-scapes. Our great poet, Longfellow, has touched this and that spot with a loving hand and endearing charm. It is he who has told us that the poets are the best travelling companions. Let us then take him at his word, in this his own native city. We have no sooner reached the brow of Bramhall's Hill than deep down beneath we see the shadowy crown

"Of the dark and haunted wood,"

where the boy Longfellow roamed and mused.

Indeed, at almost every turn, the stranger is reminded that Longfellow was born here. In the most aristocratic quarter a statue has been raised to his memory. The artist, Mr. Franklin Simmons, who is also "native here and to the manner born," has represented the poet seated in his chair, with head slightly drooped forward on his breast. The work gives us Longfellow all complete; the meditative pose of the head, his thoughtful brow, his pensive look, and even his half-sad smile of later years — the years of his "Lost Youth," perchance — are all there. It is the very man.

LONGFELLOW STATUE.

I happened to be standing by, among the crowd, on the day when this statue was publicly unveiled. As the white covering was being removed, disclosing the noble and dignified features to view, a well-dressed woman at my elbow remarked to her neighbor, "Why, he must have been a dark-complected man!" The statue itself, it is perhaps needless to add, is of a dark bronze.

Before taking many steps in Portland it is necessary, first of all, to point out one or two things, even to the casual visitor. In the first place, he finds a new city when he had expected, if not hoped, to find an old one. Then, again, there is a marked discrepancy in the looks of the west end of the town, as

DISTANT VIEW OF PORTLAND.

compared with all the rest. In one part, the mellowness that comes with age and use takes us back through many generations of builders, and has much individual character about it; in the other, the unmistakable stamp of newness is everywhere. There should be, he thinks, among the buildings of so old a place many interesting memorials of the past.

On the 4th of July, 1866, the most destructive conflagration our country had ever known — that which desolated New York in 1835 alone excepted — laid fifteen hundred buildings in ashes, and turned half the population into the streets. A boy's squib, carelessly tossed among some shavings, had undone the work of fifty years in a few hours. The day of rejoicing was thus turned into one of mourning, while men looked on to see the gradual accumulations of a lifetime vanishing before their eyes in smoke and flame. Everything in Portland naturally dates from this fire, the limits of which may be easily traced, like the crack in old china, wherever the new city joins the old.

Previous to this event Portland was more noted for fine trees than for fine buildings; but when it rose from its ashes, it was really more of a city and less like a large country town. It was no more like what it had been than a second growth is like the first, after fire has gone through the forest. For one thing, the streets were much better built, and thus a new era in architecture was begun; but where were the beautiful shade-trees which had once imparted to them a beauty and charm not to be made good with brick, iron, or stone? All gone in the tornado of flame that mowed its way through the doomed city unchecked. Some had been growing so long as to be reckoned among the most ancient landmarks. In their loss, Portland's most distinctive feature was quite effectually blotted out, and the cherished name of Forest City — so long the pride and boast of every citizen, and which every one found so appropriate — had lost its significance.

A most excellent reason therefore exists why the city seal should show a phœnix rising from its ashes, and should bear the very suggestive motto of "*Resurgam.*"

I spent part of an afternoon in loitering about Bramhall's Hill,[2] which finely overlooks the land-approaches to Portland, even as far as the White Mountains. Those noble peaks are grandly presented here across sixty miles of low country. Much of the ground is already occupied by costly residences, so distinguishing it from Munjoy's Hill, at the other end of the city, where the houses are of a more modest construction.

While he was about it, Bishop Berkely might just as well have laid down the incontestable axiom, that westward the course of fashion takes its way. For a long time, Bramhall's Hill seemed definitely consigned to the limbo of waste-places, or at least to no better use than for a graveyard, pitched at the very edge of the bluff, and destitute of every species of adornment. The improvements we now see on every hand are due to the energy and foresight of the late John B. Brown, whose charming villa and grounds form a sort of centre-piece to the circle of fine houses grouped about it.

I have often remarked the peculiarity, not confined, however, to New England towns by any means, that when you are seen to be a stranger, you are at once shown the residence of the man who cannot spend the interest of his money. On the other hand, every visitor to Portland, who has an hour to spare, first asks his way to the house where Longfellow was born.

A more attractive avenue than State Street would be hard to find in all New England. Other cities, it is true, have had such streets, but they are now only a memory and a regret. And the least we can say of it is, that if we were going to live in Portland, we should want to live in State Street. Double ranks of magnificent old elms stretch out their canopy of leafage across the broad highway, which is shaded with a cool, soft light. Every house has its shade-trees and its garden-plot ; every citizen, his own vine and fig-tree, so to speak. Strips of well-kept turf border the sidewalks, gratefully relieving the dull glare of red brick and glitter of window-glass, that is so trying to the eye. As for the large, square houses themselves, — with their black-painted front doors, big, brass knockers, and fan-shaped top-lights, — though mostly guiltless of all architectural adornment, they stand well apart, thus leaving elbow-room for the cultivation of those old-fashioned gardens beside them, where we may see fruits ripening upon the trees, and flowers blooming along the gravelled walks. We can well imagine the pride which filled every good citizen's breast when these houses were going up; for in every stick and stone they speak of substance, thrift, and comfortable living.

Then, again, there is certainly an atmosphere of old-fashioned ease and solid comfort, to which this hurrying age of ours is a stranger ; of decorous retirement belonging to an older generation than ours, and to its manners, which we do not find at all disagreeable.

State Street plainly belongs to the period when fortunes were made from ships that ploughed the main, instead of from the smoky manufactories or railways in which Portland's money is so largely invested to-day. John Neal lived here in this street, and so did Senator Fessenden, —

> "Than whom a better senator ne'er held
> The helm. . . .
> Whether to settle peace or to unfold
> The drift of hollow states, hard to be spelled."

In the short intervals of respite from political or professional activity, Mr. Fessenden's favorite amusement was gardening, which Lord Bacon, in one of his Essays, calls the purest of human pleasures. Fessenden's garden forms the theme for some verses from the pen of Elizabeth Akers Allen.

Congress Street is, however, Portland's principal thoroughfare.[3] It is laid out along the crest of the ridge throughout its whole length. At either end are the homes of the citizens, while the central portion is devoted to business exclusively. As a large part of what belongs to the daily life of Portland

THE OAKS, PORTLAND.

is transacted on this street, a walk through it is no bad epitome of that life, even if we can only give a passing glance at what we may see. Fine buildings constantly attract our attention on one or the other side, but nothing so much as those occasional glimpses of the beautiful blue sea, framed in between the diminishing walls of brick or stone that open to the right or left as we pass by. Among the more recent structures is that little architectural gem, the new public library,[4] the gift of Mr. J. P. Baxter to the city.

On arriving near the depression which we have called the saddle, Congress Street throws off three branches, which now penetrate the oldest portion of the city, as the Mississippi does its delta. The point of junction, or divergence, is called Market Square,[5] notwithstanding its triangular shape, and is perhaps the busiest single spot of ground the city can show, surrounded as it is by shops and hotels, gathering in as it does all the travel flowing from so many different directions to a common centre.

Yet we can only stop long enough to fix in our memory one or two buildings which the great fire so capriciously spared, and in which men having a national reputation have lived.

The hotel now known as the Preble House, overlooking this square, had its origin in the mansion that Commodore Edward Preble,[6] of Revolutionary fame, built for himself as a retreat for his declining days, though the original house has well-nigh disappeared from view in successive additions. Before these changes took place, John Neal says it stood alone, fronting Preble Street, with a large yard on Congress Street, and a garden full of trees running far down behind it.

THE ONE-HOSS SHAY.

The original front was scarcely a third part of what we now see, it having been extended on both sides as well as in the rear. The house was never occupied by the bluff old commodore, though built for him. He died in 1807, at just about the time that his new house was ready to receive him as its master.

Next above the Preble House, a little back from the street, stands an old, three-story brick, of very modest, not to say homely, exterior. This, we are told, is the first brick house ever built in Portland, and its appearance certainly bears out the assertion. Some fine old elms, growing at the sidewalk, cast long shadows over the paved courtyard within, and the mansion itself is further darkened by the walls of the adjoining buildings, which shoot up high above it on either side, thus leaving only a space of blue sky at the very top. In truth, the old homestead seems to have drawn back from the noise and bustle of the street, within the shadow of its aspiring neighbors, as if conscious that it did not belong to this new and crowding generation.

General Peleg Wadsworth,[7] a soldier of the Revolution, whose escape from Castine was as exciting an adventure as anything to be found in romance, began this house in 1785. It had but two stories when completed, but Stephen

PUBLIC LIBRARY, PORTLAND.

Longfellow, father of the poet, who married Zilpah, the general's daughter, enlarged it by the addition of another story, when the general moved out and he moved in, bringing with him the boy Henry Wadsworth, who had thus good Revolutionary blood in his veins, and was proud of it, too.

Mr. Longfellow once described to me his experience of travel between Portland and Boston, going back to the time when the old-fashioned stage-coach was the only means of conveyance between the two cities by land. By starting at three o'clock in the morning, one might reach Boston late at night on the same day. But this was too fast for ordinary travellers, who preferred taking the "accommodation," which made the trip in two days. In winter it was no holiday journey, the less so as the sides of the alleged stage were only curtains of common bocking, buttoned down to keep the weather out. The poet said, with a shiver that the recollection called up, that he "usually patronized the

LONGFELLOW AND HIS HOME.

accommodation, because it gave him a night's rest at Freeman's tavern, at Cape Neddock."

Another gifted poet, in another land, has left on record his views with respect to this now antiquated mode of travel, from which it will be seen how railways have reduced travellers to compulsory taciturnity. Southey remarks in one of his letters that "it is only in a stage-coach that I am on an equal footing with my companions, and it is there that I talk the most and have them in the best humor with me."

While in the vicinity it would be our own loss not to drop into the studio of Mr. Harry Brown, who, as the enthusiastic lover of the scenery of this his native city, and its truest interpreter withal, has done so much to make it known to the great world of art. A visit to his studio is almost as good as a summer vacation.

A most interesting hour may be spent among the monuments in the Eastern Cemetery, the oldest in the town. The earliest stones must be sought for among the rank grass of the southeast corner. We almost expect to see Old Mortality start up from among the head-stones here. And one can almost trace successive stages of the town's growth in the changing character of these memorials, as of emancipation from the thraldom of old ideas, associating death with all that was repulsive or hideous in the mortuary symbols.

WADSWORTH.

Commodore Edward Preble is buried in this yard; gallant Harry Wadsworth, too, who was blown up at Tripoli, has his memorial; so also has Parson Smith,[8] whose "Journal" is the source of so much of what is known about the early life of Portland. But there is indubitable evidence showing that toward none of these do the feet of most visitors turn. The ground about the graves of the three naval heroes, Burrows, Blythe, and Waters, is well trodden down. We risk nothing in saying that Longfellow's admirable commemorative lines have brought thousands to the spot who would otherwise never have known of the gallantry of these men. It is but a short way down the hillside to the old, square, wooden house in which the poet was born, — indeed, the house can be quite plainly seen from the cemetery, — so we can very well believe that the terrible sea-fight which set the whole town wild with excitement, and the solemn interment of its victims which followed, left an indelible impression on the sensitive lad's memory, which he has conveyed to us in that simple and touching language of which he was the master. Bur-

TYNG.

rows was only twenty-eight, Blythe twenty-nine, Waters eighteen. That tells where the young men were in that war.

It was pleasant to note how all had been decorated alike with flags and evergreens. Poor Blythe could not have been more honored among his own kindred.

"Mad Jack" Percival, of the old navy, used to say that the *Boxer* and *Enterprise* fought the only equal battle which we won during that war. At any rate, the victory was dearly bought. Yet the inscription to Burrows is a surprising commentary to the patriotism of the time. It reads that his monument was erected by "a passing stranger."

Rear Admiral James Alden has a fine monument in this ground. He was a man after Farragut's own heart, a sailor cast in the same heroic mould as those valiant old sea-dogs, Hull, Decatur, Stewart, who believed that victories were only to be won by fighting, and to whom the smell of powder was like incense to the devotee.

It is not much farther to Munjoy Hill, on which the observatory stands that we took note of from the harbor. Similarly to Bramhall, this name comes from a settler of the early day, who, it is said, built on or near this hill as early as 1661. The city of tents pitched on the greensward here, for the accommodation of those whom the great fire had rendered homeless, was a most picturesque and suggestive sight. At the same time the old City Hall, since demolished to make room for the soldiers' monument, was turned into a depot for feeding these poor people, and I remember seeing them passing to and fro between camp and commissariat, a few days subsequent to the fire,

OLD COURT-HOUSE, PORTLAND.

each carrying the portion of food dealt out to him for the subsistence of himself or family. It was a scene from the war over again.

Local chronicles tell of various occurrences, more or less interesting, associated with this commanding spot of ground, which, in some sort, dominates the history of Portland as it does crowding city, gay harbor, and island-studded bay. There is one among the rest that is deserving of more than a passing word.

During the exciting period that followed close upon the Battle of Lexington, His Majesty's ship *Canceaux*, Captain Henry Mowatt, commander, was stationed in this port to keep an eye on the patriots, while without his knowing it, it seems they were keeping two on him.

It seems, also, that a certain Colonel Samuel Thompson, of Georgetown, understood that with the shedding of blood war had actually begun. This very matter-of-fact person appears, moreover, to have somehow got the notion in his head that the merchants of Falmouth, as Portland was then called, among whom were some avowed Tories, were in no haste to commit themselves to the patriot side in its hour of peril, further than by way of empty professions. At any rate, Colonel Thompson was himself a man of settled convictions. So getting together some sixty of his neighbors, who thought with him that the presence of the *Canceaux* was an insult, and that a good blow struck here would strengthen the hands of their friends everywhere, Thompson landed with his men one night on this very hill, determined either to take the ship or drive her out of the harbor. And here they lay hid till the next day at noon.

At this hour Captain Mowatt, with his surgeon, was taking an airing upon this hill, wishing that he might lay hands upon some rebel to make an example of, when Thompson's men suddenly surrounded them and made them prisoners. As soon as the officer left in charge of the *Canceaux* heard of it, he put springs on his cable, piped to quarters, and swore a terrible oath that he would knock the whole infernal rebel crew into a cocked hat unless the prisoners were set at liberty by a given hour.

It may well be supposed that this threat threw the town into a ferment. But when the *Canceaux* fired two blank cartridges by way of emphasizing it, the terrified inhabitants either hid themselves in their cellars, or ran away out of the town to escape the coming bombardment. Now came some of the principal inhabitants, the men of substance who are always for peace at any price, entreating Thompson to spare them so dreadful a calamity by letting Mowatt go. The bold Thompson at first treated their prayers with scorn, but he finally gave his consent to Mowatt's returning on board his ship upon pledging his word of honor to give himself up the next day. Mowatt gave the required pledge, and went off unmolested to his ship; but when the time came to redeem his plighted word, he coolly forfeited it under the clumsy pretext that no promises were to be kept with rebels and traitors.

Though cheated of his prey, Thompson proceeded to indemnify himself by levying contributions upon some of the more obnoxious Tories of the town. His conduct was highly resented on all sides, and an appeal taken to the colonial Congress, by whom Thompson's acts were fully approved as being "friendly to his country and the cause of liberty."

This too brief relation is only the preamble to what afterwards occurred. It seems that Mowatt's self-love had received a mortal thrust, which could be healed in only one way. A captain in His Majesty's service had been insulted and no blood shed. He obtained permission from the admiral on the station to take summary revenge. So in October the slippery Mowatt again anchored off the town with three ships besides his own. He generously gave the inhabitants two hours in which to leave it, though he was induced to extend the time to nine o'clock in the morning of the 18th, when all the ships opened fire with shot and shell, and from that hour till darkness shut in, the bombardment

VIEWS IN AND AROUND PORTLAND.

went on without intermission. At the same time the town was set on fire by his orders, so that the flames might finish what the bombardment had spared. By this atrocious act, against an undefended place, about four hundred buildings were destroyed; and Captain Mowatt's wounded honor, which he had forfeited to his homespun captors without a twinge, was thereby most honorably appeased.

One more episode of the times when neighbor's hand was raised against neighbor will perhaps serve to round out the story of this eventful period. William Tyng,[9] high sheriff of the county, was a rank Tory. One day, while political animosities were running high, he and General Preble met in King Street. Hot words passed between them. The choleric Tyng called the general an old fool. "Repeat those words," cried the incensed brigadier, "and I will knock you down!" Tyng thereupon whipped out his rapier, and threatened to run the general through; but before he could make a pass the indignant veteran threw himself upon Tyng, seized him by the collar, and shook him until the bystanders parted them. The affair terminated without sword thrusts, however, upon Tyng's asking the irate old general's pardon.

When the royal troops entered New York, Tyng went with them. Upon hearing that a son of his late antagonist was then a prisoner, confined on board the Jersey Prison Ship, of fatal memory, Tyng at once sought him out. The young man was found to be suffering from a dangerous illness, which, in that "floating hell," meant nothing less than another victim or another murder. The refugee Royalist, like the noble man he was, procured the captive's release, took him to his own house, nursed him through his sickness, and finally restored him to his family and friends, who already mourned him as dead. That young officer subsequently became the famous Commodore Preble.

After passing a little beyond the observatory, which looks quite like an ancient windmill without arms, and which every stranger in Portland ascends, the bay and bay shore quickly appear before us. Here, on the high bluff rising at the shore, stands a neat granite shaft erected to the memory of George Cleeves, the founder of Portland. The four sides of the base contain the four names by which the peninsula has been known; the shaft itself is inscribed with the leading events in the life of Cleeves. Out at the left are seen Mackworth's, or Mackay's, Island and Point,[10] the home of a settler contemporary with Cleeves, and somewhat nearer the United States Marine Hospital building at Martin's Point.

Still hugging the shore, the eye now roves along Falmouth Foreside, a favorite drive out of Portland, as the road commands a view of the bay for miles around. It is historic ground, too. Here was the site of New Casco Fort,[11] built after the destruction of Fort Loyal in 1690, to which we shall presently refer. Just off this shore lies Clapboard Island, the boundary once set up by Massachusetts as her rightful charter limit.

Munjoy Hill is to Portland what the citadel is to Quebec, — the best of all positions for overlooking its incomparable bay.

Stretching out before us in the sun is the long reach of open water, beginning down at our feet and extending up between Mackworth's and Hog Island; farther and farther on, between Great Chebeague and Cousins' Island; still farther to the neighborhood of Harpswell, where the dry land grows dim and

A DAY IN PORTLAND.   169

watery, as if a wet brush had been drawn along the horizon, and the eye then fails us. That land presenting an unbroken front at our right, which we at first take to be the main, is nothing but a chain of overlapping islands, dividing the waters of the bay nearly in two; nor do we perceive our error until from some higher point the whole matchless archipelago arranges itself, like some leviathan fleet, in a series of systematic groupings, that seem to have some time belonged to the land, although now claimed by the sea. We can hardly conceive of forces adequate to this result.

From Munjoy we look down into Fort Gorges, and out to sea through White Head passage, seeing that renowned headland quite plainly. We have now had an opportunity of getting pretty well acquainted with the western approaches to Casco Bay.

The people of Portland are certainly favored above most dwellers in cities, in having a perpetual feast of scenic beauty so lavishly spread out at their very doors, — a feast embracing the choicest examples of sea, shore, and mountain, effectively combined and contrasted, and where, indeed, nature seems always keeping open house. It should be, we think, a better education for the masses than either art galleries, statuary, or schools, since many a man has felt his first emotion for nature — his love at first sight — while standing on some such spot as Munjoy.

Why, only to see Mount Washington, as I have seen it from this spot on a clear winter's day, his robe of snow faintly touched by soft, rose-tinted shadows, that came and went like the blush on a maiden's cheek, with a sky as blue as turquoise behind him, and the bright sun shining full on his gleaming breast, would be worth a day's journey to any man!

We are still loitering in that part of ancient Falmouth to which the pioneers, undaunted by repeated massacres, clung so stubbornly. Old traditions cluster thick around it. Underneath this height, near the corner of Fore and Hancock streets, George Cleeves built his solitary cabin, — the first known to have been erected on the peninsula by a white man. Hard by, at the foot of India Street, on the premises now occupied by the Grand Trunk Railway, Fort Loyal was raised as a rallying point for the settlers who had been driven away at the sacking of Falmouth in 1676, and who were yet again scattered by death or captivity, when Portneuf, Castine, Hertel, and their confederate butchers overcame the fort in May, 1690, after it had held out bravely for four terrible days.

This force of *coureurs de bois* and savages had been led to the attack all the way from Quebec. It was, at least, a strange chance that conducted the railway from the same starting point to the same spot in the interests of peace.

La Hontan extols the bravery of the defenders. He also praises the determination of the savages who, contrary to their usual custom, fearlessly scaled the palisades. Without them, he says, the enterprise must certainly have fallen through. Fort and village were given up to the flames. The survivors, including Captain Davis, were marched off to Canada.

Thus four times in her history has Portland fallen a prey to the flames.

At the corner of Fore and Hancock streets stands the house in which Longfellow first drew breath. In the poet's boyhood, only the breadth of the road separated the house from the beach. The bay view is now shut out by intervening buildings. This house is a plain, box-like structure, on the shady side of eighty, I should say, quite like so many yet standing about in odd corners, yet remarkably suggestive of the fact that no dwelling is too humble for a great man to be born in it. Indeed, an instructive parallel might be drawn between the rather homely edifice and its surroundings, and the bronze statue lately raised to the poet in the most fashionable part of the town. Longfellow's early home belongs to the period when Portland was so immersed in commercial pursuits, that every citizen wanted his house to stand at the very edge of the shore. It was evidently the case with Stephen Longfellow. And it is, perhaps, to the impressions derived from such intimate companionship with the sea, that we owe those charming verses about it from the pen of his more famous son. I know not why it should be so, but somehow one turns away from this house, which he has so much wished to see, with a feeling of keen disappointment.

LONGFELLOW'S BIRTHPLACE.

No boy who has been brought up in a seaport can fail to appreciate this touch from memory: —

> " I remember the black wharves and the slips,
> And the sea-tides tossing free,
> And the Spanish sailors with bearded lips,
> And the beauty and mystery of the ships,
> And the magic of the sea."

I am not yet old enough to have got over my predilection for mousing about the wharves of a strange seaport, and seldom fail to pay them a visit. Those of Portland no longer groan under the weight of fat puncheons of Santa Cruz, or Old Jamaica, as in days of yore; for a man named Neal Dow, whose mansion stands in the high places of the city, has done for Maine what Saint Patrick, of blessed memory, did for Old Ireland in banishing snakes from all her borders.

Speaking of wharves and ships reminds one of the very daring act done in this harbor, almost under the guns of the forts, during the dark days of the great Civil War. It was enough to have made those old warriors, who sleep on yonder hillside, turn over in their graves. One night, in the year 1863, — the battle year, — a schooner stole into the harbor, unsuspected and unchallenged. It was a Confederate privateer manned by a crew of dare-devils. Her commander laid her alongside the revenue cutter, *Caleb Cushing*, without awakening so much as a suspicion of his real designs. So the cutter was taken without firing a shot. In the morning the cutter was missed from her anchorage, and the cause guessed. A volunteer force was hurriedly embarked on board two merchant steamers, which steamed off in hot chase of the piratical intruder. She was found becalmed under the Green Islands in the bay. Seeing no other chance of escape, the Confederate captain set fire to the cutter, and took to his boats. They were soon overtaken. The cutter, wrapped in flames, presently blew up with a tremendous explosion, and the danger was over, but the fright remained for many a day, since no one had dreamed of such a thing as possible here in New England, though Wadsworth had once done something quite like it at Tripoli.

This was but a prelude to a series of depredations in our Northern waters during which the Confederate cruiser, *Tallahassee*, destroyed no less than twenty-five vessels in one day on the coast of Maine. Her commander sardonically remarked to the master of one of them, that it was his purpose "to slacken up the coasting trade, so that Uncle Abe would be glad to make peace."

---

[1] Portland: refer to the previous chapter for indications that this name first attached itself to the Cape Elizabeth side — Indian name Machigonne. Casco, also Indian, a corruption of Aucocisco, was the adopted English name, not only for the settlement here, but for the later one in what is now Falmouth. It was also applied to the whole contiguous region, more or less. The settlements here and at Cape Elizabeth were incorporated as Falmouth in 1658. In 1786 that part known as Falmouth Neck was separated from the rest, and re-incorporated with the name of Portland. Old Falmouth included eighty square miles of territory — extending from the Spurwink to North Falmouth, and eight miles back into the country. Christopher Levett built the first house, not on the mainland, but on one of the islands, supposed to be House Island. This Levett located his grant of six thousand acres "in this bay near Cape Elizabeth, and built a good house and fortified well on an island lying before Casco River" — S. MAVERICK. Willis' History of Portland is still the best. Parson Thomas Smith's Journal is a quaint and readable account of society, life, and manners in the last century. John Neal's off-hand sketches, "Portland Illustrated," is valuable for its portraits. William Goold has written some readable reminiscences. Elwell's "Portland and Vicinity" is a scholarly and appreciative guide about Portland.

[2] Bramhall's Hill, so called from George Bramhall, a settler of 1680, who was killed in the fight between Major Church and the Indians, 1689, by which Casco was saved for the time.

[3] Congress Street, formerly called Back. The three main arteries, following the general course of the ridge, took the very simple names of Fore, Middle, and Back streets.

[4] The Library building was completed in 1888. Its reading-room contains Paul Akers' "Pearl Diver." This building is also the home of the Maine Historical Society, where an hour may be profitably spent among the gathered relics of bygone times.

[5] Market Square has just witnessed the demolition of the old city building, which stood where the Soldiers' Monument is now (1890) being erected. This building was the combined town-hall and market-house, whence comes the name of the space around it; and at one time it contained the only hall for public meetings in Portland. Many citizens strongly objected to its removal on account of its interesting associations.

[6] Commodore Preble lived and died in a house on Middle Street, belonging to the brigadier, his father, and now replaced by the Casco Bank building. The Prebles came to Portland from York. It is a distinguished family, whose history is closely allied with that of Maine.

[7] General Peleg Wadsworth removed to Hiram. His escape is related in "Nooks and Corners of the New England Coast."

[8] Rev. Thomas Smith, originally of Boston, came to Falmouth as chaplain to the troops posted there in 1725, being ordained minister of the First Church in 1727, continuing in that office until the close of the year 1784. His Journal, with that of his colleague, Samuel Deane, was edited and published by William Willis in 1849.

[9] William Tyng's father commanded the colonial fleet sent against Louisburg in 1745. His grandfather died a prisoner in the Château Angoulême, in France, whither he had been sent, with John Nelson, upon the representations of Frontenac, by whom he had been taken. William Tyng was born in Boston in 1737. When, in 1767, he received the appointment of sheriff, he went to Falmouth, or Portland. Some time after the peace he returned to Maine. St. Paul's Episcopal Church, Portland, was erected under his patronage. He died in 1807, and is buried in the Eastern Cemetery.

[10] Arthur Mackworth settled here under a grant from Gorges as early as 1632. Until recently, the island has always been known as Mackay's. Mr. Baxter, the present owner, has found evidences of old Indian camps there, which are so common about the shores and islands of this bay.

[11] New Casco Fort stood on ground now owned by General J. M. Brown, of Portland. It was completed October 6, 1700, by Captain John Gyles, who had been taken by the Indians, when a boy, at the sacking of Pemaquid. A furious assault, made on this fort in 1703, was frustrated by the timely arrival of Captain Southack's relieving vessel. Penhallow gives a good account of this affair. Only a few months before, the Indians renewed their pledges of peace, made on this very spot, and commemorated by the erection of two piles of stones, called the Two Brothers! This name now attaches to the two little islands lying out beyond Mackworth's.

AFTERNOON IN AUGUST.

CHAPTER XII.

CASCO BAY.

" — where hillside oaks and beeches
Overlook the long blue reaches,
Silver coves, and pebbled beaches,
And green isles of Casco Bay." — WHITTIER.

SO long as we may keep our eyes off the clear-cut line of blue sea out in the offing, Casco Bay looks like nothing so much as some island-studded lake, like Winnepesaukee or Lake George. Mountains only are wanting to the illusion. But should we lift our eyes to the horizon, there are the sea and the ships again.

To the plain, matter-of-fact observer, this bay looks as if it had been first ploughed out of the mainland, and afterwards filled between furrows by the in-rushing water of the ocean. Even the course taken by the rock-defying share seems too plainly indicated to leave room for doubt. But what of the power that moved it? what of the forces that could rip up fields of granite as the ploughman turns his sod?

If we go to the mainland for an explanation, we shall find at the northeast corner of the bay a banded clump of long, prong-shaped ridges of hard granite, either peninsulas or islands, that are barely severed from the main, thrusting themselves out into the sea, for many miles, in a uniform southwest direction. These facts would certainly seem to elucidate the whole philosophy of cause and effect here. Mare Point, Harpswell Neck, Bailey's, Orr's, Sebascodegan islands form this extraordinary group, the coast-line of which can hardly be less than a hundred miles, if all its sinuosities be followed. If, now, we shall trace their course out to sea, we discover that the outer islands of Casco Bay, like the sundered articulations of an enormous backbone, merely prolong these peninsulas in the same southwest direction. This, then, was the course taken by that terrible ploughshare when it ripped up the coast of Maine, and left these ridges of rock to show where it had passed.[1]

We start out into this bay, therefore, with a most interesting natural phenomenon in hand, to the elucidation of which we bring our own unscientific hypothesis.

It has become quite the fashion to say that there are three hundred and sixty-five islands in Casco Bay; no more, no less. That is what most people will tell you. It is no easy matter to dislodge a popular error of long standing. In reality, there are, however, but a hundred and twenty-two, without counting mere rocks where nothing but a sea-gull finds a foothold.

The course usually sailed by pleasure steamers, in going from Portland to the Kennebec, winds in and out between Long Island and the two Chebeagues, across Luckses Sound, and out again through Broad Sound. In comparison with the outside route, from headland to headland, this is a very crooked road indeed, but it gives much the best idea of the beauties of the bay, as well as of its great extent and its peculiar form. We are so taken up with looking at the multitude of islands that time or distance is scarcely noted. And last, but not least, in the estimation of very many worthy people, the water is seldom too rough to be travelled with comfort.

We will suppose ourselves embarked, then, on board one of the swift little boats that ply these waters during the summer season. In ten minutes we are zig-zagging among that wonderful combination of capes, headlands, peninsulas, sounds, inlets, and islands for which this bay is so famed.

From the diminutive rock, which every passing wave smothers with foam, to the slumberous monsters stretched out at full length in the distant offing, islands confront us on every hand. On some we see gray old forts; on some, prim little steeples or weather-beaten farmhouses; while those lying nearest the city and devoted to its pleasures look quite like a painter's palette, in their haphazard jumbling together of colors, by which, nevertheless, some very pleasing kaleidoscopic effects are produced.

The extreme brilliancy of the greensward, its effective contrast with the warm reds or cool grays of the rocks, and rich yellows of the bladder-weed, hanging to them in thick-clustering masses, is a constant delight.

The wooded islands are prettiest. I saw nothing that pleased me better than Little Diamond,[2] with its strong-limbed oaks spreading out great clusters of green leaves over the variegated rocks. Great Diamond, too, shows quite extensive tracts of primitive forest growth. Others have succumbed to the depredations of coasting-vessels. Some, indeed, are as bare as one's hand: Cow Island, for example, is treeless. Here and there one exhibits a *peloton* of dead pines standing like scarecrows along an arid waste of burnt-up turf. But all inviting as they look, there is hardly one of them without its tale of bloodshed or its memories of shipwreck.

So we slip by Long Island,[3] and on to Little Chebeague, with its trim-looking hotel and pine-grove background. Whichever way we approach it, this island makes a charming picture from the water. It has a fine long beach, too, and is joined by a sand-bar to Great Chebeague.

At Little Chebeague, some very much sun-burned girls were fishing off the boat-landing. They had already made a good catch of cunners, pollock, plaice, or sculpins, — for all is fish that comes to a young woman's net, — though it was evident enough that they were only fishing for the sport of the thing. Yet, as often as one pulled up a cunner or a pollock, wriggling under the agonies of the hook, all the rest stood on tiptoe, and screamed in concert, until a certain dull-featured boy, with one suspender, who was supporting the capstan of the wharf, took his hands out of his pockets to unhook the fish for them.

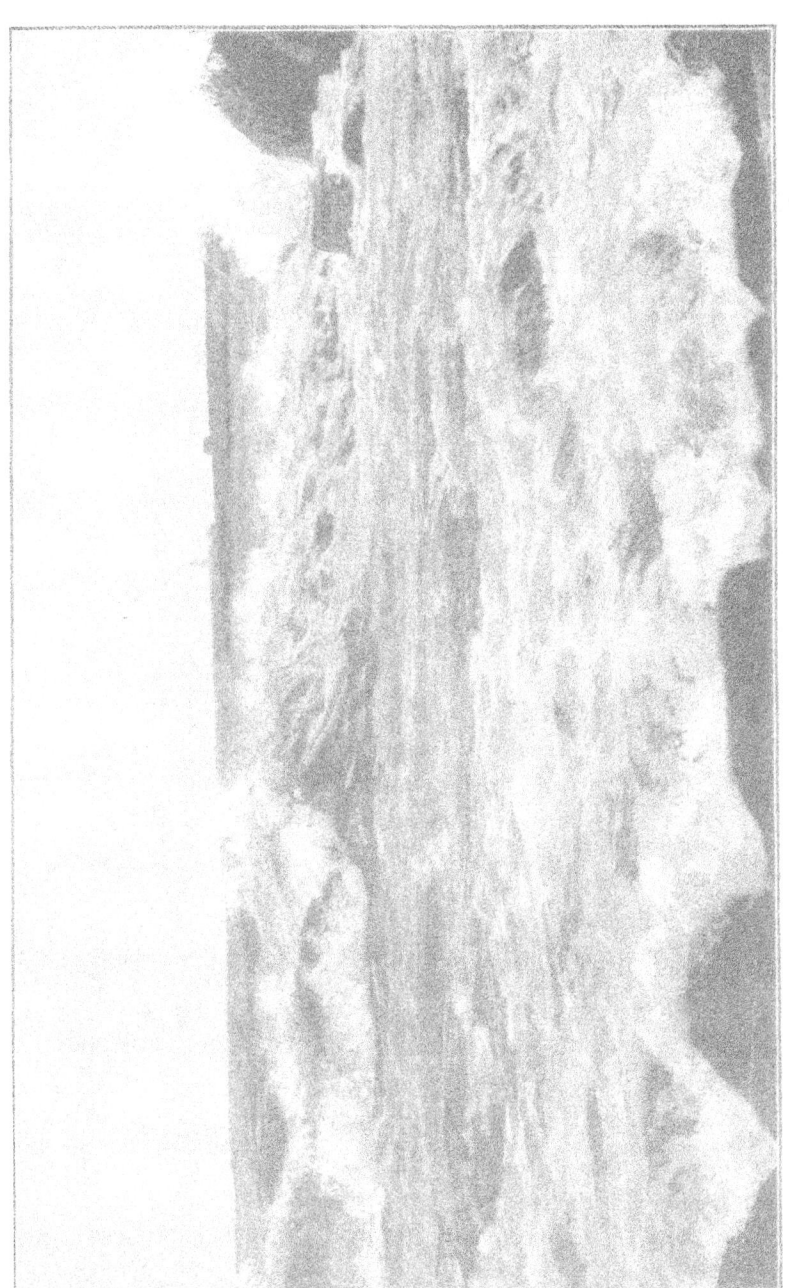

SURF EFFECTS, CASCO BAY, WITH DISTANT VIEW OF HALF-WAY ROCK.

CASCO BAY.

Great Chebeague is a little republic of two thousand acres, having its own churches, schoolhouses, and stores, with a quite large resident population. In general, the aboriginal names of Maine are jawbreakers; but we do not find those remaining about this bay so unpronounceable as those existing farther east, while as between Hog and Chebeague the relic of barbarism would certainly receive the suffrages of all travellers over the sign of civilization.

We glide on past the shores of Great Chebeague, steer between Hope and Little Bangs, out into Broad Sound, leaving Crotch, Jewell's,[4] and their satellites astern. Far out in the offing we can now make out the tall, gray lighthouse on Half-Way Rock again.[5] It is but a short run now across the sound into Potts' Harbor, at the extremé seaward point of Harpswell Neck.

MRS. H. B. STOWE.

All the world has read Mrs. Stowe's "Pearl of Orr's Island," and Orr's Island lies out in full view before us. She has told us about the lives of the people. Mr. Whittier has given us one of their most grewsome legends.

It is to be feared that nearly everybody comes to Harpswell expecting to see something out of the common, and that nearly everybody goes away disappointed.

A comparison between what may be seen by the eye of genius and the eye of a casual looker-on would be manifestly unfair; yet all of us are fond of visiting places that have been celebrated by genius. It is not, therefore, an ordinary visit we are making, but a pilgrimage.

For me, the old legendary stories of a past generation, which have their natural habitat near the sea,

THE FLYING DUTCHMAN.

have always had a peculiar charm. Not seldom they invest places, otherwise insipid enough, with a certain flavor in spite of themselves. They should not be too hastily classed with old wives' tales because their origin may be unknown, but should find a place among those secret beliefs to which all of us are more or less susceptible.

Upon this ground our venerable poet was asked for the nativity of the "Dead Ship of Harpswell," which he introduces with the following verse : —

> " ' Here,'
> He said, as died the faint applause,
> ' Is something that I found last year
> Down on the island known as Orr's.
> I had it from a fair-haired girl
> Who, oddly, bore the name of Pearl,
> As if by some droll freak of circumstance,
> Classic, or wellnigh so, in Harriet Stowe's romance.' "

Here is his reply: "Some twenty years ago I received from Miss Marion Pearl, daughter of Rev. Mr. Pearl, a well-known clergyman of Maine, a letter, descriptive of the people, habits, superstitions, and legends of Orr's Island, where, I think, the writer was a teacher. The legend of a spectre ship, as described in my poem, interested me by its weird suggestiveness. I have no doubt that a quarter of a century ago the legend was talked of on the island by the aged people. Perhaps it has died out now. The school teacher has been abroad since, and the new generation are ashamed of the fireside lore of their grandmothers."

Whoever has seen the play of the fog about the masts and sails of some passing vessel will have had a reproduction from life of the phantom ship. Like that doomed wanderer of the main, the Flying Dutchman, the "Dead Ship of Harpswell" never comes into port; for

SEAMARK.

> "Just when she nears the waiting shore,
> She drifts again to sea."

Potts' Harbor exhibits a wharf, some fish-houses, two public houses, a treeless point, with a little pebble beach under it, and a quite high island (Haskell's) lying out before it. At the eastward, Bailey's Island and Orr's Island enclose Harpswell Sound. Eagle Island is a striking landmark, it being high, round, and all one mass of greenery.

From Harpswell, or Merryconeag Neck, our course lies out through the narrow passage between Haskell's Island and Little Mark Island, on which a lonely looking monument points out the eastern portal of Casco Bay. Clearing this passage, and the dangerous ledges around it, we once more gain the free and open sea, shaping now an east-southeast course for Cape Small Point,[6] distant a dozen miles or so.

HALF-WAY ROCK, CASCO BAY.

The open sea! Ah, that is something to which a first introduction may prove no such agreeable experience, after all! It was even so to-day, judging by the sudden disappearance of the greater part of the passengers from the decks, the wholly unconventional attitudes of the few who dismally hugged the benches in sight, as well as other and even more unmistakable signs of physical prostration that the boat now presented. As I was making a zig-zag course along the lower deck, from one object of support to another, a sudden lurch threw me into the arms of the mate, who was coming from the opposite direction. "Most alluz find an old sea runnin' round the Cape," he said; then adding, "Most alluz makes more or less folks onwell, the motion doos. We had two gents aboard of us last trip. One of 'em was a lawyer. My grief, wasn't he done up, though! T'other wasn't a bit. There he sot, smoking as calm as a kitten. He was a high-up jedge goin' down to hold court. 'Can I do anything for you?' says he. 'Yes,' gasped the seasick one; 'I wish your honor would overrule this motion.'"

As we rounded the stark promontory, so sad and austere, our eyes caught the glimmer of a long sand-beach, edged with foam, stretching away from it at the east. Seguin[7] and its lighthouse now rose up before us. Pond Island, with its tower, stood out from the moving shores. These are the well-known landmarks of the Kennebec for which we were now searching with all our eyes, when suddenly the coast line parted, and out came a tow-boat, belching forth volumes of thick, black smoke, and dragging after her a long string of schooners, that were wallowing deep in the water, with the ice they carried under their hatches. They had hardly cleared the river's mouth before another similar convoy followed them.

Then there was music in the air. Up went the sails, off went the tow-lines, and out to sea bounded the eager vessels, the spray climbing higher and higher at their bows, as, with gathered speed, they threw the big seas off their gleaming sides. The sight was exhilarating enough. As one tall fellow swept past us with roaring bow and foaming sides, I could not repress an exclamation of delight — it was such a gallant sight. It was again the mate who proffered his word of information. "That head one there," he observed, "is the one that sunk the whole United States Navy."

"Did what?" I doubtingly asked.

"Why, didn't you hear of it?" he rejoined. "She run down the *Tallapoosa*, a steam corvette, or something, in the Vineyard Sound. They say orders was issued for government steamers to git out of the way of sailing-vessels in future; for if a Bath schooner could down a man-of-war in that fashion, where were we? and that's what started such a hue and cry about our not having a navy, you see."

But here we are in smooth water again, tied up to the wharf at Fort Popham, with the river flowing quietly past, as it has flowed since the beginning of time.

[1] It is a fact that all the islands do lie in three parallel ranges, topographically classed as the Inner, Middle, and Outer Range. The number is too great to be given in detail, but it is interesting to think that Cushing's Island may once have formed part of Mare Point, as the Outer Green, Jewell's, etc., perhaps did of Harpswell Neck, or Half-Way Rock of Bailey's or Sebascodegan.

[2] Little Diamond is a station of the lighthouse service for the Maine coast.

[3] Long Island is considered one of the most valuable and productive of the group. It is two and a half miles long, has two hundred and fifty inhabitants, and is separated from Peak's by Hussey's Sound, by which there is a good passage out to sea.

[4] Jewell's Island is the farthest land of Casco Bay. Half-Way Rock is farther out, but is only bare ledge. In some respects, Jewell's is the most interesting of all the islands here. In 1676 it gave refuge to the miserable remnant of the inhabitants of Falmouth destroyed, though proving by no means a safe asylum, as the Indians soon drove them off the island. At this early time there was a garrison-house here. There is a cave by the shore, which may have served the refugees as a hiding-place.

[5] This is a flashing red light. The exposed condition of the rock on which it stands will best appear from the report of the happenings of a storm in the winter of 1888-89. Mr. Alexander, one of the keepers, says that the sea ran fifteen to twenty feet high over the rock. One sea rushed by the side of the house, reaching to the eaves, which are fifteen feet above the ledge. The same sea carried away the rail that runs from the Light Tower to the Bell Tower, a distance of one hundred feet. Another sea struck the Bell Tower, a building forty feet high, set up on legs and braced with iron braces. The sea broke those braces off and bent the iron ladder so that it was left in the shape of a rainbow. Huge pieces of rock, amounting to several hundred tons, were broken off the eastern side of the rock and carried across to the western side, a distance of three hundred feet.

[6] A summer colony is located here. The locality has taken the name of Popham Beach. The sea-look from the hill, back of this beach, is remarkably fine.

[7] Seguin is very high and bold, and is well placed for performing its important function of keeper of the Kennebec. Indeed, it is one of the best known landmarks of all this coast. The light is a fixed white of great power. It shines out from a height of two hundred feet above low-water mark. Seguin is undoubtedly a corruption of Satquin, the Indian name, which first appears in Strachey's account of Popham's voyage.

CHAPTER XIII.

THE GATE OF THE KENNEBEC.

"'Tis not too late to seek a newer world;
Push off, and sitting well in order, smite
The sounding furrows."

HOWEVER historians may differ, two things seem certain: one is that somebody discovered the Kennebec, the other is that this discovery was made previous to the year 1607; because, when the first colony was sent out of England for this part of the world, it was directed to this very river and no other. The fact of discovery being thus established, the inquiry remains as to who the original discoverer may have been.[1]

There can hardly be a doubt, we think, that these colonists knew where they were going. No time was wasted in exploration. They went straight to the spot for which they had set out.

There can be as little doubt, it is believed, that the reported discovery of a great river in New England, or rather in Virginia, by one Captain George Weymouth, was the moving cause out of which this enterprise grew up. A great river is equivalent to a great key unlocking a country.

The language used in describing this river is worthy of attention: "Some of them that were with Sir Walter Raleigh, in his voyage to Guiana, in the discovery of the Orinoco . . . gave reasons why it was not to be compared to this river: others before that notable river in the West Indies called the Rio Grande." The Loire, Seine, and Garonne are all declared to be inferior.

Since it would be difficult to convince ourselves that old sailors like these did not know a great river when they saw it with their own eyes, either the narrative of Weymouth's voyage is a pure fabrication, or it was a great river and not a little one that was discovered.

If that narrative be fictitious, the details it gives are not worth considering, because the whole pith of it lies in this one memorable action.

But we know that there was a great river about where the narrative says it was. So far, then, the fact bears witness to the veracity of the narrative. We also know that Weymouth spent a whole month, wanting only a day, in exploring the vicinity. And we know, furthermore, that the colonists, who followed so closely in Weymouth's traces, neither went into any other river nor had any difficulty whatever in finding the one they were in search of, after they had once recovered Weymouth's landmarks. That some one carried the discovery of the Kennebec to England, in season for its appropriation by the colonists of 1607, is therefore indisputable.

We can go one step farther. Weymouth kidnapped five Indians, three of whom were seized by Sir Ferdinando Gorges as soon as they reached Plymouth. When they had picked up enough English to be able to give an account of themselves and of their country, they proved "the means, under God,"— these are Gorges' own words — of turning his attention to colonization. Now Gorges was himself one of the originators of the Popham colony of 1607. We have here his own story of how he became one. And we can hardly be in doubt, therefore, about Weymouth's having carried back the unimpeachable evidence of his discovery, in the persons of these Indians, since the first steps for planting a colony at the Kennebec began within a twelvemonth or so.

We know further, that when Champlain went into the Kennebec, a little later than Weymouth, the savages of that river told him that five of their men had been killed by the people of a strange ship, and her anchorage was pointed out to him.

This voyage of Weymouth, and the coming of the colonists of 1607, are things so closely related that the last was, beyond all question, the outcome of

FORT POPHAM, KENNEBEC RIVER.

the first. We find, therefore, a remarkable sequence of events pointing us unerringly to the Kennebec as Weymouth's great river.

An unfinished fort, roofed over to protect it from the weather, impotent enough in its ability to afford protection, stands out on a bare ledge, at Hunnewell's Point, where we pass into the Kennebec.[2] This point of land forms part of the ancient peninsula of Sabino, of which the Popham colonists took possession for their fort and settlement; so that the present fort stands for a memorial to the first English fortification ever erected in New England, as well as to the ill-starred colony itself.

It is probable that this colony did more to discourage emigration than to help it. It fell to pieces from its own inherent weaknesses. That it was an early failure can hardly admit it to rank with later successes, as much as we may have wished it a better fortune. The world does not take great pride in its failures.

There are, however, a good many interesting incidents connected with this colony, the first experimental effort of the great Plymouth Company, the rival of

SEGUIN ISLAND.

THE GATE OF THE KENNEBEC.

that sent out to Virginia at nearly the same time, which was meant to be the entering wedge that should break the solitude of ages. Of two good blows struck, only one took effect.

Its master-spirit was no less a personage than the chief-justice of England, and its leader his brother. The lord-chief-justice died while his colony was on the sea, his brother within six months after the landing at Sabino. The chief-justice had presided at the trial of Raleigh, and had been hissed for coarsely denouncing him in open court. Raleigh's want of success in getting gold from Guiana proved his destruction. His still fortunate enemy did not live to know whether his colony had succeeded in getting gold from Virginia or not.

George Popham, the president, was old, feeble, and timid; Raleigh Gilbert, his successor, — who bore two famous names through his kindred of blood with two famous navigators, — was, on the contrary, young, headstrong, and exceedingly ambitious, — so much so, indeed, as to make some of his colleagues feel extremely uneasy when the president's death left the colony in young Gilbert's hands. He had hopes, it seems, of reviving his distinguished father's claim to all America in himself, but these visions faded with the utter extinguishment of the colony itself.[3]

One of the ships sailed for England in two months after landing the colonists. It being found that the supply of provisions brought out would not last through the winter, in the middle of December all but forty-five of the colonists were sent home in the second

FOOT-SOLDIER OF THE TIME.

ship. Two relief ships left England in March for Sagadahoc, and in July a third. By these vessels, the colonists learned of the death of Sir John Popham, and Raleigh Gilbert of that of his brother, Sir John, whose estate fell to him.

If one may judge from the letter that Popham wrote to the king in December, by the same ship that brought out the colonists, and was then returning, his credulity was not surpassed by his other infirmities; for in that letter he says: "All the natives constantly affirm that in these parts there are nutmegs, mace, and cinnamon, besides pitch, brazil-wood, cochineal, and ambergris!" Other letters, by the same ship, gave equally glowing accounts of the natural and spontaneous productions of the soil of Maine, though they did not venture to claim for it a tropical climate, and told of the valuable deposits of alum-stone already discovered. These flattering reports were all the freight the ship brought back to England. The colonists did not want for interpreters; because Nahanada, one of those Indians who, under Gorges' tuition, had become the earliest geographers of Maine, made them frequent and ceremonious visits. We should rather suspect that, on learning what it was the Englishmen so much desired to find, the crafty savages fooled them "to the top of their bent."

Besides building themselves a fort, — for which Popham himself threw up the first spadeful of earth, and in which he subsequently found a tomb, — we know that these colonists planted gardens, whose first-fruits they may have tasted, because the roots and herbs they had set in the ground were found growing among the old walls twenty years later. After getting their fort enclosed, they next set about building their storehouse, as the ships could not unload their provisions until a shelter had been provided for. We fancy that none of these buildings were of a very permanent character. Hubbard says, speaking upon hearsay, that the ruins were visible as late as the first Indian war. By ruins, he is supposed to mean old cellars, not walls of brick or stone.

INDIAN HUNTER ON SNOWSHOES.

To think of these colonists tramping through the swamps and thickets of Georgetown, as we know them to-day, loaded down with their armor, excites a smile. Their boat journeys to the east and the west were undoubtedly productive of much better results and far less fatigue.

Though the torch had hardly been lighted before it was extinguished again, the Kennebec, or Sagadahoc,[4] as it was first called, had been cleared of its mystery. It had waited for ages, and it could wait yet a little longer. The visit of Biencourt and Father Biard, in 1612, partly to procure help for the colony at Port Royal, and partly to win over the natives to the French, tended still more to bring out the capabilities of this grand river.

Once more thrown back into its original solitude, the Kennebec flowed on "unvexed to the sea," until the coming of the Plymouth Pilgrims, whose necessities made them farmers at one place, fishermen at another, and traders at still another, but everywhere earnest men who knew no such word as fail. Bradford tells us, under the date of 1625, how, after getting in a good harvest, they sent out a boat-load of corn into the Kennebec at a venture. Their boat was only a shallop of their own building, on which they had laid a little deck amidships, to keep the salt water from the corn; "but the men were faine to stand it out all weathers without shelter." Bradford says, although the time of year began to grow tempestuous. This voyage was made by Edward Winslow, "and some of the old standards, for seamen they had none." The

THE GATE OF THE KENNEBEC.   191

"old standards" here referred to were the iron remnant of the *Mayflower's* company. It proved unexpectedly profitable, however, the corn bringing them seven hundred pounds of beaver, besides other furs. So they pressed this advantage home. In the year 1628 they set up a trading-house on the east bank, at Augusta, so that the Pilgrims were, after all, the founders of the capital of Maine. By the next year they had taken out a patent, which gave them a legal title to fifteen miles on each side of the river, and to about half as much of its course north and south.[5] With their usual sagacity, the Pilgrims had tapped the great artery of the state.

We now begin to hear of adventurous journeys made through the trackless northern wilderness, against which this lonely outpost had been set.

We have first the account of an Englishman, called Captain Young, who is reported by Père Le Jeune to have travelled all the way from the English house referred to, with a single servant, and conducted by twenty savages in canoes to the St. Lawrence. The account which he gave of himself was, that he was an explorer seeking for a passage this way to the northern sea. This happened as long ago as the year 1640. Père Le Jeune adds that this hardy explorer was not allowed to go into Quebec. He then attempted to return the way he came; but finding the difficulties insurmountable, he had at last to turn back among the inhospitable Frenchmen again, who, not knowing what else to do with him, finally shipped him off to France.

To this lone spot in the wilderness, which the wary Pilgrims had made secure with a stout palisade,—for they were far from home, and knew the crafty ways of their savage neighbors from experience,—to this harbor of rest and refuge from the perils of that long march from Canada, came, with staff and wallet, the Jesuit Druillettes, — he whom the Abenakis styled their patriarch, — with the view of planting the cross among the tribes here. He found a hospitable welcome at the hands of John Winslow, in which there was no trace of that rooted antipathy which the Puritan felt for the Church of Rome.

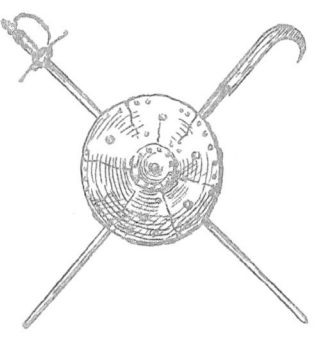

SWORD, TARGET, AND BILL.

Some one has said, "That which pleases me in history is the minor circumstances, the details of character." It is a pleasant thought, that, for once at least, the supple Jesuit and the rigid Puritan could meet on the common ground of Christian hospitality and good-fellowship; could break bread together, and both bless God for it, without harboring resentment that one should do so differently from the other.

But we are in advance of our story. In the meantime, during the summer of 1630, it so fell out that some emigrants, who styled themselves husbandmen, and their ship the *Plough*, had essayed a settlement somewhere about the east corner of Casco Bay, though the precise spot still remains unknown. After only a single year's trial of the place, they deserted it in a body for the more promising lands and more populous neighborhood of Massachusetts Bay, into which other settlers were eagerly pouring.

By order of M. Talon, the Chevalier Saint Lusson made a journey to these coasts in 1671, for the purpose of notifying the inhabitants that they were on the territory of the king, his master. He found the banks of the Kennebec, as well as all the contiguous seacoast, "sowed with habitations, all well-built and in excellent condition." Five years later the Indians had again desolated it.

Let us turn now to more alluring themes.

It is a little odd, to say the least, to find that the ice, from which the first colonists fled in terror, should not only have become the greatest of all attractions, but the chief source of livelihood, to the present inhabitants.

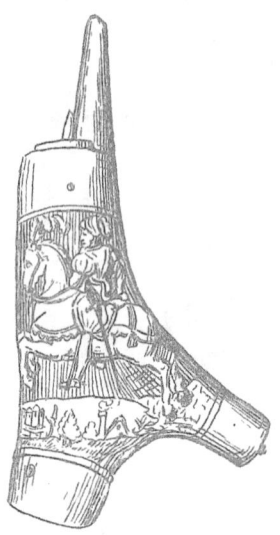

POWDER-FLASK OF THE TIME.

In one sense the Kennebec might be called the circulating medium of the Pine-Tree State.

The annual yield of the ice-fields of Maine is roundly estimated to reach a million and a half tons. And the best of it all is, that these ice-fields, so humorously called plants in the vernacular of the rivers, and unlike those of the dry land, are just as productive to-day as they were fifty years ago, and will be just as fertile fifty years hence as they are to-day. Men reap here where they have not sowed. The serpentine river is annually stripped of its frozen skin, only to put forth a thicker coat in the season to come.

When you are at Bath, in the coldest morning of cold winter, the first thing they bring you at breakfast is a glass of ice-water, in order that you may taste their staple commodity.

The ice business is by no means, however, without its attendant anxieties; for the Kennebec is often open to navigation into February, and while the crop seldom, if ever, fails, the advent of freezing weather, especially after mid-winter has come and gone, is watched for with an eagerness that no class, perhaps, except ice-cutters and ice-shippers can appreciate. Make ice before the sun shines is the maxim of the river. Zero weather means full storehouses; it means employment for thousands of laborers, and many thousand tons of shipping; it means the circulation of ready cash among farmers and storekeepers. Therefore, the lower that the mercury falls, the higher the iceman's spirits rise. It is seen, then, that no greater misfortune could possibly overtake capitalist or laborer than an ice-famine.

Yet among all the multitudinous occupations of men, it is believed that this business has no proper counterpart. Finding gold among the sands of California or Australia may perhaps furnish the nearest analogy to it.

The scenes witnessed every winter on the river, in the neighborhood of the great ice-houses at Richmond, Gardiner, and Hallowell, when the ice-crop is being secured, are very animated and interesting. It has already been our good fortune to get a glimpse of the scene, witnessed when this crop is being transported to the various ports of the Union.

It would seem the most natural thing in the world that the vessels engaged in this traffic should bear such high-sounding and suggestive names as the *Ice-King*, or the *Ice-Monarch*, or even the *Iceberg*, instead of those of their owners, or their owners' wives and daughters, which seem so puerile and commonplace. Speaking of this to a large taker of marine risks, he replied, quite off-hand, that nobody would think of taking a risk on a ship having the word "ice" in any part of its name, because such names are considered unlucky.

Ship-building began on the Kennebec with the launching of a "prytty pynnace" by the Popham colonists, with which to prosecute their explorations about the coast. She was called the *Virginia*, in honor of the country which gave her to the sea. So we are all Virginians.

Most of the ship-building of Maine is now carried on in the yards of Bath, that business having followed the inevitable law by which capital is absorbing the industrial interests of the country right and left, so weeding out weaker competition everywhere. Small yards are now maintained, and vessels now and then built only where local conditions, such as cheap labor and low taxes, permit the builder to realize a profit; since in the purchase of materials, all of which must be brought to his yard, the advantage of buying in the best market is clearly with the large buyer. Then again, in a dull season, the concern with capital is able to build vessels on its own account, as land speculators do houses when materials are cheapest, and so keep his laborers at work, till the times improve; while the individual builder, who is too poor to run risks, must let his yard grow up to weeds.

While looking over the annals of ship-building in the United States, I came across an item of unusual interest as related to that subject. The Lloyds' register of last year, the shipping chronicle of the world, contained the name of the barque *True Love*, an American bottom built at Chester, Pennsylvania, in the year 1764, or twelve years before the Declaration of Independence by the colonies. She was certainly afloat in 1887, and still seaworthy; her owner being J. S. Ward, of London, England. I doubt if there be an older American hull in existence.

There are many spots about Georgetown[6] and Arrowsic Island[7] rendered memorable by some association with the old Indian wars, or by the stirring events of later times. But we must hasten on to other scenes, without doing more than allude to the Kennebec as the highway of war, out of which swarmed the destroyers of many a fair New England home, or to the vengeance that overtook them at last in their forest hold, or to that amazing march to Quebec which

194   THE PINE-TREE COAST.

deserved, if it did not achieve, success, and is without a parallel in the military annals of the nation.

[1] Whether or not Weymouth discovered the Kennebec has been considerably discussed. There are monographs by John McKeen, George Prince, Rev. Edward Ballard, D.D., Rev. Dr. B. F. De Costa, and Rev. H. S. Burrage, with others to come. I am bound to say that most of them take an opposite view to that expressed in the text, yet the course of events seems more conclusive than the effort to make Rosier's narrative of the voyage fit impossible conditions. I have never yet seen an original narrative of this sort that was free from exaggeration, pre-eminently the vice of explorers, or in which it would not be easy to pick flaws.

[2] Fort Popham, only half completed before granite walls were found to be no defence against modern artillery, is of no particular use that I could see except as a historical monument. The work was begun under General Totten's supervision in 1861, after delays thrown in the way by Secretary at War Floyd. A memorial stone, with this inscription, has been placed within the walls of the fort: —

THE FIRST COLONY
ON THE SHORES OF NEW ENGLAND
WAS FOUNDED HERE,
AUGUST 19TH, O. S. 1607,
UNDER
GEORGE POPHAM.

[3] Sir Humphrey Gilbert was half-brother of Sir Walter Raleigh. By Anne, his wife, daughter of Sir Anthony Aucher, or Ayger, he left Sir John Gilbert, an officer of reputation, and eight other sons, all of whom died *s. p.* except Raleigh Gilbert, from whom the distinguished British major-general, Sir Walter Raleigh Gilbert, was sixth in lineal descent.

[4] Sagadahoc means in Indian the mouth of the river, or more definitely in this case, that part of the Kennebec below the junction of the Androscoggin. Colonel William Lithgow gave it the former derivation. An old sea-chart of 1723, in my possession, shows that the contiguous waters of Sheepscot Bay were also known as Sagadahoc. See also the Duke of York's patent. President Popham's letter to the king is dated "At the Fort of St. George, in Sagadahoc of Virginia, the thirteenth day of December, 1607." Champlain writes the name of this river Quinibequy, hence Kennebec, the name now adopted for its whole course.

[5] The Plymouth Trading-house patent was the foundation of the land-titles for so much as it covered. Contiguous tracts were also acquired by purchase of the Indians. See Baylies' "Plymouth Colony" and the "Additions" by S. G. Drake, showing these boundaries.

[6] A history of Georgetown is in preparation. There is an account by Judge Sullivan printed in the "Massachusetts Historical Collections" for 1806. It is running over with errors. Georgetown was Sagadahoc Island.

[7] Major Thomas Clark and Captain Thomas Lake, two merchants of Boston, bought Arrowsic Island for a trading-station in 1661. They had built a fort, storehouse, and several dwellings when the river Indians made their descent in August, 1676, driving off or killing all those found on the island, including Lake, who was mortally wounded. See Hubbard's account of this affair. The south part of Arrowsic was granted by Sir E. Andros in 1679 to Laurence Dennis and others, on condition of their settling a town there, to be called Newtown.

GETTING SEAWEED, SHEEPSCOT BAY.

CHAPTER XIV.

BOOTHBAY AND ABOUT THERE.

"Good by to pain and care! I take mine ease to-day:
Here where these sunny waters break,
And ripples this keen breeze, I shake
All burdens from the heart, all weary thoughts away." — WHITTIER.

NO happier experience could fall to the traveller's lot, I am sure, than to find himself comfortably established on board one of the boats that ply the devious Sasanoa, between Bath and Boothbay. It is the perfection of water-travel.

To say that nature, in one of her most capricious moods, has lopped off a series of long finger-like points, extending far out to sea so many successive barriers to be turned, and so many deep bays to be ascended; and by so doing has opened a network of navigable inland water, remote from the usual track, by which old ocean is fairly outwitted, and outgeneralled, would be only putting the case in its plainest terms. We also are going to steal a march on Father Neptune, as it were.

Leaving noisy Bath behind us, we steam directly out across the Kennebec, toward the opposite shore, into a channel wholly hid from view, till we have come within a cable's length of it, when, suddenly, as if some magician had pronounced his cabalistic "open sesame," the shores part before us, the land lifts its gaunt rocks and bending trees above our heads, and away we dart into a narrow strait of open water, much surprised, and not a little elated by the novelty of the thing.

THE PILOT.

And here begins one of the most enjoyable voyages I have ever made in my life.

Just as we have entered upon it, a queer old crook-backed bridge, bent with age and hard usage, spans the shores, and bars the way. The boat gives one short, impatient blast, that wakes the echoes far and wide, and pushes straight on for the obstruction. A woman comes running down the road, hastily adjusts a long iron bar with both hands, and by applying her back to it, as a man would his shoulder, turns off the drawbridge for us to pass through a space just large enough for us to pass through, and no more.

Except for the seaweed deeply fringing the rocky shores at low-water mark, we might suppose ourselves sailing on some delightful mountain lake; but here we get in perfection the pungent exhalations of briny ocean, mingled with the warm, resinous odor of the pines.

We are soon traversing a broader reach of smooth water, trending off inland, with miniature capes, reefs, and headlands. This presently narrows again, between a rising crag and low-jutting point of rocks, to a width of not more than fifty yards. It is a mere split filled with a rushing tide. Through this contracted channel the current pours with such force and swiftness that we are carried along with it, like a feather in the air, to be launched out upon the quiet water below, with just a little tension of the nerves to show that the episode is not without its excitement. After going through this Upper Hell Gate, as it is called, all is smooth and quiet again.

He was a bold navigator who first pushed his bark into this tortuous rapid! If Champlain was not that man, he is, at any rate, the first to give us an account of it; and a most amusing one it is. But let him tell the story himself:

"We passed a very narrow water-fall, but only with great difficulty; for although we had a favorable and fresh wind, and trimmed our sails to receive it as well as possible, in order to see whether we could not pass it in that way, we were obliged to attach a hawser to some trees on shore and all pull on it. In this way we succeeded in passing it. The savages accompanying us carried their canoes by land, being unable to row them. I was greatly surprised by this fall, since as we descended with the tide we found it in our favor, but contrary to us when we came to the fall. But after we had passed it, it descended as before, which gave us great satisfaction."

A FRESH BREEZE, SHEEPSCOT BAY.

It is seen, however, that the force with which the strong ebb-tide impinges against both shores here creates an eddy which carried Champlain's bark along with it for some distance into smooth water again. So the alleged phenomenon is easily explained.

We are soon up with the fine promontory called Hockomock Head, a huge mass of forest-shagged rock, thrust down from the north, on which Champlain's Indian guides each left an arrow, as an offering to its guardian spirit, whose name the headland bears. The headland is also the subject of a local legend, which, under various aliases, may be met with all over the United States.

This point forms a sort of vestibule to Hockomock Bay, a beautiful sheet of water by which vessels pass up, twenty miles inland, to Wiscasset. That nearest land, in the north, is Phips' Point, the supposed birthplace of Sir William Phips, who is said, on one occasion, to have pointed it out with the rather inflated remarks: " Young man, it was upon that hill that I kept sheep a few years ago. You don't know what you may come to." Let us likewise look to our muttons.

This endless solitude of water, woods, and rocks, how swiftly it has borne us away from all thoughts of streets, lanes, and steeples ! As we wind in and out among the intricate channels between wooded points, each twist and turn takes us to some new scene, some new surprise, some new fancy. Now it is a solitary wharf creeping out from shore, on which we leave a single passenger, or toss a mail-bag ; now it may be a drowsy little haven, like that of Riggsville, which is stirred to momentary wakefulness by our coming, but dozes off again the instant we have turned away.

Emerging at last from the labyrinth of waters, which our boat threads like a hound recovering the scent, we shoot out upon the broad bosom of Sheepscot Bay,[1] just as the low sun is silvering it with a dull lustre, and is gilding the tops of the stately pines.

ONE OF THE FIVE.

Here again we meet the open ocean, its regular swell, its briny odor, its searching breezes. Just now we were feeling ourselves a little cramped and confined, but here we have plenty of sea-room. We quickly run down the Georgetown shore to a little clump of islets that seem dropped in the water, like eggs in a nest. These are the Five Islands. Pretty cottages, a trim little steam-yacht, gay dresses, brown faces, fluttering handkerchiefs, announce a prosperous summer colony.

The form of these islands is very peculiar. They rise from the waves mere mounded rocks, on whose gray backs a few pines cling with wonderful tenacity. They nod to us as if to say, "You see, friend, I can grow where anything can." The islets, too, show exposed faces, just as the larger islands do, their scraps of forest also retreating back from diminutive forelands, showing where the waves dash fiercest.

These Five Islands command the whole range of Southport Island, opposite, on which the meeting-house holds its spire high above everything around, down to ancient Cape Newagen, and its dangerous outlying rocks. They also look down the Sheepscot, far out to sea. Directly across the water is Hendrick's Head. Higher up, the course of the Sheepscot may be traced far up into the land.

But our voyage is not to end here. We are no sooner clear of the Five Islands, than the iron-gray mass of Old Seguin looms finely in the distance.

BURNT ISLAND, BOOTHBAY.

Edging now up to the Southport shore, we approach the entrance to Ebenecook Harbor, an Indian settlement of long standing, snugly ensconced in the side of the isle; but instead of entering it, the boat rounds to at a singular protruding rock, traversed by a wide split, behind which there is a narrow cove and landing-place known as Dogfish Head.

Pitched among the retreating rocks and trees of this shore I saw tents and shanties, of most primitive design; such, indeed, as men rear who are used to camps and marches, or whom economy has taught to be their own architects. I should have called it the poor man's paradise. It was, in fact, a *bona fide* summer camp, the rigid simplicity of which in all matters pertaining to domestic economy contrasted somewhat sharply with the elaborate and even luxurious belongings of its neighbors; yet, nevertheless, pots were bubbling merrily on the coals, the men and women who stood around looked happy and contented, their attitudes were as unconstrained as their little cabins were homely, there was vigor and elasticity to their steps, and altogether it seemed as if they

BOOTHBAY HARBOR.

were getting nearly the best of life at the shore, without troubling themselves too much about those things which are making our so-called fashionable coteries, we fear, much too civilized for comfort.

There is no better summer-house than a good Sibley tent, pitched in a sheltered spot; but it should always have a floor of boards, raised above the ground a few inches, and so trenched round on the outside as to drain off all surplus water. "Keep Dry" should be the maxim of every camper-out. For a cabin, matched boards make a tight roof, which is the *sine qua non* in wet weather.

Rounding the northern point of Southport, our course now lies through Townsend Gut, past the pretty resort at Mouse Island, into Boothbay Harbor, where it is no uncommon thing to see from fifty to a hundred weather-bound craft snugly moored at once.[2] In fact, Boothbay is one of those natural harbors, so perfectly fitted to the wants of commerce, and so admirably placed for its uses, as to seem the result of intelligent provision rather than of accident.

I doubt if there are two things in this world more like each other than two New England villages.

Boothbay will be better appreciated, perhaps, for its fine ocean views, its excellent building sites, and healthful situation, rather than for any very marked features of its own. It mostly skirts the uneven edge of an inner basin, — a sort of limb which the larger harbor has pushed up into the land, — protected at the entrance by a little rocky islet, and filled with deep, smooth sea-water. The ocean may roar outside; but here it comes in like a lamb led by a little child.

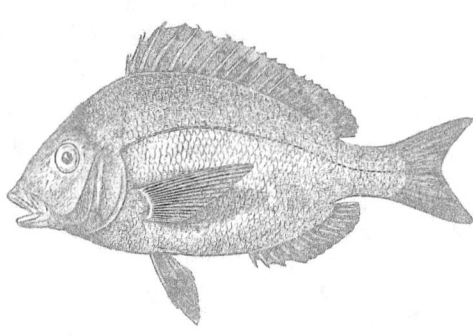

THE PORGY.

At the east side, attention is drawn to the long, high, dark-wooded tongue of land, advancing out seaward, called Spruce Point, than which there is nothing more beautiful about the environs of Boothbay. Some steps are being taken toward bringing this shore into notice; yet up to this time, Spruce Point makes slower progress in that direction than its natural charms would seem to warrant.

At the west side, the main harbor has cut out a second basin, around which a suburb has grown up, devoted to the making of fish-oil and other fish products. When I was here in August, 1888, the whistle of the porgy factory sounded for the first time in seven years. So scarce had these valuable fishes become in consequence of the war of extermination waged upon them, that the business had come to a standstill. After taking time to recuperate, the porgy has come back again to his old haunts, factories have started up, and the slaughter is being renewed. In a good season, between six and seven hundred thousand barrels of porgies have been ground up in the works in and about Boothbay. At this rate, the wonder is that any should remain alive.

STEAMING HOT.

The outlook from the head of Boothbay Harbor holds the shores of Southport, with Mouse, Burnt, and Capitol islands adjoining, as far as the extreme out-point at Cape Newagen, where the Cuckold rock raises its warning beacon.

Squirrel Island lies three miles off the harbor, to which it makes a sort of breakwater. Then comes the Damariscove group, and then, still farther out,

> " Waves in the sun — the white-winged gleam
> Of sea-birds in the slanting beam —
> And far-off sails which flit before the south-wind free."

It would need all of one summer, perhaps even a winter added, to do justice to what the eye has traversed in less time than it takes to put pen to paper. What history has to tell, or the coasts themselves to show, gives promise of a rich treat to the studious observer.

SEINERS ON THE ALERT.

Let us first go to Squirrel Island. The distance is short, so we are soon there. A cove is roughly worked out of its west side, from which the land rises to a moderately high ridge, skirted by groves of evergreen. The big trees are all gone, but there still remain some pleasant stretches of spruce and fir. Around this cove, along this ridge, in the woods, and by the shore, rise a hundred cottages, all pretty, some handsome, not a few mere cubby-houses, others with room to spare, — and all set so thick together that one looks about him for the familiar warning of " standing-room only."

The colony at Five Islands is conducted like a club; here the associated cottagers may keep house or dine out, as they prefer. They have a code of regulations; they have their chapel, their printing-office, and their reading-room; a tennis-court, croquet-ground, and bowling-alley. Their large boarding-house is also open to the public. In short, I found them excellently equipped for a summer campaign against blue-devils in every form.

I bought a copy of their newspaper, called *The Squid*, after a marine animal extremely addicted to squirting ink, as everybody knows. For all that, it is a surprisingly clean little sheet, the chronicle of all local events, apt commentary here upon the *dictum* that the first thing an American would start on a desert island would be a newspaper.

By crossing the strip of woods, which makes such an agreeable background for the parti-colored cottages, one comes out upon a waste of sallow, pie-crust ledges polished smooth by the waves, which slide up with a stealthy, panther-like movement, and fall back with a soft purring sound, but would drag you off

CAPE NEWAGEN, FROM SQUIRREL ISLAND.

your feet in an instant, if once off your guard. A deep crevasse runs across this granite terrace, against whose knife-like edges the sea makes savage lunges. Not to mention Kidd's Cave, a hole among the rocks, would be unpardonable. Yet, to judge from what we see and hear, Asmodeus and Captain Kidd must have been the pioneer travellers to these parts, for no well-regulated resort is without its legend of the one or its story of the other.

There is a custom at Squirrel of which I would rather not speak than give offence. It is this: The dignified-looking matron of the public house very graciously bestows on each departing guest a parting kiss, — a sort of *baiser de souvenance*, — without distinction of age or sex. Each visitor thus takes away with him an unfailing reminiscence and a receipt in full.

A run over to Cape Newagen [3] should by no means be left out of the traveller's itinerary. At Southport Landing the mail-carrier's wagon will take him to the end of the Cape. When he is there, the visitor will be quite ready to declare that of all the rough, inhospitable backbones of what is miscalled land, Cape Newagen caps the climax. It is sterile to emaciation. The island is long but narrow. Two excavations in the west side serve for harbors. At

Hendrick's Head, where there is a light, is the principal settlement; on the hill behind it stands the meeting-house we saw from the Sheepscot, the post-office, and two or three dwelling-houses.

Cape Newagen demands little at our hands. A few unpainted cottages and fish-houses, a few idle boats moored off them, the ruins of what were once wharves sticking up out of the water, with mourning seaweeds hanging to them, exhibit the business aspect at a glance. Little enclosures, so small that a cow would have to wait for the grass to grow between meals, — a streak of rock and a streak of sod, — zig-zag among the cottages, as if every householder had picked out his lot blindfolded, and no man got what he wanted. The battle has evidently gone against this village.

Over at the east shore there is a pretty large tract of cleared land, all of which has been taken up by the omnivorous speculator.

Newagen Harbor is small but deep. It looks quite as if the sea had made a clean breach across the point of this island, just as it has at Cape Neddock Nubble, similarly cutting off Jerry's and Hunter's islands, and leaving the one quaintly called the Ark sticking in the harbor's mouth. The two dangerous Cuckolds foam and fret just outside. Names like these indicate the antiquity of the place itself.

TURNSTILE.

This forsaken little port, so long and so early frequented, could hardly fail of being spiced with tales of piratical adventure, though we are quite at a loss to account for the absence of Captain Kidd's name from the local traditions. According to these, the notorious Gibbs once took the liberty of stretching a chain across the harbor, while he was refitting at his leisure. There was probably no one to say him nay. Another recounts how a corsair who had grown weary of cutting throats ran away from his ship here. He was adopted into the community, where he passed the rest of his days, taking a wife, and leaving descendants who are now among the living. It is said this man would sit for hours in a natural seat formed of the rocks at the shore, smoking his pipe, and gazing off to sea; and that during one of these visits a retributive breaker dragged him down from his seat to a watery grave. So perish all pirates! In proof of the story, anybody at Cape Newagen will show you Chappelle's Chair.

All the familiar landmarks show grandly here. In the southwest the double dome of gray Seguin keeps silent watch. We can look back as far as Small Point, or, by making an about-face, can run the eye along the coast to the mouth of the Damariscotta and distant Monhegan. But on this side the Damariscove Islands obstruct the view.' This is glorious indeed, you will say, and so it is; but come back here by night and see Seguin and Monhegan playing at hide-and-seek across Plutonian darkness!

The history of all these islands begins with the earliest occupation of any part of the coast for fishing purposes, and it breaks off with the rise of permanent settlements on the main shore. Damariscove has a good harbor, smooth in all kinds of weather. It is now deserted. There is little to be seen there; for fishermen raise no monuments.

---

[1] Sheepscot Bay and River give entrance to a region about Wiscasset in which there are many traces of ancient settlement. The locality was known as the Sheepscot Farms until depopulated by Philip's War, after which the settlers seem to have thought the situation too exposed to return to it.

[2] The early history of Boothbay is quite obscure. Those settlers living about here were probably included in what was known as the Sheepscot settlements, until the first and second Indian wars caused their total abandonment. A town was laid out by Colonel Dunbar, of Pemaquid notoriety, in 1730, called by him Townsend, or Townshend, a name legally superseded by the present one in 1842. Boothbay is the scene of Miss Blanche Howard's story of "One Summer."

[3] Christopher Levett came as far east as Cape Newagen in the winter of 1623-24, looking for a situation to his mind. He says that nine ships fished there in that year. At this place Levett met with the Indian chief, Samoset, whose memorable greeting to the Pilgrims, "Welcome, Englishmen," has become historical. Hearing that Cape Newagen, Pemaquid, and Monhegan were already taken up, Levett went back to Portland and located his grant there. Philip's War depopulated the Newagen settlement for a time. A fortified house was afterwards built for its protection.

[4] Altogether, the Damariscove Islands constitute a very marked group. Damariscove proper is two miles long by, perhaps, half a mile broad. It is the largest and best of the group. Fisherman's Island, next north, with Ram Island (lighthouse) adjoining, lies about one mile off Linekin's Neck, Boothbay. It is poor and forbidding. East of this, ranging also north and south, are the two Hypocrites (formerly Hippocras), mere wave-washed ledges; still farther east are the two White Islands, a good mark in sailing from Monhegan to Boothbay, as the Great White is high and bold. Next south, and due east from Damariscove, comes the Outer Heron; then Pumpkin Island, where there are bad ledges. Southwest of Damariscove are the dangerous Bantam Ledges, marked by a buoy.

The *Sparrow* fished at Damariscove in 1622, when she brought out passengers for Plymouth Colony. Bradford says, despondingly, "this boat [from the *Sparrow*] brought seven passengers and some letters, but no vitails, nor any hope of any." By this means, however, a boat-load of provisions was afterward procured, and communication opened. In 1624 the Pilgrims lost a pinnace here. At this time it was a regular resort for fishing-ships, which fact first drew the Pilgrims' attention to this quarter, of which they had previously known nothing except from Samoset.

CHAPTER XV.

MONHEGAN ON THE SEA.

"No fish stir in our heaving net,
And the sky is dark, and the night is wet;
And we must ply the lusty oar,
For the tide is ebbing from the shore." — BAILLIE.

DISCOVERY CROSS.

TEN miles off the pointed promontory of Pemaquid, in the open ocean, two islands, the one only moderately large, the other a mere lump of rock, — the nursling, as one might say, of the greater island, — emerge side by side from the bottom of the sea, like sleeping whales that lie warming their huge backs in the sun. We can hardly get rid of the notion that the ocean will swallow them up before our eyes.

Land ten miles at sea? That means a rock of danger to the sailor, in thick weather, or happily it may be the guiding mark for which two straining eyes have searched through the long watches of a wintry night. East or West, is there a sailor but knows Monhegan[1] as well as he does the old church spire of his native village, or a reader of history who has failed to recognize it as one of the stepping-stones of advancing civilization in this quarter of the globe? So true it is that a very little spot of ground may make a large figure in history.

They told me at Boothbay, that the only means of getting off to the island was by taking passage in an open boat, which carried the mail three times a week; that is, when the carrier was lucky enough to make the trip.

The voyage proved a memorable one in many respects. At a late hour of one September afternoon, we pushed off from the wharf. Long before we got clear of the harbor, the sun went down in crimson pomp behind the hills, and with the gathering dusk a dead calm fell upon the drowsy sea. A weird glow still lingered in the west. The harbor lights danced about us like so many will-o'-the-wisps in a churchyard, the sullen wash of the waves came back to us from black and brooding shores, the stars stared down out of the heavens upon us, and little by little the noises of the land died away in confused murmurings as we drifted slowly on out to sea with the tide.

Off Linekin's Bay we were perilously near being run down by an inward-bound steamer, getting from her, as she backed her engines and sheered off, a volley of abuse for being in the way. There was a minute or two of eloquent silence, while we watched the steamer's receding lights, broken at length by the skipper, who said, between puffs, as he lit his pipe: "You see, sirs, it's a stark calm. Like as not it won't breeze up before morning. Mebbee it will, mebbee it won't. You see it's a sollum row out to M'nhiggon. You see it's kinder wet and nasty like out here. I motion we go over to the light to Ram Island, where we can be in out of the doo and night air" (he said nothing about the danger he had just escaped); "then, if the wind takes a cant to the nor'ard or west'ard, we can go 'long."

The soundness of these views being incontestable, it was voted *nem con* to pay the keeper of Ram Island a visit, the more willingly because his light had for some time shed an alluring and compassionate glow upon us, and its red track on the waters even seemed foreshadowing the warmth of our welcome.

It was eleven o'clock at night when we moored our boat in the inky-black gut opening between the islands, under overshadowing crags, along which we felt our way with our hands to a friendly shelf. As we scrambled up the slippery ledges, guided by the faint glimmer of our boatman's lantern, and treading cautiously in his footsteps, we might have been taken for smugglers, treasure-seekers, or anything but honest folk "on hospitable thoughts intent."

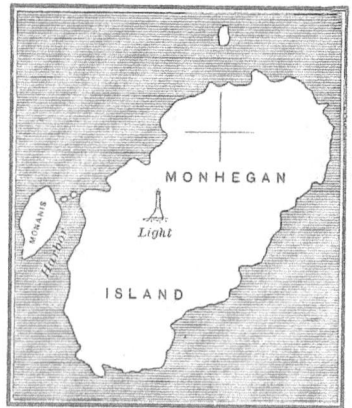

MONHEGAN ISLAND.

The keeper proved to be a bright young fellow, hardly turned of thirty, perhaps, who had lost a leg in the service of the lighthouse board, but who, nevertheless, was far more active on his one leg than most men are on two. A snug pension would seem a poor enough return for being thus maimed for life; yet, strange to say, the government's bounty does not reach this class of its servants, even to the furnishing of a wooden leg or a pair of crutches. The keeper's wife, good woman, made us a pot of tea, piping hot, and laid the cloth for her famishing visitors, after which we were shown to a tidy bedroom, wished a good night's rest, and left to make the most of the opportunity.

At four in the morning, while the stars were still shining, our boatman, remorseless as old Charon himself, called to us from the foot of the stairs to turn out. The wind was light but fair for Monhegan. So once more we groped our way out among the slippery rock-weed, which threatened at every step to trip us up, down to the landing-place, from which we presently glided out again upon the open sea.

With sails and oars we gradually worked our way up to the island by the middle of the forenoon. For me, its every secret nook and cranny — gray headland or tuft of woods — held a mysterious charm like to that surrounding some antique sea-hold of song or story; for whether the viking bold or men who sailed with Frobisher or Drake were the first to set foot on Monhegan, it is the vanishing-point down the long vista of time, the haven wherein we dimly discern the first discovery ship at anchor.

As we come up to it from the west, the island stands up from the sea, bold, robust, and aggressive, in one regular mass, its rusty red rock-armored sides receding back from the water quite like the hulk of a ship. Two conspicuous objects break its outlines. One is the lighthouse, which stands about midway of the summit of the island; the other being the fog-signal on Monanis, which does not detach itself from Monhegan till we get closer in.

But neither lighthouses nor fog-trumpets, buoys nor beacons, can put an end to the long list of disasters of which Monhegan has been the cause.

FIVE MILES AWAY.

Just before going into the harbor we saw a steam-tug coming out with a schooner in tow, stripped of sails and rigging, and much down by the head. She was so full of water that she refused to rise upon the swell as she met it, but lurched and floundered on after the tug like a balky horse hitched to a wagon-tail. A dismantled wreck is always a pitiful object. This one had gone on the rocks of Lobster Point in a dense fog, had been deserted by her cowardly crew, who cut the only boat adrift and made off with it, and was finally got afloat and brought round into the harbor by the islanders, who look upon a wreck as they would upon a big haul of mackerel. The fog-horn was going at the time, but the master was like the man who heard the sound of the trumpet and took not warning.

In this picture and its story are comprised one phase, at least, of life as it is known to the men of Monhegan.

Monanis is nothing in the world but a bald rock, chipped off at the sides, rising up sheer and stark from the water's edge. Could we imagine a giant hammering away at it in the rough, until he had wrought out some semblance to roundness and symmetry, what we see would represent the crude result. Underneath its battered sides, snatched as it were from the sea, nestles the tiny harbor — such a retreat, for instance, as Ariel tells Prospero he has hid away the king's ship in —

> "the deep nook where once
> Thou call'dst me up at midnight, to fetch dew
> From the still vex'd Bermoothes: there she's hid."

This harbor lies all open to the southwest, but is nearly walled in at the upper end by a high and dry ledge, thrust across it from Monanis, so as barely

A MONHEGAN LAD.

to leave room for boats to pass in and out this way. They call it Smutty Nose here. Upon this natural breakwater there is a signal-mast, which persistently refuses to stand up straight, though it does make a picturesque addition to the *ensemble* of the harbor, which, in spite of its having proved the salvation of many a big ship, is really so diminutive as to give you the idea of a basinful of water dipped up from the ocean.

As we forged slowly along, among the fleet of idle boats moored in midharbor, all the settlement of Monhegan, and no small part of its inhabitants, came under close inspection. It is all here, by the shore of the harbor. One can count all the houses, see what is going on out of doors, take note of sundry evidences of thrift or decay, trace the path leading up to the lighthouse on the hill, or dive down into the hollows beyond, which make an oasis in this ocean solitude.

The first step taken on the little beach inducts one into the life of Monhegan as it was centuries ago, as it is to-day, and as it is likely to be in the time to come. These same grimy dressing-stands, all this nameless litter of seafaring gear, this very heap of decaying fish-offal, might have been seen here in this very spot two hundred years ago. And the men are as like their fathers as like can be.

The beach itself is formed of about equal parts of sand, shells, and fish-bones. One man ventured the assertion that if all the fish-bones that had been thrown into the harbor could be gathered together into a heap, they would reach as high as Monanis — not so incredible a statement as it would at first seem, since they have been cutting up fish here and tossing the bones about for some two hundred and eighty years or more. But one needs constantly to remind himself that gold has no smell, since the stench is so unbearable, all up and down the shore, as to divest fish and men of all manner of romance whatsoever.

Monhegan fish are, however, highly esteemed on account of the care taken in curing them, and that is the whole secret of making good fish. If there be any knack about it, these island men ought surely to have mastered it; for they have done nothing but catch fish, cure fish, and pack fish ever since they were big enough to handle an oar or cast a line.

The men who gathered about us at the landing were mostly past middle age, — gray-haired, gray-bearded men. A good many people seem to think that by coming a hundred miles more or less they must see a very different order of human beings. They would suffer disappointment at Monhegan. I was about to ask, however, " Where are your young men ? " when I learned that the population of the island was steadily decreasing with the falling off of its fisheries. And there being absolutely nothing else to do but follow fishing for a living, the law of demand and supply has worked out its inevitable results in diminishing the number of inhabitants from 133 persons in 1880 to 101 at the present time.

I soon saw that a ripple of suppressed excitement was disturbing the wonted calm. It was on the beach, in the fish-houses, and had even made its way into the back kitchens. It seemed that the captain of the wrecked coaster we had seen being towed into port was treating the islanders unhandsomely in the matter of salvage, from their point of view, he having held out three days for a trifle of twenty-five dollars, or some such matter, which they demanded over and above what he was willing to pay. One man in particular seemed much put out about it. He very bluntly declared, in my hearing, that he "hoped another vessel never'd get ashore on Monhegan." The bystanders, on whom this thoughtless speech made a visible impression, took him sharply up for it; but he stood his ground, obstinately, though I believe he did subsequently qualify the offensive remark so far as to say that he hoped the owners would be aboard of her when she struck.

After dinner I saw the island men holding an open-air council over the matter, on the beach. As each took the attitude that suited him best, they formed a very picturesque group indeed. Two or three did all the talking. The one thing to be remarked was that the interest of one was the interest of all. Upon all questions affecting them as a body the islanders are a unit. A decision being reached, the council broke up. The schooner's sails, utensils, and furniture, from a frying-pan to a jack-plane, were all carried down to a seine-boat, put on board, and rowed off to the scow that had been waiting for them. I don't believe that a single article was missing.

The dingy, ill-favored look of the fish-houses, crowding the shore, is a little enlivened by the pale yellow lichens encrusting them. Those growing to the rocks are of a beautiful bright orange color. One has to pick his way out among splitting-stands, lobster-crates, skiffs, buoys, spare spars, nets, and killigs to come at the owners' cottages at the back, where the picture is agreeably reversed; for though no man seems to have built better than his neighbor, if we except the large, square Trefethren mansion, all the houses look neat, and some even pretty, with their bit of grass, their climbing posies at the doors, or their handful of nasturtiums under the windows. The women-folk look as neat as wax in their calico gowns and sunbonnets, and their modest demeanor announces that society rests on no insecure foundation here. Like most people who live outside the great world, they are apt to be just a trifle inquisitive about strangers; so those who may go to Monhegan hereafter may as well understand that it is no place to carry hauteur or reserve. One may ask as many questions as one likes, but should be prepared to answer two for one in return.

There is no aristocracy, no middle class, no understratum of society. The people seem more like one large family or clan than anything else. They doubtless have their family quarrels, with which it would be as unwise for an outsider to meddle as with family quarrels in general. Where one man sells his fish all the rest sell theirs. Share and share alike seems to be their unique motto in all business concerns. Indeed, they seem to have imbibed something of the spirit of modern socialism, if they do not practise all its vagaries, and this too without any teaching whatever.

There is a green lane running between the cottages; but if you want to get into it or out of it from the harbor, you must let down somebody's bars, or pass through somebody's gate. Grass land is far too valuable to be squandered upon highways. And taxes must be correspondingly light. The feeling that you are committing a trespass so soon wears away, however, that in spite of its novelty one grows bolder every hour of one's stay. This one thoroughfare goes as far as the lighthouse, and no farther. As there are neither horses nor carriages on the island, it cannot with entire propriety be called a road; and it plainly will never be a street. It suffices, however, for all the wants of the islanders. To make a circuit of the island afoot, one must follow the sheep-paths till he finds that there is no need of a guide.

Over toward the harbor mouth there is a neat little chapel, built of wood, in which occasional services are held, there being no settled minister here. Though so few in number, I understand that the islanders are as much divided as to creeds as their brethren of the mainland. The chapel, therefore, was dedicated by the generous Philadelphian, who gave it, to the use of all Christian sects alike. Under no circumstances will the islanders permit its use for any other purpose than the worship of God. Concerts, fairs, readings — everything, indeed, of a secular character — are rigidly excluded, as so many infractions of the contract.

As there is not much else to see about the harbor, we will take a stroll up to the lighthouse on the hill. Among the few houses that begin the ascent with us is the one schoolhouse of the island. A little farther on, we come to its solitary graveyard,— a square plot of ground, enclosed by white palings, showing a score of graves marked only with such rough head and foot stones as could be picked up at random. Not a line or a letter to tell who the occupants are. Others have their memorials, it is true, but these are the nameless, the forgotten ones. Nowhere do the dead go so quickly. There are thousands upon thousands of unmarked graves in New England. And the pity of it is, that a great deal of history is forever buried in them. Our laws provide for the burial of a pauper, but stop there. They should go further. They should require the marking of every grave by a suitable headstone, and make wilful neglect to comply with the provision the subject of a certain penalty. And every municipality in the land should be held responsible for the execution of this law.

Though placed in a spot quite remote from the dash and roar of the sea, Monhegan Light stands on the most commanding ground of the island. There is not a bit of that romance about it, therefore, that is usually associated with such structures. It is a solidly built, circular tower of granite, the lantern being raised one hundred and seventy-five feet above sea level. The light is a revolving one of great power. In a clear night it shows a corona of dazzling brilliancy, not the sprawling flame we are so accustomed to seeing represented in pictures. In a thick night it pierces through the blackest darkness, like a meteor, and with White Island, Boon Island, Half-Way Rock, Seguin, Matinicus, and Mount Desert Rock, so plucks safety from danger that ships now shape their course along the coast as well by night as by day. Seguin is visible in the west, Matinicus Rock at the east, each being about twenty miles distant.

I had gone no farther when the freshening easterly breeze brought down upon us the fog, — its inseparable companion in this latitude. It had been lurking outside, a long wall of gray, all the morning. Very curious it was to see the exasperating vapor streaming across the island as noiselessly as one of Ossian's ghostly armies in full flight, with the sun shining out serene and bright overhead. The fog-horn on Monanis soon began its lugubrious braying. There was no help for it but to sit down till the fog had blown over, which it fortunately did in the course of half an hour more.

CLIFFS AT MONHEGAN.

I can give a profile of Monhegan in a very few words. You first ascend the hill on the summit of which the lighthouse stands; then go down into a hollow; and then ascend again some heights at the south shore. This hollow is a deep valley driven across the centre of the island. These heights are the brow of an enormous headland that looks out over the broad Atlantic.

A walk across the valley to the south shore, short as it is, is quitting the coast for the country, for the time being. No sound, no suggestion of the sea, reaches you there. A broken rim of tipped-up land runs round the coast. The bottom of the crater-like basin around you is a morass grown up with weird, moss-bearded evergreens. When you have ascended the opposite side, you find it shoved high up above the northern shore, like all the exposed faces of all the headlands of this remarkable coast. How much land was washed away before this result came about is a problem yet unsolved.

The thin soil affords pasturage for a few sheep. Your true fisherman does not take kindly to farming, not so much for want of time, because he spends days and weeks in idleness, as for the reason that he considers farming and fishing quite as incompatible as he would the avocations of soldier and sailor. Fogs, calms, storms, scarcity, consume an undue proportion of the fisherman's lifetime. It is true his labor is always hard, often hazardous, but he can hardly be classed, I think, as a laborer, among the toilers of our great cities, with whom every day is a working day.

After climbing the short slope, to the crumbling and overhanging edge of the headland, one step more would send you headlong a hundred and fifty feet down among the breakers. You are standing upon the brow of the great cliff known on the island as White Head. So swift is the descent that I could not

BLUE-FISHING.

see to the bottom even by leaning out over the brink of the precipice, though I could hear the breakers roaring down there among the fallen rocks.

Then I went back to hear men talking about the price of mackerel.

The visitor to these cliffs should be warned against going too near the brink, as deep cracks have opened in several places at the surface, possibly by the action of frost, possibly through the undermining of the cliff by the sea.

Monanis should be visited on account of the remarkable rock inscription there, generally attributed to the Northmen or the devil.

I therefore took a wherry across the harbor, climbed the long flight of stairs by which access to the fog-station is gained, and after a short search found the inscription rock at the side of a deep gully, that may have been ploughed out of the summit of the isle, when the ice pushed across it, ages ago.

The exposed face of this rock is deeply pitted by the action of water and frost. Such as they are, the markings cover a space of about forty-five inches long, by six and a half in breadth.[2] All are cuneiform, or wedge-shaped. With trifling devia-

ROCK INSCRIPTION, MONANIS.

tion, they appear to be rude attempts to form the capital letter "N" in continuous succession, and to all appearance are as legible to-day as when first made. Assuming them to be the work of hammer and chisel, which their regular form and depth of incision would seem to indicate, we can only guess what the unknown workman's purpose may have been, — whether it embodied a story or conveyed a direction, — since no one would be likely to perform so much manual labor without a purpose. At one time I thought it possible that some one of the early discoverers might have taken the latitude and longitude of the island from this spot; at another, that pirates might have concealed treasure near it. But these are mere conjectures. Nobody has been able to make any intelligible record out of these characters. Danish antiquaries have puzzled over them in vain. There is no evidence whatever that a Northman ever set foot on Monhegan, and tradition is silent. We can decipher Egyptian hieroglyphics, but not these.

Without exception, the islanders themselves scout the idea that human hands had anything to do with making these characters. In this they are at least honest. What they may say when Monhegan gets to be a summer resort is a quite different matter. One man actually tried to dissuade me from going over to Monanis, on the ground that it would be a pure waste of time. He himself had been sitting on the beach for a full hour, whittling. Another said that some of the markings had been made within his memory. The consensus of opinion among them seemed to favor the operation of purely natural causes. But if water has really done this work, it has done it so well that one would hardly know where to look for a greater curiosity of its kind; nor would the whole conclave of Monhegan philosophers be able to convince one that these despised characters do not contain a riddle yet to be solved.

Monhegan is known to have been the resort or asylum for pirates, smugglers, or mutineers centuries ago. If what we do not know about it could be unearthed, what an interesting chapter it would make!

Monanis makes an excellent historical observatory, never so fully appreciated as when one has looked off over the leagues of water intervening between him and the distant coast.

The good ship *Archangel*, George Weymouth, commander, out of England since Easter Sunday, 1605, clewed up her sails, and let go her anchor under Monhegan on the 18th day of May, — a day now memorable in the annals of Maine. Weymouth came on shore, looked over the island, and was so well pleased with it that he called it Saint George, after the tutelary saint of England. Landward, perhaps midway between his ship and the shore, he saw a cluster of islands lying in the estuary of what seemed either a river or arm of the sea. Through this opening in the coast he could look up to where the view was bounded by what he took to be high mountains — lofty, indeed, as compared with the low coast — striking as the landmark which no sailor could mistake for anything else. We can see all this as plainly from Monanis as Weymouth did.

OLD-TIME FISHERMAN.

The next day Weymouth worked the *Archangel* up to the islands he had discovered inshore, as he desired to bring his ship into some harbor more convenient to the main; not because there was no good anchorage at Monhegan, as the Relation has it. This was found to the leeward of the larger island of the group. As it was Whitsuntide, Weymouth named it Pentecost Harbor, out of thankfulness, it would seem, that God had fixed the beginning and end of so prosperous a voyage on two great festival days of the Christian Church. Neither name has survived, though his anchorage now goes by the name of Saint George's Harbor.[3]

Monhegan was thus the island-postern through which Weymouth passed to his new world.

I looked in at the signal-station. Everybody does. The keeper solemnly averred that he had had nothing to wet his whistle with all that morning, though everything was kept ready for instant action. It is written in the book of the prophet Ezekiel that "if the people of the land take a man of their coasts and set him for a watchman," he shall forewarn them of the coming of the sword. The figure would not lose its appropriateness if applied to the coming of the storm.

[1] After the visits of Weymouth and Popham, 1605 and 1607, there is a blank of six years; but we know from Smith, who was at Monhegan in 1614, that an English ship was then fishing across at Pemaquid, "having many years used only that port." This ship belonged to Sir Francis Popham, one of the Kennebec adventurers, who was profiting by the knowledge gained in that unlucky enterprise, that "the main staple from hence to be extracted is fish," as Smith says. Two years later Smith gives us his map, with Monhegan laid down as Barty Isle. From this time onward Monhegan was more or less visited by fishing-ships, coming direct from England, or calling on their way home from Virginia, to occupy the island while making their cargoes of fish, trading with the natives, and getting in wood and water. When Samoset visited the Pilgrims, at Plymouth, in March, 1620, he could give the names of the masters who were in the habit of frequenting Monhegan or its vicinity. Though permanent occupation dates only from its sale to Abraham Jennens, in 1622, a rendezvous thus existed, holding a close relation to the Pilgrim colony and its fortunes. Jennens sold out in 1626 to Robert Aldworth and Gyles Elbridge, merchants of Bristol, England, for £50. They subsequently perfected their title by procuring a patent (1631–32) to Pemaquid, which included both Monhegan and Damariscove. Aldworth had been a furtherer of Pring's voyage. It is curious to learn that when this sale became known at Plymouth, Bradford and Winslow came to Monhegan in an open boat, thinking to buy Jennens' trading goods at a bargain. Besides a "parcel of goats," they took away goods to the value of £400 sterling. Bradford speaks of this sale as the breaking up of the plantation at Monhegan. Abraham Shurte, the agent for Aldworth and Elbridge, made his home at Pemaquid either then or soon after; so that with the settlements now springing up on the mainland Monhegan lost much of its old prestige. When, in 1676, the Indians fell upon the Kennebec settlements, the inhabitants, living east of that river, fled first to the outlying islands, and next to the west for safety. Monhegan was then deserted, but occupied at the close of the war. It was at one time called Southack's Island, probably for Cyprian Southack, of Boston.

[2] The inscription is printed in *Des Antiquities du Nord* for May, 1859.

[3] Saint George's Islands lie east by north about six miles from Monhegan. Allen's, Burnt, and Benner's, the outermost, are the ones usually called The Georges. Two bad ledges, the "Old Man" and "Old Woman," lie due south of Allen's Island, on which Weymouth is supposed to have set up his cross. George's Harbor opens at the north of Allen's Island, between this island, Benner's, and Davis' Island.

As Weymouth remained in this vicinity a whole month wanting a day (May 17 to June 16), there can be little doubt, we think, of his having explored the Saint George's sufficiently to ascertain that it was in no sense a great river. This month was spent in searching the coasts.

CHAPTER XVI.

PEMAQUID THE FORTRESS.

"I would not be a Puritan, tho' he
Can preach two hours, and yet his sermon be
But half a quarter long." — COWLEY.

WE are still climbing the coast. Our next stopping-place will be Pemaquid, that famous promontory of colonial times, that thorn in the side of our French rivals, which so well illustrates the changing aspects of political power.

After passing the pretty summer settlement at Ocean Point, the always beautiful Damariscotta[1] comes down out of some large fresh-water ponds to mingle with the inflowing tide. Some dozen miles up, at the head of the tide, are the twin villages of Newcastle and Damariscotta, both old settlements.[2] They afford most interesting ground on account of the extensive shell-heaps found in the neighborhood, which it must have taken centuries to accumulate, and which bear witness to the fixed habits of the aboriginal tribes, with whom the summer was a season of feasting, plenty, and relaxation.

To think of those lazy vagabonds with whom to work was a crime, regaling themselves, like the epicurean gods, upon oysters of such size, plumpness, and delicacy of flavor as these shells go to show, — shells of eight and even ten inches in length, — and that without either salt or pepper to give them a relish, almost reconciles us to the doom of the savage depredator himself! But if to his uncontrollable habit of gluttony we owe the extinction of this delicious bivalve, as would seem only too probable, we can regret the oyster, but never forgive the Indian.

The Damariscotta betrays the same wayward propensity to stray out of its fixed course so characteristic of all these tidal streams of Maine. It is forever pushing and pressing up against its banks, as if in search of some secret egress through which it may slip off unperceived.

Christmas Cove is a pretty nook worked out of the side of Rutherford's Island in this way. The profusion of green here is a delightful resting-place for the eye to linger upon; but as every medal has its reverse, so just below this island there is a weird stretch of black, humpbacked ledges, with deep channels between, protruding above water, and prolonging the shore with a sunken wall. They have been quaintly called the Thread of Life Ledges, and certes, they are no bad epitome of that mortal thread by which many a poor sailor's life has hung suspended, when his vessel has been tossed up here a wreck. The outermost rock of this singular group is known as the Thrumcap, — a name which seems to have found great favor with sailors of the olden time.

I will relate a single incident, which will with difficulty be realized by those who may have chanced to land on these self-same rocks, on some fair summer's day, without so much as wetting their feet.

One dirty night in November, 1889, the schooner *Belle*, outward bound, was struck by a gale when

THE OYSTER-SHELL BANKS.

off Monhegan. She was then standing eastward. Finding that she could not be kept on her course in the teeth of the increasing gale, the master put about for Boothbay Harbor, not doubting his ability to find it; but when day broke, the *Belle* was already among the breakers, with death staring all on board in the face. Both anchors were let go. It was a vain hope; for the chains snapped like rope-yarns under the tremendous strain, leaving the *Belle* to the mercy of the next breaker, which hurled her against the ledges a miserable wreck.

SETTING UP A WIGWAM.

This was the situation at seven in the morning, when the word was passed about among the men of Rutherford's Island that a vessel was ashore on the dreaded Thread of Life Ledges. Only those who have heard it can know the thrilling effect of such an announcement. Three stout fellows — common, every-day men, but heroes every one — manned their dory, and pushed off to the rescue. The sea ran so high that they were compelled to give up the attempt to reach the wreck, but, after a hard pull they succeeded in making a landing at the back side of the ledges, which they rapidly crossed over to that nearest the wreck.

Between them and the doomed vessel, however, there was an impassable gulf of raging water. The next question was how to get the crew off. The wreck was certain to break up in a few hours at most. But no boat could live a moment in that sea, nor the stoutest swimmer hope to reach the rocks with life; or if he should succeed, it would only be to meet death there in a still more horrible form. There is no life-saving station near, and the rescuers were without the means of sending off a line to the perishing crew.

With the crew, however, it was now a matter of life and death, and when that is the case, men think fast and act quickly.

First, making fast a stout rope to a piece of plank, the sailors next cast it adrift, in the hope that the swell setting so strongly in toward the ledges would carry the line within the rescuers' reach. We may well believe that its progress over the foaming billows was watched with breathless attention, for to those imperilled sailors it was, in every sense of the word, a cast for life.

After a few minutes of this suspense, to their un-

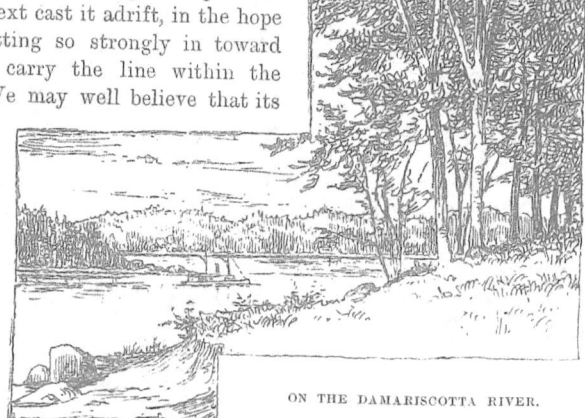

ON THE DAMARISCOTTA RIVER.

speakable relief, their plank drifted up against the rocks; but it was only with great hazard of their lives that the rescuers managed to secure the life-line, for they were more than once swept off their feet by the recoil of the waves. Then six stout arms began hauling away for dear life. A second and stronger line was quickly brought ashore by means of the first. This one being made fast to the rocks of the ledge, served as the frail bridge over which five of the crew made their perilous passage, between life and death, in safety. One man was lost.

Heron Island is anchored, as fast as rock can hold to rock, in the mouth of the Damariscotta. There is also a summer colony here. Our steamer took on a party of tourists, all of whom were chewing gum, and all shouting "Goo by! goo by!" in one and the same breath, to the friends who had come down to the pier to see them off. After setting up their peculiar shout, they fell back

PEMAQUID POINT.

upon song. The vessel then, greatly to my surprise, pushed boldly out among the ledges, through the singular hole-in-the-wall where the shipwreck took place, so letting us pass into John's Bay by a short cut, with Pemaquid Point rising before us on the opposite shore.[3]

This is another of those long, lean, uneven wedges of rock driven out into the ocean, between Muscongus Bay on the east and John's Bay on the west. A belt of rusty red granite stretches round it above low-water mark, and out into

A SUMMER IDYL.

the foaming breakers beyond. Pastures pallid from exhaustion, and spotted with clumps of melancholy firs, spread themselves out over this foundation. In the extreme corner of this threadbare robe there is a lighthouse.

You look about you in vain for those evidences of long occupation which the historic vista has opened to you in advance.

In the course of half an hour our tortoise of a steamer crept quietly up to the wharf at the harbor. Fifteen years ago a flourishing business was done at the porgy-oil factory here, thus giving some appearance of life to the place, at any rate, even if it dealt a death-blow to its sentiment. Indeed, one porgy factory is enough to create a solitude. When that business gave out, — when porgies were no longer to be caught by hook or by crook, — the large works were pulled down, and nothing has since risen on their ruins.

Before coming to Pemaquid, one should have passed an hour or two in reading up the history of the place.

A few people have put the notion into the heads of a good many more people, I find, that Pemaquid has a history going back of any existing record. Mysterious hints are dropped about an older civilization than we wot of.

Now everybody loves mystery except historians. It is their ungrateful task to destroy other people's illusions.

If a few fishermen were in the habit of coming here before settlement was ever thought of, much less attempted, what does it signify ? Our own fishermen now make yearly voyages to Greenland, with the same object. We know, indeed, that in course of time these fishermen and traders became colonists; but we may safely challenge the assumption that those first transient comers made any of the improvements now seen about Pemaquid. A booth, a wigwam, a camp-fire in the woods or on the beach, met all the wants of men who lived on shore just long enough to dry their fish, or trade off their wares, and who left no other traces of their stay behind them; nor is it usual even for actual settlers to labor at the laying down of paved streets, for instance, for which they could have no earthly use, until other and more indispensable wants are provided for.

ARROW-HEAD.
(Actual Size.)

ARROW-HEAD.
(Actual Size.)

Captain Smith, who fished and traded at Pemaquid in the year 1614, and whose name is a household word among us, saw nothing whatever to indicate the presence of European settlers. Nor did his particular friend Nahanada, sagamore of Pemaquid, who had been in England, and could speak excellent English, even hint such a thing, or Smith would hardly have failed to mention it.[4]

After speaking of his friendship for Nahanada, one of those Indians whom Weymouth had kidnapped, and Haman had brought back, Smith goes on to say that "with him and divers others I had concluded to inhabit, and defend them against their mortal enemies, the Tarratines," or in effect to set up a new Jamestown here in bleak New England. Nahanada embraced Smith's offer with "no small devotion"; but we are sorry to say that notwithstanding his association with the great ones of England, by whom he had been much caressed, Nahanada had become as much a savage as ever when he and Smith entered into this alliance, offensive and defensive.

PEMAQUID THE FORTRESS. 227

We thus have a definite starting-point, at any rate.

In the next place, William Bradford, the faithful, minute, and conscientious historian of Plymouth Colony, tells us under the date of 1623 that "there were also this year some scattering beginnings made at Pascataway by Mr. David Thompson, at Monhegan and some other places by sundry others." If to this we add what Levett says he heard at Cape Newagen in the winter of this same year, "that Pemaquid was also taken up," it is just possible that Pemaquid may have been one of those "other places" to which Bradford refers, though we find nothing to confirm such an inference.

Nothing, therefore, is more improbable than that Pemaquid was settled before Plymouth, as we have heard it sometimes asserted. The Pilgrims would have known it, we think. And they would never have long delayed opening a communication tending so much to mutual advantage. But all this is only part and parcel of that obscurity in which the earliest settlements of Maine are so hopelessly involved. The primitive settlers seem to have conducted their affairs like men who have moved out of the world, and whom the world has forgotten.[5]

I have said more than I intended, in the hope of giving some check to those loose and misleading statements which, from frequent repetition, gain credit among uninstructed visitors, and are so hard to root out. No place on the whole coast has afforded such a plentiful crop of historical nettles as Pemaquid. The indulgent reader will, I trust, therefore appreciate the endeavor to give him the true countersign, before we go the rounds together.

This tour of a spot not much larger than a country gentleman's private grounds is certainly one of the most profitable experiences old or young could possibly have; not so much for what the place has to show, though in this respect it is by no means lacking, as for the crowding recollections it calls up, the consistency it gives to things but imperfectly understood at best, and for the satisfaction one feels in walking about among scenes consecrated by history.

A short walk takes us to the rising ground, where the fortress of colonial times still marks the farthest point at which the ensign of England could assert its sovereignty in this quarter of the globe. In a short quarter of an hour one has made the circuit of the grass-grown ramparts; has peered into all the choked-up underground holes; has rebuilt in imagination the batteries, the bastions, the magazines; has looked over all the rust-eaten relics that the intrusive spade has turned up, — has brought the past vividly before him, and the dead to life.

What are they then, these mysterious conductors, which enable us to look across the centuries down the long vista of time?

The story of this fortress is the story of the settlement itself, for the fortunes of one determined the fate of the other. The settlers built their first fort on the same ground since occupied by the more elaborate works, as it was the dominating point of the peninsula. It was probably no more than a strongly built house, with a stockade around it; but such as it was, no body of settlers could feel themselves secure without its protection, for the feeling that they were trespassers made them always fearful of a surprise.

FORT FREDERICK AND ENVIRONS.

Before the weak plantation was fairly settled in some order, one Dixy Bull, a renegade English trader, whose name is found among the patentees of Agamenticus, made a descent upon it with his crew of outlaws. Bull seems to have ransacked the place at his leisure. So the history of this fortification begins with an ill omen.

Fort and settlement were given to the flames in the time of Philip's War, though not until the settlers had made good their escape to the islands. The close of this war brought with it a new order of things, as New York now assumed the government of Pemaquid, as an appendage of that province, by royal letters-patent. The very first thing done was to build a timber redoubt,

PEMAQUID THE FORTRESS. 229

with a bastioned outwork, in order to establish a rallying-point for the fugitive settlers.[6] It was completed in 1677, and garrisoned with some regular soldiers from New York. The new-comers called the place Jamestown, and the fort, Fort Charles.

Under the new régime a strictly military government was established, of which the local commandant was the head. A code of regulations — emanating from the council-board at New York, but which read as if they were drawn up on a drum-head after a conquest — was enforced, with a cool defiance of the people's rights, either in their persons or property. If the people had hitherto lived almost without law, they were now to learn what it was to be governed too much. Their domestic occupations, their out-of-door employments, were regulated by a signal-gun from the fort; and they were squeezed at every turn by the needy adventurers into whose clutches they had fallen.

The political situation was interesting. England now first asserted a determination to hold Pemaquid, by force of arms, against the claim of France to establish her boundary at the Kennebec.[7] England thus forestalled any motion toward occupying the disputed territory, — disputed ever since it had been granted by the sovereigns of both states, in turn, without bringing about any agreement as to the actual rights of either. According to the interpretation of the French court, Pemaquid was French soil; by all the traditions of the English court, the Saint Croix formed the true boundary. Whenever the two nations went to war, the quarrel over this strip of territory was revived; whenever peace was declared, the negotiators seem to have purposely left the question unsettled as something with which either party might challenge, at some future time, the good faith of the other. So poor Acadia, like Mahomet's coffin, hung suspended between the two claimants.

This state of things converted all Eastern Maine into debatable ground, one part being in the occupation of the French, and another part in that of the English, with the Penobscot forming a sort of natural barrier between them for the present; but the erection of Pemaquid into a stronghold put an end to all uncertainty about the intentions of the British court, virtually to assert control over the region in dispute; so Pemaquid henceforth assumed a political importance wholly disproportioned to its character as a fishing hamlet.

If only great interests led nations into war, then we might take leave of this history where it is; yet it seems only too evident that neither national dignity nor even national antipathy can truly account for the attitude so long maintained by two great states touching this wilderness, which neither had been able to bring under subjection to civilizing influences after a trial of eighty odd years. The true solution, we suspect, is to be sought for in the secret history of those rival monopolies, fostered by both courts; in the corrupt influences brought to bear upon high officials for the purpose of controlling the fur trade; in the perquisites derived by hangers-on; in the artfully thrown-out hints that great revenues were to be derived by keeping the region a sort of national preserve, rather than in the demands or interests of the commonweal. When monarchs play at this game, it is never difficult to throw dust in the people's eyes.

Be that as it may, the people of Pemaquid and its dependencies not only found themselves being squeezed by the rapacity of their friends, but destined to become the especial target for their enemies. In times past their very insignificance had proved their safeguard; they were destined to know what it was to be lifted into prominence.

In 1688 Sir Edmund Andros made a sudden descent upon the French trading-post then occupied by Saint Castin, and now known by his name. Andros plundered the house of its goods, little dreaming what would follow. In revenge, Castin incited his friends, the Abenakis, to dig up the hatchet. Soon the whole border was in a blaze. News of the revolution in England, and imprisonment of Andros at Boston, threw everything into greater confusion. The royalist garrison of Pemaquid partook of the excitements and the dissensions of the times. Many soldiers deserted, some were drawn off, the rest with

A SNUG HARBOR, PEMAQUID.

difficulty kept at their post of duty, while the storm of war was ready to burst upon them in all its fury.

At Castin's fort active preparations were making for the attack, Castin himself, and Father Thury, of the Indian mission, being the energetic leaders. Spies were sent out to New Harbor, an out-village of Pemaquid, to ascertain and report how the inhabitants disposed themselves about their every-day work, and what would be the best way to strike them unawares.

The blow fell one afternoon in August, 1689. A war party, sent out from the Penobscot villages, gained the eastern shore in their canoes, undiscovered. It was in harvest-time. The unsuspecting settlers had gone about their usual avocations, some to the fields, some to the shores. Vigilant eyes were watching them; and when the men were so completely dispersed as to render resistance of no avail, a furious onslaught began simultaneously at two points. It was planned with fiendish ingenuity. The main village lay about a quarter of a mile from the fort. The Farms, where most of the men were at work, were at the Falls, three miles off. New Harbor, two miles east of the fort, had some dozen houses.

The assailants divided. One band threw itself between the fort and village; the other cut off the village from the Farms. Then the butchery began. As the men at the Falls ran for the fort, they were either shot down or taken in the net the enemy had spread for them. Thomas Gyles, who was at work in his hay-field, was mortally wounded by the first volley. The Indians then rushed in and made him their prisoner, along with a number of others, among whom was Gyles' youngest son. Moxus, the chief of this band, said to Gyles, ironically, that he was sorry. The dying man replied that he asked for no favor except to pray with his children. This being granted him, Gyles was led aside and despatched, while his two sons stood by in the grasp of his murderers and heard it all.

In like manner those inhabitants who were left in the village, — and these were mostly women and children, — who made for the protection of the fort, were either intercepted, or only reached it by fleetness of foot.

The assailants next turned their attention to the fort. Some houses standing along the street leading from the village to the fort were filled with savages, who fired at every one who showed himself. In like manner the high rock that makes so conspicuous a feature of the ground to-day served to shelter more assailants, who, firing within pistol-shot, were able to drive the gunners away from their posts.

Weems, the commander of the fort, held out till the next day, when, finding but fourteen men out of thirty unhurt, he surrendered the place on condition that the garrison should be free to depart unmolested. Fort and village were then set on fire, after which the Indians marched off in triumph with their captives.

Thus, for the second time, Pemaquid was swept out of existence.

Exit Sir Edmund Andros, and enter Sir William Phips, a man born almost within sight of Pemaquid, a ruler sprung from the ranks of the people, the representative, and, to some extent also, the product of the new order of things in New England, consequent upon the dethronement of the Stuarts in Old England. Phips was not born a gentleman, though he aspired to be one; he was not a soldier, but he had soldierly instincts. His iron personality was the controlling force of his administration.

One of the royal instructions to Phips, who came back to New England clothed with the prestige of a king's favor, was to rebuild Pemaquid at once. In the summer of 1692, therefore, he personally superintended the erection of a new fortress on the site of the old one; but, unlike the old one, built in a most substantial manner, of stone, and so enlarged as to take in the rock which had proved the weak spot in the old defences. This work was called William Henry. Cotton Mather, the friend and biographer of Sir William, gives a full and, as might be expected from a person so profoundly ignorant of military affairs, a rather bombastic description of it.[8] Impoverished Massachusetts strongly demurred against being called upon to pay the bills, but Phips put both hands into the treasury and built his fort.

Frontenac saw that he must either give up his control over the savages or destroy Pemaquid; and Frontenac was not the man to let the grass grow upon his projects. He soon despatched two ships and some hundreds of savages to take the fort; but the garrison had been notified to be on its guard, and so the plan miscarried. The plain story has a somewhat romantic sequel. Frontenac held in his hands at this time a young Bostonian, whose unselfish devotion of himself at the call of his country shines out clear and bright on the dark page of the time. The prisoner's name was John Nelson. Having penetrated Frontenac's purpose, Nelson contrived, at the risk of his life, to get word of it to Boston before the enemy's ships could reach the coast; so that when they did arrive there, the French commander judged that an attack would be imprudent. Unfortunately for him, Nelson's agency in the matter was discovered. Frontenac dared not go so far as to shoot him, though he put him to the cruel test of being led out for execution; but he shipped Nelson off to France as altogether too dangerous a man to be kept in the colony. Nelson was held a state prisoner first in the Château Angoulême, and afterward in the Bastile, till the intervention of friends procured his release.[9]

But stone walls do not make a fort any more than a prison. It might have been foreseen that Frontenac's next blow would be delivered with full effect, after the failure of the first. Incapacity, however, ruled at Boston. In August, 1696, Iberville, with two war-ships and a mixed force of French and Indians, came again before Pemaquid. At this time there were about a hundred men in the fort, of which Captain Pascho Chubb held command. Castin and his Indians, who are supposed to have landed at New Harbor, at once broke ground in the rear of the fortress, where the cemetery is, thus cutting off the garrison on the land side. Cannon were landed and batteries erected on the adjacent shores and islands. The besiegers worked with so much zeal that their batteries opened fire by three o'clock in the afternoon of the day next after their landing. Chubb retorted a first summons to surrender defiantly enough. Weems had fought just long enough to save himself from the imputation of cowardice, but Chubb's courage seems to have oozed away precisely at the moment when that of a true soldier begins to rise. Intimidated by Castin's threats to show no quarter, unnerved by the explosion of a few shells inside the fort itself, Chubb hastened to open his gates to the enemy rather than fight it out like a man. The victors had not counted on so easy a conquest.

Once more the victorious enemy dismantled the works, and threw down the walls so impotently raised to be the bulwark and stay of New England. For the third time in its history Pemaquid had fallen a prey to those it was meant to overawe, perhaps subdue, and with its fall the little life it had kept in the settlements existing east of the Kennebec flickered and went out.

No further attempt to fortify Pemaquid was made until 1729, when Colonel Dunbar was sent over with a royal commission, giving him authority, as governor of the resuscitated ducal province, to rebuild the fort at the charge of the crown. This he proceeded to do on the old lines; so it is the ruins of this later work, and not of the one raised by Phips, that we now see around us.[10] Dunbar called it Fort Frederick, in compliment to the Prince of Wales, father of George III. It stood until the Revolutionary War broke out, at which time the inhabitants, taking counsel of their fears, chose to demolish it, upon the strange plea that, as they were not strong enough to defend it, the fort was an element of weakness rather than of strength. So that whether by the hand of friend or foe, Pemaquid's evil destiny was fully accomplished at last.

The history of this fortress is, therefore, we blush to say, a tale of dishonor, unredeemed by one solitary act of heroism on which we would like to dwell. Let us pass on to other things.

On approaching the fort by the street leading up to it from the east, we should first turn off to the left in order to look at the strip of pavement recently uncovered at a depth of a foot and a half below the surface of the ground.[11] The area so far exposed shows a perfectly well-laid pavement, of small cobble-stones, such as may still be seen in the court-yards of some old New England mansions. Of the genuineness of this pavement there need be no question, since the evidence of one's eyes is all-sufficient upon that point; but of its origin, there is room, perhaps, for a difference of opinion.

Some find in it — and this brings us back to the point we were discussing at the beginning — clear proof of an occupation going back — I know not how far — to the Northmen, perhaps. Some are satisfied to look at it through the spectacles of others. For my own part, I have been unable to see anything extraordinary about it. Apparently there was a street leading from the water-side, up the rise, toward the southeast angle of the fort, whence a second street led toward the cemetery, and a third toward the wharf at the north of the cemetery. Plainly, the fort was the common centre for all these streets, and to its presence here, or its needs, one may safely attribute their origin without going farther back. The removal of building-stones, heavy guns, and materials of every description, from the shores to the fort, seems to point clearly enough to the origin of paved streets, without referring it to builders who could have had no use for such things, or whose existence is not even ascertained. One experiment of dragging an eighteen-pounder gun over a muddy road would probably convince the most incredulous person that by making the approaches to the fort practicable at all times, the builders were merely saving their own labor.

THE GRAVES.

So with the old cellar-holes found scattered about these streets. Their presence is fully accounted for in the story of the second siege. And the tenor of the orders issued in Sir Edmund Andros' time warrants the inference that the present street, leading from the fort toward New Harbor, was the only one then existing on this peninsula. The accumulation of earth above unused streets or pavements is something of too frequent occurrence to have any peculiar meaning in this particular place.

The little graveyard on the hill, behind the fort, the same on which Castin opened his trenches, contains little of interest that can be recovered. Only one stone of early date remains, and that has simply the initials I-M and date of 1695. This stone was noted by a curious visitor of 1710, who found Pemaquid the solitude its destroyers left it.

It is three good miles to the lighthouse at the Point, from which, when the sun is in the west, the houses on Monhegan may be seen distinctly.

---

[1] East Boothbay (Hodgdon's Mills) and South Bristol lie on opposite sides of the Damariscotta, about three miles from the sea. Four miles up we come to the battery on Fort Island, at the Narrows. Inner Heron, with its cottages, makes an excellent landmark for this river. The smelt run up in shoals in winter, making a fishery so profitable as sometimes to be worth fifteen thousand dollars in a season.

[2] July 4, 1682, Henry Josselyn laid out the town on Sheepscot River, "the ruins of which now remain, south of Sheepscot Bridge, in the town of Newcastle." These ruins are fully described in Vol. IV., "Maine Historical Society's Collections."

[3] Pemaquid is now the local name only for this part of Bristol, instead of being, as many have supposed, the corporate name of a township. The wide use made of the old historic name by the great public is, however, a striking example of the survival of the fittest, which legislators everywhere might take a hint from.

[4] Nahanada, with four others, was kidnapped in this vicinity by Weymouth. When he arrived at Plymouth, Sir Ferdinando Gorges, who was then governor of that place, summarily seized three, of whom Nahanada was one.

[5] One John Brown has usually been considered the first settler here, under an Indian purchase of 1625. Maverick, however, refers the settlement to Alderman Aldworth's people in 1625; but inasmuch as Shurte, Aldworth's agent, made oath in 1662 that he was not sent over until 1626, Maverick's memory was probably at fault here. (The patent to Aldworth did not issue until 1632.) Aside from this we think his statement is correct. Pemaquid was outside the grant and government of Gorges. At first the settlers lived without much law, and they get a very indifferent character from friend and foe alike. Bradford accuses them of selling guns to the Indians, trading with and giving intelligence to the French, etc. Josselyn speaks of them with scorn. In 1636 the ship *Angel Gabriel* was wrecked here while on her way to Boston with emigrants. Hubbard, 1676, says, "There have been for a long time seven or eight considerable dwellings about Pemaquid." The *Boxer* sailed out of Pemaquid harbor to meet the *Enterprise*, and the battle took place between Pemaquid Point and Monhegan, September, 1814.

[6] In 1664 Charles II. granted his brother James, Duke of York, all the territory between the Kennebec and Saint Croix rivers, except the small tract bounded east on Pemaquid River. It was styled Sagadahoc in the patent, but became familiarly known as the Duke's province. The next year a royal commission visited it, and attempted to settle a new form of civil government. They also gave the country the official name of Cornwall. Having nothing behind to support it, their work soon fell to the ground.

[7] By the provisions of the treaty of Saint Germain in 1632, and of Breda in 1667, under which Pentagoet (Castine) was given up to France.

[8] Mather's description is as follows: "William Henry was built of stone in a quadrangular figure, being about 737 foot in compass without the walls, and 108 foot square within the inner ones. Twenty-eight ports it had, and fourteen (if not eighteen) guns mounted, whereof six were eighteen-pounders. The wall on the south line, fronting to the sea, was twenty-two foot high, and more than six foot thick at the ports, which were eight foot from the ground. The greater flanker or round tower, at the western end of this line, was twelve foot high. The wall on the east line was twelve foot high, on the north it was ten, on the west it was eighteen." — *Decennium Luctuosum*.

[9] Nelson did not get back to New England for ten years. The author's story of "Captain Nelson" gives most of the leading events of his life. Nelson died at Boston in 1724. His descendants are among the first families of New England.

[10] David Dunbar laid out three towns, some say four, covering in whole or in part Boothbay, Bristol, and Waldoboro'. The power he assumed of re-granting lands, as if they were vacant, brought him into collision with the old proprietors whose rights were thus ignored. The matter was referred to the crown attorneys, who declared Dunbar's acts illegal. This put an end to the existence of the new province, and also to its claim to be outside the Massachusetts charter.

[11] Though it is claimed as a recent discovery, the pavement is mentioned by both Williamson, Vol. I. p. 57, and by Johnston, "Bristol and Pemaquid," p. 223.

OUT ON A LARK.

CHAPTER XVII.

THOMASTON, ROUND OWL'S HEAD.

Polonius. "Aboard, aboard, for shame!
The wind sits in the shoulder of your sail,
And you are stay'd for." — *Hamlet.*

AFTER witnessing the struggle going on at our coast resorts for what is bizarre or purely ornamental, it is a relief to walk about in the elm-shaded streets of a downright plain, old-fashioned country village, like Thomaston, once more, where picturesqueness is achieved by simply letting things alone. It quite restores the old home feeling again. And we feel it a privilege to become a brief part of that tranquil existence, and to share in its historic memories.

Thomaston[1] is the still vigorous mother of a still more vigorous offspring. Rockland and South Thomaston are ribs taken from her side. Seated at one corner of the broad Penobscot, with half a dozen harbors in her lap, with her head reclining on a pillow of mountains and her feet in the sea, what is the wonder that the searching eyes of the early traders turned to this spot as if by instinct?

To this cause we owe that succession of events which, together, make up the checkered history of this slumberous old sea-place.

It was in some dingy old counting-house of London or Bristol that the plan first took shape. It seems that one Edward Ashley, an adventurer, who had been in New England, and whom Bradford calls a "profane young man," though allowing him "wit and abilite enough" for the business in hand, had somehow induced two wealthy English merchants, called Beauchamp and

Leverett, to take out a patent for all the territory lying between the Penobscot and Muscongus rivers, with the view of setting Ashley up in a trading business there, in opposition to the Pilgrims.

Behind Ashley was the shrewd, scheming, restless, if not unprincipled, Allerton, the originator of the scheme, whom the Pilgrims more than suspected of turning his trust as their agent to his private account, though for the present they kept their suspicions to themselves. When all was ready to go on without them, the Pilgrims were offered a partnership. It was a home-thrust at their monopoly, because this Indian trade was their main reliance for paying off what they owed in England, and they were heavily in debt there; so it caused them to make many wry faces to see how they had been overreached in the house of their friends: still, rather than be shut out from all the Penobscot region, the Pilgrims swallowed their medicine, but they prudently sent a man of their own to keep an eye on Ashley.[2]

This was the origin of the celebrated Muscongus patent, which, after passing through many hands, finally fell into those of General Knox, of Revolutionary fame, whose wife inherited certain rights from her grandfather, Waldo.[3]

General Waldo was making progress toward peopling his lands with settlers, — some from Ireland, some from Germany, and some from the older New England settlements, — when his sudden death removed the guiding hand. When the Revolution broke out, Waldo's heirs became political refugees, with the exception of this granddaughter, who had married young Knox against the wishes of her family, though by so doing she eventually preserved her rights in the Maine estates. Samuel Waldo's name is, however, stamped upon the tract in that part of the county formed from it.

Knox came to Thomaston after the war, purposing, it would seem, to take up the work that his wife's grandfather had left unfinished, to lead the life of a country gentleman, who, after many years devoted to the service of the public, found he had yet his own fortune to make. Though humbly born and reared, his military life, no less than the influence of a woman of birth and breeding so near to him as his wife, with a will stronger than his own, and much keener perceptions of human nature, had changed the young and ardent republican of 1775 into a man of aristocratic feelings, aspirations, and tastes, in 1795; so that Knox looked forward as much, perhaps, to living after the manner of the great landed gentry of England, as he did to becoming the source of all prosperity to his tenants; and this too with a people whose hatred for aristocracy in all its forms was the legitimate outgrowth of the war. So landlord and tenant met on rather debatable ground. Still, the ex-general was a man of such unfailing *bonhomie* that he soon won over most of his agrarian tenants, by the simple, straightforward honesty of his character and the magnetism of his presence.

Then, again, Knox must have looked forward to a life of retirement, even when so nearly akin to exile, with the natural longing of a man who is thoroughly sick of all the strifes and cares of office; else it is hard to account for his voluntary withdrawal from all society, which a residence at Thomaston implied. But to Mrs. Knox, the woman of fashion, the leader and oracle of Washington's drawing-rooms, the sparkling and witty support to a somewhat slow and heavy, but honest and lovable, husband, the change must have seemed nothing short of banishment.

But Knox had saved nothing in the army; he was a poor man when he laid down the portfolio of war, a family was growing up about him, and his Utopia held out hopes of a colossal fortune. So Knox, the man whom the grave Washington distinguished by his personal friendship, and Mrs. Knox, the fine lady of Washington's republican court, buried themselves in the seclusion of a

MONTPELIER, GENERAL KNOX'S MANSION-HOUSE.

frontier village. Knox began building here, in 1793, a mansion corresponding with his ideas of what a country gentleman's home should be, which, when completed, he called Montpelier. Local tradition would make it out a palace; but it seems to have been rather substantial than elegant, like the general himself. It was two stories high above the basement, with an upper half-story rising from the roof, designed, perhaps, for a lookout over the sea, a distant view of which the house finely commanded. It had a bow-front, with balconies running quite round the outside of the whole house, thus setting off the rather plain exterior, as well as allowing the inmates an extensive and secluded promenade in bad weather. To the country folk it was doubtless a wonder of wonders.

Knox was a whole-hearted, upright gentleman as ever lived, but he was not a man of business. His grand schemes for enriching himself, and of performing the duties of a public benefactor at the same time, proved a Pandora's box, out of which swarmed more misfortunes than he had ever dreamed of. He did,

PORT CLYDE.

however, start a veritable boom. He set up brick-yards, saw-mills, and lime-kilns; built houses, vessels, and dams; in short, set going a prosperity as short-lived as it was fallacious, because much of the outlay was sunk in unprofitable or useless schemes, or because it cost Knox more to make a cask of lime than it was worth in the market. He ran deeply in debt and became a bankrupt, his best friends being also his largest creditors.

So instead of the life of ease that Knox's imagination had pictured to him, he found his later years oppressed by a load of debt which, however manfully he might strive, could not be lifted off. In a little more than eleven years after he passed the threshold of his new home, full of life and hope, he was carried out over it in his coffin, a broken-hearted man.

The mansion was pulled down many years ago. Hawthorne describes it briefly as "a large, rusty-looking edifice of wood, with some grandeur in the architecture, standing on the banks of the river, close by the site of an old burial-ground, and near where an ancient fort had been erected as a defence against the French and Indians.[4] It is not forty years since this house was built, and Knox was in his glory; but now the house is all in decay, while within a stone's throw of it there is a street of smart edifices of one and two stories, occupied by thriving mechanics, which has been laid out where Knox meant to have forests and parks. On the banks of the river, where he intended to have only one wharf for his own West Indian vessels and yacht, there are two wharves with stores and a lime-kiln. Little appertains to the mansion except the tomb and the old burial-ground and the old fort."

GENERAL KNOX'S MONUMENT.

The family vault referred to was only a few rods east of the mansion. This is also described as "a spacious receptacle, an iron door at the end of a turf-covered mound, and surmounted by an obelisk of marble." The remains and obelisk were long since removed to the cemetery on the hill back of the village.

One hardly knows whether to laugh or cry over these evidences of the fluctuations of human prosperity. No demand of progress hastened the downfall of the old house that was once the envy and admiration of all the country round. A more sorry example of uncalled-for demolition could hardly be imagined. No one seems to know just why it was pulled down; its site is to this day unoccupied, save by one small frame dwelling and by the nameless odds and ends pertaining to the neighboring shipyard. Two of the outbuildings remain. One was the general's stable; the other was occupied by his servants. The stable was converted into a grist-mill; the offices, into a railway station. One old elm hangs its head in shame over the wreck of its former splendid surroundings, to which, indeed, it is the dumb witness and solitary mourner.

From this spot one looks straight down and out of the Saint George's to the twinkling, drowsy sea. Though quite broad here, at low tide the river shrinks to a thin, serpentine streak of water, winding through a muddy bed like molten silver in a mould of clay. This channel touches the shore only a few hundred feet away from the site of the old mansion. It then bends sharply to the west, and is soon lost sight of among the trees. On this commanding ground the first settlers built their block-house, with a covered way leading down to the waterside. It had been the scene of many a stubborn conflict, many a desperate onslaught and stern repulse.

Not without long search did I succeed in finding the little shabby monument standing on the spot to which General Knox's remains were finally removed, and if report speaks truly, without more show of respect than would be paid to those of a pauper.

The situation of this cemetery, with the mountains rising green and smiling behind it, the sea and shores stretched out crisp and sparkling beneath it, is beautiful indeed. But alas! the utter neglect which surrounds the last resting-place of such a man as Knox is enough to strip the landscape of its charm, the hallowed earth of its consecration. One side of the iron fence enclosing it was so broken down that the little burial plot could be entered at will. The grass was green, tall, and rank about the little shaft which recorded the name and virtues of this great man.[5] One side simply reads: —

The Tomb
of
Major General
H. Knox,
who died
Oct'r 25th, 1806;
aged 56 years.

'Tis fates decree, farewell thy just renown
The hero's honor & the good man's crown.

OWL'S HEAD, PENOBSCOT BAY.

For me these lines had a very satirical meaning indeed. Could it be true that this was the grave of that daring soldier, that invincible spirit, who forced the passage of the ice-blocked Delaware with his guns, who stemmed the tide of disaster at Monmouth, and who fired the last shot at Yorktown?

"He sleeps his last sleep; he has fought his last battle."

While sauntering among the monuments in the adjoining ground, my eye fell on a massive cenotaph of gray granite standing near the principal walk. The cap-stone bore the name of Jonathan Cilley on one of its faces,— not a word more. Yet this dumb stone has its sad story, too. Shall I break the silence it seems enjoining? Cilley, the grandson of a brave officer of the Revolution, fell in a duel with Graves, a Kentuckian, and a member of the same Congress with his victim, in February, 1838. They fought at Bladensburg with rifles, Cilley falling at the third fire. He had no quarrel at all with Graves, but his having declined to accept a challenge from James Watson Webb was resented by Graves, the bearer of it, who immediately challenged Cilley himself. This monument was raised to Cilley's memory by the contributions of his friends. Its silence aptly commemorates a life thrown away without any advantage.

It was here in Thomaston that General Peleg Wadsworth, while acting as military commandant without troops, was taken prisoner by the British, one cold February night in the year 1781, and carried off to Castine in triumph. The sentinel at the door had only time to challenge before the enemy rushed in and disarmed him. They then assaulted the house. The stout old general, who had jumped out of bed in his shirt, fought hand to hand with his assailants until a shot through the arm put him *hors de combat*, when he gave himself up.

From Thomaston it is only four miles across land to Rockland, while by water it is forty.

The longest way round is, however, always the shortest way out in these pleasant excursions of ours. In passing out of the Saint George's we leave Cushing[6] on our right and Saint George[7] at our left, soon again to be lost among the multitude of islands, great and small, with which the sea about us seems literally sowed. After getting clear of the Saint George's, and passing Port Clyde, our course lies between Metinic and the main, past Tennant's Harbor, known by its light, thence up to Whitehead Island and light, an important landmark situated in the gate to that maze of rocks, islands, and reefs known as the Mussel-Ridges.

Whitehead is considered to be the western entrance to Penobscot Bay. It is not large, but stands up high from the water, and is readily distinguished by its white cliffs and tall lighthouse, first built in 1803.

And now we are threading our way through the intricate Mussel-Ridge channel, where dangerous reefs protrude at every turn and on every side. It was one of these, just off Ash Island, so aptly called the Grindstone, that the steamer *City of Portland* went on at full speed some years ago, just at daybreak, and then and there ended her voyage. Her pilot had shaved the ledge just a little too closely. By great good luck, however, her headway carried her so far up on the ledge that, notwithstanding there was a bad sea running, the rocks held her fast, so that the passengers were taken off, much frightened, but without loss of life. Steamers often come into this crooked passage to avoid the rough water making outside the islands; yet unless every precaution is used in running the various courses from mark to mark, or from buoy to buoy, the deviation of a single fathom from the true channel means the loss of the vessel. If she had gone clear of the Grindstone, in less that five minutes the *City of Portland* would have been in deep water again.

A short run from Ash Island brings us out into the narrow passage opening between Sheep Island and Monroe's Island, and up with Owl's Head, — a name as old as the Indian wars, — a promontory familiarly known to all who have sailed these seas. Champlain says its Indian name was Bedabec. Smith says it was Mecadacut. The sleepy little lighthouse lends a peculiar appropriateness by day to its present designation.

Owl's Head ushers us at once upon a scene almost too beautiful to profane with speech when we are looking at it, impossible to find language to do it justice when memory would summon it before us again. Our pencil is no talisman. One shrinks from the attempt to reproduce the charm of life and color, its rich warmth and glow, its exquisite modulations, its masterful breadth, with our cold, lifeless imitation sketch.

Out there in the distance are the Camden Hills with the morning mists still clinging about their sunburnt flanks. One by one they slowly rise and soar away. Over all stands aged Megunticook warming his broad back in the sun. How the old fellow scowls when some truant cloud comes between it and him! Long leagues of grayish-green shores, streaked with soft sunshine, stretch on beyond the leagues of lustrous, cool gray water. Impalpable shapes rise out of the distant sea. Indistinguishable sounds are borne to us by the warm breezes from off the land. The shores glide by; the waves purr soothingly along the beaches. A shriek startles us! We look up, to see a city drawn up at the water's edge. We have been dreaming, and the dream is over.

Rockland [8] has a fairly good harbor, or will have one when the breakwater now being built out from its northeast point shall be completed. In old times it was Owl's Head Bay. The city itself is, as we have said, an offshoot of old Thomaston. No longer ago than the beginning of the century it went by the ambiguous name of "The Shore," not yet having attained even to the dignity of a village; later on it was known as East Thomaston. Ship-building and lime-burning have since brought it up step by step to its present prominence, so that Rockland lime is now known the wide world over.

There is not much here, I am free to say, that would be likely to detain the visitor.

One's curiosity touching the process of converting the native rock into lime is soon satisfied. It is a very simple matter. The business itself gives a certain unkempt, smoky, and barbaric appearance to the water-front, which is not

MATINICUS LIGHTS, PENOBSCOT BAY.

materially lessened until one gets back out of the grime and smoke of the lime-kilns. One feels, however, a certain pride in a seaport which is both self-creative and self-sustaining, as against those marts of trade which serve merely as storehouses for taking in and putting out other people's merchandise. We are told that General Knox's favorite toast — and he was a lime-burner himself — used to be, "A hoop to the barrel!" - In Rockland it should be, we think, "Cement to the Union!"

As we have now entered Penobscot Bay, we should not omit to speak of Matinicus, its lonely outpost and beacon. This island lies seventeen miles out, in the open ocean, southeast from Owl's Head. It has already had mention as one of the outer range of coast-lights. With seven other islands and rocks clustered around, it forms a local or "plantation" government, which is believed to be the most remote from land of any on our whole coast. Ragged Island, Matinicus Rock, Wooden Ball, Seal Rock, and No Man's Land are the others that have names. Matinicus is wholly inhabited by fishermen. Its insular character is perhaps a little more pronounced even than that of Monhegan; but the same general features, either as respects the people or their island, are common to both. For a long time the people came near realizing the golden world of the old writers; for they had neither laws nor rulers, nor did they ever vote in public affairs, and still lived happily. The tax-gatherer did not trouble them. Remains of stone houses are found on Matinicus, whose builders are unknown. They belong, doubtless, to the lost chapter of the earliest fisheries and fishing-stations. These islands are a bad place for wrecks. The schooner *Ida Grover* struck on Seal Rock and went to pieces in January of the present year, the crew scaling the cliff, where they struck, with difficulty.

The direct route to Mount Desert now passes, first, through the Fox Islands Thoroughfare, or between Vinal Haven, celebrated for its extensive granite quarries, and North Haven. Vinal Haven lies about midway of the entrance into Penobscot Bay, fifteen miles from Rockland. There are several good harbors in the Thoroughfare, besides Carver's, at the southern end, where the principal village is located. The route then crosses open water to coast the south side of Deer Isle, Mark Island Light being the landmark to the intricate passage through the multitude of islands cropping out on every hand between Deer Isle and Isle au Haut. At Green's Landing there are more quarries, and from here a road crosses over to the north shore at the Eggemoggin Reach. From Green's Landing the route leads on and out into Blue Hill Bay, meeting there that coming down through the Reach. Navigation among all these islands is extremely hazardous, even to the most skilful pilots, when the marks are shut out by fog.

---

[1] Thomaston is named for General John Thomas, who died while leading our army of invasion in Canada in 1775. He was a soldier of whom much was expected.

[2] The story is too long for a clear explanation in a few words. It came near causing an

open rupture between the Pilgrims and their English partners, and did bring about one with Allerton. See Bradford, p. 257 *et seq.*

[3] General Samuel Waldo, a merchant of Boston and comrade of Sir William Pepperell at Louisburg. His daughter Hannah married Crown Secretary Flucker, whose daughter Lucy married Knox. Waldo acquired a controlling interest in the patent through his efforts to have Dunbar set aside (see preceding chapter). He brought over German and Scotch-Irish emigrants, started the manufacture of lime, built saw-mills, etc. His death occurred in 1759, while he was in the act of pointing out the boundary of his lands to Governor Pownall. He was buried with military honors at Fort Point, but subsequently taken to Boston for final interment.

[4] The first defences were destroyed in Philip's War ; the next were raised in 1719-20 by the proprietors. " At this period there was not a house between Georgetown and Annapolis, N.S., except a fish-house on Damariscove Island." — WILLIAMSON, II. 97. The Indians strongly protested against building a fort here, and yielded only to necessity.

[5] As I write this, an effort is making to have the general government erect a suitable monument to this gallant soldier.

[6] Cushing had its first incorporation in 1789, and has just celebrated its centennial. It was named for Thomas Cushing, a Revolutionary patriot, who obtained the honor of a special notice from Sam Johnson in "Taxation no Tyranny." He was a member of the Old Congress, and lieutenant-governor of Massachusetts. The town was first settled by Waldo's Scotch-Irish emigrants.

[7] This township fortunately retains the name given by its first discoverers, who displayed the national spirit. It is thus identified with that interesting period when to take possession of a continent it was only necessary to set up a cross.

[8] The manufacture of lime was begun at Thomaston by Samuel Waldo, near where the State Prison now stands. — EATON's *Thomaston.* At Dix Island the manufacture of granite is carried on quite largely.

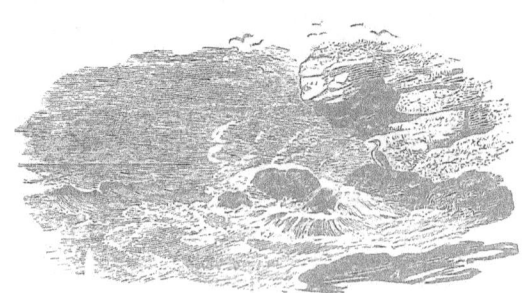

THE EAST COAST.

MORIONS OF THE DISCOVERY PERIOD.

CHAPTER XVIII.

A VOYAGE TO NORUMBEGA.

"Now from the North
Of Norumbega and the Samoed Shore,
Bursting their brazen dungeons, armed with ice." — MILTON.

WE crave the reader's indulgence for a brief season, while we turn aside from the beaten paths of modern travel into the still obscure routes of the old discoverers.

At last we are sailing in the famed waters of the ancient Norumbega,[1] its fabulous city and people, of whom old writers have so much to say, and modern writers say so little that is to the point. At last we are following in the track of sailors who lived before the Pilgrims were born, or Milton had penned his fine figure in "Paradise Lost," affixed to the beginning of this chapter.

Nothing is easier than to unsettle history. And everybody who breaks down an old tradition nowadays is said to have performed a peculiar service to history.

We will, however, venture to sail on in the well-marked channel of our earliest faith and our latest convictions. Champlain bluntly says of the Penobscot, "Now this must of necessity be the Norumbegue." No man knew better than he all the relations, all the traditions, concerning it. We accept him, therefore, for our pilot, the rather because he knows how to separate the true from the false, the actual from the fictitious.

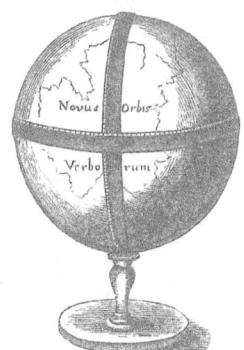

DAWN OF DISCOVERY.

There is little room to doubt that the unknown and unsung fishermen of Normandy, Brittany, and the Biscay provinces led the way into our waters, precisely as the hunters and trappers of our own great plains made paths for the so-called explorers to follow in, — the difference being that the actual discoverers kept no journals, and had no friends at court to sound their praises abroad. No sooner was it noised about that an English ship had been to a new world in the west, where fish swam about so thickly that she could scarce plough her way through them, than these Normans of Dieppe were most concerned lest their restless neighbors of Saint Malo, or those rascally Basques, whose jargon the foul fiend himself could not understand, should get the start of them. They asked for neither royal patent nor commission, charts nor soundings. A fair wind and plenty of it, a free field and no favors, were the sum of their desires.

Those old voyages of discovery in which Spanish, Portuguese, and English took part are about the most romantic episodes in our history. There is so much of the spirit of true adventure embodied in the act of hoisting sail for an undiscovered country; so much of noble emulation in the resolve to plant the flag of one's own nation before all others! And then the interest is so much heightened by the knowledge that a navigator was now and then killed and eaten!

SAMUEL CHAMPLAIN.

First comes Jean Parmentier, of Dieppe, in Normandy, the "great sea captain" of Ramusio, who has printed in his superb collection a manuscript dated in 1539, and attributed to Parmentier, in which the name of Norumbega is first mentioned in any printed work that has yet come to light. The writer of the memoir, whether it be Parmentier himself or his admiring friend and comrade, Pierre Crignon, says that Norumbega was discovered by Verrazano, who took possession of it in the name of the king, Francis I., and of the regent, Louise de Savoy, Duchess of Angoulême, and mother of the king. Napoleon said of her that she was the only man of her family. The memoir, or relation, further asserts that Norumbega was the name by which the natives called their country. There is a very curious map accompanying it, and the voyage to which it refers must have followed close upon Verrazano's, of 1524, as Parmentier died at sea in 1529.

A VOYAGE TO NORUMBEGA.

Jean Alfonse, called the Saintongeois, was contemporary with Verrazano, Parmentier, and Cartier, whose discoveries he would seem to have been desirous of emulating. His surname of Saintongeois identifies him with that fruitful old province in the west of France, that in later times gave De Monts and Champlain to the cause of American colonization.

Our judgment of Alfonse is based largely upon the verdict of writers of his time. The sonnets and other eulogistic verse addressed to him bear witness to our day how high "Ce gentil capitaine de mer" stood in the popular esteem. So also to these performances we owe about all we know, or are likely to know, of Alfonse's life, through the scanty scraps of personal history, thrown in at hazard, and to which, no doubt, the poet himself attached the least importance.

Besides these poetical effusions, of which he is the subject, Alfonse has left a manuscript "*cosmography,*" composed or dictated by himself, bearing date in

SAINT MALO.

1545, which, no doubt, served as the foundation for the very rare and curious little volume, edited by a strange hand, and printed in 1559, with the title "Voyages Aventureux du Capitaine Jean Alphonse Saintongeois." Its publication is due to Saint-Gelais and Jean de Marnef.

When Roberval followed Cartier to Canada, as the king's viceroy, Alfonse was master-pilot of the expedition. In the cosmography referred to he asserts that he had been into a bay as far as the 42d degree, lying between Norumbega and Florida; but not having searched it to the bottom, he could not well say whether this bay joined Norumbega with Florida or not. After describing the cape and river of Norumbega, Alfonse goes on to say that "up the said river, fifteen leagues, there is a town which is called Norombegue, and there is in it a good people, and they have many peltries of many kinds of furs." The inhabitants, he tells us, were dusky.

Alfonse may well be pardoned some exaggerations, and even inconsistencies, for the sake of the truths he has told. It was a credulous age, in which the fabulous held full sway. What is certain is, that Alfonse's descriptions, or delineations, of the coast itself enabled subsequent explorers, like Champlain, to identify the river of Norumbega with the Penobscot. So long as Alfonse sticks to his rôle of pilot, one may follow him without misgiving; when he attempts going up rivers and exploring the country, he is all at sea. In the

ANDRE THEVET.

words of the witty editor of "Hudibras," "Cosmographers, in their descriptions of the world, when they find many vast places of which they know nothing, are used to fill the same with an account of Indian plantations, strange birds, beasts, etc." It is to be observed that while our modern historians put aside such things with one hand, as all idle tales, they invariably set them down with the other to enliven their pages. But these stories of demons, mermen, sea-serpents, and other monsters are like the wine formerly served out at funerals; they help to reconcile us to the decrees of Providence.

Place for André Thevét, Angoumois, the chaplain of Catherine de Medicis, the companion of Villegagnon in his voyage of 1555, to Brazil, and author of a cosmography written in the spirit of the time; that is to say, quite as destitute of science as of philosophy!

It is not improper to scan this writer's credentials a little. "He was of an excessive credulity," says M. Weiss; to which Larousse adds, "To-day the 'Voyages of Thévet,' placed in the rank of those of Marc Lescarbot, and become rare, are regarded only as drolleries, everywhere full of humor." And again, "He speaks only after the home-made tales of sailors or passengers, who often amused themselves at his expense."

The ship in which Thevét took passage home to France ran up the coast as

A VOYAGE TO NORUMBEGA.

far as Newfoundland, or "Baccalaos," as it was oftener called by sailors. After speaking of Florida, Thevét goes on to say that "one of the finest rivers in the whole world presents itself, which we call Norembegue, and the natives Agoncy, and which is marked on some charts as the Grand River. Several other beautiful rivers enter into it; and upon its banks the French formerly erected a little fort, about ten or twelve leagues from its mouth, which was surrounded by fresh water, and this place was called the Fort of Norumbegue."

Notwithstanding Thevét has been hitherto classed with those who lie not wisely, but too well, his account of the more pronounced features of Penobscot Bay is sufficiently accurate to disarm criticism with respect to much more that is either downright nonsense or bold invention. One thing, however, Thevét has said before any one else. He was the very first person to formulate the name of New England. In speaking of Cabot's voyage, in his "Singularitez de la France Antartique," Thevét remarks that the English navigator purposed going to America "to people the country with new inhabitants and to establish there a New England."

Proofs crowd upon us that Norumbega was, first of all, a region of unlimited extent, reaching from Cape Breton to Florida, next contracted so as to embrace what are now New England and Nova Scotia, and finally to the territory comprised between the Kennebec and Saint John, but always covering the greater part of Maine. With the scant aid of what was taken down from the lips of roving sailors, the map-makers of the sixteenth century continued to rectify from time to time our rude coast line, or embellish their parchments with drawings

> "Of all those beasts, and fish, and fowl,
> With which, like Indian plantations,
> The learned stock the constellations."

But Champlain was the first to destroy the prevailing delusion, under which he himself had labored, touching this great river of Norumbega. It is to him we owe our first accurate account of its coasts and people. The name that had so long held a place on the maps, or in the old relations, like that of the Great American Desert of our own time, for instance, — our much-vaunted time, — vanished with the illusions of which it was an inseparable part. And with Champlain, Dame History, now sure of her ground, marches complacently on over a well-lighted route.

---

[1] Doubts have been raised as to whether the Penobscot is the true Norumbega of Verrazano, Parmentier, Rut, Alfonse, Thevét, Sir H. Gilbert, and others. Like a good many historical questions upon which opinion has become settled, this one has lately been re-opened, and all the old evidence submitted to new tests and new arguments, designed to overturn the old belief and install the new. A careful collation of this evidence makes one of the strongest presumptive cases in favor of the Penobscot I have ever known. So far as its location is concerned, Norumbega is the one initial point on the North Atlantic coast, about which the early map-makers are all agreed, which we readily identify, and to which subsequent and better

delineation of the coast, as discovery extended itself, is but the better shaping out of the crude original. The inference is irresistible that Newfoundland, with the Gulf of Saint Lawrence, and its contiguous coasts of Cape Breton and Nova Scotia, was the pivot of geographical development in this quarter. And the history of the fisheries shows how this state of things came about.

Assuming that "Norumbega" must of necessity be a word of native origin, it has been urged that it should be applied according to the genius of aboriginal tongues; that is to say, to some marked geographical feature, or some peculiar means of identification, rather than to a country. It would seem to concern us more to know what the name stood for with navigators and cosmographers of the time, than what we may think it ought to mean at the present day. On all the earliest maps Norumbega is always a country. The evidence offered that "Norumbega" is Indian is at most inconclusive. Both Hakluyt and Thevét assert that it is not Indian. The concluding syllable, as written by French authorities, means a stammerer. Attention is also called to the name of the city of Nuremberg, in Bavaria, which takes in Spanish the form of Nuromberga, and in Latin and Italian that of Norimberga. On Ruscelli's map of 1561, the name Nurumberg is, in fact, attached to the region in question.

THE ROCKLAND STAGE.

CHAPTER XIX.

PENOBSCOT BAY AND ITS MOUNTAIN COASTS.

<blockquote>
"And like a lobster boil'd, the morn
From black to red began to turn." — BUTLER.
</blockquote>

THE history of our most famous watering-places would be no bad abstract and brief chronicle of the advance the nation is making in wealth and refinement, in improved means of locomotion, in the breaking down of sectional barriers, or of that peculiar trait of the national character which makes the American the greatest traveller on earth.

Many of us can remember when Nahant and Newport were the two fashionable watering-places *par excellence* of the New England coast, when steamships crossed the ocean but twice a month, and when a journey by rail was an epoch in a man's life.

Such comparisons enable us fairly to appreciate the narrow limits in which our grandfathers and grandmothers moved about in quest of those recreations which have become a second nature to their descendants, and they also prepare us for the equally limited knowledge concerning those things lying outside of that narrow circle in which our elders travelled year in, year out. Old fashions hold their own much better than old ways of travel. Directoire bonnets, short waists, long gloves, and reticules come round again, at stated periods, like the comets; but the canal-boat and stage-coach in which our grandams and grandsires made their summer jaunts to Newport or Ballston Spa have finally gone down the coasts of time to return no more.

Under the old régime, be it said, fashion followed the dictum of certain leaders, with the passive obedience of a subject who feels himself bound to uphold the prerogative of his master at all hazards.

Mr. N. P. Willis, who was the uncrowned autocrat of the fashionable world of his day, — and his day seems but yesterday to some of us, — coldly sets down the following dictum touching our delectable eastern coast. It is well worth reproducing as one of the curiosities of literature, though it does seem just a trifle odd that Willis, the traveller, should have known so much about the Oberland and the Engadine, and so little about the region where he was born. Hear him : —

"Very much the same sort of incredulity with which one reads a traveller's account of the deliciousness of the Russian summer comes over him (*malgré* all the information to the contrary) when it is proposed to him to admire anything so near the cradle of the east wind as the Penobscot River; . . . in point of fact, when Penobscot River is mentioned, we shudder at our remembrance of the acrid blasts that have swept over us from that quarter, and image the scenery forth-drest in the drapery so well described by the captain of a Penobscot whaler, — a fog so thick that having driven his jack-knife into it on the eve of sailing for the Pacific, he found it sticking in the same spot on his return from a three years' cruise."

Now it is quite safe to say that when Willis shuddered, all the world of fashion shuddered, too; nor can we wonder that his illustrative witticism should have given the finishing stroke, so to speak, to that bleak "cradle of east winds," in which he himself had been rocked, as it went the rounds of the drawing-rooms, albeit the jest itself had already made several voyages round Cape Horn.

It took years, however, for our eastern coast to live down a slander emanating from such high authority, and consigning it so definitely to the limbo of waste places. But as the lamented Bryant has said, —

"Truth crushed to earth will rise again" :

so we have lived to see the blighting prophecy return to plague its inventors.

All this time we have been seeing the nine miles of shore extending between Camden and Rockland glide swiftly by us. And what a shore it is! Above us the Camden Mountains stand for a landmark at the western portal of Penobscot Bay, very much as the Mount Desert range does at the eastern portal, and all between them of bays, harbors, islands, or sounds must, at no distant day, become the summer home of thousands of those people who sensibly carry their home life along with them. We have now no class so unappreciative as not to demand something of the picturesque in their surroundings. And where shall these conditions be looked for if not in this always charming bay?

PUMPKIN ISLAND, PENOBSCOT BAY.

Not only is Penobscot Bay in a certain sense the distinguishing geographical feature of the whole Maine coast, but we have seen that it is equally notable for the wealth of its historical associations, which go far back into the dim twilight of discovery and exploration, and have come down to us spiced with all the romance of a wonder-loving age.

Taken as a whole, the scenic features of this bay are graceful rather than bold, suggestive of calm rather than riotous commotion. You will not see the full play of ocean as you would along the more exposed coasts, or find here those long levels of gleaming sand that echo to the mighty tread of the free Atlantic; but you will always have green islands, noble mountains, and inviting harbors on every hand — the sea shorn of its terrors, the land divested of its harsh and hideous features.

THE CAMDEN MOUNTAINS.

The north shore, when one has passed out of Rockland Harbor, shows unmistakable signs of a stimulant growth. The new resort at Bay Point is especially noticeable. One falls over head and ears in love with these velvety undulations of smooth shore land, after seeing the long leagues of unsightly ledges that tear their way through the thin crust of soil. Here all is sunny and green quite down to the water's edge. Trees grow, flowers bloom, and gardens and groves proclaim a more genial climate; nor are we insensible to the change from the rasping breezes of the open sea to the softer and more gentle winds that come off the land.

We first look into Rockport,[1] an out-village of Camden, where lime-quarrying and lime-burning is extensively carried on. There is a strong dash of picturesqueness about this village, in the haphazard way that the houses are perched one above another all along the gorge dividing it, and the life and animation given to it by the stream that comes tumbling down this gorge.

But come with me now, gracious reader, to the mountains that loom so grandly over yonder wooded point. We are going to enter upon an entirely new experience. Long enough they have played at hide-and-seek with us om afar. To-day we lay claim to a closer companionship.

ROCKPORT BASIN, LOOKING TOWARD OWL'S HEAD.

Camden Harbor[2] is finely locked in between two jutting points of land, one high, the other low, with a pretty little wooded island deftly dropped in at the entrance. Negro Island is its name. The harbor light stands on this island. Back of this, the mountains rise so near at hand that the village spires are thrown up against them in strong relief, though both houses and steeples are diminished to the size of toys by the bulging and overhanging mass of Mount Battie, which lifts its bare, bluish gray crags hundreds of feet above them all. It is North Conway among the hills again; it is Camden by the sea.

The village clusters mostly about the head of the harbor, where the business centre is located, ships are built, and lime burned; but it also follows the course of the curving shores, or stretches along the breezy mountain sides, or goes back into the pretty and secluded valleys behind them, where there are so many picturesque spots. Its old life drew it toward the country; its new draws it back toward the sea. A Camden shopkeeper sits in his door, and looks out upon the vessels constantly passing and repassing the harbor, quite as a city man would at the splendid turnouts of his avenue at home, only this highway is broader, perfectly noiseless, and never gets out of repair. Sails bathed in sunshine look like cloth of gold; masts and ropes, like cobwebs borne along by the breeze.

Some very fine vessels have been built at Bean's shipyard here; among others the *Millie G. Bowne*, a four-masted schooner, and the largest one of her class ever launched in Maine up to the time she was set afloat; but her career was short, for she was lost in a hurricane at sea while on her first voyage.

Camden is one of the later aspirants

IN BEAN'S SHIPYARDS.

HEAD OF THE HARBOR.

for public favor. One cannot help remarking the capabilities of the place in this direction, let him be ever so devoted a lover of the wilder aspects of the open coast. The mountains give to Camden a distinction all its own. There is a wondrous fascination about mountains; an endless charm in the sea. Where both are to be had in a single locality, the *ne plus ultra* of one's desires in this direction would seem to be realized.

Megunticook[3] is the principal summit. Making the ascent is not difficult enough to deter even the most timid climber. It begins with a promenade, and ends in a scramble, which continues, however, for a few hundred feet only. For half the way we walked on, quite at our ease, through a grass-grown forest road, guided by the course of a brook that came tumbling down the mountain's flank. Here the gay spirits of the climbers, whose picturesque costumes gave a most enlivening effect to the dark green of the woods, frequently broke forth in snatches of song, which would be taken up all along the route, and echoed back by the mountain itself. The impulsive ones dashed forward with disdainful looks at their slower companions; the more discreet saved themselves for the tussle they knew was only deferred. In this manner, the procession gradually elongated itself in proportion as the ascent grew steeper, until one could see a little knot here, toiling up the highest crags, or a straggler there, stopping to take breath, while admiring the constantly enlarging view. Our advanced detachment was, I grieve to say, near being routed by a devil's darning-needle that whizzed through them like a rifle-bullet, causing a disorderly retreat to begin upon the reserves. It was solemnly declared, by way of excuse, that if one flew in your face, it would sew up your eyes with its needle. Poor harmless dragon-fly, with your baboon's face and great goggle-eyes, how much appearances are against you!

But what a delicious panorama is that the summit unfolds! And how soon all fatigue was forgotten in the majesty of the scene spread out beneath us! Fifteen hundred feet below lay island-studded bay and blue-vaulted ocean: bay and ocean all one great ruffled plain of sparkling topaz, strewn about with islands of emerald, set in necklaces of foam; islands upon islands, from gray Monhegan to dim Mount Desert; shores dotted with villages and farms from smoky Rockland to drowsy Castine; ponds sparkling like gems among the crowding woods; the land rolling back into the shaggy north, streaked with brightness where some cleared spot let in the sunshine, or some lake gleamed out of its shadow and gloom, but all dark and sad where the forest lifts its huge billows against the horizon in such marked contrast with the ocean behind us. And last, but not least, beyond all, yet over all, there stood misty Katahdin and there the great White Mountains, at the east and the west, diminished by distance to such little clumps of tents or mounds that one scarce believed Megunticook was only a large hill by comparison.

FORT KNOX, BUCKSPORT, MAINE.

The western side of Megunticook is broken down many hundred feet in precipitous cliffs, washed at their feet by Megunticook Lake, a beautiful sheet of water, from which a clear stream flows out through the village into the harbor. From Camden, one may drive around the base of these cliffs and by the shores of this lake, so making the circuit of Megunticook, to the bay shore again; and the lake itself is becoming a favorite resort for all summer residents.

Thus Camden has its secret nooks as well as its fair and open expanses of blue water. The drives along the shores of the bay, either southward as far as Rockland or northward as far as Belfast, are scarcely equalled in the whole range of coast.

I saw one other feature here at Camden as noticeable as it is rare, and as agreeable as it was unlooked for. Quite a large part of Sherman's Point — the one reaching round the north side of the harbor — is covered with a plantation of oaks, — great stately

EVENING IN THE HARBOR.

trees of antique growth and noble girth, where one looks for some stray stag to break through the thicket, or hear the huntsman wind his horn. One can never quite divest our forests of pine and fir of a certain funereal feeling, so responsive are we to the force of association; but these brave old oaks, the sturdy type of a sturdy race, charm us with memories of Nicholas Poussin's bacchanalian revels, of Robin Hood's Merry Men, or of the Druids' mystic rites.

I was not a little surprised to find these groves occupied by students or graduates of the Castine Normal School, who had been in the habit of pitching their summer camp here for many years. When I asked them why they deserted their own favored locality, which so many consider the *ultima Thule* of summer resorts, I received the characteristic reply that there was such a thing as knowing a place too well, and that novelty was the salt and savor of one's idle hours even more than of one's active pursuits.

From Camden one may either coast the shores of the bay as far up as Fort Point, where it narrows to a river scarcely less beautiful, or turning aside from the travelled route to Bangor, may strike boldly out across the bay, toward Islesborough,[4] an island township full of nooks and coves and reaching points, so obstructing progress in this direction that we must turn its extreme northern head before we can shape our course for Castine, where we purpose next to put in.

---

[1] Rockport's output of lime amounted in 1889 to 337,000 casks.

[2] Camden takes its name from Lord Camden, some time Lord High Chancellor of England, whom Junius so much extols. It became the American outpost while Castine remained in British hands.

[3] Megunticook (1457 feet) is highest. Battie (1325 feet) comes next. Bald, Ragged, and Pleasant do not exceed 1000 feet.

[4] Islesborough really includes not only Long Island, which is eleven miles long and divides the Penobscot into two channels, but also the cluster prolonging it to the south as far as a point due east from Rockport Harbor. Of this cluster, Seven-Hundred-Acre, Warren's, and Job's form with the main island Gilkey's Harbor, which is shaped like a lobster's claw. The harbor light stands at the northwest point of the west entrance, and can be seen from Camden. Lassell's, Saddle, Mark, and Robinson's islands extend from north to south in the order named. In view of its topography the name is singularly appropriate. Midway, the island narrows to a few rods, so forming several little harbors east and west. This group belonged to the Muscongus-Waldo-Knox grant, from which its land titles are derived. From Rockland to Castine the eastern passage is nearest, leaving Robinson's Rock on the port hand. Long Island, on which there were a few farms, is now a growing summer resort. Turtle Head is its northern promontory.

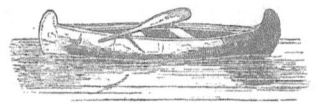

CHAPTER XX.

HISTORIC CASTINE.

"Are there any tidings from over sea?
Ah, why has that wild boy gone from me?"—LONGFELLOW.

DOORWAY, CASTINE.

A CERTAIN learned jurist, on being asked why he chose Castine to begin the practice of law in, made this naïve reply: "Why, I found that I had to break into the world somewhere, so I thought, on the whole, I would select the weakest spot."

Castine[1] is the first of our seacoast towns to greet us with a genuine French name, which we find to be the key to the romantic story of an eventful career.

It is the first to draw us quite away from the sober, even-paced life of the older English settlements into another life, embodying some elements of the picturesque, even its every-day aspects. Upon this our fancy builds its castles. It is as nothing that the Castine we know shows scarcely a trace of Castin, the founder. With the help of history, legend, and poetry our imagination supplies all deficiencies. Is it the deference that republican simplicity pays to the trappings of monarchy gone to irremediable rust and decay?

Castine is a peninsula formed as much like Portland as one almond is like another. There is the same long, high-rounded back of ridge, sloping steeply down to the water at the sides, yet blunted at the ends by precipitous headlands. The village has climbed the sunny southern slope, as far as the edge of the broad plateau at the top, where one enters the fields, the woods, and the pastures; in a word, the country itself. At this elevated point the State Normal School building overlooks the whole village, so becoming to Castine what its gilded dome is to Boston, or, as one might say, the hopeful sign of a higher education.

Its topographical features are such as to make this peninsula a natural stronghold, easily convertible into a most defensible position, — a fact to which Castine's early importance was undoubtedly owing.

Close by the shore-side, as one sails up this beautiful harbor, is the green bank which tradition makes the site of ancient Fort Pentagoet,[2] sometime the hold of Messire D'Aulnay Charnisay, and after him, of the Baron Saint-Castin. Its true history begins with the prompt reoccupation of Acadia, when Cardinal Richelieu put his powerful hand to the task of awakening colonial France from its long stupor.

As the extreme outpost of Acadia, Pentagoet was to be sustained at all hazards, and New England henceforth found an enemy at her doors, determined to resist her every attempt to regain possession of the territory between the

SITE OF FORT PENTAGOET.

Penobscot and Saint Croix; for the king's lieutenant, in his double capacity of military commandant and monopolist of the Indian trade, could be relied on to defend his personal rights even more vigorously than the national honor. Such was French colonial policy — feudalism transplanted.

D'Aulnay began by driving out the thrifty Pilgrims, who threatened his monopoly. But he had a more formidable rival in La Tour,[3] of Saint John, who held command beyond the Saint Croix. Stripped of their titles, they were really rival traders, masquerading as soldiers, who showed much more jealousy of each other than of the English; and as neither paid any respect to the limits marked out for him by his commission, a very pretty quarrel soon fell out between them.

Engrossed by their personal hatreds, each applied to the detested English for a helping hand against the other. The crafty Puritans, after first searching the Scriptures to see if they could find warrant for it, decided to assist La Tour, inasmuch as D'Aulnay was by all odds the more dangerous neighbor of the two; and seeing, furthermore, a promise of profit to themselves in allowing these adversaries to cripple each other to the top of their bent. So when

HARBOR SHORE, CASTINE.

D'Aulnay blockaded La Tour at Saint John, the Puritans helped La Tour to drive him back to Pentagoet. He was followed there and attacked in his turn, but succeeded in beating off his assailants without much trouble. For this assistance La Tour promised the Puritans freedom to trade in his territory.

D'Aulnay was attacked a second time with no better success. Biding his time, he again sallied out against La Tour's fort when the master was away with part of his men; but in Madame La Tour the assailant found a châtelaine every way worthy of her trust; for she defended herself with so much spirit that D'Aulnay had to retire, choking with wrath and mortification at the thought of being thus defeated by a woman.

He then resorted to finesse. Amusing the cunning Puritans with talk of peace, to which they listened, when he had thrown them off their guard, he suddenly fell upon La Tour again, and this time with entire success, taking his fort and stripping it of all it contained, — plate, furs, arms, everything.

INSCRIPTION PLATE.

La Tour became an exile, and worse still, for a man deeply in debt, a hopeless bankrupt. But D'Aulnay having died, and Madame La Tour also, the widower married the widow, so coming to his own again in whole or in part, and so terminating this remarkable feud in a way that none of the principals could have dreamed of.

Like all the French colonial establishments of this early time, Pentagoet was at once a fort, a trading-post, and a mission. In 1646 the Jesuit, Father Druillettes, found several Capuchin friars domesticated there under their superior, Father Ignace, and we have a possible memorial of them in a fragment of copper-plate that was picked up on the shore not many years ago, and is thought to have once decorated their chapel. Be that as it may, the conversion of the Indians to the Catholic faith was the sowing of the seed that was to bear a bloody harvest for Protestant New England when times grew ripe for it. And to this day the remnant of the once powerful Penobscots hold fast to the faith they then embraced.

PINE-TREE SHILLING.

In 1654 Sedgwick, a colonial officer of Massachusetts, conquered all the posts in Acadia from the French, Pentagoet included. Sedgwick's report is the first account we have of what the place was like. He describes it as being a small yet well-planned work, and very strong, mounting eight pieces of ordnance.

Acadia having thus passed to the control of the English, its several posts were granted to different proprietors, first by Cromwell, and afterwards by Charles II., Pentagoet falling to the share of that Sir Thomas Temple who so cleverly turned away the Merry Monarch's wrath from New England by telling him that the device stamped on the pine-tree shilling was put there in commemoration of Boscobel. But under the treaty of Breda, Acadia was tossed into the scales as a makeweight, so becoming French again.

It was not until 1670 that the French flag was again unfurled over Pentagoet. There is an elaborate description of the fort at this time, showing that it had been much enlarged and strengthened. In 1674 the place was again taken by buccaneers from San Domingo, who carried off Chambly, the commander, to Boston, where he was held to ransom.

It is at this time that the man whose name is so intimately associated with Castine first comes upon the scene.

Baron Saint-Castin had come out to Canada with his regiment in 1665. The history of this regiment is not without interest to Americans. De Tracy, the king's viceroy, had instantly set it to work building three forts on the Richelieu River, as a bulwark against the Iroquois. Captain Sorel, of this regiment, was charged with the first, at the mouth of the river; Captain Chambly, with that at the foot of the rapids; while Colonel Salières took upon himself the erection of the third, still higher up. In this way the names of Sorel and Chambly became affixed to the map of Canada.

Castin's regiment having been disbanded, both officers and men were given liberal grants of land as an inducement to stay in the colony, so as to strengthen it by the infusion of a little iron into its blood, as it were, — a very judicious move, as it proved, because many of the officers were of good family, and the men seasoned soldiers, who could be reckoned on to defend their own homes all the more zealously. Castin himself seems to have preferred casting his lot among the Indians, which gives us, perhaps, the best index to his true character. He was yet a mere lad when he is found fighting at Pentagoet, against the buccaneers, as has been just mentioned, and from that time onward his exploits caused him to be known and feared throughout New England as no other Frenchman had been before him.

Castin was equally ready to fight or trade, as the occasion might call for. He had the twin passions of a true Bearnais, — love for war and love of money. At one time he is a boon companion; at another he exhibits all the ferocity of a savage. He took an Indian princess for a wife, adopted the manners of her nation, shared in its councils, monopolized its trade, and made himself so far master of its acts as to be able to dictate peace or war when he would.

In his hands, however, Pentagoet declined to a mere trading-post, partly through the parsimony, and partly through the neglect, of those in authority. As such, it invited attack. Sometimes Castin was forced to take refuge among his wild Penobscots until the storm had passed over. In one of these hurried flights, some fugitive is supposed to have lost or concealed a large sum in silver

UNITARIAN CHURCH, CASTINE

coin, which was found, so late as the year 1840, on the old trail leading off from the peninsula.

In this vagabond life, picturesque, it is true, Longfellow found an attractive theme for his poetic fancy, to which he has given much freedom, since by all accounts both rank and manhood were degraded in Castin for the sake of lucre. Brave he was, yet in the double personality of a gentleman turned savage, and of a savage turned gentleman, — for Castin finally went back to France with a fortune "in good, dry gold," — the distinction becomes confusing.

Castin's half-breed son succeeded to his father at Pentagoet, and followed in his footsteps. He was a true chip, inheriting all his father's hatred for those "perfidious English," to whom he sold brandy one day, or fought with the next. But we lack space to chronicle all that befell in this remote corner of New England up to the time when it finally passed out of French control.

PICKED UP AT CASTINE.

Castine is certainly a very attractive village. It is also a very quiet one, except when roused to abnormal activity by the arrival of a steamboat, when about all the floating population swarms down to the landing. The stranger who is uneasy at seeing the streets full of people all hurrying in one direction, when but a moment before they were deserted, is quieted, however, at finding that the village is not on fire. Having gratified its curiosity for the hundredth time, perhaps, the crowd quietly disperses. This incident lets us deeper into the practical isolation of the place, perhaps, than anything else could.

In point of fact, one very soon realizes that the commercial prosperity of Castine is at its lowest ebb. Middle-aged people, proud of their traditions, who remember when it was different, look upon the shifting throng of giddy sight-seers with something of the same feeling that their fathers experienced when the regulars marched up the hill with fixed bayonets.

THE OLD "TUB."

This antipathy to new-fangled notions has so far left its impress on the outward aspect of things that Castine seems like a chapter taken out of an old book.

It is like meeting again the friend of our youth, to listen to the ringing of the church bells at morning, noon, and night. Here the observance might well recall that ancient chapel by the sea, — its pious call to prayers, its solemn chants and stately processions, — as something grown stronger and more sonorous with the lapse of years. How lovingly the sweet tones of the curfew seem lingering on the evening air!

"Those evening bells, those evening bells!"

But no; it is the call of Time rather than Eternity. Yet it agreeably breaks the stillness, or divides it rather into equal portions.

When one has gone through every nook and corner of the village, it becomes apparent that Castine's greatest charm lies in its eventful past. To that we once more turn as to an inexhaustible resource.

For those who never read except when they run, few places furnish better object-lessons in history. From the story of border warfare, as told by those

MAIN STREET, CASTINE.

fading mounds by the shore, we pass on, and up, to a more momentous period, as portrayed in the still solid ramparts crowning the heights. Here men of the same race have crossed swords in deadly strife.

The Main Street takes one straight up to the site of Fort George; for it was built when George III. was king, and christened with many bumpers when the flag was run up and saluted for the first time. Landor's incisive abridgment of Thackeray's "Four Georges" came into my mind quite spontaneously, as I was taking my first walk around the ramparts: —

> "George the First was reckoned vile;
> Viler George the Second;
> And what mortal ever heard
> Any good of George the Third?
> When from earth the Fourth ascended,
> God be praised, the Georges ended!"

All the islands and shores forming the harbor lie at one's feet. Here are Holbrook's and Nautilus islands, and yonder are Brooksville and Cape Rosier.[4]

Far away in the east rise the dim humps of Mount Desert and the solitary cone of Blue Hill — striking landmarks, all.

> "Sweet odors and bright colors swiftly pass —
> Swiftly as breath upon a looking-glass."

Southward, lies the flat expanse of Penobscot Bay, smoking with the morning mists, almost tropical in its dull and glassy brightness, with Long Island reposing in its midst. The Camden Hills are over beyond. "Ah, this is beautiful!" you say to yourself; and then you look down at the embattled walls under your feet, and mentally add "This was worth fighting for!"

Fort George seems good for another century, at least. It is a spacious rectangular earthwork, from which everything but the bare walls has disappeared. Its present owner, Mr. George Witherle, has, I am pleased to note, the historic instinct for preserving these relics of the past, which no visitor to Castine

FERRY, BAGADUCE RIVER.

should neglect seeing. When I saw it last, a game of tennis was in progress, and balls were being tossed about of quite a different kind from those which had passed between besiegers and besieged when playing the game of war.

In the course of the day, however, the scene changed to one of pathetic interest. The grass-grown parade was again filled with soldiers, — veterans of the Civil War, met here to fight their battles over again. What a grizzled, battered, hard-featured band they were, to be sure! Some hobbled painfully along on crutches, or limped awkwardly in the rear. There was nothing left of that old elastic swing and jaunty air with which they first marched off to the war. They tramped heavily and even gloomily up the hill, passing a word or a jest with the bystanders, who looked on with something of awe in their faces, yet without showing the admiration that a militia company in full rig would have called forth. One poor fellow said apologetically, in reply to something he overheard about his lagging in the rear, "Young man, I guess you would lag, too, if you had seven buckshot in you." The scoffer turned away as red as fire.

These men's eyes were dim, their shoulders bent, their joints stiffened with advancing age, old wounds, or lurking diseases; but in them the grand spirit of brotherhood in arms was a sacred fire to be kept alive to the last survivor. Once more the roll was called. How many failed to answer to their names! The dead far outnumbered the living. In silence they stood around the tattered flag they had fought for. Then the loud drums rattled out again as of old. The fifes struck up "Dixie," each veteran straightened himself up like an old war-horse at the trumpet's sound, and with indescribably martial port the column marched down the hill, — yes, down the hill.

The war for independence had been on four years before Castine again assumed importance in a military sense. At this time the British ministry determined to isolate the settlements lying east of the Penobscot from those at the west. The war-worn peninsula was therefore promptly seized upon. In June, 1779, a force sent from Halifax under General MacLean broke ground on these heights. Massachusetts hurriedly got together a homespun army, formidable only in name, to expel the invaders. Novices in war as the soldiers were, their officers were scarce better fitted to lead them. There was a fleet, numerous but inefficient, like the army. In a word, it was a force hastily scraped together for the purpose of executing a brilliant *coup de main*, from which its authors expected to reap both glory and profit. Always brave, when mere bravery sufficed, our soldiers gallantly scaled the steep cliffs of the southern headland under a galling fire. Any one who will take the trouble to visit the spot must appreciate the daring of the act. One bold effort would undoubtedly have won the day; but after clearing their way to the fort, which was not then half completed or half armed, the besiegers wasted three precious weeks in looking at their adversaries from a distance, because Saltonstall, the naval commander, dared not push his squadron into the

FERRYMAN.

KINCH'S MOUNTAIN.

harbor against the enemy's ships and batteries. This delay was necessarily fatal. On one of those foggy mornings so prevalent in this bay the watch-boats caught sight of seven heavy ships bearing down upon them under a press of sail. It was Sir George Collier's squadron coming to raise the siege. With the greatest exertions our land forces were safely drawn off the peninsula; but the fleet was completely destroyed, most of the ships being driven ashore and burnt to the water's edge. It would be difficult to conceive a more disastrous rout. From Castine to Bangor the shores were literally strewed with wrecks, while the woods swarmed with fugitives.

John Moore, then a young subaltern in the 82d Foot, began here that remarkable career which was so gloriously terminated in the trenches of Corunna in 1809, and is commemorated through all time in Wolfe's fine ode, —

"Not a drum was heard, not a funeral note."

The invaders kept undisputed possession until after the conclusion of peace, though the memory of the defeat they had inflicted on our untrained soldiers gave rise to occasional projects for dislodging them. But the first effort had quite robbed the enterprise of its charms. Rochambeau and La Peyrouse offered to undertake it, and would have done so if more important services had not called them to another field. That would have been a curious instance of history repeating itself, if the French flag had been again planted on the heights of Pentagoet, through the intervention of those very colonists who had been the most inveterate in their efforts to pull it down.

From this vantage-ground the British began their wanton depredations on the neighboring coasts and harbors, — a warfare exclusively aimed at the destruction of property.

Castine remained in our hands until 1814, when it was abandoned without a fight to another strong invading force, who again made it the centre for plundering and burning the coast towns east and west, levying forced contributions, setting fire to half-built vessels, — all with the view of crushing out not only the ability for resistance, but the spirit also. At this time Belfast was visited, Hampden pillaged, and Bangor taken. In a very short time Eastern Maine was as good as subjugated. At Boston these acts were believed to foreshadow a formidable invasion of all New England. After a stay of eight months the British garrison took its final leave of Castine in April, 1815, leaving behind such memories of balls and routs, of levees and amateur theatricals, as sufficed for the tea-table gossip of a whole generation.

In view of all these ups and downs, the unwritten history of Castine would, no doubt, prove far more interesting than the dry recital of what has been so many times repeated. One would like an account of some of the *soulagements* of garrison life, — the flirtations, the promenades, the boating-parties, the dinner-parties; in short, to know whether those perfidious Britons carried off with them the susceptible hearts of the Castine maidens.

RELIC OF THE OCCUPATION.

The most agreeable stroll out of the village that I know of begins at the old fort, and follows the shore round to the lighthouse at Dice's Head, past the summer colony that has sprung up in the neighborhood, through the woodland paths skirting the brow of the high cliffs of that shore, — those enduring monuments to unavailing valor,[5] — on past Blockhouse Point, where the landing was made, and out again into the open plain that is everywhere furrowed with vestiges of the siege of a hundred years ago. Some are the remains of trenches, and some merely serve to show the positions of old camps pitched outside the fortress.

By descending the hill a little, from the northwest angle of the fort, a well-preserved battery shows how strongly the land approach was guarded. Still lower down a deep moat was cut across the isthmus, thus wholly severing it from the mainland, the passage to and fro being made over a bridge. Strict guard was kept here. Yet it was by this dangerous route that Wadsworth made his escape through the sentinels to the opposite shores; so that his name has become attached to the cove opening into the bay, at the left here.

Although Castine lies somewhat off the direct route from Rockland to Mount Desert, the Penobscot Bay steamers afford frequent communication with that island. It would be difficult to trace out a more beautiful excursion than is thus placed at the visitor's disposal, or one from which he could derive equal pleasure for so small an outlay.

GOOSE FALLS, CAPE ROSIER.

HISTORIC CASTINE. 287

After passing out of the harbor, the route skirts the curiously stratified rocks of Cape Rosier, another locality which has been bought up by improving speculators. It then turns sharply away to the east to enter the far-famed Eggemoggin Reach, or Naskeag, as the old charts name it, a narrow strip of water separating the shores of Brooksville, Sedgwick, and Brooklin from those of Little Deer and Great Deer Isle.[6] For a dozen miles, or from the entrance at Pumpkin Island out again at the Devil's Head, no sail could be more charmingly diversified, more full of scenic surprises, or more free from actual or hidden dangers. One cannot look in any direction without seeing some new picture. Then the water is everywhere deep and unobstructed by sunken ledges, and so still that but for the occasional appearance of a landing or a fisherman's skiff, one might easily fancy himself sailing on some calm stream of an undiscovered country. At Indian Cove, on Little Deer Isle, there is a sprinkling of cottages, built by the light-keeper for the accommodation of summer visitors of moderate means, or who do not care a penny for fashion or show. Life here is essentially amphibious. There's many an islet where one thinks he would like to make a Crusoe of himself for one summer at least. Pure air and vigorous exercise quickly convert pale cheeks and flabby muscles into bronze and brawn. This is surely the common-sense side to a summer vacation. "What is the country but a means of returning to our earliest youth, of finding again that faculty of happiness, that state of deep attention, that indifference to everything but pleasure and the present sensation, that facile joy which is a brimming spring ready to overflow at the least impulse?"

After looking into Sedgwick, a really picturesque village at the head of a pretty harbor, the boat glides swiftly on through the Reach, past a clump of low-lying islets, clears Naskeag Point with a rush, and shoots out into Blue Hill Bay,[7] with nothing between us and the frowning summits of Mount Desert but the long ocean swell, which comes rolling steadily in, and is piled up on the foaming shores about us. Our boat seems courtesying to the slumberous old mountains, as she ploughs her way steadily on toward that haven of marine luxury, — the far-famed Desert Isle.

---

[1] Castine was known to the English as Penobscot, and to the French as Pentagoet, that being their rendering of the Indian name. Champlain first gives it to us in this form. Upon the division of the old county of Lincoln into the two counties of Hancock and Washington, in 1790, Penobscot was made the shire town of Hancock, and Machias of Washington. Castine was set off from the old township of Penobscot, as it had been first incorporated in 1787, and given corporate rights, with its present name, in 1796. Previous to this the peninsula of Castine somehow acquired the local name of Bagaduce, though no very satisfactory reason is found for it beyond what is stated by Williamson, II. 572. Castine River was the name formerly given to the water extending inland into Penobscot, northwardly, and Moxus' River to that between Brooksville and Sedgwick. Dr. G. A. Wheeler has written the history of Castine.

[2] Fort Pentagoet is on the property of Mr. George H. Webb, situated about a quarter of

a mile south of the steamboat landing. Excavations made with the view of establishing the locality in question have brought to light some foundation walls, with other remains that would seem to confirm the local tradition, but the work of time or demolition, or both, has rendered identification difficult, the more as the fort had gone to decay long before the French finally abandoned the place. Some part was doubtless of stone and some of wood. Unfortunately for the success of later inquiry, the settlers probably helped themselves to such materials as they wanted; so that the stones of Fort Pentagoet would probably have to be sought for among the foundation walls of the village.

[3] For a more ample account of La Tour, refer to Winthrop's "Journal," Hutchinson's "Massachusetts Bay," Murdock's "Nova Scotia," "Sir William Alexander" (Prince Society's Series), etc.

[4] It is not known to the author just how this promontory got its name. It is generally supposed to have been given in honor of James Rosier, the journalist of Weymouth's voyage.

[5] There is a tradition connected with Trask's Rock, running to the effect that a drummer-boy belonging to the storming party ensconced himself behind this rock, where he kept up his inspiriting rataplan while his comrades were toiling up the steep ascent under a sore and heavy fire. There is a small portrait of Israel Trask, the hero of this exploit, in the rooms of the Maine Historical Society at Portland.

[6] Deer Isle, largest of the Penobscot islands, is nearly severed at the middle, leaving two large lobes, of irregular shape, uneven surface, and cove-dented sides. The easternmost side is crushed all to pieces, its debris being the score of large and small islands which at one time undoubtedly formed part of the main island itself. The water entering its west side leads to the principal village, situated at the isthmus. Decline of the fisheries, and consequent loss of population, is a rule to which Deer Isle offers no exception. Isle au Haut rises at the south, Mount Desert at the east, the Fox Islands west, with the Camden Mountains, the common scenic property of all this glorious bay, for a background.

Isle Haute (High Isle), as Champlain well named it, is considered the eastern limit of Penobscot Bay. It was attached to the township of Deer Isle until set off in 1874. The population is small, poor, and decreasing. This aquatic township also comprises all the smaller islands lying off south of the passage so whimsically named Merchant's Row, perhaps for Anthony Merchant, an early settler. The shores rise up sharply from the water, like the tip of a half-submerged mountain. Some soil has collected in the hollows, the upland being fit only for pasturage. The inhabitants eke out a poor living by raising a few sheep, fishing a little, and farming a little, and by gathering blueberries, which grow plentifully on most of these islands. The island catches the eye from all outer approaches to this bay.

Blue Hill Bay reaches up fifteen miles to the village of Blue Hill, on the west shore, receives Union River still higher up, by which vessels ascend to Ellsworth, forms part of the water separating Mount Desert from the mainland, here called Western Bay, and like all the bays of Maine is strewed with islands from one end to the other. North of Naskeag Point are the noted marks, the Ship and Barge, so called from the trees once growing on the larger islet; the Barge is nothing but a dry rock. Southerly of Naskeag, in the mouth of the bay, is the large Swan's Island, or Burnt Coat, also surrounded by its tributary cluster of smaller islands, thus forming a "plantation," of which outer Long Island is perhaps conspicuous above all the Maine islands for the semi-civilized character of its fishermen. It is said that for the want of animals they harness themselves to the plough. Next to Mount Desert Rock it is the last land in these waters. Swan's Island has about eleven hundred acres, with a good harbor at its westerly side. Marshall's lies southwest; Pond, Calf, John's, and Black lie out north, toward Naskeag.

ANEMONE CAVE, MOUNT DESERT.

BASS HARBOR, MOUNT DESERT ISLAND.

CHAPTER XXI.

MOUNT DESERT ISLAND.

" May I turn oyster and drink nothing but salt water." — MARLOWE's *Faustus*.

EVEN so late as the year 1857 a writer plucked up the courage to say that he thought a visit to Mount Desert might prove a grateful experience, — a remark thrown out by the way, to note, it would seem, if the drift of popular prejudice had yet set in a truer direction. Yet, as recent as it seems, this date does not accurately fix the new discovery by some years. The old stigma was not yet removed. If some one happened to let fall the remark that Mount Desert was said to have fine scenery, it was instantly countered with "So has Labrador."

There is, however, a class of discoverers who accept no man's dictum,—worshippers of nature, devotees of art. At Mount Desert, as at many another spot that might be mentioned, our landscape painters were the advanced guard, whose pictorial bulletins first set in motion the grand army of tourists, ever insatiable for new worlds to conquer. Thomas Doughty is said to have been the first painter of note to reproduce on canvas the fine scenery of Mount Desert, he having sketched here before 1840; and Doughty was more or less closely followed by Cole, Fisher, Church, Gifford, Bierstadt, H. Brown, and others, who have been pioneers of American landscape art in the truest sense of the word. If that group of men could not make Mount Desert famous, nothing could.

And so this beautiful island of the sea was not only newly discovered, but redeemed from the obloquy that a flippant paragraph and infelicitous name had so long cast about it. Visitors dropped in by twos and threes, by scores, by thousands. The simple island folk awoke to find themselves engulfed by a wave of phenomenal prosperity, which has carried some of them on to riches as unlooked for as a capital prize in the Louisiana Lottery; and the end is not yet. The whole history of American summer resorts may be safely challenged to show another such instance of rapid growth, or of a popularity more firmly established or better deserved. That statement invites us to a survey of the island itself, though it may seem a good deal like threshing old straw to go over ground so well known as Mount Desert is to-day.

Long ago, when a few storm-beaten explorers were groping about the coast, seeing everywhere nature seemingly intrenched against civilization, this region obtained the romantic name of Acadia. The French voyagers who adopted it, or coined it, as the case may be, hastened to secure its official sanction by letters-patent bearing the spacious scrawl of Henri Quatre, "that lusty gallant, that very devil," who then and there extended his royal sceptre over all New England, and much besides.

This was the celebrated patent of 1603 granted to the Chevalier De Monts,[1] governor of Pons, in the old province of Saintonge, where both he and his distinguished *confrère* Champlain first drew breath.

Each scrap of history that we now pick up seems flavored with that spice of romance, of gallantry, of chivalry, which is so appetizing after the savorless records of a purely practical people.

Mr. Parkman tells us how this Acadia looked, and what it was like: "Rude as it was, Acadia had its charms, and it has them still: in its wilderness of woods and its wilderness of waves; the rocky ramparts that guard its coasts; its deep, still bays and foaming headlands; the towering cliffs of the Grand Manan; the innumerable islands that cluster about Penobscot Bay; and the romantic highlands of Mount Desert, down whose gorges the sea-fog rolls like an invading host, while the spires of fir-trees pierce the surging vapors like lances in the smoke of battle."

A single episode of history, scarcely serious in its origin, but tragic enough in its sequel, has imparted much sentimental interest to this island of late.

I speak of the time when, after exhausting every other resource, it was the fashion to be pious at court, and every noble lady have her father confessor. In those days of war and intrigue Madame the Marquise de Guercheville[2] was seized with a burning desire to become the founder of a religious colony, or mission, to the heathen of Acadia, under the inspiration and guidance of the Jesuits. She herself was above all reproach; but the notorious profligacy of the regency of Marie de Medicis is too well known to need further comment. This proposed mission was to be the root through which the powerful order of Jesus should spread itself out over all Acadia, disconcert its enemies, both lay and church, and assume sole charge of the souls of the benighted heathen, for whom, be it said, there was then no probationary period after death. That illustrious sinner, the queen regent, set the example to her ladies by opening her own purse. The whole court hastened to follow the fashion. With the moneys thus obtained the Marquise fitted out one small ship, which set sail amid the prayers of its pious patroness. This vessel cast anchor under Mount Desert in the month of May, 1613, after experiencing an encounter with the fogs of Grand Manan which put all on board in great peril of their lives. In gratitude for their deliverance from shipwreck, the fathers called their first anchorage Saint Sauveur. While the colonists were debating among themselves what course to steer next, some Indians paddled off to the ship, and piloted her into the noble sound that parts the island in two, and is its natural haven. Although their fixed destination was the Penobscot, the colonists, conceiving that the hand of God had led them here, decided to begin their habitations where they were. Without seeking further they therefore set themselves to the task before them; but they were hardly settled in some order on shore, with their half-manned bark lying out at anchor in the stream, when an English ship bore down upon them with guns shotted, colors displayed, and matches lighted.

GENTLEMAN.

At this moment the French ship offered an easy prey; for as the stranger approached, she poured in a destructive broadside, to which her defenceless antagonist could make no reply. In vain Flory, the French captain, screamed to his men to fire: no one seems to have had the courage to obey, except Brother du Thet, who, being on board, bravely snatched up a match and fired the first shot. Seeing they would be sunk at their anchors, the French sailors then cut their cable, which caused them to drift out of the fire. To meet this manœuvre, Argall, the English commander, quickly wore round and gave them another broadside, which decided the combat. Brother du Thet fell across the tiller, with a musket-ball through the body.[3] Flory and several others were wounded. The French then cried out that they surrendered, and firing ceased.

GENTLEWOMAN, 1605.

Argall made equally quick work of the colonists ashore. Some were carried off captives to Virginia, and some suffered to make their way back to Port Royal as they could, with the warning not to be again found trespassing on English ground.

The hopes of the founders of this colony were thus completely wrecked. Its brief life and sudden overthrow, the swiftness with which the action passed, leaves us in doubt to this day what spot of ground was thus consecrated by the blood of its founders. It is true that up to the time that the island became famous, nobody seems to have thought the matter worth wasting time upon. The incident itself was hardly remembered; nor can local tradition lift the veil.

The English of that day seemed equally determined to obliterate everything that might serve to identify the island with French occupation or establish a claim; so when the Boston colonists of 1630 sighted this island as their first land, they were told it was called Mount Mansell,[4] and Governor Winthrop has set down in his "Journal" how a pigeon flew on board the ship, like another dove returning to the Ark, to tell them that the dry land had once more risen from the sea; and how the sweet air, wafted to them from the shore, was like the smell of a garden, and did much refresh them.

From this time down to the middle of the eighteenth century, Mount Desert was given over to its primitive solitude, broken only by the rude encampments of wandering savages who came to fish, or hunt the moose, or mustered there in arms for some bloody foray on the war-worn New England coast.[5] Possibly the dark tale of Saint Sauveur may have been drawn upon to stimulate their hatred the more, if their fathers had kept the tradition alive over their council fires. At such times the mountains surrounding Somes' Sound have echoed to the songs of rugged bands inured to war, and animated by its spirit, whose miserable descendants now come, with the print of a degenerate and ignoble race upon their faces, to peddle gimcracks among their conquerors.

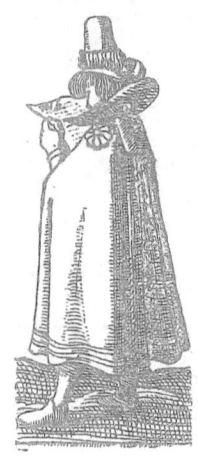
LAWYER.

In the year 1747 a vessel that was employed in transporting a colonial re-enforcement to Annapolis, Nova Scotia, was cast away on Mount Desert in a snow-storm. The weather was very severe, and seventy or eighty persons perished. The survivors underwent great hardship and suffering. At that time there was not a house on the island, nor had they the means of leaving it. Hope and resolution did not desert them, however. With materials saved from the wreck they built a boat, by means of which news of their deplorable situation was carried to Townsend.

This long lapse in the history of Mount Desert brings us to the period of its second occupation by white men.

Measures looking to permanent settlement here were initiated by Governor Francis Bernard, of Massachusetts, who so won over the General Court of that colony by his first speech, that they made him a present of Mount Desert outright.[6] This was in 1762. The governor had laid out a town at Southwest Harbor, which he intended making the island metropolis; and he had taken some steps toward bringing in settlers also, when the troubles that rendered his administration so unbearable caused his recall. By this time the donors, who had been so carried away by the charm of his oratory, would have hanged him with a good conscience.

After Bernard came the Revolution with its check to all prosperity, its confiscations, and its hatreds. Bernard's property went with the rest; but after the war was over, his son John, who had remained in the country, a quiet spectator of passing events, succeeded in getting restored to him the west half of the island. The other half was also restored, not to Bernard's heir, but to Madame Thérèse de Gregoire, the granddaughter and heiress of La Motte Cadillac,[7] and to her husband, Barthelémy, who thereupon settled at Hull's Cove, where they afterwards lived and died as American citizens. The claim of these Gregoires to Mount Desert was allowed, not so much on its merits, — for in that light it was a pure gift, — as an exhibition of that abounding gratitude toward our French allies which made even the most obsolete claim a debt of honor.

SARGENT'S MOUNTAIN, FROM THE SOUND.

Having thus swept the historic horizon through the medium of musty records, we are all the more impatient to get acquainted with those picturesque features through which the island has acquired its later prestige.

It is as if the granite hills of New Hampshire had been transported to the shores of the Atlantic to form a more imposing display. And though there are so many ways of reaching the island, none, I am sure, shows off its rare combination of shore and mountain to so much advantage as the approach from sea, — the way of the discoverers and explorers.

But we shall sail without wind and ride without horses.

As we come toward the island, out of the west, we first make out what seems a solitary mountain, darkly blue, cool as an iceberg, lifted up above the coast. By what chance has this freak of nature heaved or lodged itself against these shores?

Upon getting closer, the mass expands into a crown of barren summits, more before steam took the place of wind, may be seen at a glance. In point of fact, this was the great thoroughfare of the island before the day of summer travel came.

The sea was always, however, the road that the islanders were most accustomed to travel, and the one they liked best.

Southwest Harbor experienced a loss of prestige as soon as Bar Harbor was discovered. It maintains, nevertheless, a sort of dignified rivalry which not a few travellers prefer to the ostentatious newness of Mount Desert's acknowledged summer capital. For one thing, it preserves its old simplicity. Have we come seeking repose for mind and body? One look announces a haven of rest. Its land-locked harbor, its circlet of islands, its background of mountains, its sound conducting to new scenes or storied shores, declare Southwest Harbor to be in no way deficient, either in natural attractions or scenic beauty.

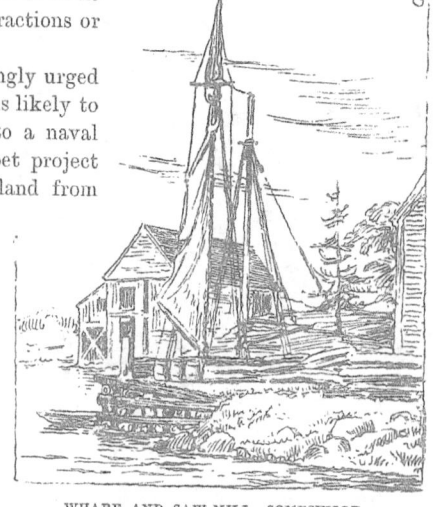

WHARF AND SAW-MILL, SOMESVILLE.

Years ago General Totten strongly urged upon the government the advantages likely to arise from turning this harbor into a naval and military arsenal. It was a pet project of his. The remoteness of the island from centres of population caused the scheme, however, to sleep the sleep of oblivion. Newport has its fortress, its naval reviews, its infusion of military life into the more prosaic civil life. So has Point Comfort. Perhaps this may be the one thing wanting to fill out the full measure of Mount Desert's many attractions.

Northeast Harbor is a sequestered nook, rising to wooded heights, in which one imagines no end of sylvan retreats. The air grows warmer, and is heavy with the fragrance of the pines. And the faces that look down at us from the wharf are as brown as berries. Then, too, there is a refreshing atmosphere of quiet about the little village, with its neat dwellings and modest chapel, that makes it seem closer to nature than any we have yet seen.

For an hour longer our progress round the high eastern shore shows us one continuous wall of naked rock, or rather the crushed and ponderous fragments of one, now broken into by coves, now bulging out in grim headlands, now retreating again under the shadow of the mountains of which they are the outworks. On this battered front is written the story of a thousand storms and a thousand battles.

MOUNT DESERT ISLAND.

Threading our way through the difficult channel here, we soon leave Long Ledge and its lonely bell-buoy, rocking and tolling on the passing swell, to coast along a natural sea-wall formed of broken rock, which here skirts the shore and breaks off the sea. This has always been accounted one of the curiosities of the island. But we have now entered a broad road, the vestibule of Somes' Sound, at a point where the great hills before us are cleft at the very centre of the line, as if some enormous wedge had been driven straight up into the heart of the island. Strange thoughts come over us as we look up through the sundered mountains! Nothing but an earthquake, followed by the rush of an ocean, could have pierced that embattled front of granite.

Two harbors are hid away at opposite corners of this sound. Southwest Harbor opens at our left; Northeast Harbor, at our right. We steer for the first, to find something like the whole population awaiting us at the pier.

As the natural gateway of the island, Somes' Sound controls its topography. Thus Southwest Harbor may be considered as the strategic capital for the western half, as Bar Harbor is for the eastern. The Sound soon wanders off among the mountains.

All the summits are now in plain sight.[10] Those rising at the east are superbly massed in one great group, and look highest; those lifted in the west stand well apart, so as to be easily distinguished, and in their gray coats and rounded backs look like a herd of elephants marching majestically across the island.

The village at Southwest Harbor being the oldest on the island, most of the traditions naturally cluster about its neighborhood. For example, the sup-

SOMES' SOUND.

posed site of Madame de Guercheville's ill-starred colony is only two miles above, on the west shore of the Sound, at Fernald's Point. At least, that spot seems to best answer to the description given by Father Biard, who was one of the company: Seven miles up, at the head of the Sound, the little village of Somesville is a sort of centre upon which all the roads of the island converge; and as one of them crosses to the bridge, joining Mount Desert with *terra firma*, the importance of Southwest Harbor, before steam took the place of wind, may be seen at a glance. In point of fact, this was the great thoroughfare of the island before the day of summer travel came.

The sea was always, however, the road that the islanders were most accustomed to travel, and the one they liked best.

Southwest Harbor experienced a loss of prestige as soon as Bar Harbor was discovered. It maintains, nevertheless, a sort of dignified rivalry which not a few travellers prefer to the ostentatious newness of Mount Desert's acknowledged summer capital. For one thing, it preserves its old simplicity. Have we come seeking repose for mind and body? One look announces a haven of rest. Its land-locked harbor, its circlet of islands, its background of mountains, its sound conducting to new scenes or storied shores, declare Southwest Harbor to be in no way deficient, either in natural attractions or scenic beauty.

Years ago General Totten strongly urged upon the government the advantages likely to arise from turning this harbor into a naval and military arsenal. It was a pet project of his. The remoteness of the island from centres of population caused the scheme, however, to sleep the sleep of oblivion. Newport has its fortress, its naval reviews, its infusion of military life into the more prosaic civil life. So has Point Comfort. Perhaps this may be the one thing wanting to fill out the full measure of Mount Desert's many attractions.

Northeast Harbor is a sequestered nook, rising to wooded heights, in which one imagines no end of sylvan retreats. The air grows warmer, and is heavy with the fragrance of the pines. And the faces that look down at us from the wharf are as brown as berries. Then, too, there is a refreshing atmosphere of quiet about the little village, with its neat dwellings and modest chapel, that makes it seem closer to nature than any we have yet seen.

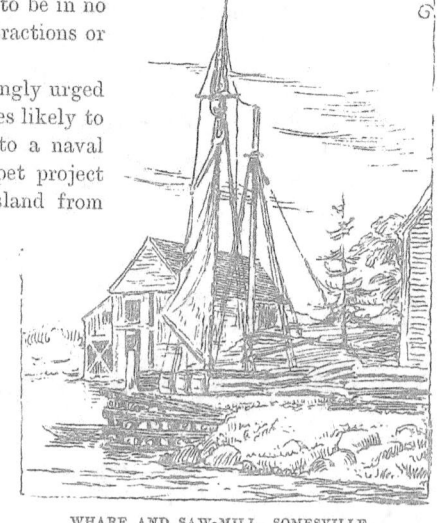

WHARF AND SAW-MILL, SOMESVILLE.

For an hour longer our progress round the high eastern shore shows us one continuous wall of naked rock, or rather the crushed and ponderous fragments of one, now broken into by coves, now bulging out in grim headlands, now retreating again under the shadow of the mountains of which they are the outworks. On this battered front is written the story of a thousand storms and a thousand battles.

So, sailing on, our next landing will be at Seal Harbor, where another summer settlement appears in its holiday dress. It is from here that the romantic region lying about Jordan's Lake is reached by a cross-road striking directly off from the shore into the heart of the mountains; but the improvements now in progress are designed to carry travel still further through this absolutely virgin wilderness of woods and lakes, quite across the mountain range, and out upon the shores of Eagle Lake, some three miles from Bar Harbor, and on the reverse side of the mountains. The route will thus penetrate into the most secret nooks of the island.

ROCKS, MOUNT DESERT.

And now we are passing out from the shelter of outlying islands, to be lifted again on the swell of the open sea.

Here begins an exhibition which no one should grudge coming a hundred miles to witness, — the stony feet of mountains washed by the obedient ocean. But it is no labor of love, truly! One by one, swift, stealthy, and noiseless, the great wallowing waves heave themselves up against the rugged masses of rock with prodigious force. The hidden ledges are passed at a bound, but their sharp tusks gore and tear the breaker into tongues of foam, which dart hither and thither, hissing like angry serpents. Its momentum is checked, but the next sea forces it on again: the Atlantic is behind it, and on it must go. Once more the broken billow shakes its white mane, and rushes on into the old piled-up breaches with a roar of defiance. Crash goes the water! up leaps the spray! A hundred pitfalls open to suck it down. Its flurry and foam seem like the torment of some expiring monster, brought forth by a Dantesque imagination. Little by little, one by one, the smothered rocks struggle up out of the whirlpool of emerald-green, crackling water. For a moment it seems as if the ocean had exhausted itself with this effort. Then the coast opens wide its streaming jaws again to the coming wave.

Passing still on by Otter Cove and its high eastern cliff,[11] which are finely presented, we are soon up with Great Head, that colossal torso of gray-white granite, bulging far out, and heaved high up above the surrounding wrack, of which it seems, indeed, the sole survivor. It is fearfully dented and beaten in by storm and frost. We see the deep holes that the sea has worked out at its base; we cast our eyes up to get an idea of its altitude, and we make a mental calculation as to how long it will be before this cliff, undermined in its turn, will come crashing down like those of which the ruins are the only remaining evidence. But we do not know where to begin. The cliff counts the ages as we count the years.

We now get sight of a still longer headland advancing out from the shore before us. It is Schooner Head, a promontory thrown off by Newport Mountain, which gets its name legiti-

OTTER CLIFF, MOUNT DESERT.

mately enough, notwithstanding the efforts made to cry it down, from the rude outlines of a vessel accidentally formed on its vertical wall. More than once I have heard it roundly declared a humbug, a phantom ship, or a caricature. All these are libels. This picture on the wall must be seen in the right light, instead of being condemned like the mediocre pictures of our exhibitions, because it happens to be badly hung. If, for instance, the noonday sun is shining full upon the cliff, it will be vain to look for the resemblance; but when the face of the cliff is in shadow, let us say in the afternoon, the pictured schooner, riding under mainsail and jib, stands out as clear and distinct as one could wish to see it.

SCHOONER HEAD.

The Spouting Horn, a deep rift in the rock, driven up through this cliff from base to summit, is seen to the best advantage only when there is a heavy sea to set it in full play, when a jet of fine spray is thrown high above the top of the cliff. Schooner Head, four miles from Bar Harbor, with its romantic Anemone Cave, situated a little south of the Spouting Horn, is one of the favorite resorts of the island.

Near by is the Lynam homestead, long a favorite haunt of those artists whose pictures first made Mount Desert famous. This certifies that we are among the most picturesque scenes of the island. Now and then the road to Bar Harbor comes in sight, to disappear again in the thick woods of Newport Mountain, like a girdle that has cut into the superabundant flesh. Here is little Thrumcap, to which we must give a good berth in passing. But cottages by the shore, and sailing craft on the sea, announce that we are nearing our port. Newport Mountain now rears its grisly cliffs high above our heads. A third cluster of islands, wilder and more forbidding than any we have yet seen, — all bald rocks below, with a headgear of bristling pines above, — stretches a broken line across our course. Through the intervals we look off north into the sparkling expanse of Frenchman's Bay. More islands, more mountains, more mysterious blending of land and water in the distance, meet us whichever way we look. At our right the mainland rises again in a cluster of misty summits, — the landmark of this bay, the sharply dented Schoodic Hills. Out before us is a roadstead thick with pleasure craft of every sort and size. And here at last is our summer city of pleasure itself. But we have seen enough for one day; we want to sit down where we can think it all over in quiet.

---

[1] De Monts' efforts to plant a colony under his patent are treated of in the chapter on Eastport.

[2] The patent granted to De Monts had been revoked at the instance of the merchants, who saw their trade cut off by it. They denounced the patent as a monopoly hurtful to the interests of the kingdom, but especially ruinous to the maritime ports, precisely as the English merchants subsequently did the privileges granted to Sir Ferdinando Gorges. Clashing interests worked out the same results in both cases. The merchants had the most influence at court, or rather the most money, which in those days of venality and intrigue meant nearly the same thing. Madame de Guercheville first procured the transfer of De Monts' rights to herself, and then obtained a new patent from the king, covering nearly the entire seaboard of the United States. Her colony was destined for the Penobscot, probably upon the report made by Champlain, or perhaps by De Monts himself.

[3] The martyrdom of Du Thet has furnished Mr. A. A. Hayes with the *motif* for a novel entitled "The Jesuit's Ring."

[4] The name Mount Mansell was probably given in honor of Sir Robert Mansell, vice-admiral of James I. It obtained among the English as late as 1676, but would not stick. The natives called the island Pemetiq, meaning in their tongue "at the head," and preserved in one of the summits.

[5] The island offered a convenient rendezvous for the Penobscot and Bay of Fundy tribes. In Hubbard's narration of the captivity of Thomas Cobbet, 1676, an account will be found of the way the Indians passed their winters on the island.

[6] Governor Bernard was one of those men who can be sometimes useful, but never popular. When his mind was not taken up with enforcing the Stamp Act, it was occupied with such schemes as that narrated in the text. Just what he contemplated doing is not very clear; but the settlers who are found on the island during the next few years doubtless came with his sanction or his aid. Abraham Somes came as early as 1760, as his grandson informed me, settling at the head of the sound which has taken his name. He was of Gloucester, Mass. In the course of the next decade a good many followed him, and by the close of the next there were 744 inhabitants. See Williamson's "Maine." John Bernard, son and heir of the governor, took the title of baronet upon his father's decease. See chapter on Eastport.

[7] Antoine de la Motte Cadillac, sometimes styled Lord of Mount Desert, received in 1688 a grant of this island from the French king, as the reward for distinguished services in Canada and Louisiana. He is considered the founder of Detroit. See Charlevoix's "New France"; Parkman's "Frontenac," etc.

[8] The Placentia Islands are Great Presench, or Black Island, the outermost one, Little Presench (northwest), and Gott's (northeast). Little Presench is named on a chart of 1723.

[9] Great Cranberry has five hundred acres, and makes the west channel into the sound; Little Cranberry, which the new residents call "Islesford," lies to the east with two hundred acres; Sutton's, formerly Lancaster's, lies west of north from Little Cranberry; Baker's, on which there is a lighthouse, south, with a reef joining it to Little Cranberry. The eastern channel into the sound is between Sutton's and Bear Island (lighthouse), the latter being also

the mark for Northeast Harbor. All the Cranberry Islands are inhabited and have growing summer colonies. They came within the Gregoire grant; were set off from Mount Desert and incorporated in 1830. They have a Methodist church, schoolhouses, and a public library. They owe their rise to fishing, and their name to a cranberry bog of two hundred acres. In very stormy winter weather the task of the mail-carriers is often dangerous, but they seldom miss making their trip, though the postmaster's wife has said it made her hair "stand on end" to watch the progress of the mail-boat when standing across for the island close-reefed.

[10] Those east of the sound are Brown's, Sargent's, the Bubbles or Twins, Pemetic, Green, Dry, and Newport; those at the west, Robinson's, Dog, Flying, Beech, and the two peaks of Western Mountain, in the order named. All lie in parallel ridges trending north and south. Between these ridges are a number of fresh-water ponds. Subordinate elevations prolong the seven principal ridges, but are of no great height. For instance, the Beehives and Peak of Otter are outworks of Newport Mountain, coming to the shore behind Great Head. In like manner Mount Kebo is thrown off from Dry Mountain at the north. Green, Dry, and Newport form the background at Bar Harbor. Green, 1527 feet, is the highest of all; Dry, 1268 feet, is separated only from Green by a deep cleft; Newport, 1260 feet, is perhaps the most marked in its outlines. These three peaks establish the topography of the east shore. Brown's, 860 feet, and Sargent's, 1344 feet, wall up the sound at the east; and Robinson's, 750 feet, Dog, 670 feet, and Flying Mountain, 300 feet, at the west. Western Mountain's east peak is 1073 feet; west peak, 971 feet. McFarland's, 751 feet, is the northernmost summit, lying a little north of west from Bar Harbor. Though not mountainous, the northern section of the island is hilly.

[11] Otter Cliff is five miles from Bar Harbor by the road through the Gorge. It makes the precipitous sea-face of Otter Creek Point, and is greatly admired for its bold castellated outlines. This headland makes with Great Head, next east, a cove partly formed of Newport Beach, and having the Beehive and Peak of Otter behind it.

TURTLE LAKE, MOUNT DESERT.

CHAPTER XXII.

IN AND OUT OF BAR HARBOR.

"'Fore God, you have here a goodly dwelling, and a rich." — *King Henry IV.*

ACCURATELY speaking, Bar Harbor is no harbor at all, but a roadstead only half sheltered by the Porcupine Islands,[1]—five weird lumps of granite, protruding above water, a little way off the land, the largest of which has a submarine attachment with Mount Desert, formed of a strip of shingle that is bared at low water, all awash at high tide, and covered again at the flood. This bar and island make clear the genesis of the name of Bar Harbor.

The other islands of this group stretch off irregularly round the roadstead, a kind of broken-down barricade, with deep water between to show where the sea has breached it.

There is a farmhouse on Bar Island, and some land under cultivation there, — a strip of greensward and a shag of woods, — but we notice that the farmer-owner, who awoke one fine day to find himself a millionnaire, has also fenced in the bar joining his island to Mount Desert, with a row of saplings, so getting the benefit of the crops of herring, mackerel, or porgies that are brought up by this weir, and left stranded by the tide, when one would only have to gather up his loaves and fishes, so to speak.

This simple statement will elucidate the whole philosophy of life at Bar Harbor up to the time when the golden shower began falling, and every one who owned a little land ran out to hold his hat. Some men are born rich, but here it would seem as if wealth had literally been thrust upon them.

Not a few of our best-known seashore resorts are but the natural expansion of decaying villages, — the evolution of the grub into the butterfly, so to speak,

— to which the advent of summer visitors has given a new lease of life; others are so many evidences of a cold purpose to turn out a watering-place to order. While there is a certain not unpleasing mellowness about the ready-made article which is wanting to the product of a day, yet it is not to be denied that a great many very worthy people look upon country life as a species of exile, and country living as but another name for actual privation. At Bar Harbor they find their Arcadia; so that odd but not uncommon feeling that one is being cheated if he happens into a place where money will not procure him luxuries finds nothing to feed its egotism upon at Bar Harbor, where money will buy everything. Indeed, Choate's famous *mot*, "Give me the luxuries, and I will do without the necessaries of life," might be taken as the accepted creed of a very large following.

A BIT OF BAR ISLAND.

The sum of the matter is that few places afford ground for a more instructive study of character than a fashionable watering-place; and now I think of it, why may not that be a primary cause for the rise of a new literature, — the literature of the summer resort, in fact, — since even one summer must furnish no end of affairs of the heart?

The study might appropriately begin with the arrival of the boat at the pier. The millionnaire gets into his carriage and rolls off to his cottage, followed by admiring looks; the half-millionnaire goes to the most exclusive hotel, pursued with obsequious attentions; the hundred-thousand-dollar man, to the most pretentious one, hardly noticed at all; the man with a salary, to a respectable one, whose guests receive him much as a garrison that is already short of provisions might an unlooked-for re-enforcement; and so on, down to the unfortunate who has to reckon on the cost of everything beforehand, and who feels it a privilege to be allowed to slip away unobserved to some modest corner. Everybody is subjected to the same magical touchstone. Consequently head-waiters who can tell how much a guest is worth, simply by noticing the way he walks into the dining-room, are sure of being engaged for the next season.

Nobody quite realizes what Bar Harbor is like until he finds himself absorbed among the crowd. To your utter surprise, you find Broadway among the mountains of Mount Desert, New York six hundred miles away from New York. "You meet again with the rustling of dresses, the confused hum of conversations and steps, the offensive splendor of artificial lights, the obsequious and wearied features of traffic, the skilful display of the shops, and all the sensations you wanted to leave behind."

A person who had not visited Bar Harbor for fifteen years would have to turn often to the mountains, the sea, and the islands to convince himself that he was really standing on the site of the puny village of that day. Without doubt, it is the most notable example of rapid growth New England can show in this direction, and unless all signs fail, it bids fair to hold a proud preeminence as "the capital of polite life, the mustering-place of the pleasures of the world of fashion."

It is curious to observe, however, that while fashionable people came here to get away from the crowd, they have drawn the crowd after them.

BAR HARBOR, FROM BAR ISLAND.

But what was it that first drew these fashionable people here, — the people of cultivated taste, travelled people, refined people, who know Nice and Naples, and Monte Carlo and Venice, and are not easily carried off their feet by the noisy applause of the *claque?*

Twenty-two years ago Bar Harbor began to draw to it a little of the travel that, before that time, had centred wholly about Southwest Harbor and that shore. It came overland, by way of Somesville, at first; for there was then no wharf at Bar Harbor at which a steamer could land. Tobias Roberts, who was the pioneer landlord here, built the first public house, the "Agamont," in 1867. Roberts was also the storekeeper and general factotum of this out-of-the-way little hamlet. Daniel Rodick, the owner of Bar Island, built soon after Roberts; and so late as 1874 there were, perhaps, twenty buildings all told, strung out at intervals along the lane then leading down to the landing-place — those for the public being flimsy, hastily built structures, half furnished and half finished, kept by fishermen or farmers turned landlords for better profit; because, as one of them very honestly said, he could make more money out of one summer

EAGLE LAKE, MOUNT DESERT ISLAND.

boarder, in a single season, than from the labor of three men on his whole farm. These worthy landlords are now represented in the second generation, as the first indifferent accommodations are by the great hotels over which they preside.

It is hardly possible to discover a trace of this petty village in the long rows of buildings now stretching far out into the country on every hand, or of the primitive hotels in the monster hostelries now occupying the same sites, or of the landlords themselves,—raw products of this rough, strong soil, that they were, — in the spruced-up personages who own the same surnames. Certainly it is no discredit to the guild that men who are island born and bred should have known how to compel the wave of prosperity to carry them along with it.

Though of imposing appearance, these Bar Harbor hotels, with their pie-crust decorations. are cheaply built, and, with few exceptions, cheaply furnished. They appeal strongly, however, to the national demand for the biggest of everything. If crowded, they are insupportable; when there are only a handful of guests, they are inexpressibly dreary. The landlords say, "We must have a big net to make a big haul." That is true, except when the fish have struck off.

TENNIS-PLAYER.

Bar Harbor is conspicuously lacking in the charm imparted to Newport by its delightful historic associations. It is not so much as mentioned in the standard history of the state. Hence no other resource is open but our eyes and ears. Our excursion of yesterday did not skim off all the picturesqueness or all the poetry.

I have just returned from a stroll through the suburbs. The day's routine was evidently just beginning. A string of carriages lined the curb from the

Rodick as far as the Grand Central. Two or three omnibuses were already in waiting to take passengers to Green Mountain, the top of which is in full view from the streets. For the longer drives to Schooner Head, Great Head, or Somesville, most tourists seemed to prefer the mountain buckboard wagon, a most democratic sort of vehicle, partly suggestive of riding on a rail, and partly of being tossed in a blanket. You are reassured, however, on being told that if one is overturned, the vehicle ordinarily escapes without injury.

The most striking thing I saw about the throng in the streets was the singular medley of costumes. One gets the impression that most of the visitors have travelled hundreds of miles in order to play at tennis. The aquatic side of life is also well represented. I came frequently across the gilded sailor, who is always shivering his timbers at the "hops," or smashing his tarry top-lights in the tennis-courts. Upper-tendom rolls languidly by in elegant turnouts; sharp-set land agents

THE BUCKBOARD WAGON.

lurk in the open doorways; florists, caterers, milliners, photographers, all have spread out their most appetizing or enticing displays for the expected customers. There goes a gun in the harbor! Another nickel-plated yacht has come to anchor. Another floating *salon* tenders its round of visits, receptions, and *petits-soupers* to break the monotony of life.

The winding shore path leading to Cromwell's Cove is still as charming a promenade as ever. You enjoy the open sea-view, the bracing sea-air, the splash of the waves at your feet, the gliding sails, the tasteful cottages, with their spaces of bright turf, their variegated colors, their carefully tended shrubbery and flowers. You see grave-looking men tossing pebbles into the water with boyish satisfaction, peering into crevices, picking up shells, or attentively examining what they may never have thought worth noticing in the whole course of their lives.

CLIFFS, SARGENT'S MOUNTAIN, FROM JORDAN'S LAKE, MOUNT DESERT.

There is something in that, at all events.

I found it quite different, however, when walking in the street skirting this fine bit of shore. . Here the inhospitable warnings, "No Thoroughfare," "No Trespassing," or "No Passage," stare one in the face as often as some inviting by-way tempts one to turn aside. Would not such of our seashore towns as have any ocean-front left, show a wise forecast by setting apart some portion of it for the use of the people, — the common people?

In going a little farther on, I ran up against the ill-favored camp of some peripatetic Indians. A sharp contrast, truly! Wild-eyed, bareheaded boys and girls were bringing bundles of fagots out of the neighboring thickets, on their heads. They were not a bit frolicsome, like other children, but had a hunted look, as if they had been sent out to steal and expected detection. Some well-dressed ladies stopped their carriage to admire these dirty brats of dirty parents. Once an Indian, always an Indian. This is the net result of two hundred years' close contact with civilization, — civilization in the land of schools, colleges, churches, the Maine law, and foreign missions. How, then, shall we hope to civilize the savage of the plains? These Indians were fully as squalid as their fathers. But then, their squalor is so picturesque! Besides, there is a prevalent notion that a real live Indian adds something to the attractions of the place. He is a feature. So have him we must.

Strange to say, these gypsies are everywhere allowed to hew and hack the woods unchallenged. You can hardly turn off the road to right or left without seeing some noble birch stripped of its bark to make knickknacks of. That means death to the tree. You meet them slinking about after nightfall with loads of basket-stuff on their shoulders. Their fathers knew how to split skulls; these fellows know how to split basket-stuff.

Apropos of basket-making, the Indians possess the secret of dyeing wood to a degree of perfection not yet attained by our most skilful workmen, though it is believed that the former make use of vegetable substances only. The secret seems to have been handed down among them from a remote time, and they are shrewd enough not to divulge it.

A turn around the skirt of the village brings one up to the high ridge which overlooks it at a distance, like the seats of an amphitheatre. In this place, those builders who found the shore-front already taken up have intrenched themselves, as it were, against the advancing village, which is fast closing in upon them. Here, they are far from the madding crowd; at least, for the present. And here they may enjoy that seclusion which is no longer attainable on the shore or in the village itself. Beautiful residences of almost every known type — rare products of the most correct taste, the best skill, the most lavish expenditure — stand thick among the evergreen groves, from which a warm, resinous odor exhales, mixed with the salt breezes from the bay. This hill colony stretches a belt of mottled colors around the skirt of the village, of which it is the fashionable citadel.

Not unfrequently, when deep in the woods, I came across a sort of skeleton tower, looking quite like an oil derrick; at least, if it had been in the oil region of the Keystone State, I should have had no doubt about it whatever. A closer examination, however, showed them to be lookouts, run up above the surrounding woods, so that by ascending the rounds of a ladder for seventy or eighty feet, intending purchasers might get an idea of what the view would be from the roofs of imaginary houses. Is the Eiffel Tower but an adaptation of the Bar Harbor land-agent's fertile invention?

But every picture has its light and shadow, and so Bar Harbor has its slums, too. Quite a large portion of the bay-front, extending northward from the steamboat landing, has been handed over to its least valuable population. It couldn't

TRAVELLERS' ROOM, SOMESVILLE HOUSE.

be a city of pleasure without its vices. This neighborhood is crowded with cheap frame buildings, which mostly stand on leased ground; and as they pay a handsome rental, the proprietor refuses to sell. In short, Bar Harbor presents at once all the extremes, — all the varied phases of metropolitan, suburban, and seashore life, — the fierce struggle for wealth, the dead weight hanging to the heel of progress, the clashing of permanent with ephemeral ideas, the sudden fluctuation in values, from which many have deduced the coming downfall of the place. That is certainly one way of bringing about the undesirable result.

I should say that the greatest drawback to the future prosperity of Bar Harbor lay in the ever-present menace of a disastrous conflagration. A city of boards, built on a bare, treeless plain, can offer little resistance to the spread of the flames.

One of the Desert Mountains, which Champlain first brought to the light of history, rises back of the village; yet so far as I have been able to discover, the name of Champlain is nowhere commemorated on this island. This is Green

WOODS, TURTLE LAKE, MOUNT DESERT ISLAND.

Mountain, and the view held from its summit easily ranks first among Bar Harbor's many attractions. There is a house of entertainment there for the convenience of tourists making the ascent. It is said that the windows of this house flash out their "good morning" as far as Belfast[2] and Montville, fifty and sixty miles away.

Visitors go to the mountain in vehicles as far as Eagle Lake, a beautiful little piece of water two miles long, lying underneath it near the Somesville road. They are then taken across in a steamboat, and finish the ascent by means of a railway sixty-three hundred feet in length. There is also a carriage road to the summit. Pedestrians who are not afraid of a little healthy exertion find little difficulty in climbing up through the ravine opening a wide gap between Green Mountain and Dry Mountain.

By whichever route he may have arrived, the visitor will hardly be able to keep back an exclamation of delighted surprise at the wonderful and memorable panorama of sea and shore which he is looking down upon, perhaps for the first time in his life. For many a year will those seas and islands float through his memory as he strives to recall the scene from the mountain top. Long will he treasure up the image of those lovely lakes set like gems in that "silent sea of pines." Never will he forget how suddenly, as if a veil had dropped from his eyes, a new, an absorbing sense of the sublimity of nature came over him, or the almost tender realization that he had been lifted up in his whole being, out of the world below, almost to see as the immortals see.

CLOCK, SOMESVILLE.

The tribute may even be something bizarre withal, though sincere, like this one. Once upon a time two of my countrywomen stood here, the dumb witnesses to the glories of the sunset. All at once one broke out with, "Oh, isn't it gorgeous? isn't it grand?" The other, who pressed closely to her companion's side in a kind of ecstasy, replied with decision, "Yes, 'Manda, it is slick!"

Although not a high mountain, this one is so commandingly placed that a very wide arc of land and sea is thrown open to the eye. You do not, however, lose the sense of proportion or perspective as you would from some higher summit. Under favorable conditions everything is clearly seen,—the swarm of islands advancing out into the vast sparkling plain of the sea from the grim bastions of the coast like a cloud of skirmishers, the far-off islands emerging like monsters rising to take breath, the leagues on leagues of forest rolling back their billows into the north. Lonely old Katahdin stands there at the edge like a spectre whom the day has surprised. Statuesque Blue Hill guards his lovely bay. The Camden Hills send greeting from the west; the Schoodic Hills, from the east. Then the eye drops down among the deep gorges of the island, rude cradles of the little lakes which seem turning their bright faces up to their shaggy guardians to be kissed.

Driving is by all odds the favorite pastime, one might almost say the favorite occupation, at Bar Harbor, and it lends an agreeable diversity to the almost numberless excursions by water. Indeed, that is where Bar Harbor, or Mount Desert rather, claims pre-eminence over all other seashore resorts of the Union. One may drive a hundred miles without even going off the island at all, and yet never be more than twenty or thirty from his starting-point.[3]

Well do I remember my first visit to Somesville and its modest inn, where I was the only guest. I could have wished there had been another to divide with me the attentions of the landlord, the hostler, and the errand-boy, which I found so embarrassing.

And now after exhausting the day's round of boating, bathing, driving, exploring the shores, or roaming the woods, of tennis, bowling, or billiards, the evening brings back city life again as certainly as flood follows ebb, with its teas, visits, hops, and receptions, its concerts, readings, and private theatricals for the young people, its quiet rubber of whist, or a book — it need not be the latest novel unless one likes — in some retired nook or corner, for the elders. This double life suggests the figure of a contribution-box into which every one is expected to drop his bright idea, and for which he is to get a recipe against blue-devils out of the common fund. It follows that the great man here is by no means the senator, the general, or even the millionnaire; he is the man of original ideas, who can not only devise new schemes for killing time every day and hour, but put them in successful execution. One has only to look in at some hotel parlor of an evening to see what zest the pursuit of out-door pleasures all at once imparts to all those in-door amusements which seemed so insipid when they were one's sole resource at home.

---

[1] The Porcupines are Bar Island, Burnt, Sheep, Round, and Long Porcupine, the latter being the outermost. Round Porcupine was once the property of General Fremont. At a sale by the state it was knocked down for $37.50. It is now claimed by William and Tobias Roberts under a title from Massachusetts.

[2] Belfast can be plainly seen from the summit on any clear day.

[3] The Ovens are a series of shallow caves worn into the rocky bluff, near Sand Point, by the action of the waves. They can be entered only at low tide, and from the beach underneath. Not far from the Ovens is the Cathedral, a detached fragment of the cliffs, from which it is separated by an opening called the Via Mala. This locality is about six miles from Bar Harbor. Salisbury's Cove, a short distance west, is the political centre of Eden, the township in which Bar Harbor is situated. Citizens of Bar Harbor have to go there to vote.

THE OVENS, MOUNT DESERT.

MOUNT DESERT, FROM SULLIVAN HARBOR.

CHAPTER XXIII.

AROUND FRENCHMAN'S BAY.[1]

"When thou haply see'st
Some rare noteworthy object in thy travels,
Make me partaker of thy happiness." — SHAKESPEARE.

WET.

CROSSING over to the eastern shore of the Penobscot, the country begins to wear a different look. It is more like what one would expect to see when passing out of the borders of civilization. Settlements grow less frequent, villages smaller, routes of travel more primitive and difficult, and in many ways the people themselves show a more marked individuality than their western neighbors. They seem, indeed, more like native products of the wild woods and rocks among which they have been born and reared. There are long stretches of coast where the improving hand of man has scarcely left a trace of itself. There are broad tracts of untouched forest reaching far back into the shaggy interior. Clearing these away seldom means opening the land to cultivation, as it would in the west, but oftener exposes the barrenness they have hid for centuries; so that with few exceptions the axe has really converted the face of the country into a worse wilderness than before.

To the observing or thoughtful traveller all this is a revelation for which he was quite unprepared. He now sees why this far coast, with so old a history, shows so little progress; and the wonder grows, not so much that communities everywhere fall away in population, as that men could be found willing to try conclusions with such an iron land, where a bare subsistence is the rule and the attainment of wealth the rare exception.

But, on the other hand, this state of things is by no means unpleasing to the sentimental traveller, for whom every indication of civilization is something of a disappointment. He wants the woods let grow, the deer preserved, the ponds stocked with fish, and he thinks the villages quite large enough as they are. The actual residents, strangely enough, look upon the summer resident as a means to that development which the penury of natural resources has denied them.

To the established prestige of Mount Desert the rise of the flourishing colonies at Lamoine, Sullivan, Sorrento, and Winter Harbor is undoubtedly owing.

Broadly speaking, Lamoine[2] occupies the east half of that peninsular part of the mainland from which Mount Desert is divided by the narrow strait

A SUNNY POINT AT LAMOINE.

joining the waters of Blue Hill Bay with those of Frenchman's Bay. The Lamoine peninsula roughly resembles an eagle hovering with outspread wings and uplifted beak on the inner shore of Frenchman's Bay, Jordan's River being under one wing, and Skilling's Bay under the other. Two deep coves form the beak, which is turned toward Frenchman's Bay.

The first settlers here came from Biddeford, Maine, to Old Point in 1774. There were also various French settlers, or owners, who held their land by purchase from Madame de Grégoire of Mount Desert, and from one of whom the township takes its name; but most of them vanished away without leaving more distinct traces of their sojourn.

The position of Lamoine renders that shore of Mount Desert extending between the Ovens and the Narrows even more accessible here than from Bar Harbor itself, while much of the interior of the island may be as readily visited from Lamoine as from most of the island resorts proper.

Just across Skilling's Bay, Hancock Point[3] is pushed down Frenchman's Bay toward Bar Harbor. This pretty peninsula is the extreme limit of railway communication with the out-coast at this time. From this point, passengers reach Bar Harbor refreshed by a sail of eight miles made in a swift and comfortable steamer, no less than by the exquisite views of the island, shores, and mountains which are impressively introduced.

Crossing tide-water again, we next set foot on another of those long peninsulas that everywhere elbow their way out from the mainland as if to obtain the best views of ocean and mountains.

We are now at the very head of Frenchman's Bay, in the little village and coming resort at Sullivan Harbor.[4]

The transition from the bustle of Bar Harbor is perhaps the first thing noticed here, or rather, one has not been fully aware how much the activity of

BITS OF SULLIVAN HARBOR.

Bar Harbor is like that of any other city, or how easily he has become part of it, until one has landed at some such quiet and secluded nook as Sullivan.

Upon landing, I saw a strip of gravel beach bordered by grassy banks, back of which the village is seated. Instead of a heavy sea pounding it, the waves rippled gently up the strand, diffusing a feeling of drowsiness to which the warm breeze blown off the pines added its narcotic effect. A little way offshore, in the tideway, which is here swift and strong, the black water was overspread with a network of foam as like lace worn upon velvet as anything could be, while fleeces of spume spun round in the eddies like so many Portuguese men-of-war setting out for a warmer clime.

From the narrow gorge above came the roar of falling water. This passage leads into Taunton Bay, a fine basin which extends up several miles farther inland; so that every tide fills it full with the clearest sea-water. But when the tide turns, the water cannot escape from this inner basin, through its confined outlet, as rapidly as it falls in the outer bay. It is thus forced out through the Narrows, by the pressure behind it, making a fall of ten feet in its descent to the basin below, and at the same time churning itself into suds against the sharp rocks as it goes. The roar of this fall was the only sound that broke the stillness, during my stay at Sullivan, except the occasional zip of a grasshopper. The local name of Falls Village is, therefore, easily traced.

It would be impossible to have a more delightful companion for one's thoughts than the long vista of island-studded water, over which the Mount Desert range lifts itself in the distance. It is a present delight and unfading memory. Nowhere do their rugged lines stand out more sharp or distinct than from here. The wide cleft of Somes' Sound, the rotund bulk of Green Mountain, the deep hollow carved out between that mountain and Newport, are all open to the play of light and shade, now in the dazzling sunrise glow, or again in the black wrath of the storm. From the piazza of the Waukeag House one catches the faint glimmer of Bar Harbor casements, and the white flash of sails against the mountain sides. And then the variegated spots of color peeping out among the sombre greenery, as one turns this way or that, make little eye-catching points of rare effectiveness as regards the whole picture.

From the harbor shore the ground slopes back easily to where it meets the forest. Behind this lies a wilderness of woods, mountains, and lakes, as wild and romantic as the unvisited regions of the White Mountains or Adirondacks. And back of this again a belt of hairy-breasted hills swings round to meet the Schoodic chain, of which these hills are the outworks. Avenues and drives lead to the most commanding outlooks, that from the Moorish pavilion at Ossipee Hill, four hundred feet above the sea, disclosing all this mass of tree-tops, rising hills, and sunken lakes beneath.

Hard by this airy perch, and extending out between two arms of the bay, which almost insulate it from the mainland, is the promontory formerly known as Waukeag Neck, but more recently as Sorrento. Sorrento is the name of a town in Italy. Every one who goes to Naples is supposed to visit Sorrento; but to visit Sorrento it is no longer necessary to go to Naples.

This is another attempt to realize that Happy Valley of Rasselas, the ideal resort. Formerly it merely grew up; now it has become an affair of capital, — of capital intelligently directed to bring about a union of the best conditions of urban and suburban life, minus their drawbacks or restraints.

A truly charming spot is this Sorrento, with its cordon of green islands thrown out before it in such a way as to form a snug little road, in which small

AROUND FRENCHMAN'S BAY.

yachts or large run no risk of being swept away from their moorings, blow high, blow low.[5] Then the peninsula itself is pushed far down and out into the bay toward Mount Desert, so as to hold that peerless island from the truest point of perspective, perhaps, for a thoroughly satisfactory survey. It follows that æsthetic residents of Bar Harbor have to come over to Sorrento in order to see what their own island looks like, before they can pretend to know how really beautiful it is.

Still lower down the bay — for we are slowly working our way out to sea again — we come to Winter Harbor, in Gouldsborough, where there is a lighthouse at the entrance to show us the way in. This is another candidate for public patronage. It should not be confounded, however, with the ancient settlement at the mouth of the Saco, where we have already spent some hours. This Winter Harbor lies across the bay from Bar Harbor, with which it has communication by a steam ferry.

When Schoodic Point[6] is doubled, we shall get sight of Petit Manan Light, standing up gray and tall on its rock at the eastern limit of Frenchman's Bay, to which it is the guide and beacon.

But before quitting this bay it would be an unpardonable omission not to say a word or two about its lone sentinel and farthest outpost, its rock of danger, in fact. Mount Desert Rock is the farthest land on which a New England coast lighthouse shows its warning "light in the window." Its gray tower is too distant to be seen from the island, as six or seven leagues of water roll between; but I warrant that not a few of my readers have seen it by night or by day, — a strange sight, indeed, in a strange place! — rising above the waves like the last monument of some buried city of antediluvian times.

PETIT MANAN LIGHT.

Here now is a spot where the terrors, the solitude, of ocean might well appall the stoutest heart. There is no need to have recourse to rhetorical metaphors. What is it but a prison, a walled-up dungeon, a horrible solitude ? A bare rock, drenched by every gale, holds the light-tower high above the waves. Drenched, indeed! There is an enormous bowlder lodged on that rock which the power of the sea, during some terrific storm, has split as cleanly as if it had been done with a quarryman's hammer and wedge. Not only has it done this, but the ponderous fragments have been forced fifty feet apart by the resistless power of the waves. How did this happen ? Did the toppling breaker throw its tons of water upon the rock and crush it by sheer weight ? By no means ; the rock was first lifted up clear of its bed, and then brought down again with such force as to crack it apart as easily as a schoolboy would crack a ripe cocoanut by flinging it down upon the pavement.

There is another bowlder that looks as if it might defy the power of steam to stir it a hair's breadth. Its great size and enormous weight render it to all intents a part of the isle on which it rests. However it may have come there, to all appearances it is likely to remain till doomsday, one would say. So, indeed, it would seem. Yet stay a little. Upon stooping down, we discover to our surprise several pieces of driftwood that have become tightly wedged underneath the huge mass, — " dunnaged up," as the keeper described it to me.

On one of those mild spring-like December days when Winter relaxes his grip only to take a firmer hold, I stepped again on the deserted wharf at Bar Harbor. Could it be the same place I had seen all alive with people only a few short weeks before? One lank mail-pouch was flung out after me. One bareheaded boy picked it up and started off with it up the absolutely lifeless street. I followed this lad to the one small inn, that furnished ample accommodations, however, for all travellers. Not a shop was open, not a creature stirring in all that long line of street.

THE WHARF IN DECEMBER.

It was a wild night. Nothing could approach the island in the morning, as the gale drove such a sea before it that one continuous roar went up all around the shores. On land and sea everything was in commotion. Now and then some mountain peak would struggle up through the clouds that rolled over them in great billows, like waves to the strand, showering down volleys of hail and sleet in their track. This silent combat in the heavens was in marked contrast with the loud cannonade of the surf below.

When the clouds lifted a little, Green Mountain had a white tablecloth spread out on its summit. I had entertained the idea of climbing this mountain this very day and hour; but, certes, it was no day for a picnic, and the warfare of the storm was far more suggestive of the poetry of Ossian than the poetry of Whittier.

By one of those sudden shiftings which has made the New England climate the subject of a treatise from that eminent philosopher, Mark Twain, the wind veered round from northeast to northwest, knocking down the sea, freezing the sloppy streets to the hardness of stone, and incrusting everything with a treacherous rime which tripped up the unwary pedestrian's heels in a twinkling. The stanch little *Sebenoa*, however, resolutely steamed out into the tossing bay, in the teeth of the gale, now wallowing deep in the trough, now getting a staggering blow right in the eyes as she rose out of it, which sent the frozen spray flying high over her funnel, yet always forging ahead with a hop-skip-and-jump-like motion, as if all this pounding did but put her on her mettle. A good sea-boat that, even if half the voyage to Sorrento did seem to be made under water.

Out in the offing we saw the revenue cutter towing a disabled coaster into port. This common enough incident proved the *open sesame* to the silence prevailing among those of us who preferred fresh air to that of the stuffy cabin below. The talk instantly fell upon shipwrecks and disasters at sea. I took down from the lips of an eye-witness of what he related, the following account of how a ship was saved, so remarkably illustrating the ascendency of a superior mind in wellnigh desperate circumstances, that I cannot refrain from briefly repeating it here.

During her voyage home from Singapore the deeply laden ship had met with nothing but gale after gale, from the effects of which she had become so badly strained as to make a resort to the pumps the only means left of keeping her afloat. The pumps were therefore rigged, and all hands set to pumping. Meanwhile the ship's course was laid for the nearest land, supposed to be about four hundred miles distant. After many hours of hard labor, disheartened at finding that all they could do

WHISTLING-BUOY, SCHOODIC POINT.

would barely keep the leak from gaining on them, the crew, to a man, refused to work at the pumps longer. In vain the captain commanded, implored them to return to their duty as the one hope of saving all their lives. Too panic-struck to care for either orders or entreaties, the men sullenly refused to stir. Seeing his authority was at an end if the crew continued in this state of fatuity, yet fully realizing the straits to which he and they would be reduced in a few hours more at farthest, the captain put his trumpet to his lips and gave the unheard-of order to unship the brakes and draw the boxes from the pumps. The men mechanically and wonderingly obeyed; but their astonishment was turned to dismay when they saw the captain fling over the ship's side, into the sea, the implements on which he had but just now asserted that all their lives depended.

"Now, my men," shouted the aroused commander, "you refuse to pump, do you? So be it, then; we will all go down together." By one of those sudden revulsions of feeling which a lofty mind sometimes inspires, the desire for life returned as soon as the last chance of saving it seemed disappearing before their eyes; and though they had just flatly refused to work the pumps, the crew, with one voice, now besought the captain to give his orders, declaring that they would go down, if they must, like men. All hands were instantly set to work bailing. "No words," said the captain afterward, "can begin to describe the way in which the men worked to keep down the leak." By superhuman exertions, the sinking ship was kept afloat until the gale abated, when the intrepid master had the inexpressible satisfaction of taking his ship, with her valuable cargo, safely into port.

Our humane societies award medals for the saving of a single life. Why should there not be a national decoration for the heroism that preserves a hundred lives?

---

[1] This name was originally given to the Bay of Fundy, in remembrance of the adventure of Nicolas Aubry, a priest of De Monts' company, who came near starving to death, while lost in the woods, before his companions found him. The vessel was then at Saint Mary's Bay, N.S.

[2] Lamoine formed part of Trenton until set off in 1870. The first settlers were Isaac Gilpatric and his son-in-law, Edward Berry. The French families of Des Isle and De Laittre found homes here. Professor J. C. Winterbotham has written an account of Lamoine.

[3] The forty-two miles of railway connecting Hancock Point with Bangor and the railway system of New England should be counted among the attractions of Mount Desert, since no similar example of natural scenery is known on this side of the Alleghanies. For many miles the route passes through a region in which it seems to have rained stones, many of which are as large as an ordinary tenement, — so large, indeed, that the engineers were compelled to carry the line around them. A straight road was impracticable. Nothing grows there except a few sickly birches. It is without doubt the track of an old glacier; such weird sights commonly show themselves from the tops of our mountains only.

[4] Sullivan, formerly New Bristol, was one of twelve townships laid out between the Penobscot and Saint Croix in 1762. Six were east and six west of Union River, which derived its name from that circumstance. Sullivan was No. 2 of the eastern group. It was incorporated in 1789. During the fever for silver-mining which raged throughout Eastern Maine a dozen years ago several shafts were opened at Sullivan, into which the companies put more silver than they took out. They have either been abandoned or filled up. The first settlers came from York, Maine. Besides David Bean, there were Daniel Sullivan, Josiah and Paul Simpson, Nathaniel Preble, and others. They had increased to forty families when the Revolution broke out, but were reduced again to twenty by the harassing raids to which their isolation exposed them. Thus, in February, 1781, a British armed vessel from Castine burnt Bean's and Sullivan's houses, turning the inmates out to the inclemency of the season. Quite recently a cannon-ball was dug up at Sorrento, supposed to be a relic of this affair.

[5] These islands form part of the chain stretching along the east shore of this bay, all the way from Schoodic Point to Sullivan. Ironbound, the largest, ranges with the Porcupines, and with them serves to break off the force of southerly gales from the bay. Jordan Island is next, and Stave Island next, north of Ironbound. Then Calf, Preble's, and Dram islands swing off across Flanders' Bay, thus making the harbor of Sorrento. Bean's Island lies out between Sorrento and Hancock Point. Seward's is east of Sorrento, in Flanders' Bay. Sorrento is thus well flanked on all sides by islands.

[6] Schoodic Point has a whistling-buoy, placed to mark a dangerous reef that makes out from it.

A FISHERMAN'S COTTAGE.

CHAPTER XXIV.

FROM PETIT MANAN TO MACHIAS, CUTLER, AND QUODDY HEAD.

"Wave after wave
Breaks on the rocks, which, stern and gray,
Shoulder the broken tide away." — WHITTIER.

AFTER passing beyond the limits of Frenchman's Bay, there are about forty miles of coast as yet scarcely known to the vacation rambler. If possible, it is more deeply eaten into by bays and indents, more and more cut up by outflowing streams, worse and worse tattered and torn about the edges, than the region through which we have just come. No less than four large bays strike boldly up into the land, and one of them receives the waters of two considerable rivers.[1] Beyond these, again, Machias Bay performs a like office for the watershed of a forested region lying behind it, which is fast being stripped of its timber for the supplying of domestic or foreign markets.

Petit Manan is an island of about twenty-five acres, prolonging Petit Manan Point, between which and the island itself a bar extends. Pigeon Hill is the prominent feature of the shore-line here, deeply indented as it is by numerous coves, one of which nearly severs the pointed backbone of granite, called Petit Manan Point, from this hill at its base. The portage — of some forty rods across — retains its old name of the Carrying Place, and the cove forming it that of Carrying Place Cove. By availing themselves of this short cut, the red Indians were saved a long, tedious, and sometimes perilous *détour* when journeying to and fro on their warlike expeditions. Many a dark file of savages has crossed here, bearing their birch canoes on their shoulders, and many a noble buck has been struck in the neighboring woods.

The eastern shore of Petit Manan Point, looking toward Frenchman's Bay, is now thrown open to summer residents and summer visitors; so that in the near future we may expect it to become quite as well known as the older resorts, especially as it is only a dozen miles from Mount Desert; though, to my mind, the wise ones are those who skim off the cream of a place before the crowd comes in with its staff of surveyors, architects, landscape-gardeners, and innovators of all sorts, to show us that, if nature defies art, art quite as often defies nature.

Among the villages that occasionally dot the green hillsides of this interminable series of points and bays — patient waiters for the wave of a coming pros-

THE CARRYING PLACE.

perity to make itself felt — is that little one of Jonesport, lying up behind Mooseabec Reach. Let us look in at Jonesport.

We find a sober, plodding, undemonstrative people, engaged in fishing, ship-building, lobster-canning, and the like humdrum occupations. A more unpromising soil to nourish delusions in one could scarce imagine. Yet it was from this very place, and under this same cold sky of Maine, that a colony of religious enthusiasts, whose zeal outran their worldly wisdom, set out for the Holy Land, some twenty-five years ago, with the avowed object of raising up a new Palestine on the decrepit civilization of the benighted Moslem. They were to be the vanguard of a reflux movement toward the hoary East. These people

AVERY'S ROCK, MACHIAS BAY.

were not driven to do this, as the Latter-Day Saints were in founding Utah, but embraced their voluntary exile in the self-sacrificing spirit of a new-born zeal.

A roving itinerant had come among them, preaching this new crusade. He possessed the dangerous gift of natural eloquence, seemingly without judgment or practical wisdom to give it useful direction. When pushed for an explanation of how this or that thing was to be done, by some of the more cautious ones, he would tell them "that the Lord would provide, and to throw themselves upon the Lord." To make a long story short, he induced his converts to sell their household goods, houses, and lands, in order to carry out this visionary scheme of his; and with the means thus obtained, the colony of Jonesport Redemptionists put to sea, and in due season landed at Jaffa, the port of Jerusalem.

Here the scales fell from their eyes. They found Palestine anything but a land flowing with milk and honey. Laws, manners, customs, language, — every-

SAND COVE, PETIT MANAN.

thing, in short, — were all new and strange, all so many stumbling-blocks in their path. Nobody did any other work except to beg. The "unspeakable Turk" looked upon them with lofty disdain. The leader whom they had so blindly followed proved not only a false prophet, but untrustworthy guide, and his promises a snare and a delusion. Recrimination and distrust soon followed. Too late they found they had come on a fool's errand. But even here the Yankee character asserted itself. One enterprising fellow started a stage-line from Jaffa to Jerusalem, thus distancing the patient camel and the methodical ass of old renown. The colony was, however, broken up, as a body, and its visionary projects abandoned to the necessities of the hour. Without employment or money, the members soon fell into destitution, from which they were rescued by the intervention of our resident officials, who procured them transportation back to their native land, where they finally arrived, something wiser if not better, it is to be hoped, than when they left it.

Machias [2] comes into the history of the coast of Maine at a quite early day; just how early no one can say; yet the indications we find pointing in that direction do not, so far, resolve themselves into certainties. That the French frequented it more or less from their first coming into these waters is as good as settled with those who have taken the trouble to look into the matter, although we do not find tangible traces of their visits, until our English chronicles begin. The first part of the history is torn out of the book; and we must therefore begin with the fragment left us.

It appears that in disregard of the treaty of 1632, by which Acadia reverted to the French, those free-traders in the broad sense, Isaac Allerton, of Ply-

ALONG SHORE.

mouth, and Richard Vines, of Saco, — two of the more distinguished minor characters of the time, whose antecedents we know something of already, — made an ill-advised attempt to establish a trade with the Indians of this bay as early as the year 1633. La Tour, of Saint John, promptly came and put them out by force.[3] Allerton and Vines lost heavily by the venture, and the Pilgrims, with whom Allerton had been playing fast and loose, could not conceal their satisfaction at the summary way in which La Tour had ousted their once trusted associate. There is nothing to show where this short-lived trading-house stood, — a mere wigwam of brush and bark, perhaps, — though conjecture locates it somewhere about Machiasport.

This village of Machiasport first hugs the foot of a hill, and then makes a dash up the steep ascent to scatter itself about the brow, like a column of skirmishers broken and halting to take breath. From this commanding height, the meeting-house, with its graveyard sloping off behind it, looks up and down the farthest reaches of the tranquil bay, and the whole scene, as I saw it lying out before me, at the close of a summer's day, was certainly as sweet and restful a picture as mind could conceive or heart desire.

In the cool of the evening, when the air was heavy with the scent of new-mown hay, I took the road which follows the shore, but does not touch it, till the falls are reached, at Machias, which is built around, above, astride, and underneath them, as if to intercept every drop of water that comes down through the foaming gorge.

Here is the water-power which drew settlers to the place [4] as long ago as 1763; and here are the all-devouring mills through which whole forests have passed, — a mournful procession, driven like sheep to the shambles, from which proceed loud cries of distress as a log is seized, pinioned, stretched on a sort of rack, and pushed into the jaws of the machine that instantly tears it in pieces and spits the fragments out again. Just above, are the logs that the river has brought down; just below, are the wharves, the boards, the sawed lumber, and the vessels taking in their cargoes. Around this centre of its activity the village spreads itself out with a charming irregularity and freedom.

Not to mince matters, the business quarter of Machias is homely; the residence portion, homelike. As the shire town, it is provided with a court-house and jail; as the political centre, with two excellent hebdomadals.

The inhabitants of Machias are justly proud of their military history. To the firmness and intrepidity of their fathers we owe the preservation of this extreme outpost of the colonies, throughout the Revolutionary War, though so little has been said about it that the fact is hardly known outside of the locality itself. Fortunately there were leaders equal to any emergency, and a spirit equal to any sacrifice.

It was in June, 1775, that two sloops arrived at Machias, under the protection of the armed schooner *Margaretta*, to be loaded with lumber for the use of the British troops, then mustering to put down rebellion at Boston. The feeling of resistance, which had united the people farther west as one man, seems not to have crystallized here as yet, so the vessels took in their cargoes without hindrance. But there were bolder spirits abroad who were determined to prevent the sailing of the vessels at all hazards. Their plans were quickly laid. A party of them first took possession of the sloops. Emboldened by this easy conquest, it was then proposed to take the *Margaretta* also. But for this hazardous venture the patriots could only muster twenty muskets and a few axes and pitchforks. They spiritedly resolved, however, to make the attempt, with such arms as they had, and having manned the sloops, set sail in pursuit of the *Margaretta*, which had dropped down the river, out of gunshot. One of the sloops soon got aground. With the other, Jeremiah O'Brien kept on out to sea, laid his vessel alongside the enemy, and carried her after a brief struggle, in which the British captain was mortally wounded.

Not satisfied with this day's work, however, the men of Machias next resolved to carry the war into the enemy's territory. They looked forward to an easy conquest, it is true, because at this time quite a large part, if not a majority, of the people of Nova Scotia were at heart favorable to the American cause. Relying, therefore, more upon this fact than in his own numbers, Colonel Jonathan Eddy[6] led an attack against Fort Cumberland in 1776. It not only proved unsuccessful, — disastrously so, indeed, — but was productive of great hardship to those friendly settlers who had been led to commit themselves, by word or deed, or had aided or abetted the invasion, in any way, many of whom were shortly driven out of the province or thrown into prison.

From this time forth Machias became the especial mark for British vengeance, which was only deferred until a sufficient force could be got together for the purpose in view. The rebel nest was to be blotted out of existence.

The occasion came when, on the 13th of August, 1777, three British frigates and a brigantine were discovered standing up the bay, with all sail set. This display of force would seem to have been enough to put all idea of resistance out of most men's heads; but the Machias men were not made of that sort of stuff. So under the lead of such men as Jonathan Eddy, John Allan, George Stillman, Stephen Smith, and Benjamin Foster, they resolved to fight it out then and there, and fight it out they did with a will. They sent off their women and children to the woods, called in Chief Neptune's friendly Quoddy Indians, posted themselves along the narrows of the river, and then waited for the enemy to come and attack them.

Machias is not an easy place to attack with large vessels, as they can only get up to it when the tide is well toward the flood. When it is down, they lie aground. From this cause Sir George Collier could only send his smallest vessel up to destroy the town. There is a point of land below the village called the Rim, at which the east and west rivers come together, thence running on in one stream. The Machias men had thrown up a temporary breastwork here, besides obstructing the channel with a boom. As the brigantine came up within range, in tow of all her boats, our people poured in so hot a fire from the banks and the battery, that she hastily let go her anchor below the Rim. Nothing further took place that afternoon. The next day, however, the enemy landed, under cover of a fog, drove the defenders out of the battery, cut away the boom, and set fire to some houses and a mill in the vicinity unopposed. Nothing now hindered an advance upon the village itself, except the stalwart arms and resolute purpose of its defenders, among whom none showed more conspicuous bravery than Neptune's warriors. Its destruction seemed inevitable, however, when the brigantine was seen warping up within gunshot, stripped for fighting; but the sight of large bodies of men advantageously posted to repel a landing, the demoniac yells of the Indians, who could be seen running from point to point in order to get a shot, seems to have decided the British captain to give

OLD MAN'S ISLAND.

over the attempt even after his boats were manned, after firing a few harmless shots. It was no such easy matter, however, to get out of the trap he was in. The boats were again set to towing the brigantine out of the river under a galling fire of cannon and musketry, with which the Americans plied them from every cover and at every turn, until the harassed and discomfited British tars found safety under the guns of the fleet, which soon sailed away leaving Machias scarcely harmed. Sir George Collier reported in his despatch to the admiralty how thoroughly he had cleaned out the rebel nest.

Although we have seen that Castine fell into British hands in 1779, Machias was successfully held against the enemy throughout the war. It yielded, however, in 1814, on the approach of an invading force. The circumstance that no garrison was found in the fort, except a number of bullocks, gave rise to considerable merriment among the invaders, one of whom wittily declared that American forts were far more suggestive of ox-parts than ramparts.

East Machias is the twin village of the other — identical in looks, interests, and situation. These three villages once formed a single township. As each one is four miles from the other, it was found expedient for each to set up for itself, thus again proving the old adage that two of a trade can never agree.

From East Machias to Cutler it is fourteen miles by a very roundabout route. For half the distance the road skirts the greater bay; it then winds round the head of Little Machias Bay into the wild and shaggy region surrounding the harbor at Little River, the name by which that part of Cutler has been known to sea-faring people in former years.

The long outlooks over the water, as successive hill-tops are climbed, the queer little hamlets occasionally encountered when least expected, would make this route seem a short one to the traveller, even if the cool stretches of fir and tamarack were not shorn of their loneliness by our loquacious driver's "swift and sententious" chatter about the deer he has seen walking these woods in broad day, like the "native burghers of this desert city." When a stream is crossed, he tells us about the red-speckled trout that laugh and grow fat in the shade of the alders. On this particular day, however, we saw neither deer nor trout, alive or dead. It is a thinly peopled half wilderness, between Machias and Cutler. One solitary hamlet was pointed out as being a settlement of Latter Day Saints. I have heard of such things before about Eastern Maine, but had put no great faith in them, until, on arriving in such or such a neighborhood, I found them to be a matter of common notoriety. My informant could not say whether polygamy was practised or not, but he gave his face a very meaning expression, all the same.

I saw also that the young growth of firs — the old has long ago disappeared — was being cut off right and left for supplying a comparatively new industry, — the Christmas-tree market, in short. These trees are shipped off by deck-loads, by car-loads, by whole train-loads, to our great cities, sold for a few cents apiece, perform their temporary office for pleasing the young folks, or in decorating the churches, and are then cast into the fire. What I saw were the acres of stumps. Farewell to the forest! The Dutch, who cut down most of the valuable trees in the Spice Islands to raise the price of those which remained, were sages in comparison with these wholesale destroyers of the young growth. The bake-apple, a species of wild berry somewhat resembling the raspberry, but getting its name from a peculiar flavor of its own, grows among these openings. But it is the blueberry that must be reckoned among the valuable products of Maine. One thousand acres of otherwise unproductive land, owned by the town of Brunswick, are said to yield an annual crop of blueberries worth five thousand dollars, and give employment to many poor people. I know of a family who picked enough berries in a day to buy a barrel of flour with on their return from the berry-fields.

As I have said, our driver was a chatty fellow who paid little or no attention to his horse, — he himself being occupied exclusively with his passengers, — except now and then turning to give the animal a cut of the whip which was enough to take off the hide.

And so we went on, crawling up one hill or clattering down another, stared at with wild-eyed astonishment by barefooted children from the roadside, bawled at by men at work in the fields, taking a letter here or a parcel there from women who had snatched up the first thing that came ready to their hands to put on their heads, — that being most often a man's straw hat, — until the very last of the great granite swells was surmounted that roll themselves together about the little hollow harbor of Cutler.

As we descended the hill toward the cluster of houses extending only part way along the edge of the harbor below us, a ragamuffin of a boy, who had grown out of his clothing at both ends, called out to us derisively, "The dog-fish have come!" For the information of such of my readers as may be ignorant on the subject, I would remark that this is the name now given to summer visitors along shore, in retaliation for that of "natives," which the visitors find so appropriate to the actual residents.

> "For as on land there is no beast
> But in some fish at sea's exprest,"

so the first name was undoubtedly suggested by the fact that those pests to the fishermen always make their unwelcome appearance at the same time that the summer boarder does his.

We have a moment or two to spare, so I may be permitted to relate an anecdote illustrating the feeling with which these "natives" are sometimes regarded. On a certain afternoon two city ladies were driving out for an airing, when they met a man walking in the road. The lady who was driving bowed to him as to an old acquaintance. Americans are not deficient in politeness; so the bow was returned, and the man passed on his way. "Why," said the other lady, "do you know that man you have just bowed to?" "Not at all," was the reply; "but I do it because it makes a bright spot in these people's existence."

ENTRANCE TO LITTLE RIVER HARBOR, CUTLER, MAINE.

By common consent there is no prettier or safer harbor on the whole coast of Maine than this same Little River. It has something of a new-old look, consequent upon putting off the old dress and putting on the new and strange one. It has hardly got used to its new garb. Its ancient tavern has thus been converted into a summer hotel; its old homesteads are being remodelled, or disguised with red and yellow ochre. In a word, there has been a discovery, followed by an invasion. It is a most romantic little nook sunk deep into the hills, which seem to have opened here on purpose to let in the sea. The rough hillsides, rising around, are shaggy with woods and bits of rusty crag. A high, rocky island, bristling with tapering spruces, blocks up the entrance so completely that, but for the lighthouse standing guard over it, a stranger would hardly find his way in at all, except by hugging the shore. It was probably this fact which led to the adoption of the unique sea-marks one sees pictured out on the opposite headlands, at the entrance. The one at the right has three horizontal white stripes painted on the rocks; the one at the left shows three disks, — symbols extremely suggestive of Jack's intimate acquaintance with the pawnbroker's shop. One of these headlands is traversed by a deep fissure which makes a fine spouting-horn of it.

In times past Cutler was better known, or known only, perhaps, as a harbor of refuge, or as a station for Bay of Fundy pilots, except to those who had the bad luck to be cast away in its neighborhood; with them it bore no enviable reputation. Even when I saw it the harbor looked far more like a marine graveyard than honest port; for in walking only a short distance I counted no less than eight old wrecks rotting upon the beach. Strange tales these sodden old hulks could tell! One had met her doom on the dangerous Murre Ledges of Grand Manan; others had been boarded when abandoned or disabled, and towed in here to be "wrecked," as the saying is, — plundered, in plain English, — under the shadow of the church on yonder hill.

From Little River to West Quoddy Head, a distance of five leagues, no shore could wear a more weird or forbidding appearance. Look where you will, nothing is to be seen but wild waves lashing an iron shore, with a pine here and there rearing its tall head above the dark fringe of vegetation. Except about Moose Harbor and Haycock's Harbor, which afford some little shelter, the coast shows an unbroken front of half-mountainous ranges of ashen cliffs, a league or more in width, from which monster headlands protrude far out, and against which the sea breaks so violently as sometimes to throw the water a hundred feet in the air. But rough weather and inhospitable coast are not the worst enemies the navigator encounters here.

Perhaps nothing could so well illustrate the character for lawlessness, which has made this locality a by-word among sailors, as the following story of a wreck taken from the columns of the *Eastport Sentinel*. The disaster it speaks of happened no longer ago than the winter of 1888.

"The story told by the crew of the schooner *Flora*, recently ashore at Boot Head, just a little to the west of Quoddy Head, is such a one as might be expected from castaways on some robber and outlaw infested shore, but hard to believe as happening on this Eastern Maine coast. Captain Henry Cram, who was in charge of the crew while Captain Lee came to Eastport for help, says that a gang of fifteen or twenty men from the vicinity of Bailey's Mistake came upon them Sunday night, and by every means they could devise tried to drive the crew away from the vessel and such cargo and property as they had got ashore, so that they might plunder and wreck the stranded craft. The shipwrecked crew were continually pelted with stones and ordered to leave their charge upon threats of the direst kind. Obliged to seek shelter from the stones hurled by cowardly thieves concealed in bushes near by, they huddled together at the water's edge, with their vessel offering a shelter for them till the tide drove them behind the jutting crags and into the deep crevices of the inhospitable shore. Thus the night was passed, the worst night, says Captain Cram, who has spent a half-century or more navigating this coast, that he ever put in. The next morning the West Quoddy life-saving crew came to their aid, and helped them out of their trouble."

I was further informed by persons of credit that when Mr. Havemeyer's yacht went ashore on Sail Rock, off Quoddy Light, and while he had gone after help to get her off, the wreckers, who seem to scent their prey like vultures, looted the vessel of her movables and silverware. Now you hear a great many well-meaning people say that this is a disgrace to the name of a civilized people, and so it is; that these pirates ought to be hunted down and rooted out with an unsparing hand. That is also quite true. You do not find, however, even in the large county building at Machias, where you would be apt to look for it, any evidence whatever that public opinion has asserted itself in the only feasible way by which the fair fame of the state could be cleared from the stigma of such acts.

The dangerous, low-lying Seal Islands, on which there are two lights, lie far out in the offing, surrounded by a perpetual surf. They are a mark for vessels coming from the southwest, and bound into Quoddy Bay. But the greatest of all landmarks here is that magnificent wall of indestructible rock, sixteen miles long and three hundred feet high, blue in the morning, purple at night, which lifts its towering bulk into view almost before Mount Desert has sunk in the distance. What other island could it be but the peerless Grand Manan?

---

[1] Steuben, the township lying next east of Gouldsborough, named for Baron Steuben of Revolutionary fame, is everywhere deeply indented. At the west, Gouldsborough Bay divides it from that town; Narraguagus River and Bay wash it on the east; at the south, Pigeon Hill Bay and Dyer's Bay enclose Pigeon Hill, and its extension, Petit Manan Point, between them. Steuben Harbor is at the head of Gouldsborough Bay. Narraguagus Bay cuts deeply up into Millbridge and Harrington, at its head, besides washing the shores of Steuben and Addison at its sides. The entrance is lighted by Pond Island (Narraguagus) and Nash Island lights. Millbridge is a shipping point for the lumber manufactured on the Narraguagus, the village being at the mouth of this river, at the head of navigation. Pleasant Bay, which

receives Pleasant River, at its head, mingles its waters with those of Narraguagus Bay, at its mouth. The distance across from Bowbear Island, on the Steuben side, to Cape Split, on the Addison side, is three leagues. Cape Split has a good harbor. From Cape Split we enter Mooseabec Reach (corruptly Moose Peak), a strait separating Jonesport from Beal's, Head Harbor, and other islands, among which safe anchorage is found. Mooseabec Light is on Ship Harbor Island, and a very lonely place it is. Leaving the Reach and skirting the numerous islands lying out before Mason's Bay, a run of seven miles brings us up with Libby Island Light, at the entrance to Machias Bay.

[2] Machias is called, on the map in Charlevoix, 1744, *Havre des Rois Magi* (Port of the Wise Men of the East), and the Seal Rocks, *Rochers Magi.* According to Morse, the Indian name was Mechisses. Whether the more poetic designation was derived from the Indian, or *vice versa*, is not ascertained. Bellamy, the pirate, went into the river to careen his two vessels; he built intrenchments and landed his men and guns. Church, in his expedition of 1704, found a Frenchman named Lutterelle living on one of the islands about the bay, and removed him. George S. Hilliard, lawyer, scholar, and traveller, was a native of Machias. There are some rock-markings at Burke's Point, which are supposed to have been made by the Indians. I was not able to examine them.

[3] For further information about this affair, see Winthrop's "Journal," II. 151, 152.

[4] The first settlers of Machias came from Scarborough, Maine.

[5] Colonel Jonathan Eddy was a native of that part of Norton, Mass., now incorporated as Mansfield. After the French war of 1758, in which he served with credit, Eddy, like many other New Englanders, settled in Nova Scotia. The town of Eddington, Maine, to which he removed after the war, takes its name from him. See Kidder's "Eastern Maine and Nova Scotia."

WHERE THEY PRY UP THE SUN.

CHAPTER XXV.

EASTPORT AND QUODDY BAY.

"*Ferret.* No fern-seed in my pocket; nor an opal wrapt in bay-leaf in my left
fist to charm their eyes with." — *The New Inn.*

BEHOLD us at last arrived at the point where, figuratively speaking, they pry up the sun with a crowbar, — at that elusive, and still debatable, Down East which is the fruitful source of so many quips and quirks to our transmontane population!

The passage through all the rocky galleries of the Pine-Tree Coast culminates at Quoddy Bay in a masterpiece.

Upon rounding West Quoddy Head,[1] and its zebra-striped lighthouse, Lubec lifts its one central and dominating spire above the dome of white houses, like the spike on a grenadier's helmet. It seems but a moment ago since we were breasting the open sea, with the wild waves tearing themselves to tatters

WEST QUODDY HEAD, LUBEC, MAINE.

EASTPORT AND QUODDY BAY. 349

against the iron ribs of an iron coast, and the strong tide whirling and surging up against our prow, as if to dispute the way with us; now we have glided into a long reach of smooth water, narrowing here, expanding there, disappearing yonder behind a multitude of islands, capes, or headlands, which lie stretched out luxuriously under coverlets of green on all sides of this delectable basin. Some lie in shadow, some in light; some are a dark green, some a bright yellow or faded brown; in truth, it is a variegated patchwork of colors from Dame Nature's own hands, yet always standing out in strong relief against blue water and azure sky.

Presently, through the open strait, which we are nearing at racehorse speed, we dimly descry the blur of red and white houses confusedly thrown up against a distant hillside, which is again topped by an odd-looking structure resembling a martello tower raised for defence. This can be no other than our destined port, the coming end of our journeyings together; the line, in short, across which Jonathan and John have so long looked askance at each other, but which mutual interest, social intercourse, and the feeling of a common destiny are fast effacing from the map.

The run up through Quoddy roads is made all too quickly, the shifting shores are passed all too suddenly for memory to hold what the eye grasps only for a single moment, and then sees receding in the foaming wake behind. Almost before we are aware, our great white steamer is tearing through the narrows, having on one hand the wharves of Lubec so near that the idlers exchange greetings with us; seeing on the other the light-keeper's honest face as he answers our deep-mouthed salute with a wave of his hand. This must be Mulholland's Point of Campobello. Yes, and out beyond us there is the Friar's Head. Out we dart into another still basin, to which this passage is only the vestibule.

There at our left are three rounded islands; here at our right the tawny cliffs of the Friar's Head glower upon us for a moment, as they echo back the beat of our paddle-wheels. Over beyond, stretched along the edge of a gravelly beach, we see the little village and harbor of Welchpool, with Eastport, on its island, advancing out toward it from the opposite shore; on one and the other side we see the Red Cross of England and the Star Spangled Banner waving amicably in the same breeze. At our right hand the green fields of Campobello glow warm in the sunshine; at our left the arid area of housetops seems impatiently thrusting back the country. Is it an epitome of national character? We shall soon see.

From this pictorial Eden one is presently turned out to meet the disenchanting aspects of unpaved streets and wooden walks, from which, on every side, handsome buildings, exhibiting the date of 1887, stand for so many memorials of the great conflagration which laid Eastport in ashes.[2] Notwithstanding the heaps of rubbish still lying about in odd corners, there is evidence of rapid if not complete recovery. The town is certainly better built, though appearances would indicate that the rebuilding proceeded with too much haste for a new era of good taste to come in with it. To that extent the fire was a lost opportunity. What is new has a raw, unfinished look; and what is old seems older still by its contrast with the new.

The island on which Eastport is built rises from the water, by a sharp ascent, to the summit of a high, rocky spur, precipitous and nearly inaccessible on one side, from which one gets a most delightful prospect of land and sea. This eminence was once crowned by Fort Sullivan, an earthwork dating from the War of 1812, but the embankments have been mostly levelled to make room for the iron water-tower, which looms up so conspicuously from every point of approach. There are scores of wood-built towns in Maine which might well take a leaf from Eastport's experience, before having resort to the old adage of shutting the stable door after the horse has escaped.

This hill offers an excellent vantage-ground for a picturesque reconnoissance of the surroundings.

At times a "very ancient and fish-like smell" pervades the air here, from which, however destructive of the romantic it may be, there is no escaping. This proceeds from the sardine factories by the harbor shore below us. The American sardine is simply a young herring put up in cotton-seed oil, and labelled with the trade-mark of some reputable French packer, — *Sardines à l'huile*. It is argued that what everybody knows to be a fraud is no fraud at all. This circumstance has given rise to no little sarcasm on the part of members of Congress who hail from the South, where the oil is produced, when they have been asked to protect an American industry.

Never having seen this delicacy prepared for the market, I obtained leave to inspect one of the factories; and if what I saw there be a fair sample of the methods in general use, then I can truthfully say that the desire to taste these toothsome little fishes again was then and there eradicated. Nothing could be more simple than the operation itself. In every factory there is a large oven, to the inside of which a rotary framework of iron is fitted, just like those in use in the cracker bakeries. This machine is capable of being turned by a crank from the outside. After washing, the fish are put in shallow iron pans, which again are placed within the machine, and the oven door shut, when the operator turns the crank until the batch is sufficiently roasted, after which the fish are taken out, to be packed away in little tin boxes, either with oil or a preparation of oil and mustard. They are then sealed up and are ready for market.

In 1888 there were seventeen of these factories in and about Eastport, from which, in good seasons, a very large pack is turned out; that is to say, when the herring-sardine is plenty and plump, and prices are remunerative.[3] At the time of my visit, the season's catch was not only poor in quality, but had been so light that work only went on intermittently in the factories. When the boatmen brought in a sufficient quantity, the works would start up and run until the supply gave out. The price formerly obtained has rapidly fallen off with the quality, inasmuch as competition has tended to make the packers more and more careless, in the desire to cheapen their product.

Most of the operatives whom I saw at work were young girls or boys between the ages of twelve and sixteen, perhaps, who were as lively as crickets on an October day, but to whom the use of soap and water seemed as a lost art. I went out of one of the filthiest places I ever was in, with a feeling that the old adage ought to be newly rendered for the benefit of all purveyors of food products whatsoever, somewhat in this manner, "Cleanliness is the first law of nature."

Besides the sardine factories, Eastport does a great business in putting up smoked and salted herrings for shipment to every nook and corner of the land. And her harvest-field is at her doors.

I heard a story here at Eastport most singularly illustrating how human pride may cling to a shattered intellect, like ivy round a ruin. For full forty years this man had lived the life of a hermit. Though he shunned all intercourse with his fellows, he was always courteous and affable enough when approached; but it was evident that he had found the world too much for him and would be apart from it. His poverty was a matter of common notoriety as well as of anxiety among his neighbors, for he was too proud to beg, and how he managed to live was a mystery that few knew the secret of until the day of his death. It seems that the recluse had somehow become possessed of the strange notion that the rocks lying about the place where he lived alone contained valuable silver ores. Under the influence of this infatuation he would every now and then wheel a load of them into town to sell them among his neighbors, who, it appears, were willing to supply the poor fellow's wants clandestinely, as they could not do so openly. They therefore arranged with a storekeeper who was in the secret, to buy the rocks of him from time to time, giving what the man needed in exchange. This novel barter went on for several years, during which time it is estimated that the hermit had wheeled upwards of twenty tons of worthless stones to his charity market, without ever suspecting the deceit being practised upon him. Surely this must have been what our old friend Hudibras meant when he wrote that enigmatical couplet: —

> "Doubtless the pleasure is as great
> Of being cheated as to cheat."

Eastport has no early history worth mentioning, and but little of its romance. At the close of the Revolution it contained only a single family. All this border was debatable ground — a source of chronic irritation between the two countries that threatened an open rupture at any moment — down to the time when a final adjustment of the vexatious boundary question brought peace to the settlers. A British vessel is reported to have bombarded Eastport in 1807, or long before the occurrence of actual hostilities. During the War of 1812 this part of the coast was harried with impunity by British expeditions fitted out from Halifax. Then, as now, Halifax was the standing menace to these remote coast villages. Halifax is still there, but where is the American stronghold? where, oh, where is the American Halifax?

In one of these hostile expeditions Eastport was surrendered, without resistance, to a land and naval force under the command of Sir Thomas Hardy, the friend and brother-in-arms of the gallant Nelson. This happened on July 5, 1814. A permanent garrison was posted in the town, which Hardy declared it to be his intention to hold as British territory, under the treaty of 1783. No vindictive severities marked the occupation. The inhabitants were required either to take the oath of allegiance to the Prince Regent, and thus become British subjects, or leave the place, — a course many preferred to a compliance with the order to denationalize themselves. Eastport continued to be a British post for three years after this war had closed, and under the pretence that the island on which it stands —Moose Island— belonged to New Brunswick.

I fancy, however, that Eastport will be found mainly attractive on account of its uncommonly interesting surroundings. In this respect it offers a rich field to the lover of natural scenery. There is a generous breadth about everything which commands respect.

In the first place, Eastport is part and parcel of a system of coast and inland navigation simply wonderful in its extent and picturesqueness. Go where you will, there is seemingly no end to the novelty or charm of its environment. And there is such a variety of water excursions at command that one is quite

EASTPORT AND QUODDY BAY.

at a loss to choose among them, and so usually ends the matter by leaving the decision to chance.

First and foremost, there is Campobello Island lying out before you for nearly its entire length. At almost any hour of the day you may go to Campobello. Then there are Lubec and the Narrows, with the five miles' drive thence around the shore to Quoddy Head. These two excursions will render us familiar with the shores and entrance to West Quoddy Bay, of which Campobello is the great sea-wall, and Eastport the metropolis. After these comes the charming sail up the bay, into the beautiful Saint Croix, to Saint Andrews and Calais, and Saint Stephen. Having thus carried the outworks, as it were, having sailed in smooth waters to our heart's content, there still remains the crowning achievement of an ocean voyage of twenty miles to Grand Manan, or of fifty to Saint John.

Eastport is thus exceptionally favored in respect of her superbly landlocked water front, no less than her outlying coasts and harbors, and is lacking only in the proper equipment of a summer resort to render all these natural gifts, so lavishly bestowed, thoroughly available.

Looking off across the water from the Eastport wharves, Campobello shows a background of low wooded hills stretching behind the more gentle undulations of the bay shore. Directly before us the bay makes a graceful curve inward between two headlands, so forming a broad, still basin from which the ground slopes back to a spacious tract of sunny upland that extends quite across the island in its narrowest part. This is the village and harbor of Welchpool. The southern promontory is the Friar's Head; the indentation, Friar's Bay; and the adjoining strip of high shore just pointed out is the admirably chosen site for the hotels and cottages of the Campobello Land Company, an American association which, by acquiring most of the island, have thus taken the preliminary steps toward annexation. Either we must have this island, because in the event of hostilities Eastport would lie at its mercy, or diplomacy must do what force could not for the defence of the American shore, by declaring it all neutral ground.

THE INVADER.

Campobello is indeed beautiful to look at of a summer afternoon when the low sun lights up, with an intense brightness, all the scattered cottages dotting the island shore from Windmill Point to Friar's Head.

Where we see so many evidences of the value of our shore fisheries, and where every one is more or less dependent upon them for his daily bread, we can but feel an active interest in all that pertains to a business that has worked so many miracles in its time and season. "And what sport," says the redoubtable Captain Smith, with true poetic feeling, "doth yield a more pleasing content than angling with a hooke, and crossing the sweete ayre from isle to isle over the calme streames of a summer sea? And is it not pretty sport to pull up twopence, sixpence, and twelvepence as fast as you can hale and veare a line?"

HIGH AND DRY.

The shores round about us are fringed with weirs for taking herring. But the prettiest sight of all, to a landsman, is the one witnessed on every forenoon here, when the Campobello boats go out into the northern passage to catch the pollock, which run in shoals here until the turn of the tide carries them out into the Bay of Fundy again. To this cause the Passamaquoddy presumably owes its name, which, in Indian, means Great Pollock Water. Hundreds of boats are then seen tacking to and fro among the tide-rips, like gulls hovering over a school of mackerel, until the pollock strike off for other feeding-grounds, when the whole fleet bears up for Deer Island or Campobello to land their catch. The boats used here are of the whale-boat pattern — sharp at both ends, deep in the water, and broad of beam — as the most weatherly, roomy, and quickly worked craft that a fisherman can have. The fish cured here, and called English pollock, are preferred by many people even to the codfish for a fish dinner.

I went over to Campobello impressed with the notion that there was quite too much "Taffy" about all those Welsh names that sound so outlandish to unaccustomed ears. Then again, this quarter of the world has always had such an unenviable reputation, on account of its fogs, that fog and Fundy have come to be synonymous terms with most people. "Why," said a man I met by the way, "you'd be a settin' there, with clear sky all around you, and in half an hour the fog would be thick enough to drive a nail into and hang your hat on it. Fog! Bah! Mount Desert's a paradise to it. I don't know but you could shovel it up and cart it off by the wheelbarrow-load if it would fetch anything."

Though haunted by the fear of fog from day to day, I am bound to say that, out of the ten days I spent in the neighborhood, only one brought the exasperating vapor along with it. And in this instance it soon disappeared under the ardent rays of a noonday sun.

To an artist in search of studies of fish and men, Welchpool is the ideal fishing-village, — oppressively quiet, strongly tinctured with the odor of smoked herring, and wearing a look of contented indigence. When the tide is out and the pretty beach of fine dark gravel is uncovered, all the lumpy fishing-smacks lie high aground, and all the wharves are left high in the air, so giving the place the appearance of having been swept by a tidal wave which has just subsided.

This makes us aware that we have come within the influence of the abnormally heaped-up tides of the Bay of Fundy.

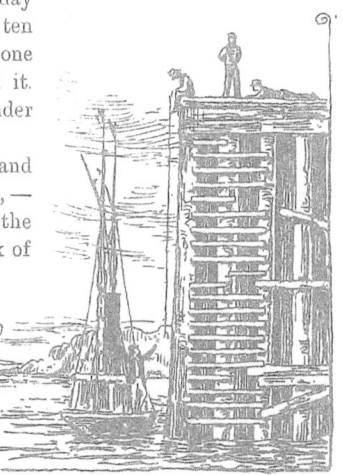

LOW-WATER MARK.

Of all the natural marvels that assail the understanding of an inland-bred man, this ebb and flow of the tides is perhaps the greatest, the most inexplicable. I have heard of people getting up out of their beds at two o'clock in the morning in order to go down to the shore and see the tide come in for the first time in their lives.

In this bay the tides rise and fall some twenty-five feet. This overturning of the laws of gravity, as applied to the visible universe, gives one who is acquainted only with the unchanging level of our great inland seas and lakes, a veritable sensation; nor is he, as a general thing, more than half satisfied with the explanation of Kepler or Sir Isaac Newton touching this wonder-working phenomenon, which has only become real to him when it has become a present, an active — why not say a living ? — fact. All the marvels of creation pale to that man's perceptions before this clock-like movement of the great waters, — the majesty of ocean obeying the majesty of God.

Apart from the influence of tidal flow upon the weather, — and great storms at sea invariably begin on the coast with the turn of the tide, — I know of people who believe firmly in some mysterious relation of the tides to human life, as, for example, that a sick man will not die till the ebb goes out.

A friend of mine once overheard a Western man asking a negro sailor if the tides came in and went out at any particular times. The reply was unique:

MEADOW BROOK COVE, CAMPOBELLO.

"Well, dat's mighty onsartin', sah ; sometimes dey rises in de day-time and sometimes dey rises in de night-time."

There is little enough to detain us about the beach. Clots of bladder-weed hang thick about the grimy wharves, like rags upon the shrunken shanks of a mendicant. The slippery stairs and ice-cold recesses beneath them, where the tide is heard washing darkly about, seem tomb-like in comparison with the warm air and genial sunshine outside. There is a deal of picturesqueness about all these lonely little hamlets, yet the look of stolid indifference one sees in the faces of those he meets awakens a doubt whether even an earthquake would make them go a step faster. Nobody seems in a hurry. The briskness

EAST QUODDY LIGHT, CAMPOBELLO ISLAND.

so noticeable in their American neighbors is altogether wanting. And the uncertainty attendant upon their one occupation seems to stimulate no desire to find a better. "We are fishermen," they say, "and our fathers were fishermen before us," as if this were the "say all and the end all" of the matter. And this is the type of the provincial fishing-village everywhere, as I have seen it.

While I was walking in the village street, a bell began tolling. Presently I met the funeral train itself coming up the hill-side, the bearers carrying the coffin on their shoulders, in the old, primitive way, a few mourners walking behind it with downcast looks. A pall bearing a red cross was thrown over the coffin. The procession soon turned aside into a thick clump of trees, from which the measured strokes of the bell still came, and I saw it no more. I afterwards learned that it was the burial of an aged person, who had become a

AN ARM OF PASSAMAQUODDY BAY.

resident here through his having been wrecked on the "Wolves" sixty years before.

The situation of the summer colony here presents the reverse of the picture as we saw it from the heights of Eastport, with different groupings and a larger perspective, however, and possibly, too, with a fuller sense of that panoramic luxury which every one acknowledges by a deep-drawn breath of delight. Campobello is just about large enough to admit of easy drives or rambles; there are roads leading all up, and down, and across the island, and the visitor here commands all the water excursions for which Eastport is the proper point of departure. At Herring Cove, on the eastern shore, there is a fine beach, from which the cliffs of Grand Manan loom grandly in the distance, and the Bay of Fundy rolls its dreaded waters before you. At the extreme northern end again, Head Harbor thrusts a long, natural breakwater off into that bay.

Here are certainly as picturesque surroundings as can be met with in a region preëminent everywhere for its fine scenery.

We have already noted that the Friar's Head is a prominent landmark, either when coming in or going out of this glorious bay. This name, which belongs, first of all, to the headland itself, comes from an upright column of gray rock standing a little out from the base of the cliff, of which it once formed part. Before a senseless piece of vandalism destroyed the resemblance, the figure was taller by a head than we now see it. The story goes that during the War of 1812 the head was shot off by a British man-of-war to show her skill in gunnery.

The large island lying out between Lubec and Friar's Head is Treat's, formerly Allan's, Island.[4] It was once the residence of that Colonel John Allan

CHAMCOOK MOUNTAINS.

whom we have seen defending Machias, and who, by his prudent management in bringing the local tribes over to the American cause, succeeded in erecting a living barrier against British aggression from the side of Nova Scotia during the Revolutionary contest. It is vain to comment upon the stupidity which allows this obliteration of historic names to pass unheeded. So long as it shall continue, Old Mortality's chisel can never be idle among us.

Though the excursion to Calais may be made with a historic purpose, or with no purpose at all except the gratification of sight-seeing, it should never be omitted from the tourist's itinerary.

The swift little steamer *Rose Standish* makes daily trips between Eastport and Calais. From first to last it is an excursion full of enjoyment. First comes the passage of the whirlpools, set in motion by the crashing together of the opposing tides, that meet and struggle for mastery in the narrow waters between Deer Island and the mainland. It is, indeed a novel sensation to see enormous funnel-shaped water-holes twenty, forty feet wide open suddenly to right and left as if to swallow boat and all. This never fails to cause a ripple of excitement on board, similar to what is experienced in running the Lachine rapids or the Niagara whirlpools. No sooner has the boat entered the area of broken water than her headway is checked as suddenly as if an invisible hand had seized her prow. The shores creep by. Woe to the unlucky boatman who should be drawn within reach of all this foam and fury; for stanch as she is, even our gallant steamer reels like a drunken man as she fights her way through it foot by foot!

Getting clear of this tumult, we are once more free to scan the shores that bound these narrow seas with walls of rugged strength, fertile slopes, or mystic headlands.

Cleaving the crystal water, down in whose depths the graceful medusæ flit by, like lilies on the bosom of

ALONG THE WHARVES, SAINT ANDREWS, NEW BRUNSWICK.

some clear inland lake, we see, at our left, a green hill-side, thinly sprinkled with houses, that slopes to the bay. Conspicuous among them is a chapel. This is Pleasant Point, the home of what are left of the Passamaquoddy tribe,[5] impotent remnant of those valiant and dreaded warriors who once filled New England with mourning. One solitary figure, erect and motionless in his canoe, stands gazing at us with uplifted paddle as we sweep past him. Is he wondering why God first gave his fathers the land for a dwelling, and then took it from them to bestow upon this strange, hurrying race?"

Close upon our right rise up the masses of gray crag, moss-grown and forest-crowned, that make the shores of Deer Island. How cool and inviting they look! From top to bottom their sides are crossed by deep cracks from which stunted firs lean out over the water; while mosses and trailing vines spring from the seams with a highly decorative effect. Down at low-water mark, where the cliffs have been deeply worn into, the surf plays finely among the hidden nooks and crannies and ice-cold caves. But suddenly the side of this island breaks away toward the east; we pass out upon the bosom of a noble bay, and there opens before us a picture of land and water, which for breadth, for that harmonious blending of one with the other, — of mountains tossed up here, of low, wooded points creeping out there, of villages and farms on the hill-sides; or again, the long leagues where you look in vain for any sign of a human habitation, — seems almost perfection itself. Then it is so land-locked on every side that we speed along over water as calm as a mill-pond, following with our eyes the hazy outlines of the New Brunswick coast in one direction, till it waxes faint as the moon in the day-time, or coming back to scan the American shore again in the other, over which the Chamcook Hills seem asserting a sort of sovereignty that not even national treaties can shake off.

A BIT OF JOE'S POINT, ON THE SAINT CROIX.

Crossing this bay to Saint Andrews,[6] once a port of some note, but now exhibiting those unmistakable symptoms of decay that seem so peculiarly adapting it to the demands of a watering-place, we stop only long enough for a rapid survey of the waterfront, where the many facilities for doing business make its absence all the more impressive. The site of Saint Andrews is charming. The pointed peninsula on which it stands is washed on either side by the Passamaquoddy Bay, or the Saint Croix River. Three miles behind it is Chamcook Mountain, with its lovely lake, like Agamenticus, at the west, — the lone sentinel of all this border.

Beginning our zig-zag voyage into and across the Saint Croix, we next touch at the pretty village of Robbinston, on the American shore. Then for a sail that in some respects rivals the beauties of the far-famed Hudson itself.

EASTPORT AND QUODDY BAY.

Two miles and a half above we leave a little wooded islet on our left, having before us, and a little at our right, another and larger island, showing a gravel bluff, as we approach it, crowned by a lighthouse. As we come nearer

DE MONTS' ISLAND.

still, a part of this bluff separates itself from the rest, thus forming a detached knoll of land, overgrown with bushes, but joined with the main island by a dry ledge. The whole island is, in fact, a bank of gravel and sand rising up from a long ledge of rocks in the middle of the Saint Croix, and exposed as it is to the abrasion of ice on all sides, was probably much larger two hundred years ago than we see it to-day.

The island is, however, firmly anchored in history. It is famous as the harbor in which the Sieur de Monts and the faithful Champlain wintered so long ago, — some time called Neutral Island from its position as an international landmark, but more frequently Dochet's, or Docie's, Island by the people living on both sides of the line. Even at this distance of time all those features which Champlain has handed down to us, with so much painstaking care, are easily distinguished. So, too, are the drawbacks which told so heavily against a successful occupation, but were not perceived till too late. We cannot wonder when Champlain says they were deceived by the attractive appearance of everything around them, or feel surprise at the remark that one must pass a winter here to know what it is like.

UNDER JOE'S POINT, SAINT ANDREWS, N.B.

To build their houses, the island was stripped of its wood. All winter they suffered for want of firewood. In their haste to get under cover they neglected to dig a cellar, even for their storehouse; in consequence of this error all their provisions and liquors were frozen. They dug a well, but the water proved bad and insufficient for their wants at that. Scurvy attacked them, and they had neither the knowledge nor the means requisite to check its fatal progress from day to day. The ice locked them up as in a prison, notwithstanding they were only a gunshot away from the shores, because the anchor ice made launching a boat too dangerous a thing to attempt even when they were so sorely pressed for those two common necessaries, wood and water. So they were virtually prisoners in their island. In short, they had set themselves in an inaccessible position, only to be starved out by an enemy that had first closed every avenue of escape.

But stranger than the strange story itself, and harder to believe, is the sequel to it. Will it be credited that this episode of history had so far faded from the knowledge of men, or that time had so thoroughly effaced every trace of the colony, that in less than two hundred years it required a special search to determine its site?[7]

---

[1] West Quoddy Head is the extreme southeast corner of Maine and of the United States. The highest point is elevated one hundred and fifty feet above sea-level, though the bluff on which the lighthouse stands is but ninety feet above it. This light was built in 1808, and is the important landmark to the western passage into Quoddy Bay, as that on East Quoddy Head, at the northernmost point of Campobello, is to the eastern entrance. In clear weather the tower, with its alternate red and white stripes, is a very conspicuous object; and in thick weather its fog-signal enables the mariner to feel his way along the shore, guided by the sound; but just off this light the dangerous conical ledge known as Sail Rock protrudes its ugly head above the waves with deep water all round it. It was on this rock that Mr. Havemeyer's steam yacht struck during a fog, and while being got off sunk in fifteen fathoms of water. A new lighthouse is now (1889) being built on the site of the old wooden beacon in West Quoddy Bay, which, when completed, will greatly facilitate the navigation of this crooked channel from the Head up to Lubec. The southern end of Campobello is a dangerous place for vessels making West Quoddy Bay in a storm. Two were wrecked there in one night during the winter of 1888.

[2] Eastport, first called Moose Island, took its name at its first incorporation as a town in 1798, and from its local situation. It then had about thirty families, and comprised all of what is now Lubec, with the islands between them; but that town was set off in 1811, mainly growing up from the withdrawal to it of citizens averse to living under British rule. Accounts differ about the date to which settlement should be referred, some fixing it as early as 1772; while Williamson, who is probably nearer being correct, places it at about 1780. One authority puts Colonel John Allan, with others, refugees from Nova Scotia, at Lubec, as early as 1776; but this is plainly unwarranted, inasmuch as Allan made Machias his headquarters until the war was over. In a letter of August, 1777, he speaks of Machias as "the frontier of the state, the last retreat . . . and key of the eastern country." At this time there were, perhaps, a few settlers living about Passamaquoddy Bay, chiefly on Campobello and at Saint Andrews. Eastport, or Moose Island, was granted to Sir Francis Bernard, along with Mount Desert (see that chapter). Before the restoration to him of Mount Desert, his son John

dwelt some time at Pleasant Point, in Perry, where the Passamaquoddys now live, in a hut built by himself, and with no other companion than a dog.

³ The output of the sardine factories is about three hundred thousand cases annually. The fishermen get eight dollars the hogshead on an average for this fish. When fully employed, the factories give work to from eight hundred to one thousand hands, men, women, and children, who earn, perhaps, eight thousand to ten thousand dollars per week. The smoked herring business produces about two million boxes yearly. The waters around Eastport are usually very productive. Cod, haddock, pollock, hake, halibut, and lobsters are taken in them. Railroads are wanting to give increased facilities for business, as well as to bring in summer travel.

⁴ Treat's (Allan's) Island contains about seventy acres of good land. I have been informed that the first canning business in Maine was begun here. The house on it, "with two doors," used to be the sailor's mark, in running for Eastport, before the day of lighthouses or beacons. The smaller island, lying to the southwest of Treat's, is called Dudley's on the United States coast survey charts; and the little, high, round one, next the ship channel, Pope's Folly. The boundary line runs through it, making it convenient for smuggling in times past. This cluster of islands, including Eastport itself, covers the entrance into Cobscook Bay on the northwest. They were determined to be ours under the treaty of Ghent, and were formally surrendered to us July, 1818, when our flag was again hoisted over Eastport. At this period there were earthworks on Treat's Island.

⁵ Passamaquoddy is said to mean the "Place of Pollocks," or, according to some authorities, "Great Pollock Water." The tribal reservation is in the town of Perry. Charlevoix calls the Indians of these parts Etechemins, or Malecites, distinguishing them from the Penobscots on one side and Micmacs on the other. The following clipping from an Eastport newspaper may be thought somewhat whimsical. "With the increased material prosperity enjoyed by the Pleasant Point Indians in late years, has also come a desire for better government. At planting time this year a tribal meeting was held by authority of Governor Lola, and besides electing policemen, certain regulations or by-laws were adopted, some of which have a striking resemblance to the old-time blue-laws of our fathers. One section of the by-laws reads as follows: 'Any woman out walking 'bout after dark, policeman he 'rest him, take um back home.' And another, 'Any cow found loose in village, policeman he 'rest him.'" The tribe numbers about six hundred persons, mostly engaged in basket-making for a living. Some few go winter fishing. There are about one hundred pupils in schools, taught by sisters of charity. The native tongue is fast dying out, as the children are brought up to learn English. These Indians are wards of the state of Maine.

⁶ Saint Andrews is a decayed seaport at the mouth of the Saint Croix, in a situation of great natural beauty. It is now coming into prominence as a summer resort, but my plan and purpose do not admit of a more extended notice at this time.

⁷ In 1796 commissioners appointed by the two governments were led to visit this island with the view of determining which of the three rivers emptying into Passamaquoddy Bay was the true Saint Croix. Heretofore this river had been called by its Indian name, the Schoodic. The American commissioners contended for the Magaguadavic, the eastern river. Naturally, the solution of the dispute turned upon the identification of De Monts' settlement, since it was he who first named the Saint Croix. Remains of an ancient fortification found on the island served to settle the question, beyond reasonable controversy, in favor of the Schoodic, and it was so determined by the agents of the two nations. Since then cannonballs, and other evidences of the French occupation, have been dug up about the island. See Holmes' "American Annals," p. 149, notes; "N. E. Hist. and Gen. Regr." XIII., p. 160.

BOAT-HOUSE AND WHARF, GRAND MANAN.

CHAPTER XXVI.

A RUN ACROSS GRAND MANAN.

"I shall no more to sea, to sea;
Here shall I die ashore." — SHAKESPEARE.

BEAUTIFUL as it is, the first blossoming of the wayside golden-rod does not bring unmixed satisfaction to the summer idler, since it but too surely prefigures the term to his capricious wanderings as all too nigh.

Having had the good fortune to meet with an old and respected resident of Grand Manan, of goodly countenance withal, and a full man besides, we talked the matter over before a rousing fire one evening, with the result that when the *Flushing* steamed out of Eastport the next morning, I found myself on board of her. On some of the large steamers that ply these waters, the inquiring traveller more often gets a curt answer than a civil one; but on any of the smaller coastwise vessels, where there is less red tape and gold lace, one finds a refreshing willingness to give information which, as it adds so much to the interest of the voyage, while it costs the giver nothing at all, one will not be slow to appreciate. This is well. Even a steamboat captain may sometimes entertain angels unawares.

I wish every one might have as perfect a day for the voyage as I did. The run out into the open sound occupied scarce an hour. The boat was then headed straight for the island in order to take advantage of the eddy formed by the rushing up of the ebb out of the Bay of Fundy, against the northern head of Grand Manan, by which the hurrying flood is deflected off the shore of the island.

We now held the coasts of Campobello and of Grand Manan under the eye from stormy cape to frowning headland. Away off to the eastward of this passage, the low-lying clump of rocks called the Wolves could be dimly made out. They are aptly named, for a more hungry-looking pack never beset the bewildered mariner's stormy path. Manan was yet distant when we first made out three or four white specks clinging or floating, one could scarce tell which, about the water's edge, and down at the very bottom of a deep fissure opening in the cliffs above. This forlorn little spot is Dark Harbor; no harbor at all, but a place where a few fishermen have their huts in summer, on account of a natural herring-pond formed there by the sea-wall under the cliffs. The fish run into this pond at the flood, and are taken out in shoals at the ebb. Once there was something of a cove here, but in some great gale the sea sealed it up to everything larger than a fishing-boat, and so it remains.

From every distant point the resemblance of Grand Manan to a long and regular wall of rock strikes every one alike. Sometimes it looks like the edge of a storm brooding over the sea. But on getting closer to it, what has appeared to us like a regular wall now breaks up into a series of monster headlands over which the upper forest rolls cataracts of green half way down the cool gorges between. There they meet the naked rock. Out of these billowy masses the stark and mutilated cliffs force their way into the sunshine, seamed with a thousand scars and glistening with moisture. Except the handful of cabins seen at Dark Harbor, all these long leagues of shore, all this immense lift of cliff and forest, is one unbroken solitude, — a fact going far to augment its terrors with sailors.

On closing with the island we found deep water and bold shores. Soon we were cutting through the glossy black shadows that the Northern Head flings down, — a dark-browed, beetling giant, so hewed and hacked about its base, so bulging and impending overhead, that one's thoughts are soon busy with the notion of how easily it could crush our egg-shell of a boat. That is one way of taking account of its height. How slowly we creep by it! That helps us to form some idea of its mass. And how disdainfully it seems brushing aside the torrent that comes pouring out of the Bay of Fundy as if ocean's flood-gates had been suddenly opened to its foam and fury! Now we are among the tide-rips, and it is now steam against a waste of leaping water into which the colossal headland has forced its iron beak. We make a bold push through it, however, leaving two or three fishing-boats bobbing helplessly up and down in our wake; for the wind has died away under the cliffs, and tugging at the oar is but slow work here.

Having left behind the isolated rock called the Bishop, which the great Northern Head seems dandling on its huge club-foot, Whale Cove quickly comes in sight. The side of the island seems actually gouged out to make room for it between the deformed crags of Fish Head, at the east and the equally hideous

Eel Brook Point at the west. A fog-horn is located on the high bluff here to warn vessels off, or guide them by its sound. Here, too, was the scene of a dismal wreck, which no islander has yet forgotten, though it happened full forty years or more ago. We are soon up with Swallow-Tail Point, another murderous-looking heap of naked rock, on whose prostrate neck the lighthouse seems planting its conquering foot and lifting its flaming spear. Turning this last point, the *Flushing* slipped quietly into Flagg's Cove, and up to her wharf, which is ascended by means of an inclined plane, extremely suggestive of the roof of a house rising out of a submerged village.

Flagg's Cove is not much of a harbor, it is true. But one hardly expects to find either so large or so neat-looking a settlement in such an out-of-the-way place. Boats dot the water; fish-houses skirt the beach; a tier of cottages rises at the back. I found it but the type of many a secluded nook of the New England coast, or perhaps it may be better described as an assemblage of one and two story houses, all cast in the same mould. As there yet exist no osten-

TREND OF THE HEADLANDS.

tatious exhibits of wealth to make the fisherman's poor cottage seem poorer, one accepts the prevailing stamp of democracy as the product of native, not of forced growth. By the same token we may dismiss it as readily for its want of interest.

We have just seen the great western coast-wall of Grand Manan, inaccessible alike to foot of man or wrath of storm, throughout its whole length. We now see that behind this wall the land makes a gradual descent to the sea-level at the Bay of Fundy shore, though even this low-lying coast is bolted to the great western wall with ribs of rock that at intervals run quite across the island into the sea, thus forming several harbors between them. It looks tame, however, in comparison with the precipitous side. Then again, this eastern side is all crushed away, so forming islands which serve to defend the harbors and break off the sea, while the western admits nothing and harbors nothing. One might say that the island turned its back to Maine, but opened its arms to Nova Scotia.

Grand Manan Island is said to have been discovered by Champlain in the year 1604. He is supposed to have put into Whale Cove for a harbor.

CLIFFS AND BEACH, GRAND MANAN.

Long ago, even before it was inhabited by white men, and possibly before it was inhabited at all, since we are without any definite record of its ever having been a permanent residence of the natives, this island was the known landmark for the Saint John River, and is so set down in old French charts. But its forbidding coast, its baffling currents, and outlying shoals, among which it was equally dangerous to get becalmed or be driven by stress of weather, were looked upon with dismay, rather than delight, so that it was seldom visited by sailors. On the other hand, its isolation was a stumbling-block to settlement. Thus it was left to slumber on, in its ocean cradle, until some exiled Royalists from New England pitched upon it for their home.[1]

The observing Champlain, who saw almost everything worth seeing on our coasts, calls this island Mathane, probably because his native interpreters gave it that sound in naming it to him, and he quite correctly estimates its length at six leagues; but he has little else to say of it except to indicate its position and bearings. The learned Charlevoix, who was ever on the alert for what was marvellous, tells us that "three-quarters of a league off Grand Manan there is a rock, almost always under water, which is nothing but one great lapis-lazuli. They say, moreover," he continues, "that the Commander Razilli broke off a piece which he sent into France, and that the Sieur Denys, who saw it, said it was esteemed worth ten crowns the ounce."

Whether the whole of this rock was carried into France, or sunk in the ocean by the gnome who guarded it, it is certain that it is not laid down on any chart or found in the cabinet of any museum. Coming as they did from the pen of a holy father of the Church, such tales were undoubtedly buzzed about the seaports of France as gospel truth, so turning many eyes toward the new Eldorado across the sea.

As touching the islanders themselves, visitors are apt to feel disappointment because they do not show singularities as striking, in their way, as the scenery of their island. Hard labor, simple manners, and enforced economy make very plain folk. But there are neither barbarians nor cannibals on this island. A man is considered well off who owns a fairly good house, a mowing-lot, a few sheep, some pigs, and two or three cows. If he have a horse besides, he would be an object of envy to his neighbors. But every one has his boat, his nets, and his smoke-house. Each little settlement, too, has its churches and schoolhouses; and a common-school education is all that these people can afford or even aspire to. They maintain, in their isolated situation, a sort of sturdy little republic in which a man who should appeal to the law against his neighbor is considered a bad citizen. In consequence, I believe there is not a lawyer on Grand Manan. So long as the fishery holds out, matters go along smoothly enough; the real strain comes when there is a falling off in that one resource. That means a season of grinding poverty. The young men grow discontented and leave the island; the old folks get along as best they may. Now the only man who can live exclusively on fine scenery is the summer visitor. It follows that he is looked upon as the apostle of a new life, and his coming eagerly waited for.

One thing struck me as worth noting down here, possibly because the demonstration came unawares. The refining influences of city life and city associations are nowhere more observable than in the men and women who have gone out of the home village and come back to it after the lapse of years to visit their

SWALLOW-TAIL POINT, GRAND MANAN.

kindred. I have seen two brothers come together in this way who looked, acted, talked, and dressed so differently that no one would have suspected the intimate relationship existing between them. I had to look twice before it was possible to detect the stamp which nature puts on a man's face as a sort of family trademark.

All the cliffs and coves that are contiguous to the Northern Head are easily reached from Flagg's Cove; but all are best seen from the water. Loitering about these headlands is a favorite occupation with visitors, who like to explore every nook and corner within reach. It is a pleasant walk, of an evening, over to Swallow-Tail Light and Point, a strange, rambling heap of trap-rock, split off the shore by a deep and ragged gully, through which the tide pours with wicked gurgling noises. A few sheep were cropping the grass-tufts among the ledges on which the lighthouse stands, from which the whole eastern shore of Manan is spread out to view as on a chart. As one looks around on the crimson sea, at the shadows creeping up the swart faces of the great cliffs, into the black gorges underneath, or off upon the fading shores that hedge these seas about, it is hard to realize that the island is sometimes cut off from the mainland for months at a time, or surrounded with such terrors that a good offing and sharp watch constitute the mariner's best hope.

While the keeper went about the very simple task of lighting up, which he did by taking an ordinary kerosene hand-lamp from a shelf and putting it inside the magnifying lenses, I remarked to him that he was using the old-fashioned burner with one wick. He then said, by way of explanation, that not long before he had heard of a new burner which, he was assured, would greatly increase the power of his light. A bright idea struck him. He would buy the new burner with his own money, give it a trial, and if it proved what had been claimed for it, he would then notify his inspector, with the full assurance that his action would be suitably received and commended. The double burner was accordingly tried and found to work to a charm. In great glee, the keeper posted a letter to his inspector, setting forth his discovery as modestly as possible. By the return post he received a peremptory order to restore the old burner again, and there it is now.

No visitor to Grand Manan should miss seeing the cliffs at the Southern Head. As well go to Rome without seeing Saint Peter's, or to Buffalo without seeing Niagara Falls. Moreover, as the one road traversing Grand Manan from end to end joins the several settlements together, all being on this eastern shore, this excursion allows one to see all the inhabited parts both going and returning, besides affording an excellent survey of the island itself.

For this excursion my landlord provided me with a horse that could easily do four miles an hour — five, perhaps, with urging. There are sixteen miles of road. That would make four hours for the trip, though I had reckoned on doing it in three at the outside. Eight miles are good, two more indifferent, the rest positively bad. The road mostly hugs the shore, often giving delightful glimpses off upon the bay or out among the islands. Thus the ocean was always close at hand; though at low tide one gets the impression that it has forsaken its bed.

I passed through in succession the villages of Centreville, Woodward's Cove, Grand Harbor, and Seal Cove, all of which lay in a Sabbath-like stillness. Sometimes the road would dart out upon a strip of shingle, within reach of the bounding waves; sometimes it cut through a forest of firs, or wound itself round one of the long ribs I have spoken of as crossing the island.

The soil is everywhere thin and stony. A very small breadth is brought under cultivation, though there is now and then a fairly good farm. Grass grows indifferently, but the Grand Mananer's favorite crop is potatoes. Both fruit and shade trees looked undersized and scrawny. Now and then I stopped to ask a question or two. As everybody seemed to know the horse I was driving, he served my turn as well as a letter of introduction could have done.

At Seal Cove I found the prettiest of all the island settlements. It lies about the hollow of the hills, one of which rises high above it, through which a stream runs down into the sea. Over this stream a bridge is thrown. You cross the bridge and climb the long hill-side to a meeting-house at its top, finding it a guiding landmark in a double sense. This is the last cove before reaching the land's end.

Beyond Seal Cove the road dwindled to two deep ruts, either miry or well sprinkled with loose stones, over which I jolted for another hour. At the end of this jaunt I ran up against a gate closing the road just where a brook crosses it. Pulling the horse through by the bit, and pushing the gate to after me, I found the land suddenly heaved up in front of me in one great curving embankment. Plainly my journey's end was near. This, too, was surmounted. Upon reaching the hill-top, the building which serves as both dwelling and lighthouse showed itself at the far edge of a grassy plateau, the first habitation seen for miles, and the last on Grand Manan.

The road is indeed long and tiresome, but the arrival pays for all.

Perched like a sentry-box on the wall of some gigantic fortress, the lighthouse is the only object attaching you to the world you seem to have left. One cannot choose but surrender at discretion to the spell that surrounds this charmed shore.

A path serpentines along the grassy rim of the cliffs, where harebells nod as you pass. But caution is necessary, as a single false step would send you headlong three hundred feet from top to bottom.[2] For an hour I walked on without either knowing or caring where I went, sometimes in the open, sometimes in the woods, and as often as I turned aside to look over the dizzy edge at my side the same startling sight was repeated, the same enormous shapes rose up dark and threatening out of the profound depths below.

"Can anything be sweeter than the certainty of being alone? In any widely known spot you are in a constant dread of an incursion of tourists; the hallooing of guides, the loud-voiced admiration, the bustle, whether of fastening horses, or of unpacking provisions, or of airing opinions, all disturb the budding sensation; civilization recovers its hold upon you. But here, what security and what silence! nothing that recalls man; the landscape is just what it has been these six thousand years."

The path zig-zags in and out in order to turn the tremendous breaches made at intervals in the side of the cliffs. The shore is therefore notched like the teeth of a saw. Now a headland starts out before you; now you are coasting the edge of a deep and wild gorge, with your back turned to the ocean; or if just a little venturesome, you may be edging your way cautiously out, in order to look over the brink into the pit below, though not until after taking firm grasp of some friendly sapling. But one such look will usually suffice.

SEA-GULL CLIFFS, GRAND MANAN.

The peculiar form of this shore is such as to make the walk around it a notable experience. I have explained that the cliffs do not extend in a regular line at all, as one might suppose, but at short intervals they bulge out great elephantine heads, all flowing down with savage grace into the foaming surf beneath. Some show a scarce broken front, some are shattered as if by a Cyclopean hammer. And there they stand braced to meet the thunderous roll of the Atlantic ground-swell.

These protruding masses form again deep gorges. At the bottom there may be a little strip of beach, but more often a heaped-up wall formed of blocks of stone that have come crashing down from above, followed by an avalanche of loosened earth. The trees that creep down into these gorges are stunted, misshapen, and interlaced, as if for mutual support. But trees are dwarfed, everything is dwarfed, by comparison with the cliffs. Then again, the peculiar structure of the cliffs themselves is an interesting study, because on inspection the fleshless backbone and ribs of natural rock are found imbedded in clinging masses of indurated earth or conglomerate that take wonderfully weird forms, but which the pitiless gnawing of wind, frost, and storm have stripped off, so exposing the gaunt skeleton itself, with its monstrous bones protruding. The prevailing color is a reddish brown, like iron-rust, which shines with a dull brightness. In some spots the crevices were blue with harebells. Never flowers bloomed in wilder place, or more quickly turned one's thoughts away from the shuddering horror of the precipice to which they clung trembling!

The mutilation everywhere evident — although the waves have torn away the cliffs in some spots more than in others — tells more eloquently than words how the conflict rages here when the storm king comes with his chariot and his horses.

> "Then comes, with an awful roar,
> Gathering and sounding on,
> The storm-wind from Labrador,
> The wind Euroclydon,
> The storm-wind!"

Just a word more about these cliffs, without which one would be apt to fancy it a scene of magnificent desolation.

At first the silence was something not to be described. But at the moment when I showed myself at the top of a deep and wide gorge, the whole dark interior grew suddenly alive with white-winged sea-gulls that have their rookeries among the nooks and crannies of these crags. In a twinkling the whole colony rose screaming in the air. It was a beautiful sight, — a redeeming sight, — this myriad of white wings sailing or wheeling in graceful evolutions about the dun walls of the chambered crags, or circling up around my head. The air was all alive with the creaking of wings and cries of alarm. It was, indeed, as if some enormous sea-wave had suddenly sent its foam high up among the cliffs; for, on finding that I meant them no harm, the gulls settled back among the rocks again by twos and threes, and but for their plaintive little cries all was as quiet as before.

From these creatures the locality has taken the name of Sea-Gull Cliffs.

It seems that these gulls were in danger of extermination until the people of the island awoke to the necessity of preserving them as one of its attractions. In the first place, some thoughtless person introduced foxes to the island. These animals soon drove the gulls to retreats inaccessible either to man or beast. Then came the caprice for wearing the snow-white breasts and wings on ladies' bonnets. This brought a swarm of eager hunters down upon the gulls, and soon drove them to make their rookeries still farther out, so that few remained in their old haunts. At this stage the law was invoked for their protection, much to the amusement of the law-makers, be it said, who could not see why such a useless thing as a gull should be made to occupy their serious attention.

"I will tell you why, gentlemen," said the champion of the gulls of Grand Manan. "We islanders get our living by fishing. Now for one thing, the gulls show us where fish are schooling, for they fish as well as we; and so where we see gulls sailing about the water we steer our boats. We don't want them killed off, because, dumb creatures though they are, their instinct helps us to live."

By this time the provincial legislature had settled itself to listen.

"For another thing, gentlemen," the spokesman for the gulls went on, "our men are often caught out in the bay in a fog; and when that happens, the screams the gulls set up if a boat or a vessel comes near the cliffs — for you must know, gentlemen, that a gull can see enough farther than a man — often does us a good turn in a bad place, by letting us know where we are. We don't want the gulls destroyed, because they help to keep us from death by shipwreck. That's all I have to say."

The bill was passed without further speech-making.

I have not yet said a word about the natural curiosity so long known to sailors as the Old Maid, but more recently rechristened as the Southern Cross.

It so happens that in very many pl ces the cliffs bristle with splinters of upright rock, sticking up out of the shattered waste, like monuments to the ruin that surrounds them. As these pointed rocks, or pinnacles, are warm and dry, they are a favorite perch for the gulls, and when one is thus occupied, the lonely stone has also its symbolic dove. It is one of these detached shafts of stone, standing on a pedestal of broken, weed-shagged ledge by the shore, that is rudely but strikingly worked out in the form of a cross. Though it is easily reached from below, I found the place extremely difficult of access from the top of the cliff.

One of the singularities of this island is that, while it is only sixteen miles long, vegetation is more forward by a full fortnight at the northern than at the southern end, thus reversing the climatic law existing on the mainland. This fact was vouched for by several respectable persons. It is owing, perhaps, to

SOUTHERN CROSS, GRAND MANAN.

A RUN ACROSS GRAND MANAN. 381

the greater prevalence of cold fogs, with their accompanying humidity, which renders a fire as indispensable in summer as in winter here.

Upon going up into the lantern of the lighthouse,[3] I saw the long blue line of the Nova Scotia coast, in one direction, thirty to forty miles distant, and by a slight change of position, looked directly into the mouth of Cutler Harbor, in Maine. On this side, the Machias Seal Rocks, distinguished by their twin towers, stood up, sharp and clear, from the low-lying ledges, while on the other, the lonely Gannet Rock lifted its warning shaft far out to sea.

But the afternoon was wearing away. Already the ocean was taking a deeper tint as the sun neared his journey's end, yet seemed to linger, that we might look on the enrapturing scene just a little longer. Every moment the sunburned faces of the aged cliffs grew a deeper red, so bringing sharply out all the myriad ridges, and leaving in shadow all the myriad grooves, that furrow them from top to bottom. The red glow seemed to diffuse itself about the air, which grew warm and ruddy. A thin, blue haze — transparent as gauze, delicate as incense — stole up out of the black gorges, curling from rock to rock, hanging its draperies to this pinnacle and that knob, as if each hideous cavern were being prepared for a *fête* of the fairies. No noise but the languid wash of water in and out among the rocks. Even the gulls nestled close in their rookeries. There was nothing to mar the exceeding peace that fell on land and sea. The dark-browed cliffs seemed bowing their heads in silent adoration. The ocean fell to a slow and regular motion. Twilight drew her cool hand across the slumberous waters; and as the light of day faded out, a faint glimmer from the lighthouse tower told us that the watchman was there at his post. It was time to turn homeward. It would soon be dark. No; there glided the moon up out of the ocean to light me on my way.

---

[1] The island forms the Parish of Grand Manan, which contains about twenty-eight hundred inhabitants, though the number fluctuates from causes mentioned in the text. A good many able-bodied young men ship on board American vessels. Of late the island is not holding its own. Two councillors attend to local affairs. Small suits, involving not more than eighty dollars, are tried before a local magistrate. Other causes have to go to Saint Andrews, the shire town. About half the acreage of the island, including most of the woodland, is owned by a land company ; the rest is in small holdings. There is some ship-timber remaining, but it is only a few years since forest fires destroyed much the greater part. Most of the woodland is on the west shore. Manan has an average breadth of four miles.

[2] The height of the cliffs had been variously estimated at from three hundred and fifty to four hundred feet, until Professor Baird found them to be three hundred feet by actual measurement.

[3] Gull Cliff Light shows alternately red and white. It lights the entrance to the Bay of Fundy.

INDEX.

A.

Acadia, given up to the French, 334.
Agamenticus, Mount, a landmark, 45 ; tradition of, *note*, 60 ; route to, 75 ; from Kennebunkport, 97.
Agamenticus (York) River, 45.
Akers, Paul, sculptor, *note*, 172.
Alden, Admiral James, his burial-place, 165.
Aldworth, Robert, buys Monhegan, *note*, 219 ; *note*, 234.
Alfonse, Jean, his voyage to Norumbega, 255.
Allan, Colonel John, defends Machias, 336 ; at Eastport, 360.
Allen, Elizabeth Akers, 158.
Allen's Island (St. George's), *note*, 219.
Allerton, Isaac, plays the Pilgrims false, 237 ; at Machias, 334 ; *note*, 345.
Andros, Sir Edmund, plunders St. Castin, 230.
Appledore, township formed of Isles of Shoals, 35.
Appledore Island, Isles of Shoals, 33 ; belongs to Maine, 34 ; a summer resort, 42 and *note*.
Argall, Sir Samuel, breaks up Colony at Mount Desert, 293.
Ark, the, C. Newagen, 205.
Arrowsic Island, *note*, 194.
Arundel, now Kennebunkport, 107.
Ash Island, 245.
Ashley, Edward, 236.
Aubry, Nicolas, for whom Frenchman's Bay is named, 328.
Augusta, site of Plymouth Trading-post, 191.

B.

Badger's Island, ships built at, 18.
Bagnall, Walter, at Richmond's Island, 139 ; killed, 140.
Bailey's Mistake, 344.
Bake-Apple, described, 340.

Baker's Island, Mount Desert, *note*, 302.
Bald Head Cliff, 67 ; described, 69, 70 ; wreck at, 71.
Bangor, taken, 284.
Bar Harbor, Mount Desert, approach to, 301, 302 ; back-ground of mountains, *note*, 303 ; roadstead described, 305 ; character studies, 305 ; cosmopolitan character, 305 ; its remarkable growth, 306 ; its rise and progress, 306 ; its hotels, 309 ; routine of a day, 309 ; its habitués, 310 ; shore promenade, 310 ; Indian camp, 313 ; Eagle Lake, 317 ; the drives, 318 ; in winter, 326.
Bar Island, Mount Desert, 304 ; *note*, 318.
Bass Harbor, Mount Desert, 296.
Bass Harbor Head, 296.
Batson's River, 111.
Baxter, James P., *note*, 60 ; *note*, 148 ; donates library building to Portland, 161 ; *note*, 172.
Bay of Fundy, fogs and tides, 355.
Bay Point, Penobscot Bay, 263.
Beal's Island, *note*, 345.
Bean, David, at Sullivan, *note*, 328.
Bear Island, Mount Desert, *note*, 302.
Bernard, Francis, owns and settles Mount Desert, 294 ; *note*, 302 ; *note*, 364.
Bernard, Sir John, acquires half of Mount Desert, 295 ; *note*, 302 ; *note*, 365.
Berry, Edward, *note*, 328.
Biard, Father Pierre, at the Kennebec, 190 ; describes the colony of St. Sauveur, 297.
Biddeford Pool, the name, 113 ; the beach, 114 ; the settlement, 114, 115, 116 ; Indian fort and village, 117 ; changes of name, *note*, 119.
Biencourt, of Port Royal, at the Kennebec, 190.
Bill Tynham's Rock, 103.
Black Point. *See* Scarborough, and *note*, 148.
Blockhouse Point, Castine, 284.

383

384   INDEX.

Blue Hill Bay, 287, and *note*, 288.
Bonnybeag, from Kennebunkport, 97, and *note*, 101.
Bonython, John, of Saco, 118; *note* 8, 120.
Bonython, Richard, of Saco, first *de facto* government begins in his house, *note*, 120.
Boon Island, 30, 57, 59, 60, and *note*, 61.
Boothbay Harbor, 201; described, 201, 202; early history, *note*, 206.
Boot Head, disaster at, 343.
Bourne, Edward E., *note*, 84; *note*, 110.
Bowbear Island, *note*, 345.
Bradford, William, at Monhegan, *note*, 219; his account of early settlements, 227.
Bramhall's Hill, Portland, 157; *note*, 172.
Brave Boat Harbor, 25.
Bray, John, shipwright, 23.
Brooklin, 287.
Brooksville, 280.
Brown, Harry, his studio, 164.
Brown, John, at Pemaquid, *note*, 234.
Brown, John B., 157.
Bristol, *note*, 234.
Bull, Dixy, plunders Pemaquid, 228.
Bunkin Island. *See* Cape Porpoise, 103; wreck at, 104; *note*, 110.
Burdett, Rev. George, of York, sent to England in disgrace, 53.
Burke's Point, Machias, markings at, *note*, 345.
Burnt Coat. *See* Swan's Island.
Burnt Island, Boothbay, 202.
Burroughs, Rev. John, legend of his arrest, 82, 83.

C.

Calais, excursion to, 360, 361.
Calf Island, *note*, 328.
Camden, the harbor, 264; its shipyards, 265; its mountains, 265, 266; its lakes, 269; Sherman's Point, 269; its name, *note*, 270.
Camden Hills, first sight of, 246; a landmark, 260; Mount Battie, 264, and *note*, 270; ascent of Megunticook, 266, and *note*, 270.
Cammock, Thomas, at Scarborough, 133, 134; dies, 136.
Campobello Island, first view of, 349; from Eastport, 353; should be made neutral, 353; its fisheries, 355; the islanders, 359; points of interest, 359; *note*, 364.
Cape Arundel, Kennebunkport, 98.

Cape Elizabeth, approach to, 138; Bowery Beach and Richmond's Island, 138; Two Lights, 140, 141; Portland Head, 143; islands off, 144, 147; Indian fight at, 147; *note*, 148.
Cape Elizabeth Lights, 141; life-saving service, 142.
Cape Cottage, 144.
Cape Neddock, York, 64; described, 67, 68.
Cape Neddock River, the settlements at, 68.
Cape Newagen, 198, 202, 204, 205.
Cape Porpoise, the original settlement of Kennebunkport, 106; Indian assaults on, 107; called Arundel, 107; odd settlement of boundary dispute, 108; gallant defence of, 109; singular manners, 109; islands belonging to, *note*, 110; the name, *note* 3, 110.
Cape Porpoise Light, from Cape Arundel, 100, 105; *note*, 110.
Cape Rosier, 280, 287; *note*, 288.
Cape Small Point, 180.
Cape Split, *note*, 345.
Capitol Island, Southport, 202.
Caraway, the, grows wild, 105.
Casco Bay, southern entrance to, 140; islands next Cape Elizabeth, 144; White Head, 144; Cushing's, Peak's, House, Great and Little Diamond islands, 144, 147, 175, *et seq.*; singular geological structure, 175; Long, Great, and Little Chebeague islands, 176; Hope and Little Bangs, Crotch, Jewell's, 179; Broad Sound, 179; Harpswell Neck, 179; Bailey's, Haskell's, Little Mark islands, 180; Cape Small Point, 180; *notes*, 184; early settlement in, 192.
Castine, given up, *note*, 234; routes from Rockland, *note*, 270; its name, 271; the village, 271; as Fort Pentagoet, 272-279; customs, 279; Fort George, 280, *et seq.*; invaded, 282; military operations at, 282, 283; again becomes a British post, 284; southern headlands, 284; later annals of, *note*, 287.
Cedar Island, Isles of Shoals, 34.
Chambly, Captain, taken prisoner, 276.
Chamcook Mountain, situation of, 362.
Champernowne, Francis, his residence and grave, 26; *note*, 28.
Champlain, Samuel, at Biddeford, 117; names Richmond's Island, 139; in the Kennebec, 186; his winter in Maine, 363.

Chappelle's Chair, Cape Newagen, 205.
Christmas Cove, 221.
Christmas Trees, rise of that industry, 340.
Chubb, Pascho, surrenders Pemaquid, 232.
Church, Major Benjamin, 147.
Cilley, Jonathan, his fatal duel, 245.
Clam-digging for profit, 132 ; *note*, 148.
Clapboard Island, a colonial boundary, 168.
Clark, Thomas, of Boston, at the Kennebec, 194.
Cleeves, George, 136, 140 ; *note*, 148 ; his residence, 169.
Cobbet, Thomas, captivity of, 302.
Cobsecook Bay, *note*, 365.
Cole, William, of Wells, 78.
Collier, Sir George, raises siege of Castine, 283 ; attacks Machias, 336.
Constitution, Frigate, at Kittery, 19, 20.
Converse, Captain James, defends Wells, 79, *et seq.*
Cornish, Goody, executed for murder, 49.
Cranberry Islands, 296 ; *note*, 302, 303.
Cuckold Rocks, Southport, 202, 205.
Cushing, 245 ; *note*, 250.
Cushing's Island, Casco Bay, 144.
Cutler, route from Machias to, 339 ; its harbor, 343.
Cutt's Island, 26.

D.

Damariscove Islands, 203 ; described and named, *note*, 206 ; included in the Pemaquid patents, 219.
Damariscotta, situation of, 220 ; mammoth shell-heaps near, 220.
Damariscotta River, 220, 221, 222 ; *note*, 234.
Dark Harbor, Grand Manan, 367.
Davis, Captain Sylvanus, captured, 169.
D'Aulnay, Charnisay, at Penobscot, 272 ; takes La Tour's fort, 275.
Deer Isle, Penobscot Bay, 287, and *note*, 288.
Deer Island, Whirlpools near, 361, 362.
DeGregoire, Thérèse, acquires half of Mount Desert, 295.
De Guercheville, Marquise, her mission in Acadia, 292, 293 ; *note*, 302.
De Medicis, Marie, contributes towards a mission, 292.
De Monts, Sieur, at Biddeford, 116 ; his patent, 202 ; *note*, 302 ; his winter quarters, 363.

De Monts' Island, site and history of, 363, 364 ; rediscovery, *note*, 365.
Dennis, Laurence, settles at Arrowsic I., *note*, 194.
Devil's Armchair, 98.
Devil's Cartway, 98.
Devil's Head, Penobscot Bay, 287.
Dice's Head, Castine, 284.
Dix Island, quarries at, *note*, 250.
Dochet's, or Docie's, Island. *See* De Monts' Island, 363.
Dogfish Harbor, Southport, 201.
Dogfish head, Southport, 201.
Doughty, Thomas, paints at Mount Desert, 289.
Dow, Neal, 171.
Dram Island, *note*, 328.
Druillettes, Father Gabriel, visits the Kennebec, 191 ; visits Castine, 275.
Dunbar, Col. David, rebuilds the fort at Pemaquid, 233 ; *note*, 235.
Dunstan (Scarborough), 130.
Durell, Philip, attacked by Indians, 96 ; *note*, 101.
Du Thet, Gilbert, killed at Mount Desert, 293 ; *note*, 302.

E.

Eagle Lake, Mount Desert, 299, 317.
Eastport, first glimpse of, 349 ; traces of the great fire, 349 ; earthworks at, 350 ; sardine packing, 350 ; boundary dispute, 351 ; held by the British, 352 ; as a centre for summer travel, 353 ; its fisheries, 354 ; tides at, 355 ; its history, *note*, 364.
East Quoddy Head, *note*, 364.
Eden, *note*, 318.
Eddy, Col. Jonathan, invades Nova Scotia, 336 ; sketch of him, *note*, 345.
Eddington, how named, *note*, 345.
East Boothbay (Hodgdon's Mills), *note*, 234.
East Machias, situation of, 339.
Ebenecook Harbor, Southport, 201.
Eel Brook Point, Grand Manan, 368.
Eggemoggin Reach, described, 287.
Elbridge, Gyles, buys Monhegan, *note*, 219.
Ellsworth, water route to, *note*, 288.

F.

Falmouth Foreside, 168.
Fernald's Point, Mount Desert, 297.
Fessenden, William Pitt, residence, 158.

Fish Head, Grand Manan, 367.
Fisherman's Island, Boothbay, 206.
Fishing Rocks, Kennebunkport, 98.
Five Islands, Sheepscot Bay, 198.
Flagg's Cove, Grand Manan, described, 368.
Flanders' Bay, note, 328.
Fort Charles, Pemaquid, 229.
Fort Cumberland, N. S., attacked, 336.
Fort Frederick (Pemaquid), 233.
Fort George, Castine, view from, 280; muster of army veterans at, 281, 282; when and why erected, 282; is attacked, 282.
Fort Gorges, 147.
Fort Loyal, site of, 169; sacked, 169.
Fort Mary, Biddeford, remains of, 116; note, 120.
Fort McClary, site of, 21.
Fort Pentagoet, Castine, site of, 272; its history, 272, et seq.; note, 287.
Fort Point, Penobscot Bay, 270.
Fort Popham, location of, 183, 186; note, 194.
Fort Preble, 147; note, 149.
Fort Scammell, 147; note, 149.
Fort Sullivan, Eastport, 350, 351.
Fortune's Rocks, location described, 111, 112.
Fort William Henry (Pemaquid), 231.
Fox Island's Thoroughfare, 249.
Foxwell's garrison, 130.
Friar's Head, 349, 353; the name, 360.
Friar's Bay, 353.
Frenchman's Bay, first glimpses of, 301; shores of, 321, et seq.; in winter, 326; the name, note, 328.
Frontenac, Count (Louis de Buade), decides to destroy Pemaquid, 232.

G.

Garde, Roger, of York, note, 60.
Garrison Houses described, 54, 55; note, 61.
Gentian, the, first noticed on the coast, 105.
Georgetown, note, 194.
Gerrish's Island, points of interest at, 25, 26; wreck at, 27.
Gibson, Rev. Richard, preaching at Isles of Shoals, 34; is banished, 35; chaplain at Richmond's Island, 140.
Gilbert, Bartholomew, with Gosnold in his voyage to New England, 32.
Gilbert, Sir Humphrey, his descendants, note, 194.

Gilbert, Raleigh, at the Kennebec, 189.
Gilkey's Harbor, islands forming it, note, 270.
Gilpatric, Isaac, note, 328.
Goat Island, Cape Porpoise, 109.
Godfrey, Edward, of York, defamed, 49; builds at York, note, 60.
Gooch, John, of Wells, 78.
Goose Fare Brook, 122.
Goose Rocks, its situation and name, 111; the way there, and summer colony, 111.
Gorges, Sir Ferdinando, 26; note, 28; his charter of 1622, 33; patent of 1631, 34; charter of 1639, 34; has no monument, 46; his career outlined, 46; seizure of his province, 53; note, 60; seizes Maine Indians, 186; they turn his mind to colonization, 186.
Gorges, Thomas, deputy-governor, 53; notes, 60 and 61.
Gorges, William, nephew of Sir Ferdinando, sets up a provincial government at Saco, note, 120.
Gosnold, Captain Bartholomew, runs away with Raleigh's ship, 32, 33.
Gosport, see Isles of Shoals, 36; demolished, 42.
Gott's Island, described, 296; note, 302.
Gouldsborough Bay, note, 344.
Grand Manan Island, approach to, 344; from Campobello, 359; tides of, 367; the west coast, 367; Flagg's Cove, 368; the east coast, 368; its history, 371; the people, 371; Swallow-Tail Point, 372; humors of the Lighthouse Service, 373; the island thoroughfare, 373; Seal Cove, 374; Gull Cliff Light, 374; the cliffs, 374, et seq.; the gulls, 377, 378; Southern Cross, 381; note, 381.
Graves, W. J., shoots Cilley in a duel, 245.
Great Chebeague, Casco Bay, 179.
Great Cranberry Island, note, 302.
Great Head, Mount Desert, 300.
Great Presench Island, note, 302.
Green's Landing, 249.
Green Mountain, the landmark of Mount Desert, 296; note, 303; the way there, 317; the view, 317, 318; in winter, 326.
Grindstone Rock, the wreck at, 245.
Gull Cliff Light, Grand Manan, note, 381.
Gyles, Captain John, in command of Casco, note, 172; taken at Pemaquid, 231.
Gyles, Thomas, killed, 231.

INDEX. 387

H.

Haley, Samuel, his improvements at the Shoals, 38; *note*, 43.
Half-Way Rock, Casco Bay, 144, 179; *note*, 184.
Hammond, Elizabeth (Hunnewell), *note*, 148.
Hampden, pillaged, 284.
Hancock Point, situation of, 322; route to Bangor, *note*, 328.
Harding, Stephen, keeps a ferry, 92; story of his escape, 93.
Hardy, Sir Thomas M., at Eastport, 352.
Harpswell Neck, 179; legend of, 180.
Hart's Beach located, 83.
Hawthorne, Nathaniel, on the Isles of Shoals, 29.
Haycock's Harbor, 343.
Hayes, A. A., *note*, 302.
Head Harbor Island, *note*, 345.
Hendrick's Head (Southport), 198, 205.
Heron Island, Damariscotta River, 221; *note*, 234.
Hilliard, George S., at Machias, 345.
Hockomock Head, its legend, 197.
Holbrook's Island, Penobscot Bay, 280.
House Island, Casco Bay, 147.
Hull, Rev. Benjamin, preaching at Isles of Shoals, 34; Winthrop's mention of him, *note*, 61.
Hull's Cove, Mount Desert, settled, 295.
Hunnewell, Richard, *note*, 148.
Hunnewell's Point (Kennebec River), 186.
Hunter's Island, Cape Newagen, 205.
Hypocrites, the, *note*, 206.

I.

Iberville, takes Pemaquid, 232.
Ice in commerce, 192, 193.
Indians, inhabit at York, 45.
Indian agriculture, 117.
Ironbound Island, *note*, 328.
Isles of Shoals, their literature, 29–31; history, 32–42; first frequented, 32; first named, 32; and described, 32; first settled, 33; divided between Gorges and Mason, 33; set apart to Maine and New Hampshire, 34; and annexed to Kittery and Newcastle, 34; preaching at, 34; Massachusetts claims jurisdiction, 34; granted local court, 35; population, 35; its character, 35; removal to Star Island, 36; Indian depredations, 36; religious annals, 36, 37; improvements at Smutty-Nose Island, 38; degradation of the Islanders, 41; church rebuilt, 41; reported haunted, 42, and *note*.
Isle au Haut, described, *note*, 288.
Islesborough, Penobscot Bay, 270, and *note*.

J.

Jamestown (Pemaquid), 229.
Jennens, Abraham, buys Monhegan, *note*, 219.
Jenness, Job, starts a public house, Kennebunkport, 89.
Jerry's Island, Cape Newagen, 205.
Jewell's Island, Casco Bay, *note*, 184.
Job's Island, Penobscot Bay, 270.
John's Bay, 225.
Jonesport, its colony to Palestine, 330, 333.
Jordan Island, *note*, 328.
Jordan, Rev. Robert, at Cape Elizabeth, 140; *note*, 148; *note*, 149.
Jordan, Samuel, of Biddeford, *note*, 120.
Jordan's Lake, Mount Desert, 299.
Josselyn, Henry, at Scarborough, 134; marries the widow Cammock, 136; is taken by Indians, 136, 137; *note*, 148; lays out town, *note*, 234.
Josselyn, John, at Scarborough, 134, 135.

K.

Katahdin, Mount, from Mount Megunticook, 266; from Green Mountain, 318.
Kennebec River, discovery of, discussed, 185; *note*, 194; Champlain at, 186; settlement in, 188; visited, 190; Plymouth trading-post on, 191; Saint Lusson visits, 192; settlements destroyed, 192; *note*, 194; ice business, 192, 193; ship-building, 193; settlements at the mouth, 194.
Kennebunk Beach, curiosities of, 83, 84.
Kennebunk, lower village, 83; *note*, 84.
Kennebunkport, 86, *et seq.*; decline of its ship-building, 87; becomes a watering-place, 88; the two villages, 89; drinking customs, 90; old ferry, 91; Wading-place, 92; the piers, 93, and *note*, 101; Durell's bridge and its story, 96; the river, 95; shore front, 98; Sandy Cove, 100; *see also* Cape Porpoise; *also* Arundel; incorporated, 109, and *note*, 110.
King Philip's War, in Maine, 118.
Kittery, its situation described, 18; Kittery

Navy Yard, 19; Kittery Point, 22-25; *notes*, 27, 28.
Knox, Gen. Henry, at Thomaston, 237; builds there, 238; becomes bankrupt, 241; his tomb, 241, 242.

L.

Laighton, Thomas B., lightkeeper at Isles of Shoals, 31, 41, 42.
Lake, Captain Thomas, killed at the Kennebec, *note*, 194.
Lamoine, its situation, etc., 322; *note*, 328.
La Motte Cadillac, 295; *note*, 302.
Lassell's Island, Penobscot Bay, *note*, 270.
La Tour, his feud with D'Aulnay, 272, 273; his marriage, 275; *note*, 288; drives the English from Machias, 334; *note*, 345.
Leighton's Point, Biddeford, 119.
Le Jeune, Father Paul, his *Relation* referred to, 191.
Levett, Christopher, at Cape Porpoise, 110, 111; at Saco, *note*, 119; at Cape Newagen, 206.
Libby Island Light, *note*, 345.
Lime Manufacture, its beginning, *note*, 250.
Linekin's Bay, 207.
Littlefield, Edmund, of Wells, 77; his house described, 78; site of, 78; *note*, 84.
Little Cranberry Island, *note*, 302.
Little Deer Isle, 287.
Little Diamond Island, Casco Bay, *note*, 184.
Little Machias Bay, 339.
Little River, Cutler, 339.
Little River, Goose Rocks Bay, 111.
Little River, Old Orchard, 130.
Little Presench Island, *note*, 302.
Londoner's Island, Isles of Shoals, 34.
Long Sands Bay, 64.
Longfellow, H. W., his statue, 154; his early home, 161; his birthplace, 170.
Longfellow, Stephen, 162, 170.
Long Island, Casco Bay, *note*, 184.
Long Island, Penobscot Bay. See Islesborough, 270.
Long Ledge, Mount Desert, 297.
Long Porcupine Island, 318.
Lord, George C., his residence, 85.
Lowell, James Russell, on the Isles of Shoals, 30.
Lygonia, or Plough Patent, limits of, *note*, 148, 149.

Lubec, comes in sight, 346, 349; taken from Eastport, *note*, 364.

M.

Machias, early annals of, 334; its situation and business, 335; its military history, 335, 336; naval attack frustrated, 336; is taken, 339; early names, *note*, 345.
Machias Bay, its watershed, 329; its light, 345.
Machiasport, its situation, 335.
Mackworth, Arthur, *note*, 172.
Mackworth's Island, Casco Bay, 168.
MacLean, Col. Francis, defends Castine, 282.
Maine Historical Society, home of, 172.
Malaga Island, Isles of Shoals, 34.
Mansell, Sir Robert, *note*, 302.
Mark Island Light, 249.
Mark Island, Penobscot Bay, *note*, 270.
Marshall's Island, *note*, 288.
Mason, Captain John, founder of New Hampshire, his charter of 1629, 33; death, 34.
Mason's Bay, *note*, 345.
Massachusetts asserts her claim to Maine, 53.
Massacre Pond, Scarborough, 133.
Mather, Cotton, his account of Fort William Henry, 231; *note*, 235.
Mathes, Nathan, builds at Isles of Shoals, 42.
Matinicus Island, described, 249.
Matinicus Rock, 249.
Maverick, Samuel, account of York, *note*, 60.
McMaster, John B., *note*, 101.
Megunticook, Mount, 265; the ascent, and view from summit, 266; *note*, 270.
Merchant, Anthony, 288.
Merchant's Row, Penobscot Bay, 288.
Metinic Island, 245.
Millbridge, location of, *note*, 344.
Mogg, an Indian chief, attacks Scarborough, 136; is killed in a second attack, 137.
Moody, Rev. Joshua, at Isles of Shoals, 36.
Monanis, 209, *et seq.*; *see* Monhegan; fog-signal, 214; the inscription rock, 217.
Monhegan Island, 207; disaster at, 209; the harbor, 209; the settlement, 211; fishing annals, 211; island manners, 212; lighthouse, 213; the cliffs, 214; character of the island, 214; Weymouth's visit, 218; *see* Monanis; historical sketch, *note*, 219.
Monroe's Island, 246.
Moore, Sir John, fights at Castine, 283.
Mooseabec Light, *note*, 345.

INDEX.   389

Mooseabec Reach, note, 345.
Moose Harbor, 343.
Moose Island (Eastport), 352; note, 364.
Morse, Rev. Jedediah, at Isles of Shoals, 41.
Moulton, Jeremiah, taken at sacking of York, 55.
Mountains, of Camden, 264; of Mount Desert, note, 303; Schoodic, 302.
Mount Battie, 264; note, 270.
Mount Desert, route from Rockland, 249; from Castine, 284, 285; note, 288; its rise as a summer resort, 289; artists who have made it famous, 289; in Acadia, 292; French settlement at, 293; is broken up, 293; is called Mount Mansell, 294; a rendezvous for savages, 294; shipwreck at, 294; English settlement begins at, 294, 295; approach from sea, 295; its mountains, 296; Bass Harbor and Placentia Islands, 296; Cranberry Islands, 296; Somes' Sound, 297; Northeast and Southwest harbors, 297; the sea-front, 298; Seal Harbor, 299; Otter Cove and Cliff, 300; Great Head, 300; Schooner Head, 300, 301; Spouting Horn, 301; Anemone Cave, 301; Newport Mountain, 301; approach to Bar Harbor, 302; notes, 302; names and heights of its mountains, note, 303; Bar Harbor and environs, 304, et seq.; the Ovens, Cathedral, and Via Mala, note, 318; approach from Frenchman's Bay, 323; from Sullivan, 324, 325.
Mount Desert Rock, what the sea has done there, 325.
Mount Mansell. See Mount Desert; note, 302.
Mousam River, 83; note, 84.
Mouse Island, Southport, 201.
Mowatt, Captain Henry, seized at Portland, 165; bombards the town, 167.
Moxus, the chief, at sacking of Pemaquid, 231.
Mulholland's Point, 349.
Munjoy Hill, annals of, 165, et seq.
Muscongus Bay, 225.
Muscongus Patent, history of, 236, 237.
Mussel-Ridges, position of, 245.

N.

Nahanada, the chief, enters into alliance with Captain Smith, 226; note, 234.
Narraguagas Bay, note, 344.
Narraguagas River, note, 344.
Nash Island Light, note, 344.

Naskeag. See Eggemoggin, 287.
Naskeag Point, 287; note, 288.
Nautilus Island, Penobscot Bay, 280.
Neal, John, 144; residence, 158.
Negro Island, Camden, 264.
Nelson, John, romantic episode of his life, 232; note, 235.
Neptune, the Quoddy Chief, at Machias, 336.
New Casco Fort, site of, 168; note, 172.
Newcastle, situation of, 220; note, 234.
Newcastle, Duke of, anecdote of, 25.
New England, causes moving to its settlement, 46.
New England, the name, 257.
Newport Mountain, Mount Desert, 301; outworks of, note, 303.
Newtown, note, 194.
Northeast Harbor, 297, 298; mark for, note, 302.
Northern Head, Grand Manan, 367.
North Haven, 249.
Norumbega, Champlain locates it, 253; first accounts of, 254–256; note, 257, 258.
Nottingham Galley, wreck of, 59.

O.

O'Brien, Jeremiah, at Machias, 335.
Ocean Point, Boothbay, 220.
Ogunquit, approach to, 72; Perkins' Cove, 73; land speculation. 74.
Ogunquit River and beach, 75.
Old Orchard Beach, from Biddeford Pool, 114; how named, 122; Bay View, 124; the summer city, 126; its diversions, 127; singular bathing custom, 127; great gale at, 128; fight at, 130; annals of, note, 131.
Orr's Island, Casco Bay, 179.
Otter Cliff, Mount Desert, 300; note, 303.
Outer Heron Island, note, 206.
Outer Long Island, Penobscot Bay, note, 288.
Owl's Head, situation and names, 246.
Owl's Head Bay, 246.

P.

Parkman, Francis, quoted, 292.
Parmentier, Jean, his account of Norumbega, 254.
Parsons, Charles, his improvements, 85.
Passamaquoddy, the name, 354; note, 365.
Passamaquoddy Indians, residence of, 361; note, 365.
Peak's Island, Casco Bay, 147.

390   INDEX.

Pemaquid Harbor, 225, 226; popular errors concerning settlement at, 226, 227; tour of the fortifications, 227, 228; their history, 228-231; called Jamestown, 229; under New York, 228, 229; New Harbor, 231; fort captured and destroyed, 231; rebuilt and called William Henry, 231; again taken, 232; again rebuilt as Fort Frederick, 233; street pavements, 233; notes, 234.
Pemaquid Patent, note, 219; note, 234.
Pemaquid Point, described, 225.
Pemetiq (Mount Desert), note, 302.
Penhallow, Samuel, note, 84.
Penobscot Bay, west entrance to, 245; its landmarks, 246, 249; Fox Islands Thoroughfare, 249; earliest accounts of, 253, et seq., 259; is read out of the category of summer resorts, 260; Camden Mountains, 260; Rockland, Rockport, and Camden Shores, 263; Fort Point, 270; its two channels, note, 270.
Pentagoet. See Castine, 272.
Pentecost Harbor (St. George's), 218, note, 219.
Pepperell, Andrew, son of Sir William, 20; note, 28.
Pepperellborough. See Saco.
Pepperell, Lady (Mary Hirst), residence of, and death, 21.
Pepperell, Madam (Margery Bray), 23.
Pepperell, Sir William (First Baronet), makes his grandson his heir, 20; his residence, 23; his influence, 24; made commander at Louisburg, 24; Saco named Pepperellborough for him, 119.
Pepperell, William, Senior, 23.
Perry, residence of the Passamaquoddys, note, 365.
Petit Manan Island, 329.
Petit Manan Light, 325.
Petit Manan Point, its situation, 329; eastern shore, 330.
Phillips, William, settles at falls of Saco, 118; is attacked by Indians, 118; note, 120; site of his fort, note, 120.
Phips, Sir William, rebuilds Pemaquid, 231.
Phips, Sir William, 25.
Pigeon Hill, located, 329.
Pine Point, Scarborough, 131; note, 148.
Pine, Charles, residence of, 131.
Placentia Islands, 296; named, note, 302.
Pleasant Bay, location of, note, 344, 345.

Pleasant Point (Perry), 361; note, 365.
Plough Company, their settlement, 191.
Plymouth Trading-Post (Kennebec), note, 194.
Poison Ivy (Mercury), how detected, 103, and note, 110.
Pollock Fishery, 354.
Pond Island Light (Kennebec), 183.
Pond Island Light, note, 344.
Poor, John R., builds at Isles of Shoals, 42.
Popham Beach, note, 184.
Popham Colony, 188, 189; relics of it, 190.
Popham, George, at the Kennebec, 189; his death, 189.
Popham, Sir Francis, note, 219.
Popham, Sir John, heads New England colonization, 189.
Porcupine Islands, Mount Desert, 304, and note, 318.
Porgy oil manufacture, 202.
Port Clyde, 245.
Portland, the harbor, islands, and forts, 144, 147; its topography, 153; the great fire, 157; State Street, 158; Congress Street, 158, 159; Public Library, 161; old ways of travel, 162; Eastern Cemetery, 164; old City Hall, 165; bombarded, 165; the Observatory, 168; Cleeves' monument, 168; the bay from Munjoy Hill, 168, 169; destroyed by French and Indians, 169; Confederate depredations, 171; note, 171.
Portland Head and Light, 143.
Post-routes established, 81.
Potts' Harbor, Harpswell, 179.
Preble, Commodore Edward, his residence, 161; burial-place, 164; saved from the prison-ship, 168; note, 172.
Preble, General Jedediah, anecdote of, 168.
Preble's Island, note, 328.
Preble, Nathaniel, at Sullivan, note, 328.
Prout's Neck, 132, et seq.; Indian atrocities at, 133, 136, 137; surroundings of, 137.
Pumpkin Island, Boothbay, note, 206.
Pumpkin Island (Penobscot Bay), 287.

R.

Ragged Island, 249.
Raleigh, Sir Walter, furnishes a ship for New England, 32.
Ram Island, note, 206, 208.
Rice, Arabella, a benefactor of Kittery, 18.
Richmond's Island, annals of, 138, 139, 140; note, 148.

INDEX. 391

Rigby, Sir Alexander, buys Lygonia, or Plough patent, note, 148.
Robbinston, 362.
Roberts, Tobias, of Bar Harbor, 306.
Robinson's Island, Penobscot Bay, note, 270.
Robinson's Rock, Penobscot Bay, note, 270.
Rockland, 236 ; its harbor, 246.
Rockport, situation of, 263 ; output of lime, note, 270.
Rodick, Daniel, of Bar Harbor, 306.
Rogers, Thomas, of Saco, 122.
Round Porcupine Island, 318.
Rutherford's Island, 220, 221.

S.

Sabino, peninsula, 186.
Saco, face of, and note, 119 ; called Pepperellborough, note, 119.
Saddle Island, Penobscot Bay, note, 270.
Sagadahoc (Kennebec), 190 ; note, 194.
Sagadahoc Province, note, 234.
Sail Rock, wreck at, 344 ; note, 364.
Saint Andrews', N.B., site of, 362 ; note, 365.
Saint-Castin, in the attack on Wells, 80 ; attacks Pemaquid, 230 ; at Castine, 272, 276 ; his character, 276, 279 ; his son, 279.
Saint Croix River, England claims to, 229 ; sail to Calais, 363 ; is declared the boundary, note, 365.
Saint George, 245 ; note, 250.
Saint George's Islands, situation and names, note, 219.
Saint George's River, 244, 245.
Saint Sauveur, Mount Desert, 293.
Salisbury's Cove, Mount Desert, 318.
Saltonstall, Captain, is defeated at Castine, 282.
Samoset, the chief, note, 206 ; note, 219.
Sardine packing, processes of, 350 ; annual product of, note, 365.
Sasanoa, The, voyage in, described, 195-197.
Sayward, Jonathan, of York, 56.
Scarborough, from Old Orchard, 123 ; islands of, note, 131 ; Prout's Neck, 132, et seq. ; Josselyn's account of, 135, 136 ; depopulated, 137 ; summer colonies at, 137.
Schoodic Hills, 302.
Schoodic Point, 325 ; whistling-buoy at, note, 328.

Schooner Head, Mount Desert, 300 ; its name, 301.
Scottow, Joshua, at Scarborough, 131, and note.
Scottow's Hill, Scarborough, note, 131 ; his fort, 133 ; note, 148.
Sea-Gull Cliff, Grand Manan, 374, et seq. ; note, 381.
Seal Harbor, Mount Desert, 299.
Seal Islands, situation of, 344 ; early name of, note, 345.
Seal Rock, wreck at, 249.
Sea-Urchin, its names and uses, note, 131.
Sedgwick, 287.
Sedgwick, Robert, takes Castine, 275.
Seguin Island, 140 ; Light, 183 ; note, 184.
Seven-Hundred-Acre Island, Penobscot Bay, 270.
Seward's Island, note, 328.
Sheep Island, 246.
Sheepscot Bay, 198 ; note, 206.
Sheepscot Farms, depopulated, note, 206.
Sheepscot River, town laid out on, note, 234.
Sherman's Point, Camden, 269.
Shillaber, B. P. (Mrs. Partington), on the Isles of Shoals, 30, 31 ; on chowders, 103.
Ship and Barge, note 7, 288.
Ship-building, its decay, 87 ; and annals, note, 101.
Ship Harbor Island, note, 345.
Short Sands, York, the neighborhood, 67, 68.
Shurte, Abraham, at Pemaquid, note, 219 ; note, 234.
Simmons, Franklin, sculptor, 154.
Simonton's Cove, fight at, 147.
Simpson, Josiah, at Sullivan, note, 328.
Skilling's Bay, 322.
Smith, Captain John, names Isles of Shoals, and describes them, 32 ; at Monhegan, note, 219 ; and Pemaquid, 226.
Smith, Rev. Thomas, his burial-place, 164 ; note, 172.
Smutty Nose, or Haley's Island, one of the Isles of Shoals, 34.
Somes, Abraham, at Mount Desert, 302.
Somes' Sound, 296, 297 ; site of French colony, 297 ; entrance to, note, 302.
Somesville, situation of, 297.
Sorel, the name, 276.
Sorrento, its situation, 324 ; its harbor, 328.
Southack, Cyprian, note, 219.
South Bristol, note, 234.

Southern Cross, Grand Manan, 378.
South Thomaston, 236.
Southwest Harbor, Mount Desert, settled, 294; the village, 297, 298.
Sparhawk, Nathaniel, 20.
Sparhawk, William, son of Nathaniel, becomes second Sir William Pepperell, 20.
Spruce Point, Boothbay, 202.
Spurwink River, 138.
Squirrel Island, described, 203, 204.
Stage Island, Biddeford, 114; note, 120.
Stage Island, Cape Porpoise, 105, 106.
Staples, E. C., pioneer landlord at Old Orchard, note, 131.
Star Island, becomes seat of government for the Isles of Shoals, 36.
Stave Island, note, 328.
Steuben, topography of, note, 344.
Storer Garrison, Wells, site of, 79; attacked, 79–81.
Stowe, Mrs. H. B., at Orr's Island, 179.
Stratton's Island, Saco Bay, 131.
Sullivan, Daniel, at Sullivan, note, 328.
Sullivan Harbor, its aspect, 323; its environs, 324; its annals, 328.
Sullivan, James, quoted, note, 121.
Sutton's Island, Mount Desert, note, 302.
Swallow-Tail Light, Grand Manan, 372.
Swallow-Tail Point, Grand Manan, 368.
Swan's Island (Burnt Coat), situation of, note, 288.

T.

Taunton Bay, located, 324.
Temple, Sir Thomas, his witticism, 276.
Tennant's Harbor, 245.
Thaxter, Celia, at the Isles of Shoals, 31.
Thevét, André, his voyage to Norumbega, 256.
Thomaston, situation of, 236; early history, 237; early fort, 241; burial-ground, 242, 243; its name, note, 249; defences destroyed, 250.
Thompson, Captain Samuel, seizes Mowatt, at Portland, 166.
Thompson, David, settles at the Piscataqua, 227.
Thread of Life Ledges, disaster at, 221.
Thrumcap, Damariscotta River, 221.
Thrumcap, Mount Desert, 301.
Thury, Father, incites the Penobscots to war, 230.

Tides, Bay of Fundy, etc., 355.
Timber Island, location, 111; wreck at, 112.
Townsend Gut, 201.
Treat's (Allan's) Island, 360; note, 365.
Trelawny, Robert, takes a patent for Richmond's Island, etc., 140; note, 148.
Trott's Island, Cape Porpoise, 109.
Trowbridge, John T., 101.
Tucke, Rev. John, at Isles of Shoals, 36, 37, 38.
Tucker, Richard, at Cape Elizabeth, 140.
Turtle-Head, Penobscot Bay, 270.
Trundy's Reef, wreck at, 142.
Two Brothers, Casco Bay, note, 172.
Tyng, William, his burial-place, 164; anecdote of, 168; note, 172.

U.

Union River, why so named, 328.
Upper Hell Gate (Sasanoa River), 196.

V.

Vinal Haven, 249.
Vines, Richard, at Biddeford, 117, and notes, 119, 120; at Machias, 334.

W.

Wadsworth, Henry, burial-place, 164.
Wadsworth, General Peleg, 162; note, 172; taken prisoner, 245.
Waldo, Hannah, refuses Andrew Pepperell, 20; and marries Thomas Flucker, note, 28.
Waldo, Samuel, his patent, 237; notice of, note, 250.
Warren's Island, Penobscot Bay, note, 270.
Webb, James Watson, 245.
Webhannet River, Wells, 78.
Weems, James, surrenders Pemaquid, 231.
Welchpool, approach to, 349, 353; glimpses of life there, 355, 356.
Wells, its rise predicted, 76; its villages and situation, 76, 77; first settlers in, 77, 78; Indian attacks on, 79, et seq.; First Parish of, 82; east boundary of, 83; note, 84; also, 108.
Wells Bay at Ogunquit, 74, 76–85.
Wells Beach, 75; way to, 79.
West Quoddy Head, and Light, 344, 346; note, 364.

INDEX. 393

Weymouth, Captain George, discovers the Kennebec, 185; at Monhegan, 218.
Whale Cove, Grand Manan, 367.
Wheeler, G. A., *note*, 287.
Wheelwright, Rev. John, at Wells, 77; *note*, 84.
Wheelwright, Captain John, of Wells, bloody ending of a wedding at his house, 82.
Whitefield, George, his connection with Louisburg expedition, 24.
White Head, Casco Bay, described, 144, 147.
Whitehead Island and Light, 245.
White Island Light, 22, 30.
White Islands, Boothbay, *note*, 206.
White Mountains, from Kennebunkport, 97; Josselyn's account, 134; from Scarborough, 138; from Portland, 157, 169; from Mount Megunticook, 266.
Whittier, John G., Legend of Harpswell, 180.
Willis, N. P., on the Penobscot region, 260.
Wincall, Captain, his fight with Indians, 130.
Winslow, Edward, of Plymouth, at the Kennebec, 190; at Monhegan, *note*, 219.
Winslow, John, at the Kennebec, 191.
Winter Harbor, Biddeford, 114; *notes* 1 and 2, 119.

Winter Harbor, Gouldsborough, 325.
Winter, John, at Richmond's Island, 140.
Witherle, George, 281.
Wolves, the, 367.
Wood Island, location of, 114; *note*, 120; from Old Orchard Beach, 122.

Y.

York, depopulated by plague, 45; how to get there, 47; meeting of the old and new, 47; meeting-house, 47, 48; first called Bristol, 48; called Agamenticus and Gorgeana, 49; annals of crime in, 49; sacked, 53, 54; the harbor, 55; picturesque neighborhood, 56; Stage Neck, 59; authorities on the settlement, *note*, 60; and limits and government, *notes*, 60, 61; shore front, 63; Long Sands, 63, 64; Cape Neddock, the Nubble, 64, 67; Short Sands, 67, 68; Bald Head Cliff, 69; Ogunquit Village, 72.
York Nubble, 63; how reached, 64; sea view at, 67.
Yorkshire County, Maine settlements erected into, 35.
Young, Captain, ascends the Kennebec, 191.

www.ingramcontent.com/pod-product-compliance
Lightning Source LLC
Chambersburg PA
CBHW051625230426
43669CB00013B/2183